Darkest Before Dawn

DARKEST BEFORE DAWN

Sedition and Free Speech in the American West

Clemens P. Work

UNIVERSITY OF NEW MEXICO PRESS

❖

ALBUQUERQUE

Frontispiece: Intrigued by freighter Martin Wehinger's story of killing a bear with an axe, pioneer photographer L. A. Huffman took this studio portrait of him in the 1890s. Convicted of sedition for criticizing the United States' participation in World War I, Wehinger spent eighteen months behind bars. He died, toothless, in 1920, four months after his release from prison. L. A. Huffman, Courtesy of Coffrin's Old West Gallery, Bozeman, Montana.

PAPERBOUND ISBN-13: 978-0-8263-3793-1
PAPERBOUND ISBN-10: 0-8263-3793-7

11 10 09 08 07 06   1 2 3 4 5 6

Library of Congress Cataloging-in-Publication Data

Work, Clemens P., 1944–
Darkest before dawn : sedition and free speech in the American West /
Clemens P. Work.
p. cm.
Includes bibliographical references and index.
ISBN 0-8263-3774-0 (cloth : alk. paper)
1. Freedom of speech—Montana—History—20th century.
2. Sedition—Montana—History—20th century.
3. World War, 1914–1918—Protest movements—Montana.
4. Industrial Workers of the World—History—20th century.
5. Dissenters—Montana—History—20th century.
6. Montana—Politics and government—20th century.
7. Montana—Social conditions—20th century.
8. World War, 1914–1918—Social aspects—United States.
9. Freedom of speech—United States—Case studies.
10. Sedition—United States—Case studies. I. Title.
JC599.U52M98 2005
323.44'3'09786—dc22

2005009967

DESIGN AND COMPOSITION: *Mina Yamashita*

❖

To Cecily, Alyssa, Brendan, Bryan, and Claire

❖

Contents

Acknowledgments / ix

Introduction / 1

Chapter 1: The Rebel Girl / 7

Chapter 2: Fellow Workers and Friends / 20

Chapter 3: Harvest Stiffs and Shingle Weavers / 34

Chapter 4: The Hymn of Hate / 47

Chapter 5: Fire in the Mountain / 60

Chapter 6: Patriotism and Propaganda / 74

Chapter 7: Up in Smoke / 90

Chapter 8: Standing Against the Mob / 107

Chapter 9: On the Wings of a Snowstorm / 119

Chapter 10: The Pot Boils Over / 133

Chapter 11: Liberty Can Wait / 148

Chapter 12: No Possible Means of Escape / 164

Chapter 13: "Good Night with Mr. Damned Wilson" / 181

Chapter 14: The Wine Salesman's Tale / 194

Chapter 15: A Contest of Wills / 212

Chapter 16: "The Agitation of the Billows" / 228

Chapter 17: The Dawn of Free Speech / 244

Appendix I / 260

Appendix II / 262

Notes / 264

Selected Bibliography / 300

Index / 310

Acknowledgments

MY FIRST, AND BIGGEST, DEBT OF GRATITUDE is to Jerry Elijah Brown, dean of the University of Montana School of Journalism. Jerry was behind me from day one of this project as sounding board, reader, cheerleader, leave arranger, front man, and resident therapist. Jerry also engineered a generous Kurtz Family grant to help fund my research. He was backed up by my colleagues at the school, especially editor extraordinaire Bob McGiffert. I also owe a debt to Maurice Possley of the *Chicago Tribune,* a Pollner fellow at the Journalism School in 2003, who read several chapters and made valuable suggestions.

Other colleagues at the University of Montana, including Dave Emmons, Harry Fritz, and Jim Lopach provided advice and keen insights. I also wish to thank former associate provost Fritz Schwaller, who first put me in touch with and enthusiastically promoted my book idea to UNM Press. Editor-in-chief David Holtby and managing editor Maya Allen-Gallegos made the publishing experience relatively painless with their patient, thorough guidance.

A succession of dedicated journalism students helped with historical and genealogical research including Jason Mohr, Lindsey Lear Chapman, and Lucas Tanglen.

A work such as this would not have been possible without the professional guidance of excellent archivists around the country, including Ellen Crain, director of the Butte-Silver Bow Public Archives; Brian Shovers, Molly Kruckenberg, Lory Morrow, and Katie Curey at the Montana Historical Society in Helena; Fred Romanski at the National Archives and Records Administration; Don Spritzer at the Missoula Public Library; Karen Stevens at Parmley Billings Library in Billings, as well as archivists at the New York Public Library, Wayne State University, and the Bancroft Library at U.C. Berkeley.

Several Montana newspeople contributed their enthusiastic support, particularly Chuck Johnson in Helena, Larry Tanglen in Laurel, Jan Anderson in Jefferson City, and Derek Pruitt in Butte.

When I first phoned Phyllis Rolf in Atwater, Minnesota, and told her that her grandfather, Fred Rodewald, had once been in prison, she was momentarily speechless. But she recovered, bless her, and provided me many insights into this gentle and peaceful man. She also provided a number of family photos, as did Mike Wehinger's great grandniece Connie Miller. Thanks also to Judy Gordon for the first lead to the great portrait of Wehinger by L. A. Huffman, and to Joy Fisher for help on homestead files. I also want to thank other descendants of some of the players in this drama, including George "Duke" Crowley, grandson of Butte lawyer Matt Canning, who defended the rancher Ves Hall, and Lester H. Loble II, grandson of the Lewis and Clark County prosecutor.

Finally, my heartfelt thanks to my family for their support, patience, love—and hard work. Before leaving for college, my daughter Alyssa whipped the endnotes and bibliography into excellent shape, no small feat. My wife and fellow journalist, Lucia, read the entire manuscript twice, squeezed the fat and the highfalutin language out of it and added a dose of common sense. Without them, this book never would have seen the light of day. ✤

Introduction

TWO WEEKS AFTER THE UNITED STATES declared war on Germany in 1917, Lewistown, Montana, in the very center of the state, put on a parade. Hundreds of children waved flags as they marched down the main street. Prominent citizens gave patriotic speeches about the nation's "life and death struggle." Communities across the country indulged in much the same sort of exercise, rallying 'round the flag as the symbol of the nation's crusade to "make the world safe for democracy."

Less than a year later, a mob of five hundred Lewistown residents grabbed German text books from the high school, piled them in the middle of Main Street and burned them as the crowd sang "America" and the "Star-Spangled Banner." A man suspected of being "pro-German" because he resisted buying Liberty Bonds was dragged before citizens in a pool hall and found guilty of sedition. The high school principal was made to kiss the flag. Another man was nearly lynched. And then the citizens, now two thousand strong, held another parade with more speeches, while the "crowd cheered lustily." A month later, the high school burned down.[1]

How had patriotism become so perverted?

In the following chapters, I attempt an explanation. What happened in Lewistown is just one example of a tragedy that blighted the nation. I focus on how the ugly events in this most beautiful state came to influence that most precious gift, freedom of speech.

I begin one hundred years ago, with the birth in Chicago of a radical labor organization, the Industrial Workers of the World, formed in angry reaction to the injustices caused by a growing gap between the great wealth produced by America's industrial might and the miserable working conditions suffered by the lower rungs of society on whose backs, they believed, such wealth had been created. Within a few years, the IWW's in-your-face confrontation of industrial ills and its absolute hatred of capitalism had spread to Montana and other parts of the West, where it met equally intransigent corporate and political powers.

This often-violent impasse escalated to an entirely different dimension with America's entry into the world war against Germany in 1917. The national emergency engendered by the declaration of war quickly built into a climate of fear and hysteria. Suppression of dissent was couched in patriotic terms, giving citizens permission to engage in the kinds of extreme actions that would have repelled them in ordinary times. In this climate, most citizens cheered—or at least did not protest—governmental and private actions against dissenters and troublemakers. The cancer of fear metastasized and spread throughout the body politic.

In Lewistown, as elsewhere, clues to this cancer were all around. On the day of the first parade on April 22, ex-Congressman Tom Stout, publisher of the Fergus County *Democrat-News,* said this:

> We are done with the days of a divided allegiance in this broad land of liberty. With our sacred honor and our liberties at stake, there can be but two classes of American citizens, patriots and traitors! Choose you the banner beneath which you will stand in this hour of trial.[2]

For the immigrants who comprised one-fourth of the town's population, the warning served to underline the terrible events of the day. As in so many towns, Stout the publisher was Stout the patriot, spreading fears of "pro-Germans" and tales of sabotage by radical groups such as the IWW. Encouraged by the governor and the state Council of Defense, loyalty and "third-degree" committees questioned those suspected of disloyalty. Over the next eighteen months, the hysteria so starkly displayed on the streets of Lewistown would envelop the whole state. In February 1918, Gov. Sam Stewart would sign a sedition bill severely punishing anyone who said anything "disloyal" or "contemptuous" about the government, the flag, the Constitution, or the nation's wartime efforts.

Ordinary people would be swept up in a hysterical hunt for radicals and dissenters. Some were cruelly suppressed for expressing their views. Others, ordinarily compassionate, became their oppressors. It was a huge price to pay for some immeasurable—and perhaps illusory—incremental increase in the nation's security.

Similar events were transpiring across the country, but often to a more virulent degree in the West. Montana was both a microcosm and a crucible of these tragic events. It was home to one of the largest corporations in the country, the mighty Anaconda Copper Mining Company—that dominated the state as much as any company has ever dominated any state. With its enormous political clout, the Anaconda used America's entry into the war to influence the passage of laws intended to eliminate dissent.

Montana's leaders, such as Senator Thomas Walsh and U.S. Attorney Burton K. Wheeler, were players on the national stage. Therefore, what happened in Montana influenced national events to a considerable degree. Montana's senators boosted the state's repressive laws onto the national agenda. Congress adopted Montana's sedition law three months later—with only three words changed.

Those who did not stand foursquare with the nation's policies were repressed. Their voices and their opinions were blocked or severely attenuated. The constitutional liberty of free speech was a hollow freedom.

Of course, the United States had experienced previous periods of repression. A sedition law passed in the administration of John Adams to suppress critics of the Federalist government had led to a number of prosecutions—and directly to the end of the Federalists' hold on power. The Civil War had seen dark periods for civil rights, with suspension of habeas corpus and raids on newspapers. The internment of Japanese citizens after Pearl Harbor is still a fresh wound. But the darkest, most widespread and in some ways least remembered acts of government repression of dissent occurred in the lifetimes of our grandparents and great-grandparents—before, during, and after World War I. These events were long enough ago that very, very few remain alive to bear witness to their horrors. Yet they were recent enough to continue to influence how government and the governed conduct their affairs today.

Montana was not alone. Terrifying acts of political repression occurred in many states. Montana can't take the blame more than any other state or the federal government for these shameful acts. But the sordid events that occurred here were symbolic of, and influenced, this morbid, fearful national climate.

The beatings, lynchings, raids, censorship, and jailings did not end with the Armistice in 1918, but continued in a second round of hysteria with the Red Scare of 1919–1920. Fortunately, there is a silver lining, a dawn to the darkness. After the postwar paroxysm of fear had played out by late 1920, a national reaction set in, an awakening to not only the injustices visited upon those who had spoken out in dissent, but to the dangers that their repression posed to our freedoms of speech and press guaranteed by the Bill of Rights. For the first time, the U.S. Supreme Court began to debate the boundaries of free speech in a democratic society. So did intellectuals and ordinary people. Out of that great national conversation arose a deeper and broader understanding of such rights, which in turn fostered a more solid commitment to enforcing those rights in courts and legislatures and city halls.

This recognition was not like a light bulb turned on in a dark room. It did not happen suddenly. It was more like a dawning of the First Amendment, which had lain wrapped in semi-darkness for 130 years or so since its ratification in 1791.

And so, my last chapter ends with a different parade, a parade of words on paper written by Supreme Court Justice Louis Brandeis in 1927 that expressed fresh hopes for a dawn of free speech, hopes that succeeded probably beyond their author's wildest dreams.[3] The freedoms of speech, of the press, of association so wisely reserved for the people in 1791 would finally begin to fulfill their promise. Workers, racial and ethnic minorities, women, angry radicals, schoolteachers, cranks, and corporations, would be able to express their desires and dreams. The views of minorities, even Nazis, Klansmen, IWW Wobblies and other social and political outcasts, would not be shut down, no matter how repugnant their views.

As we cherish it today, freedom of expression guarantees political dissent. This is the freedom that U.S. Supreme Court Justice William Brennan so eloquently expressed in *New York Times v. Sullivan* in 1964, affirming the constitutional right to criticize government without fear of punishment and reaffirming "a profound national commitment to the principle that debate on public issues should be uninhibited, robust, and wide-open . . ."[4]

The last seventy-five years or so has not, of course, been an unalloyed golden age. Periods of repression as in the Communist hysteria in the early days of the Cold War remind us that the guarantee of free speech is fragile. Laws and actions by the administration after September 11, 2001, bring home that truth once more. Events such as the passage and implementation of the PATRIOT Act; the increase in surveillance activities by national and state governments; the repression of political street demonstrations; and the warrant-less arrest, detention, and harsh treatment of persons targeted in the "war on terror" have shrunk everyone's civil liberties and heightened the danger to expression guaranteed by the First Amendment.

But these same actions have also provoked vigorous debate and considerable opposition. Court decisions have sharply criticized the denial of due process rights for detainees and allowed somewhat more access to terrorism and immigration proceedings. All the more imperative becomes Santayana's famous dictum, "Those who cannot remember the past are condemned to repeat it."

By focusing on this darkest period in America's history, it is my hope that certain truths may become self-evident: That freedom of expression is indeed the bulwark of our liberty, that its exercise is crucial to democratic self-governance and ultimately to the pursuit of happiness, and that we alone can preserve it. Only with this awesome power can we presume to call the United States a great nation. By looking into this dark mirror, when our freedoms were under siege, we can see ourselves as we once were, and as we might become.

—Clemens P. Work
Missoula, Montana
November 11, 2004

ONE
The Rebel Girl

The Industrial Workers of the World Target Capitalism, 1905–1909

A HORSE-DRAWN STREETCAR NEGOTIATED THE CORNER, past the striped barber poles in front of the Florence Hotel. The driver barely tugged on the reins as the pair turned north from Front Street onto Higgins Avenue, trudging their familiar, dusty, downtown path. It was a golden September afternoon in Missoula, Montana, with a full, blue sky and a hint of crispness in the air. The weather was perfect for the Apple Show, now less than a month away, perfect for showing off the little city of twelve thousand, a "clean and attractive little place"[1] nestled in the confluence of five mountain valleys.

The past year or so had been one of rebuilding. In early June 1908, after thirty-three straight days of rain, the Clark Fork River had burst its banks. The flood washed out all the bridges in town, severing all telephone and most telegraph connections. By now, though, a new steel bridge had been built at a cost of $110,000. Permits to build were being handed out at a record pace. A new courthouse was nearing completion. A second rail line, the Milwaukee, had come into town four months earlier. The recently completed Harnois Theater was considered one of the finest in the West. Across the river, the state university was starting its second decade of classes. Orchards and gardens bloomed in profusion, giving the little city its nickname.[2]

To be sure, the streets of the Garden City were still unpaved, the sidewalks were rough planks, bawdy houses and honky-tonks on West Front did a roaring business and train robberies near town were a recent memory.[3] Still, Missoula was positioning itself as a center of commerce and culture in western Montana. In the hopeful prose of a promotion pamphlet, Missoula was "an ideal spot [where] from the cot of the laboring man to the mansion of the millionaire there is a spirit of cosy content, [and where] everyone takes pride in making the city beautiful."[4]

The "spirit of cosy content" was not shared by all. Migratory lumberjacks and harvest workers, whose cots were rough indeed, floated in and out of town by the thousands. Men constantly jumped from job to miserable job. In the summer, loggers often worked as railroad construction workers; in the fall, men worked fruit and grain harvests, and with the winter snow came the work of felling and hauling logs and turning them into lumber.[5] Freight trains—"side-door Pullmans"—were the transportation of choice, carrying men from job to skid road and back. With riverfront entertainment, rail lines, and mercantile business, Missoula was a well-worn stop on the migrants' route.

On a downtown street corner that golden fall afternoon, a Salvation Army captain was attempting to salvage souls. "Are you living in sin?" asked a captain. "I don't know if that's what you call it," one lumberjack heckled in response, "but it's a lousy bunkhouse out in the woods."[6]

On the wooden sidewalk, under a canvas storefront awning, nineteen-year-old Elizabeth Gurley Flynn heard the riposte while she waited impatiently for the captain to fold up his Salvation Army banner and go home. She and her husband Jack Jones had a different gospel to preach. They were about to turn Missoula inside out. Within weeks, the pregnant, auburn-haired beauty would be carrying out her mission on a bigger stage; within a few years she would become one of the most feared and despised women in America. Her ultimate goal was to topple capitalism, and the ragged men who swarmed the dusty street would help her do it.

The Girl Orator

Gurley Flynn, as she was commonly known, was no bomb-throwing anarchist. But she might as well have been to her enemies, who perceived little difference in her intent. Instead of a bomb, she carried a suitcase. It was filled, not with shrapnel, but with literature and songbooks of the Industrial Workers of the World. Like the Salvation Army soldiers and the "sky pilots" whom she often mocked, her mission in Missoula was to save souls—not from the vulgar 10-cent shows at Big Bertha's Mascot Theater and the red-brick cribs on West Front but from the inhumane grasp of capitalism. With her broad sombrero and open-neck blouse, the young woman must have presented a charismatic image to the "floaters" and the hobos who had drifted into town looking to blow one stake and buy a chance at another.[7] It was her fiery words and forceful gestures, however, and her ability to speak directly to the rough men whom she was trying to reach, that really drew the crowds.

Elizabeth Gurley Flynn had been born in Concord, New Hampshire,

Figure 1. Army troops from Fort Missoula parade outside the Florence Hotel in Missoula in 1910. 84–305, K. Ross Toole Archives, The University of Montana-Missoula.

on August 7, 1890. She was the oldest child of Irish immigrants forced to leave their homeland because of their revolutionary ideals. Although her father had worked his way through Dartmouth and become a civil engineer, the family lived in poverty in the slums of Manchester and later in the South Bronx. Radical influences were all around her as Gurley (her mother's maiden name) grew up. Irish revolutionary James Connolly, a family friend, took a special interest in her intellectual development.

Gurley rejected the "stodgy" socialists, the party of her parents, and joined the IWW in 1906, the year after its formation. "[W]e felt a desire to have something more militant, more progressive and more youthful and so we flocked into the new organization," Flynn recalled years later.[8] "The working class and the employing class have nothing in common," the preamble to the IWW constitution began. The radical labor organization seemed to offer a no-holds-barred response to the ravages of capitalism.

In 1907 Flynn was elected a delegate to the third IWW convention in Chicago and made her first paid speaking tour after it concluded. She earned a twenty-dollar gold piece.

The "girl orator," as she was often called, had a reputation as an eloquent and fiery street-corner speaker. She earned her first arrest for street-speaking in New York when she was sixteen. An early newspaper account of a speech by Gurley in Philadelphia records "Her lithe little figure, her flaming red tie, her beautiful oval face with the broad clear brow and mischievous eyes . . ."[9] When she took over the podium, "Immediately a crowd assembled. Corner loungers, drunks, women of the street, children—all stood hypnotized as phrases from Mirabeau, the poetry of Byron, the prose of George Eliot, and the social philosophy of Maxim Gorky flowed from the lips of the girl, who salted her impassioned tirade with flashes of saucy patter and pungent wit."[10]

Flynn left high school and went to work full-time as an IWW organizer. In the Mesabi iron range of northern Minnesota, she married Jack Archibald Jones, an organizer for the Western Federation of Miners. Jones was fresh out of prison after a ten-year stretch for arson. The couple moved to Chicago, where they had met, but their marriage soon developed cracks. In the early summer of 1909, Flynn took the train for Butte to speak at the annual Miners' Day celebration on June 13. In northwest Montana, she encouraged striking IWW loggers. She remained the rest of the summer in Spokane as an IWW speaker, protesting the practices of the crooked employment agencies.[11]

It was there that she probably began to put into practice the advice of Big Bill Haywood, the executive secretary of the IWW: Speak simply and directly, as one would speak to children. Use short, clipped sentences and only the simplest words.[12] This rhetorical tactic was tailor-made for the migratory laborers Flynn would be addressing. Flowery phrases, the poetry of Byron, and theoretical nuances would be lost on most of them.

Flynn joined Jones in Missoula before Labor Day, 1909. It would be the only time the couple worked and lived together. They rented the basement of the Harnois Theater, next to the Chamber of Commerce building.

Contemporary accounts give the gist of that fall afternoon in Missoula. Backed by a large IWW banner with slogans painted on it, held aloft by local Wobblies, as IWW members were called, Flynn stepped onto a platform supported by boxes and barrels.[13] Starting with the customary Wobbly greeting, "Fellow workers and friends," she lit into the shady practices of the "sharks," the Spokane-based employment agencies such as the O. K., the Red Cross, and the Square Deal.[14]

Bindlestiffs and Timber Beasts

Many of the men in her audience had already been bitten by the sharks.

One Wobbly's tale of his treatment, later published in a socialist newspaper, illustrates why Flynn and other IWW organizers were able to recruit members so successfully:

> Over three thousand men were hired through employment sharks for one camp of the Somers Lumber Co. (Great Northern) last winter to maintain a force of fifty men. As soon as a man had worked long enough to pay the shark's fee, the hospital dollar, poll tax, and a few other grafts, he was discharged to make room for more slaves, so that the fleecing process could continue. These different fees are split, or cut up with the bosses. In most cases these fees consumed the time of several days' labor, when the men were then discharged and paid off with checks ranging from 5 cents and upwards. The victim of the shark in the most cases gets the check cashed at the first saloon, and takes a little stimulation. Why not? What is there in life for them? The strong, barbed-wire whiskey makes things look bright for awhile. Then the weary tramp goes to town with his bed on his back.[15]

Flynn may have repeated the joke that the slave market scheme was so slick, supplied by a seemingly endless stream of new suckers, that it was said the sharks had invented perpetual motion: one man going to a job, one man on the job, and one man leaving the job.[16] To this, she would have contrasted the "glad tidings of a great revolutionary union. 'An injury to one is an injury to all. Workers of the world, unite, you have nothing to lose but your bed on your back. You have a world to gain. Labor produces all wealth, and those who produce it are tramps and hobos.'"[17]

Flynn developed a deep empathy for the men, colored by a somewhat romantic image of them. In her memoirs, Flynn described "the majority [as] American-born Eastern youth of adventurist spirit, who had followed Horace Greeley's advice: 'Go West, young man and grow up with the country!'"[18]

In fact, few of the 3.5 million men roaming the West had simply been seized by the spirit of adventure and wandered west in some idle quest.[19] Most were searching for work to stay alive in brutal circumstances: miserly pay for most "wage slaves" and rough working conditions. At McKees Rocks, Pennsylvania, just down-river from Pittsburgh, workers in the Pressed Steel Car Company, the leading railroad car firm in the country, earned as little as $6.50 for ten days and two nights' work as riveters.[20] With one day off per week, such starvation wages would total $169 per year at a time when $700 was considered the bare minimum to raise a family. Nearly one-third of the men who worked in American factories and mines earned less than $10 a week. Half the women received less than $6.[21] Unskilled workers, whose unemployment rate was more than double the national average of 4.9 percent, continued to grow in numbers.[22] Of the U.S. population of about 80 million in 1904, at least 11 million were living in dire poverty.[23] "Scientific" assembly-line systems wrung out maximum profits, forcing laborers to work at a frenetic pace to satisfy production targets or be penalized.[24]

Many of the dispossessed floaters came from large families, their parents unable to care for them. Some were younger sons of farmers, squeezed out of any land ownership. Most had left already overcrowded cities and slums. In the last forty years of the nineteenth century, the urban population of the United States had quadrupled, from 12 million to 48 million.[25] Other floaters—a disproportionate number according to historian Robert L. Tyler—were "feeble-minded, neurotic runaways from middle-class homes, wife-deserters, unattached aliens, and the variously deracinated."[26]

Whatever it was they were uprooted from, the migrants found little succor in the West. The boundless horizons were illusory. Their dreams were hollow. Their prodigious, back-breaking work profited their bosses but rarely improved their own station in life. As a classic IWW lament went:

> *It is we who plowed the prairies; built the cities where they trade;*
> *Dug the mines and built the workshops; endless miles of railroad laid;*
> *Now we stand outcasts and starving, 'mid the wonders we have made.*

The Western lumber industry, the biggest employer of the men standing in the dirt street that day in Missoula, depended upon these homeless, hungry men as much as they depended on lumber for their erratic livelihood. It was a sinister symbiosis: Plagued by chronic overproduction and subsequent plunges in demand and prices, employment in this seasonal industry spiked and plummeted like a roller-coaster. Yet the industry profited most when jobs constantly turned over—and it rewarded its workers with some of the worst living and working conditions in the country.[27]

Working in the woods was a catalog of dangers: felling and cutting

Figure 2. Loggers in western Montana often encountered difficult conditions in winter, the prime logging season. 77–270, K. Ross Toole Archives, The University of Montana-Missoula.

large trees, dragging logs and slash in rough terrain, using powerful equipment, often in wet, cold conditions. The prime logging season was in the winter, from October through April. Because men were forced to pack their own bedding, rolled in "bindles," from camp to camp, and because they couldn't wash their bedding, bedbugs and lice were endemic.

"They have been treated not quite as good as work horses, for usually there was more ventilation in the barns than in the bunk-houses," wrote F. A. Silcox of the Forest Service in Missoula. "A 'get-the-hell-out-of-here' philosophy was to too great an extent in vogue when any of the men complained about the conditions."[28] Logging camps were also remote concentrations of "lonely, womanless men, without any social attractions or any means of recreation," according to a memorandum prepared for the U.S. secretary of labor.

For the IWW and its organizers, such men were ripe for the picking. "His eyes are dull and reddened," wrote Rexford Tugwell of the typical timber beast in the Pacific Northwest. "His joints are stiff with . . . rheumatism; his teeth are rotting; he is wracked with strange diseases and tortured by unrealized dreams that haunt his soul. . . . The blanket-stiff is a man without a home. . . . The void of his atrophied affections is filled with a resentful despair and a bitterness against the society that self-right-eously cast him out."[29]

Tapping the resentment of the ragged men who stood before her, Flynn called on the workers to unite as one union to fight the bosses. She may have used rhetoric like this, from a column in the *Industrial Worker*, the IWW's Spokane newspaper, printed while she was in Missoula: "If you slaves were wise, you would not need the capitalists any more than you need bedbugs in your sleeping quarters who suck your blood. Now here, you wage slaves! Don't you think it is high time for the slaves to get togeth-er to fight these social parasites?[30]

The Anxious Versus the Desperate

While the timber beasts and the bindlestiffs clung to the bottom rungs of the economy, those at the top were riding the swells of a huge sea change in American life. Industrialization, which had been accelerating since the Reconstruction era, had transformed the landscape. America was no longer an agrarian nation. In just forty years from 1870 to 1910, the nation's city dwellers had grown from a quarter to nearly half the population.[31] Free from practically any restraints, a handful of America's leading capitalists controlled the lion's share of the nation's industry and capital. J. P. Morgan, the Wall Street financier, had formed the first billion-dollar corporation, United States Steel.[32] John D. Rockefeller, founder of Standard Oil, was well on his way to becoming the first billion-dollar individual. George Weyerhaeuser, the Northern Pacific Railroad, and the Southern Pacific Railroad would own a fourth of all the privately owned timberland in the Northwest by 1914,[33] estimated at 237.5 billion board feet of standing tim-ber.[34] In turn, these capitalists were one of ten groups that collectively monopolized 1.2 trillion board feet of timber, more than 40 percent of all the timber in the United States—"enough standing timber to make a float-ing bridge more than two feet thick and more than five miles wide from New York to Liverpool," IWW organizer James Rowan noted.[35]

Only a few drops had trickled down to the poor. In 1901, just four thousand millionaires owned 20 percent of the wealth.[36] The nouveau-riche upper crust seemed to have little social conscience, but a tremendous appetite for ostentation. In 1895, one social-climbing New York family had spent $369,000, more than $5 million in today's dollars, to convert the Waldorf-Astoria Hotel for one night into a faux Versailles.[37]

In the West, industrial concentration and accumulation of awesome wealth occurred rapidly. In the enormously lucrative business of industrial mining of precious metals and other less glamorous minerals such as lead and zinc, ore extraction evolved within a generation from panning to large-scale underground mines. Cripple Creek, Colorado, became the "greatest gold camp in America." Copper-rich Butte, Montana, was "the richest hill on earth." Mining became dominated by large corporations and groups of wealthy investors. In 1899, during a colorful "war" between the copper kings Marcus Daly, William A. Clark, and Fritz Augustus Heinze, the hill's wealth had come under the control of the Rockefeller interests, doing business as the Amalgamated Copper Company and its subsidiary, the Anaconda Copper Mining Company.

Large corporations like ACM had the advantages of economies of scale. They had better bargaining power with suppliers, vendors, and railroads and could better underwrite the huge costs of exploration and extraction. But what they gained in efficiency, large corporations lost in humanity. Workers became invisible to distant bosses and stock-watching investors. Decisions were made at the home office, usually on the East Coast. Consequently, conflicts between labor and management weren't easily resolved and often bred anger and frustration. "This divorce between ownership and local management," noted IWW historian Melvyn Dubofsky, "this geographical gulf between the worker and his ultimate employer, led to violent industrial conflict."[38]

The schism would become the key to a series of bloody labor battles from 1893 to 1904 in the mining districts of the Rocky Mountain West, primarily in Idaho and Colorado, that came close to class warfare. And from that crucible of violence would arise the Industrial Workers of the World.

The pattern of conflict began to emerge around 1890 in the Coeur d'Alene mining district of northern Idaho, a narrow belt rich in silver, lead, and zinc. Distant investors who saw hard-rock miners merely as figures on balance sheets brought in managers to boost production and hold down costs. Unions refused to concede wage cuts. Managers responded with lockouts, shutdowns, more wage cuts, and spies who kept them and police informed of union plans. Further union intransigence and escalating violence were met with strikebreakers, court injunctions, troops, and mass arrests.

In self-defense, miners formed the Western Federation of Miners in March 1893. The WFM threatened the interests of the mine owners, touching off a new round of even bloodier strikes in the Coeur d'Alenes in 1899 and in Colorado from 1903 to 1905. This time, there was a new element: the business-led "Citizens Alliance" movement in Colorado, pumped-up with a get-tough attitude that gave no quarter to labor—no unions and no negotiations. As historian Tyler encapsulated it, "an anxious and violent conservatism" met "an equally desperate radicalism."[39]

The result: more deaths, and privately-financed militia and martial law imposed by viciously anti-labor governor James H. Peabody and enforced by former Rough Rider Sherman Bell. His orders, Bell averred, "were to 'wipe 'em off the face of the earth.'"[40] With martial law came suspension of habeas corpus—about which he cracked, "Habeas corpus be damned, we'll give 'em post-mortems!"[41] The bombing of the Independence railroad depot at Cripple Creek, Colorado, on June 6, 1904, resulting in a score of deaths and many more injuries, touched off an orgy of vigilantes, mob violence, and forced deportations. The miners were whipped.

One Big Union

At a secret meeting in Chicago in early January 1905, mine union leaders and a score of other labor bosses began to lay plans for a radical reform of the American labor movement. That summer, on a sweltering late-June day in Chicago, William Haywood, secretary-treasurer of the Western Federation of Miners, grabbed a board for a gavel, banged on the podium in the smoke-filled auditorium, and called the 203 delegates to order as "the Continental Congress of the Working Class." The Industrial Workers of the World would be "a working class movement that shall have for its purpose the emancipation of the working class from the slave bondage of capitalism . . ."[42]

No more half measures. No more attempts to work with management, to conciliate. "[N]o compromise and no surrender."[43] Capital and labor had nothing in common. The revolution would not be successful until it had brought about the death of capitalism, an end to the wage system, and a general union across all industries—One Big Union. The revolution would be carried out by stages. A series of strikes would culminate in a general strike that would paralyze industry and bring capitalism to its knees. Workers would seize control of the machinery of production, appropriate all profits, and govern through a workplace-centered democracy.

How to get there was not at all clear. The IWW would be nearly

THE MAN UP A TREE

Figure 3. This cartoon shows the IWW's contempt for capitalism and the mainstream press. Published in *One Big Union Monthly*, Chicago, vol. 1, no. 3, May 1919, p. 30. Butte-Silver Bow Public Archives.

wrecked in the next few years by factional disputes as members worked out its philosophy and roadmap to the promised land. In the process, the IWW managed to alienate many of its Socialist midwives. Eugene Debs, the country's leading Socialist, had joined in railing against the pro-capitalist AF of L at the IWW's founding convention. But it wouldn't be long before he and other Socialists left the IWW, annoyed at its undisciplined nature and indifference to Socialist ideology.[44] Even the Western Federation of Miners, now dominated by more-conservative members, parted company in 1907.

The biggest change in the IWW, however, came in its decision to disavow political action. The Wobblies would not fight the class struggle at the ballot box, because that was a political mechanism of the "master class." As Father Thomas J. Hagerty of New Mexico had put it, "The ballot box is simply a capitalist concession. Dropping pieces of paper into a hole in a box never did achieve emancipation for the working class, and to my thinking it never will."[45] Hagerty, a tall, black-bearded priest credited with the IWW's famous preamble, had had his views shaped in southwestern

Colorado, where his exhortations to miners to take what rightfully belonged to them earned him a suspension from the archbishop.[46]

Instead, the IWW would embrace direct action. Members would use strikes, job actions, sabotage, and other forms of confrontation. If there was a single moment where the young organization tilted toward direct action, a fateful step that cast its image so negatively in the public's mind, it might have been on the opening day of the 1908 convention, when chairman Vincent St. John invited the "Overalls Brigade" to sing that revolutionary anthem, the "Marsellaise."

The brainchild of Western IWW organizer John H. Walsh, the Overalls Brigade had sung its way east from Portland, riding the rods, sharing mulligan stews in track-side "jungles with hoboes and fellow Wobblies," and stopping in small towns along the way to evangelize. Walsh chronicled the group's quixotic adventures for the *Industrial Union Bulletin*:

> Two blasts of the locomotive whistle are heard and the train is starting on its journey, and simultaneously nineteen men, all dressed in black overalls and jumpers, black shirts and red ties, with an IWW book in his pocket and an IWW button on his coat, are in a 'cattle car' and on our way. . . . We had scarcely gotten out of the city limits of Portland, when we saw the campfires of the "boes" along the road, and we have never, as yet, been out of sight of those camp fires. . . . In Missoula, we had some of the best meetings of all the places along the route. . . . We put the Starvation Army on the bum and packed the streets from one side to another. The literature sales were good, the collections good, and the red cards containing the songs sold like hotcakes . . . [47]

Energized by the Brigade's epic, the Bummery—another derisive term that the Westerners adopted with pride—emerged victorious at the convention. The IWW would dedicate itself to industrial unionism and direct action. Its course was now set westward, toward the miners and the sawyers, the migratory loggers and harvest workers who had infected it with a fresh zeal. "With such men in the ranks," the *Industrial Union Bulletin* gushed, "the IWW may confidently hope that success will crown their persistent efforts towards industrial emancipation."[48]

Western timber workers, noted historian Melvyn Dubofsky, would be "perfect IWW recruits. Mostly native [-born] Americans or northern Europeans, they spoke English, lived together, drank together, slept together, whored together, and fought together." With an industrial depression throwing men out of work, dues (which had been kept at no more than fifty cents a month) were just trickling in. Organizers would have to support themselves by selling literature and buttons out of their suitcases.

One thing organizers like Flynn would not have to worry about was encountering people who had never heard of the IWW. By 1908, the Wobblies were already infamous, thanks to the sensational murder trial in Boise, Idaho, the year before. Former Gov. Frank Steunenberg had been slain on December 30, 1905, at his home in Caldwell by a bomb that exploded when he opened his garden gate. Harry Orchard, a drifter, had planted the bomb, perhaps as revenge for Steunenberg's role as governor in harshly breaking the strike in the Coeur d'Alenes in 1899.

Orchard implicated Haywood, WFM president Charles Moyer and George A. Pettibone, a former union member. Although they could not be extradited from Colorado, all three were kidnapped by federal agents in Denver and spirited in a heavily guarded special train to Boise, where they were kept in jail. Defended by Clarence Darrow in a trial that received strong coverage across the country, Haywood and Pettibone were acquitted; charges against Moyer were dropped. Orchard was condemned to the gallows but his sentence was commuted to life in prison.[49] Widespread news about the trial, much of it sensational focus on the violent labor conflicts of the past dozen years, had helped fix the IWW in the public's mind then and for years to come as a bloody, anarchist organization bent on destroying capitalism.

Many of the floaters to whom Gurley Flynn directed her pleas would also have known the outlines of the Idaho case. Soon, she and her band of supporters launched into a couple of songs by Joe Hill and Ralph Chaplin, two of the best-known Wobbly songwriters. In five meetings that week, Flynn and Jones sold forty-four Little Red Song Books and 273 IWW papers.[50] But gathering pennies and nickels was not her forte. What she excelled at was agitating, and the fight she was about to pick would set a pattern that would make the Wobblies even more infamous. ✦

TWO
Fellow Workers and Friends

Elizabeth Gurley Flynn Touches Off the IWW Free Speech Fights, 1909

MISSOULA HAD HAD AN ORDINANCE ON THE BOOKS since 1899 effectively prohibiting street speaking, but the local police were inclined to ignore it.[1] They
limited their duties to making sure things were peaceful and that speakers
took turns in an orderly manner. That benign attitude began to change after
Frank Little, "the hobo agitator," slipped into town in the fall of 1909.

Already legendary for his courageous union organization work, first for
the Western Federation of Miners then for the IWW, Little seemed to
show up whenever there was a battle brewing, hopping freight trains all
around the West. The son of a Cherokee Indian mother and a Quaker
father,[2] he was missing an eye from a beating. Photos show him to be lean
and muscular, with a "weather-beaten yet ruggedly handsome face."[3]
According to an old friend, James P. Cannon, Little "was always for the
revolt, for the struggle, for the fight. Wherever he went he 'stirred up trouble' and organized the workers to rebel . . ."[4]

Little was also one of the most effective of the Wobbly "jawsmiths,"
speaking passionately off the cuff. Within hours, perhaps even minutes, of
his arrival in Missoula on September 22, 1909, he was giving a short talk,
having been spotted in the crowd by Flynn and invited up to the soapbox.
A special policeman who had been monitoring the Wobbly meetings told
Flynn, "He's too radical, he'll have to cut it out."[5] Little ignored the "bull"
and finished his talk. The next evening, Little spoke again. "You're too
rank," the same policeman said. "You'll have to cut it out or I'll take you
off the box." Little went on speaking.[6]

Little's defiant attitude may have encouraged the others. Calling to
some well-lubricated soldiers from Fort Missoula who were passing by,
Flynn offered them free literature because they always seemed to spend all
their money on booze. The following night, perhaps fearing retaliation
against the Wobblies from the infantry contingent, the police were out in

force. Flynn did not seem grateful for the added protection. "Our meeting," she wrote, "was continually annoyed by these obstreperous defenders of the law and order, who probably never heard of the Constitution of the United States and its guarantee of free speech."[7]

By the middle of the following week, with the men still soapboxing and Flynn strategizing and passing out literature, police tolerance of street speaking came to an abrupt halt. On Wednesday evening, Little had just gotten out the title of his talk ("On Temperance") when he was hauled down. So was Jones. A young logger named Appleby took his place. He started to read the Declaration of Independence and was cuffed. Then Herman Tucker, a civil engineer for the Forest Service who had been watching from an upstairs window, rushed down from his office and took over the reading of the Declaration. He too was arrested.[8]

Each received fifteen days in the county jail for violating the ban on public speaking. Judge Small offered to suspend the sentence if the men would stop. "Without exception," reported the *Butte Miner*, "they spurned the generosity of the court and were remanded to jail."[9]

Flynn realized she needed reinforcements. She telegraphed Spokane, about two hundred miles northwest. On September 30, this call to arms appeared in the *Industrial Worker*:

FREE SPEECH BATTLE;
FIGHT OR BE CHOKED
. . . IT MAY BE NECESSARY TO FILL THE MISSOULA
JAIL AND IT IS UP TO YOU, IWW MEN, TO GO TO
MISSOULA AND, IF NECESSARY, BE ARRESTED FOR
THE CRIME OF SPEAKING ON THE STREET. THE
UNIONS OF THE IWW INVITE EVERY FREE BORN
"AMERICAN," AND EVERY MAN WHO HATES THE
TYRANNICAL OPPRESSION OF THE POLICE, TO GO TO
MISSOULA AND HELP THE WORKERS THERE TO WIN
OUT.
ARE YOU GAME?
ARE YOU AFRAID?
DO YOU LOVE THE POLICE?
HAVE YOU BEEN ROBBED, SKINNED, GRAFTED ON?
IF SO, THEN GO TO MISSOULA AND DEFY THE

POLICE, THE COURTS AND THE PEOPLE WHO LIVE
OFF THE WAGES OF PROSTITUTION.
Notice—We would suggest to the Missoula police, that no
IWW men be shot nor clubbed. That no IWW women be
raped nor insulted.
THIS STRUGGLING UNION, NO. 40, IWW, CALLS ON
ALL REVOLUTIONISTS TO HELP![10]

By the time the *Industrial Worker* issue with the call to arms made it back to Missoula, some of those "troops" were already arriving. As the IWW motto went, "An Injury to One Is the Concern of All."

The ringleaders led the way into jail. Those who were released climbed back on the soapbox, gave their four-word speeches ("Fellow workers and friends . . .") and were arrested again. By October 1, the disturbances had begun to attract larger crowds that filled the intersection of Higgins and Front. Mayor Andrew Logan, a blacksmith, ordered the fire chief to bring out the hose wagon. The *Daily Missoulian* viewed the affair with humor (" . . . the firemen . . . tried out the water pressure [and] . . . nobody's clothes were spoiled."[11]). Flynn's own account notes "townspeople protested vigorously after several people were hurt."[12]

The sympathy factor was enhanced by Flynn's own arrest two days later for organizing yet another street meeting. Even though her pregnant condition was probably not known, a nineteen-year-old girl in the county jail created an uncomfortable situation for the city fathers. Two days later, Flynn was freed and her case dismissed. She later recalled she had been "treated with kid gloves by the sheriff and his wife."[13] Evidently, Gurley Flynn herself was too hot to handle.

When Mrs. Edith Frenette, sent in as Flynn's replacement, was arrested after attempting to speak, a large crowd followed, jeering and hooting, demanding the woman's release. Someone hurled a rock, striking a policeman on the arm. Outside city hall, where one jail was located, the IWW organizers spoke to the crowd. Inside, the Wobblies, "accompanied the speakers with the hymn of the organization, set to the air of the 'Marsellaise' and gave their compatriot a spirited welcome as she was locked up."[14]

Prisoners in the city jail a few blocks away had also been "making battleships," raising a ruckus in IWW slang. They were locked in cells with dirt floors directly beneath the stalls of the fire wagon horses, whose urine and manure was dropping down upon their heads. The stench "made this place so unbearable that the IWW prisoners protested by song and speech, night and day," Flynn recalled.[15] "They were directly across the street from the city's main hotel and the guests complained of the uproar."

The pressure was mounting. By October 6, the two jails held more than forty Wobblies, described by the *Butte Miner* as "particularly rabid of speech."[16] Each demanded a separate jury trial. Another 250 men were "riding the rods and the blinds, occupying the available empties" from Seattle, Portland, Spokane, and northern Idaho.[17] All the action had helped Wobbly recruiting, too. About two dozen new members joined over the weekend.[18]

The confrontation had its humorous aspects. The rough-cut lumberjacks were hardly polished speakers. "Some suffered from stage fright," Flynn wrote later.[19] "We gave them copies of the Bill of Rights and the Declaration of Independence. They would read along slowly, with one eye hopefully on the cop, fearful that they would finish before he would arrest them. One man was being escorted to jail . . . when a couple of drunks got into a pitched battle. The cop dropped him to arrest them. When they arrived at the jail, the big strapping IWW was tagging along behind. The cop said in surprise: 'What are you doing here?' The prisoner retorted: 'What do you want me to do—go back there and make another speech?'"[20]

Polished or not, the protestors were growing in numbers by the hour. Charged up by an evening demonstration in the Harnois Theater basement, the Wobblies, now in the hundreds, marched on downtown, "singing their battle songs."[21] Another thirty-five speakers were arrested, but released on their own recognizance, probably because there was nowhere left to put them.

With three days to go before the Western Montana Apple Show opened, with five hundred more Wobblies about to descend on Missoula, and with the growing realization that law enforcement tactics weren't working, the city council capitulated.[22] At a special meeting on the night of October 8, "the council declared that the IWW orators might speak where and when they pleased on the streets of Missoula, provided only that they do not impede traffic."[23]

The next sentence contained a powerful truth destined to be virtually ignored in the years ahead: "When this announcement was made, a crowd gathered and the IWW orators began to speak, but without a fight to keep things warm the interest faded, and as the night was cold, the assemblage adjourned to the hall."[24]

Progressive city officials who let the Wobblies and other street speakers have their say realized that doing so avoided free speech fights. New York Police Commissioner Arthur Woods was among the few law enforcement officials in the nation to let this valuable insight guide his policies. He believed that the job of the police was to protect citizens' rights of free expression and assembly by maintaining a discreet presence at public gatherings and by enforcing reasonable regulations.[25] "It cannot properly be considered as provocative of immediate disorder if speakers criticize, no matter how vehemently, the order of things . . . ," Woods said in 1914.[26] But the Wobblies knew they could count on police overreaction and brutality in most cases.

Flynn and her fellow Wobblies had won a clear and convincing victory in Missoula. They had won the right to speak freely on the streets, where recruits to their movement would most likely be found. More importantly, they had validated a tactic that seemed almost too good to be true. Assuming one could find enough Wobblies willing to get themselves arrested and overwhelm the prisons (and Missoula indicated this was no problem), one could create a public relations nightmare. By making martyrs of themselves, by creating scenes of victims suppressed by brutal means, by polarizing the situation, they would create public sympathy for their cause, leading to greater publicity and more financial support.

Filling the jails and clogging court calendars as a tactic of non-violent civil disobedience was not invented by the IWW—just improved. In the 1880s and 1890s, Salvation Army ministers frequently invited arrests and jailing to put attention on restrictive street-speaking laws.[27] Socialists used the tactic to protest curtailment of the right to speak in 1907 in Seattle and in 1908 in Los Angeles.[28]

For the next few years, the IWW's brand of free speech fights would suit its goals admirably. As a union attempting to organize the un-organizable, the millions of floaters who roamed the West in search of jobs, the IWW knew how vital a forum the street was. Organizing on the job was virtually impossible. Union sympathizers were fired, often blacklisted, and frequently beaten. Halls for unions, especially ones as radical as the IWW, were difficult to rent because few landlords were willing to take the risk.

"The street corner was their only hall and if denied the right to agitate there then they must be silent," wrote a Wobbly organizer.[29]

Moreover, the ability to educate the working class in any large-scale way via the printed media was thwarted by the anti-labor bias of almost all general circulation daily or weekly newspapers. Negative news about unions, such as arrests of members, was often the only news printed about them. Papers often ignored rallies and other organizational activities unless arrests were made. Therefore, the IWW recruited agitators and propagandists who could speak directly to the masses.

In a time before electronic media, the street was also the traditional forum for speaking; indeed it was the center of much of community life before telephones, radio, and air-conditioning. Vendors and peddlers selling crepe hats or cough drops, boys playing hoops, couples promenading—much of life was lived on the streets. Those who wished to air their thoughts spoke on the streets, some for hours on end, and oftentimes with considerable give and take with the audience. Many municipalities had restrictions on times and places of speaking, but they were enforced irregularly at the discretion of police.

Sweatboxes in Spokane

Spokane's free speech fight followed almost immediately. It lasted four months, from November 1909 to March 1910. IWW organizers had been defying a street-speaking ordinance that allowed only the Salvation Army to speak. Holding street meetings directly outside the offending employment offices on skid road, organizers gave specifics—times, places, amounts, and names of workers who were fleeced.[30] The agencies appealed to the police and the arrests began. More than six hundred Wobblies from as far away as Maine responded to the calls to arms. They flooded into the city, jumped up to give their "four-word speeches" and got arrested. Within three days, they had overloaded the city's jail, which the police and judges were only too eager to fill.[31] The IWW newspaper in Spokane, the *Industrial Worker*, was shut down and five successive editors (Flynn the last) were arrested.[32]

Spokane police were far more brutal. Three Wobblies died in an unheated school used as an auxiliary jail. More than a thousand others were hospitalized, some from beatings, many with pneumonia. It was standard police practice to strip prisoners, put them under a scalding spray, and then rinse them in icy water before sending them to their freezing quarters in the school.[33] As the IWW Spokane Free Speech Defense, relocated to Coeur d'Alene, Idaho, described the situation in an appeal for funds: "While incarcerated, many of the men have jaws broken, eyes blinded, teeth knocked out, and otherwise maltreated, besides being fed on one small slice of sour old bread twice a day; as a result, scurvy set in, and the men were soon too weak to walk across the floor or even to stand up. . . . There are yet over one hundred men in the jails suffering the tortures of the Black Hole of Calcutta, in their endeavor to safeguard the weapons of our class, Freedom of Speech, Press, and Public assemblage."[34]

More than twelve hundred men—as well as Flynn and Frenette—were arrested. As many as twenty-eight prisoners at a time were herded into six-by-eight-foot "sweatboxes" in the city jail. As Flynn recalled: "The steam was turned on until the men nearly suffocated and were overcome with exhaustion. Then they were placed in ice-cold cells and forced to work on the rock pile."[35]

Government officials and the business community reacted in predictable fashion. The Spokane Chamber of Commerce began to organize a citizens' militia, with plans to offer "enlistment bonuses" of gold watches. Gov. M. E. Hay proclaimed, "The IWWs do not seem to be able to understand the idea of our form of government. . . . They desire no laws that interfere with their way of thinking. If we were all of that opinion, we would soon have no law but anarchy . . ."[36] But it was the government that did not get it—at least until the costs began to mount. Faced with damage suits for $150,000 from brutalized IWW members, and incurring expenses of $1,000 a week[37], the city officials finally ran up the white flag on March 5, 1910. In return for dropping all damage suits, the IWW would be allowed to speak freely, its newspaper would be free to publish and all Wobbly prisoners would be released.[38]

The next free speech fights, in Fresno in 1911 and in Aberdeen, Washington, in early 1912, began to provoke more concerted reaction by the business community. Vigilantes, joined or led by law enforcement officers, would terrorize the IWWs in jail and drive them out of town. As Harrison Gray Otis, publisher of the *Los Angeles Times*, said, "During the visit of the Industrial Workers of the World they will be accorded a night and day guard of honor, composed of citizens armed with rifles. The Coroner will be in attendance at his office every day."[39]

Otis, a Civil War veteran and a brigadier general in the Spanish-

American War, had a special animus toward labor radicals: His forceful anti-union, open shop attitude had precipitated the October 10, 1910, dynamiting of the Times building, resulting in twenty deaths. Brothers J. J. and J. B. McNamara pleaded guilty in 1912 in a life-saving plea bargain engineered by their lawyer, Clarence Darrow.

Clubs and Black Snakes

Encouraged by Otis and his friend John D. Spreckels, a sugar magnate who owned the *San Diego Union*, vigilante counter-tactics came into full play in San Diego in an eighteen-month free speech fight that began in January, 1912. As Wobbly Joe Hill remarked, San Diego was "not worth a whoop in Hell from a rebel's point of view."[40] But the IWW, numbering fifty or fewer, began to hold street meetings in town as early as late 1910.[41] Its attempts to invite the streetcar men into its fold infuriated Spreckels, who owned the local streetcar franchise. Employers pressured the city's Common Council to enact an ordinance banning street speaking in a forty-nine–block area encompassing the city's commercial district.

The call went out. "This fight will be continued," vowed IWW general secretary Vincent St. John, "until free speech is established in San Diego if it takes twenty thousand members and twenty years to do so."[42]

When IWW members and supporters began to descend on San Diego, they unleashed a paroxysm of violence by citizens determined to defend their sunny little city of fifty thousand. Wobblies were imprisoned for saying a few words on the street or for being in IWW headquarters. They were also forced to kiss the flag and run through gantlets of vigilantes armed with clubs, whips, guns, ax handles, and wagon spokes. Harris Weinstock, commissioned by Gov. Hiram Johnson, a progressive Republican, to investigate the free speech fight, told this story in his report:

> Arriving at Sorrento (the city limits), 15 or 16 autos were found lined up along the road, with lights burning low. There were between 60 and 75 men there, with lanterns, while others openly displayed revolvers, knives, nightsticks, black jacks, and black snakes. None wore disguises. The insignia of the order, or band, was a white handkerchief, tied at the elbow of the right arm.[43]

The Wobblies were made to mount a platform of boxes, kneel and kiss the flag. Then they were clubbed for ten minutes, made to sing the national anthem (and beaten until they remembered the words), and trucked to the county line at San Onofre, where they were placed in a cattle pen and slugged and beaten some more. The next morning, with no food or drink for more than eighteen hours, they were run through another gantlet and "belabored with clubs and black snakes."

Harris continued: "Then the flag-kissing episode was repeated, after which they were told to 'hike' up the track for Los Angeles and never come back. They reached Los Angeles after a tramp of several days, sore, hungry, practically penniless and in deplorable physical condition."[44]

Newspapers applauded this action. In an editorial on March 4, 1912, the *San Diego Tribune* said of the Wobblies: "Hanging is none too good for them and they would be much better dead; for they are absolutely useless in the human economy; they are the waste material of creation and should be drained off into the sewer of oblivion there to rot in cold obstruction like any other excrement."[45] Spreckels' *San Diego Union* suggested citizens had a right to take the law into their own hands.

"[The editorials] were enough to stir men's blood to action," investigator Weinstock observed in his report. "The young, the thoughtless, and the adventurous among the respectable elements of the community could not but be powerfully influenced by such preachments. Men, such as these, backed by the support and approval of the commercial bodies and the leading daily newspapers, representing . . . much of the intelligence, the wealth, the conservatism, the enterprise, and presumably also the good citizenship, of the community, felt impelled to play the part . . . of patriotic heroes . . ."[46]

With warnings of impending disaster, Spreckels and his fellow businessmen tried to interest Washington in their problem. The chamber of commerce warned Attorney General George W. Wickersham that the IWW "anarchists" threatened to assassinate the chief of police and the district attorney and blow up the water works. Behind the free speech campaign, they advised, "is a design at an opportune moment to cross the Mexican line, take forcible possession of lower California where they may loot and murder with impunity."[47]

Through the summer, officials continued to plead for indictments of the "anarchists" under either federal treason laws or statutes punishing those who conspired to overthrow the government of the United States by force. Wickersham refused. No prosecution of the IWW was possible under existing U.S. law, he replied, because there was nothing indicating a specific attack upon the government.

Nonetheless, the events in San Diego precipitated the first discussion of sedition prosecution for the Wobblies. As abhorrent as the 1798 Alien and Sedition Acts might have been, the *San Diego Union* editorialized, something like them would be needed to stop those who advocated anarchy.[48]

In his report to Gov. Johnson, Commissioner Weinstock blistered both sides. "It was the purpose of the invading IWW incidentally to test the validity of the so-called anti-free-speech ordinance, but primarily to clog the machinery of and to overwhelm the city and county government . . . and to put upon the taxpayers . . . the greatest possible burden. . . . [T]here can be no excuse for men, collectively, to conspire needlessly to hamper the machinery of government."[49]

Of their attackers, he said, "Every blinded member of the so-called vigilance committee has . . . made of himself . . . a far greater criminal than those whom he brands as 'anarchists,' 'revolutionists,' 'dynamiters,' and 'scum of the earth.'"[50]

Despite the criticism, San Diego businessmen continued to try to get Washington to take action. Republican National Committee bigwig Frank W. Estabrook suggested that Taft could make political hay by taking forceful action before the general election, now just two months away.

Taft was intrigued by the suggestion, for he was being challenged for the presidency not only by Democrat Woodrow Wilson but also by his former patron Teddy Roosevelt, now a candidate of the Bull Moose Party, and T. R.'s running mate, California Gov. Hiram Johnson. He shot off a note to the attorney general: "We ought to take decided action. The State Government of California is under an utterly unscrupulous boss (Johnson) who does not hesitate to . . . cultivate [the anarchists' and the IWW's] good will, and it is our business to go in and show the strong hand of the United States in a marked way so that they shall understand that we are on the job."[51]

Wickersham balked. "There is no doubt in my mind that the State officials have been most derelict in the performance of their duties, but . . . care should be taken to avoid getting the federal government into assuming the burdens which properly belong to the State."[52]

The attorney general's principled refusal to act against the IWW would stand in sharp contrast to his successor in the victorious Wilson administration, Thomas W. Gregory. To be sure, the nation's wartime footing would force the Justice Department and other agencies in the administration to take the Wobblies more seriously. However, under the leadership of reactionaries like Gregory and Postmaster General Albert S. Burleson—and with the repressive laws handed them by Congress—the Wilson administration would bludgeon the IWW and other radicals into submission.

Securing the Right to Speak

The IWW leadership realized that the pressure tactics inherent in the free speech fights were probably the best way of enforcing their members' right to speak freely, because the ballot box and the courts weren't available in practice. The Wobblies had no voting constituency. They were despised outsiders. Yet outsiders were exactly what they wanted to be. In embracing direct action, the IWW had rejected "dropping pieces of paper into a hole in a box."[53]

The courts could not be counted upon to protect their free-speech rights. Judges may have paid lip service to freedom of speech, like the Spokane police magistrate who in 1909 convicted all the Wobblies arrested under the city ban on street-speaking, even as he called the right of free speech "an inalienable and God-given right."[54] But courts showed little sympathy for those who challenged street-speaking ordinances.

First, there was no established notion that streets or parks were a protected forum for speech. This was reflected in a *San Diego Evening Tribune* editorial in 1912, which argued that citizens could rid themselves of street speakers "as an individual citizen would rid himself of a gang of gypsies camping on his lawn or in his back yard."[55] The writer had ample precedent to back up his opinion. Justice Oliver Wendell Holmes Jr., as a judge on the Massachusetts Supreme Court, had said much the same thing in an 1895 opinion rejecting a preacher's right to proselytize on Boston Common. Holmes had declared that a ban on public speaking in a park "is no more of an infringement of the rights of a member of the public than for the owner of a private house to forbid it in his house.[56]

Because expression had little special value, it was routinely balanced against other rights. Business owners believed their property rights were at least as important as IWW speech rights—an attitude that received general assent in a period when property rights were king.

Further, many court decisions dampened free expression by holding that a person abused the liberty of speech by, for example, breaching the peace or being a public nuisance. Thus a petty misdemeanor was enough to trump any free speech protection. Worse, under the prevailing law, speech would be judged by its *tendency* to breach the peace or lead to some crime, no matter how remote. Moreover, those applying this very loose standard would be jurors and judges applying middle-class beliefs, fears, and prejudices to their task, practically insuring a high rate of conviction.[57] In addition, neither the law nor public sentiment was sympathetic to speech rights of the minority. The common belief was that the majority could legally snuff out dissident viewpoints.

Finally, hardly anyone—no court, certainly—believed that the First Amendment even applied to state and local government actions. It would be almost another generation before the U.S. Supreme Court would expand First Amendment protection to the states, by holding that free expression guarantees were fundamental rights assured to all citizens under the due process and equal protection clauses of the Fourteenth Amendment.[58]

This constellation of ideas spelled doom for virtually any legal challenge by the IWW or other dissident group to street-speaking laws. And in the atmosphere of hysteria and fear that would soon follow during the First World War, these concepts would apply far beyond street speaking. They would make it easy for state legislatures as well as Congress to pass sedition laws severely restricting speech rights, and would spell prison time for those who spoke out against government, particularly in an angry or abusive manner.

Were the Free Speech Fights Worth It?

Two dozen more free speech fights would follow in the next four years before America's entry into the war. But even early on, some IWW leaders questioned their efficacy. Back in 1911, Wobbly tactician John Pancner had said, "Organize the wage slave, not the bourgeois, the street moocher, and the saloon soak." The latter types had been easy to recruit for free-speech duty, but they weren't necessarily swayed to the IWW cause. Others noted that passive resistance, the core of the free speech fights, put the membership at a terrible disadvantage; Wobblies should at least be allowed to protect themselves. The cream of the movement was being hit hard by jailings, beatings, and bread and water diets. Still others pointed out that committed "fighters" scattered once the victory had been won, "vagging" by freight train to the next fight. Wobbly editor Ben Williams reflected in 1913, "We are to the labor movement what the high diver is to the circus. A sensation, marvelous and nerve-thrilling. We attract the crowds. We give them thrills, we do hair-raising stunts. . . . As far as making industrial unionism fit the everyday life of the workers we have failed miserably."[59] These doubts, and the additional heat put on the IWW after the United States entered the war, would end the free speech fights.

Undoubtedly, the free speech fights raised the IWW's profile. But did IWW leaders manipulate the constitutional guarantees of freedom of speech, assembly, and association to achieve this end? There is some evidence that some members saw the free speech fights as merely a tactic to help achieve its ultimate goal, but not as an ideal in which the organization was fully invested.[60]

Yet the IWW leadership also recognized that these freedoms were essential to their political ends. Standing up for those rights—in an era when few others were willing or courageous enough to do so—was necessary for the IWW to achieve its goals of recruiting workingmen and to publicizing its grievances with the working conditions of early twentieth century America. And by doing so, the IWW helped raise consciousness about a basic principle of American democracy—which its members believed had been perverted. As an editorial in the *Industrial Worker* noted in November 1909, "[M]ultiplied thousands will continue to speak and protest against its denial, for they realize that in the imprisonment of one class of men in defiance of all constitutional guarantees, the liberties of all are invaded and placed in peril."[61]

In their own inimitable way, the Wobblies shook up the "spirit of cosy content" they had encountered first in Missoula. As writer Courtenay Lemon wrote in *Pearson's Magazine*: "Whether they agree or disagree with its methods or aims, all lovers of liberty everywhere owe a debt to this organization for its defense of free speech. Absolutely irreconcilable, absolutely fearless, and insuppressibly persistent, it has kept alight the fires of freedom, like some outcast vestal of human liberty. That the defense of traditional rights to which this government is supposed to be dedicated should devolve upon an organization so often denounced as "unpatriotic" and "un-American" is but . . . the unfailing irony of history."[62]

In the next few years, the IWW would leverage its notoriety, elevated by the free speech fights, to gain in strength and numbers. It would become a more disciplined group—although never monolithic. The many-sided organization would make real advances in organizing laborers spurned by the trade unions. As the Great War descended on Europe in 1914, rising demand for labor to produce goods and commodities for the combatants (chiefly the Allies) lifted wages and spurred efforts to improve working conditions. But the advances were hardly enough to negate the Wobblies' raison d'etre. They continued to play the role of despised dissenter to the hilt. ❖

THREE
Harvest Stiffs and Shingle Weavers

The IWW Gathers Strength and Focuses Westward, 1912–1917

WHEN IWW EXECUTIVE SECRETARY Big Bill Haywood came to Butte in 1910, he boasted that the IWW would "nail the red flag to the mast of No. 1 [the Butte Miners' Union Hall] and the [copper company] officials would climb up there every morning and get down on their knees to it."[1]

Haywood's fantasy never came true, but in the years after he waved the red flag in the company's face, the IWW became a much bigger threat. Particularly after the free speech fight in San Diego, from 1912 to 1917, the IWW grew in numbers, potency—and infamy. In those five years, the IWW did an impressive job of organizing workers across the country and spurring reforms. Despite itself, the IWW became a force to be reckoned with.

Ben Reitman, a lover of anarchist Emma Goldman (and one of many who was brutalized in the San Diego free speech fight), wryly observed in 1913 after an IWW convention: "God! Is it possible that this bunch of pork-chop philosophers, agitators who have no real, great organizing ability or creative brain power are able to frighten the capitalistic class more than any other Labor movement organized in America? Is it true that this body of politicians were able to send five thousand men to jail in the various free-speech fights? Are the activities of these men forcing the A. F. of L. and the sociologists to recognize the power and necessity of Industrial Unionism?"[2]

The answer, Reitman concluded, was yes. The problem was that when the Wobblies smelled success in the class struggle, others smelled gunpowder and revolution.

IWW successes and the reactions they provoked established a recurring pattern in the pre-war years: Wily, dedicated IWW ideologues would organize underpaid, maltreated workers to strike for better pay and conditions. Intransigent employers, citizens, governments—and the more moderate trade unions of the AFL—would react in alarm to "outside agitators" and over-react with violence and brutality even more lawless than that which they sought to extinguish. The IWW would inevitably be blamed for the bloodshed. Its members would be tried and often jailed, resulting in martyrdom for Wobbly victims. The publicity would help the IWW over the short-term. Workers would sometimes see real economic gains but often the advances would be fleeting. Each cycle would result in an accumulating demonization of the IWW, enthusiastically abetted by newspapers and opinion leaders across the country. Finally, each magnification of the IWW's "evil" nature would result in more calls for action by industry leaders and politicians, demanding that the federal and state governments act immediately to crush the IWW menace.

The IWW's successes were fashioned from a variety of circumstances, each demanding a unique strategy. In Lawrence, Massachusetts, for example, the non-violent tactics and nose for good public relations seen in the IWW free speech fights were adapted brilliantly in a 1912 strike of woolen mill workers.

Living in squalid conditions along the Merrimack River valley north of Boston—36 percent of mill workers were dead by age twenty-five—a workforce of mostly recent southern European immigrants struck when employers moved to reduce pay that averaged $6 to $9 a week.[3] IWW leaders, including Flynn and Haywood, led the walkout by some fourteen thousand textile workers. The strikers maintained their peaceful, high-spirited, song-filled protests in the face of bullying by police and acts of provocation by private citizens, such as planting dynamite. Endless chains of picketers wore white armbands reading, "Don't be a scab."[4] A banner carried by mill girls in a peaceful protest parade, which read "We Want Bread and Roses Too" became the slogan of the strike, signifying not only the workers' chronic malnutrition but their hunger for higher aspirations. The IWW also urged railroad men to "Lose their cars for them!" and telegraphers to "Lose their messages for them!"[5] To greater effect, they swiftly put together an efficient relief effort for the starving workers, who eventually reached twenty-three thousand in number.[6]

To further emphasize the child labor horrors in the mills, IWW leaders launched a masterful public relations offensive with a "Children's Crusade."

About 150 of the strikers' obviously malnourished children were sent to

Figure 4. Elizabeth Gurley Flynn and IWW executive secretary Big Bill Haywood with children of striking mill workers in Paterson, New Jersey, 1913. Walter P. Reuther Library, Wayne State University.

more affluent temporary foster parents in Barre, Vermont, and New York City, where they were paraded down Fifth Avenue.[7] The spectacle made great copy, creating instant villains of the wool trusts and instant sympathy for the IWW. When local police, in a block-headed attempt to stop more children from leaving for Philadelphia, pulled out truncheons and began to club the foster mothers, the resulting national publicity and political heat virtually ensured that the IWW's strike relief coffers would overflow.

Two months after the strike began, the textile companies capitulated, offering wage increases of as much as 25 percent to thirty thousand textile mill workers.[8] The victory lent the IWW more credibility as a labor reformer, at a time when publicity from the San Diego free speech fight was painting the Wobblies as a bunch of lawless hooligans. Membership in the IWW local in Lawrence rocketed from two hundred and eighty-seven[9] in 1912 to more than fourteen thousand in 1913, organizers claimed. The following year, however, membership in the same local had fallen back to near its starting point.[10] As workers' short-term practical needs—higher wages, shorter hours, safer working conditions—were met, their ardor for revolutionary principles evaporated.

In the West, the IWW found that nuts-and-bolts organizing worked effectively among the "harvest stiffs" or migratory agricultural workers who nightly bedded down in straw stacks, barns, or vermin-infested bunkhouses, and received a pittance for their backbreaking work. Numbering approximately one hundred thousand in the mid-west grain belt, they were part of a larger population of floating workers estimated at between 2 and 5 million.[11]

An excerpt from the field notes of Peter Speer, a tireless investigator for the Commission on Industrial Relations, gives a flavor of a typical migrant worker, interviewed in a hobo jungle near Redfern, South Dakota, in July 1914: "Age 24 years, Dane. Seven years in this country. Came to America because it is the best country in the world. The best opportunities to better himself. (High school) education. Started out as a sailor [frozen out by union]. . . . Started for the West . . . beat his way down to Missouri. . . . Asked farmers for job. Begged. Got one job at 50 cents a day for five days, when the job was done. After buying some clothing, 25 cents left. . . . Went into Nebraska—westward. Several days without eating, except apples. Got a job, with a German farmer, haymaking, $1.50 a day, 10 to 11 hours. Good board, slept in the barn. Treatment was fine. Six days, the job was done. . . . Continued his way toward West . . . Got a job on a farm in Nebraska, $18 a month. Chores and general farm work, 10 hours . . .

As Joe Hill had put it in the refrain to one of his best-loved songs: *You will eat, bye and bye; In that glorious land above the sky; Work and pray, live on hay, You'll get pie in the sky when you die.*

Because harvest stiffs were constantly on the move, IWW organizers had to go to them. Equipped with "a little black case in which they had membership books and buttons and literature and dues stamps and all the paraphernalia of organization," IWW "camp delegates" would work, eat, and bunk with potential recruits, spread IWW propaganda and organize the men to press for better working and living conditions.[12]

IWW organizers shaped the campaign for workers in the wheat fields around bread-and-butter issues. They called for decent room and board and a minimum wage of $3.50 a day with overtime after ten hours (farmers were said to have the eight-hour day—eight hours in the forenoon and eight hours in the afternoon). Farmers anxious to harvest their crops proved receptive to the union demands—backed where necessary by a dose of direct action. This usually meant "withdrawal of efficiency," slacking on the job, until demands were met. While some rural communities organized "pick-handle brigades" to drive Wobblies out of town, violence was usually muted because wheat prices were soaring to meet European war demand. Thus more farmers could afford to raise wages, improve living accommodations and reduce working hours.

When violence did occur, employers shifted the blame to the IWW and used it as further proof of the organization's danger. Yet the organization's membership rolls would often increase. After a 1913 riot of nearly three thousand hop-pickers in California's Central Valley in which a district attorney, a deputy sheriff and two workers were killed, two Wobblies were convicted of murder and sentenced to life in prison. The publicity drove up IWW membership to more than five thousand in rural California in 1914 and also spawned Progressive reforms that improved migrant labor conditions. But the same reformers pleaded for federal intervention to stop the IWW's "reign of terror," pointing to its direct action tactics that they said had resulted in widespread property destruction and arson. As with the San Diego free speech fights, the U.S. Department of Justice decided to watch, but take no action yet.[13]

As word of the IWW successes spread, so too did the value of the red membership card, particularly as a safe conduct pass on the freights. This was no minor benefit in a period when most migrant workers had to ride the rails to travel quickly to the next ripening crop. Violence on the railroads was common. According to labor investigator Carleton Parker, nearly twenty-four thousand rail trespassers, most of them hobos, were killed just between 1901 and 1905 (an average of fifteen men per day!).[14] Drunks, holdup men, bulls (railway detectives), train crews, and local police all posed threats for riders. Tales circulated constantly of riders being ditched—thrown off a moving train—sometimes by IWW's themselves if they could not produce a paid-up red card.

Sabotage and Non-Violence

Tales also circulated widely about IWW sabotage, of poisoning crops and burning bales, of spiking trees and derailing rail cars. The "proof" often offered was Elizabeth Gurley Flynn's pamphlet, *Sabotage.*

Flynn had written *Sabotage* after the silk workers' strike in Paterson, New Jersey in 1913. The AFL's motto, she noted, was "a fair day's work for a fair day's wage." Sabotage was just the reverse: "an unfair day's work for an unfair day's wage." It could take a variety of forms: reducing the quantity or quality of work in exchange for short pay, interfering with the quality or durability of goods, delivering bad service, bad-mouthing a product or service to customers, slavishly following the rule book, and work slowdowns. Flynn had also argued that violence was sometimes a legitimate response to employer violence in putting down strikes.[15]

Unfortunately, the youthful Flynn's exuberant defense of sabotage was naïve, because more destructive forms of sabotage had certainly been advocated and used by Wobblies, although not nearly to the extent that employers claimed they had. Sabotage was often impossible to prove. But it was the Wobblies who were most closely identified with sabotage. They even had a special symbol for sabotage, a thin black cat with an arched back, known as the sab cat or sab kitty.

Little wonder that, in an era when property rights were supreme, angry bosses and the officials to whom they complained seized upon sabotage as proof that the IWW sanctioned the destruction of property. Flynn's *Sabotage* was among the key exhibits sent to U.S. Attorney General Thomas B. Gregory in November 1915 by the California Commission for Immigration and Housing. In fact, the documents proved nothing. They were merely a compilation of IWW pamphlets, threatening letters, and publications like *Sabotage*, more bark than bite.

Already by 1916, the IWW's General Executive Board could see that continuing to endorse sabotage openly would only distract from the more serious organizing work being carried out, in which it now hoped to engage more deeply. The General Executive Board decided to stop publishing the pamphlet and back away from it.

The bans on Flynn's pamphlet and *Ta-ra-ra-Boom-de-ay*, a Wobbly song that celebrated sabotage, were symbolic gestures, for everyone realized that sabotage would continue.[16] If the bans made a statement that the IWW was growing up, however, their enemies chose to ignore the evidence. Flynn's pamphlet, which she later conceded had been written "in my young and hot-headed and heedless days," was regularly introduced at Wobbly trials and submitted to the Justice Department as evidence of the IWW's evil intent. It even popped up when Flynn was hauled before the

Subversive Activities Control Board in the Red-hunting 1950s. "I was as embarrassed as a man of 60 might feel if he were confronted with a love letter he wrote when he was 17," Flynn recalled.[17]

The executive board's newfound caution may have had more influence internally. Agitators like Frank Little, who favored the property-destruction form of sabotage, found themselves less in the loop for a while. At the 1914 IWW convention, Little had been quoted as saying, "Wherever I go, I inaugurate sabotage among the workers. Eventually the bosses will learn why it is their machinery is spoiled and their workers slowing down."[18] But Little, a veteran of internecine disputes, undoubtedly reasoned that the game wasn't over.

The Wobblies were, in fact, more often the victims of violence, not the perpetrators. Although there is some anecdotal evidence to the contrary, such as the stories of Wobblies throwing people out of trains for not having red cards, scholars of the period seem to agree with the leading IWW historian, Melvyn Dubofsky, that "While the IWW preached defiance of bourgeois law and capitalist justice, 'law-abiding' American citizens practiced it."[19]

The IWW, argues historian Joseph Conlin, eschewed violence from a practical standpoint, realizing it was outgunned and outnumbered in most of its fights. More importantly, the organization recognized that non-violent passive resistance could better achieve its aims—including winning public sympathy and support from the violence directed against its members. Haywood and other IWW leaders had often preached the "power of folded arms."[20] Despite their fearsome image, Conlin notes, "no Wobbly was ever convicted of driving a spike into a log or igniting a wheat field." In fact, he adds, "despite dozens of prosecutions and the investigative powers of a dozen states, the Federal Bureau of Investigation, the Immigration Bureau, and the Justice Department, *no Wobbly was ever proved to have committed an act of violence* [Conlin's italics]."[21]And yet the public, flooded by negative messages about the IWW, continued to believe otherwise.

Timber Beasts

Success in agricultural organizing—although somewhat inflated by the war demand—inevitably led IWW leaders to use the same methods in the lumber industry, especially in the West. Their success in the next two years in organizing men into the IWW and in improving wages and working conditions would come at a great cost, however. The strikes that it played a major role in starting stirred the wrath of powerful, intransigent employers "practicing classic nineteenth-century capitalism in a twentieth-century world."[22] The clash of these forces would lead to tragedy and also to more strident calls to state and federal officials to put the IWW out of business.

Conditions in timber camps were abysmal. In each bunkhouse, thirty to forty men slept in louse-infested bedrolls, two to a double bed (four to a bunk), often on top of rotten hay that horses would not touch. Poles next to a stove held smelly wet wool socks and wool underwear. "The sweaty, steamy odors of a bunkhouse at night would asphyxiate the uninitiated," wrote Rexford Tugwell.[23] Men washed at a wooden trough at the end of the bunkhouse, dipping cold water out of a barrel, recalled former Montana logger Donald Mackenzie, who worked for Anaconda Copper Mining Company's lumber department.[24] They only took baths on weekends, although Finnish loggers often constructed rough saunas that other loggers used. The food cooked by the "belly robber" and his "flunkies," his assistants, was "worse than you'd feed animals . . . what wouldn't go into a stew, they would squeeze through a sack and give it to you in hash for breakfast." One time, Mackenzie remembered, the men got so fed up at the grub, they "threw plates at the lamps and the place went into darkness." Garbage was usually dumped outside the cookhouse door, breeding flies and maggots. In summer, the stink of the rotten garbage competed with the open toilets only a short distance from the cookhouses.

Wages were typically $2.40 a day for a swamper or common laborer for a ten-hour day, and $2.60 for teamsters. Their pay had hardly gone up at all in the past decade. Records of ACM's lumber department show that laborers were paid $2.25 a day in 1902.[25] When men did get paid (in gold, cash, or checks), they found that compulsory deductions for board, hospital fees, poll tax, employment fees, spring mattresses sold over and over again to successive loggers, and other commissary supplies such as socks or snus (snuff), had reduced their net pay to some minuscule amount. "Pay checks have been issued to first-class lumberjacks in Montana by no smaller a corporation than Jim Hill's railway [Northern Pacific] for amounts ranging from 5 cents and up," the *Industrial Worker* noted in 1910.[26]

Inherently risky logging and milling operations were sometimes made more dangerous by new laborsaving technology. About 1910, the laborious work of moving logs from the woods to the mills started to be taken over by overhead cable yarding. The "flying machines" improved efficiency and allowed logging to be done year-round, avoiding the need to haul logs over snow, mud, and rough terrain. However, they demanded coordination among experienced crewmembers, something that the high turnover of loggers worked against.[27]

Western lumber companies routinely spied on their own men in order to check on employee discontent and root out IWW agitators. Written reports, such as those filed in 1913 by an operative for the Anaconda's Lumber Department, give a flavor of the working conditions and the atmosphere:

> May 1, 1913 from St. Maries, Idaho: ". . . The men who were getting $2.75 for sawing are quitting and coming in. 12 men came in from Falcone last night . . . said all the 28 sawyers are going to quit today on $2.75, all Greeks. Down in this country there are all kinds of camps to work for and they can change around . . . If they don't like one foreman, they can go someplace else . . ."
>
> May 7, Purdue, Idaho, close to Camp 8 of the Potlatch Lumber Co.: "You can see men going out to work on every train, but they don't stay, and you can see men coming in on every train. . . . Where the land is level and the timber green, they do not pay so much, as men will stay; where the ground is hilly and timber is black, burned over [probably from the enormous fires of 1910], they pay more, but the men do not stay . . ."[28]

IWW organizers urged men to stay put and fight it out, with strikes and picket lines. In 1913, organizer John Pancner urged Northwest lumber workers to "buy a fish line, put part of your money in the grub fund and camp out where you can, picket the camps, mills, railroad yard, docks, and employment offices. . . . Don't run away from the battle."[29] But strikes were less successful than membership drives. Before 1916, most IWW-led strikes in the industry were spur-of-the-moment, heated affairs. They were soon broken as much by worker confusion and lack of solidarity as by employer resistance.

Intransigence and Terror

Timber bosses and lumber company owners were unyielding for the most part to any needed improvements in pay, hours, or conditions. Self-made, rugged individualists who had risen through the ranks, most chose not to recognize the problems. Most operators would not budge from a ten-hour day, arguing that they needed the longer hours to compete with Southern timber operations, which had the advantage of being closer to bigger markets, thus having lower transportation costs. They dismissed union efforts to improve conditions as "impertinent tamperings with economic law and the prerogatives of property ownership."[30] Confronted with demands, they refused to budge, fearing any concession would open the floodgates. "As has often been said by the employers," noted national forest supervisor F. A. Silcox from Missoula, "'If those men get bath tubs they will only want something else.'"

One exception appears to have been Kenneth Ross, the manager of the Anaconda's Lumber Department. A gruff and flinty-eyed Scot who had no use for Wobblies, Ross was evidently concerned for the welfare of his men. In 1913, logger Mackenzie recalled, Ross investigated a brief wildcat strike over terrible living conditions. He fired the foreman and the timekeepers and replaced the cook. "Then he went to all the managers of the outfits in the northwest [part of Montana] and said, 'Look here now, fellas. These people are human same as we are.'" Blankets and beds (and bacon and eggs) soon followed.

With a sharp upsurge in war orders in early 1916 leading to a tighter labor market, lumber employers organized an open-shop campaign, seeking to counter the IWW's Lumber Workers Industrial Union No. 500, recently created in Spokane. The new IWW union immediately started organizing in the Kootenai River valley in northwestern Montana, not far from the Canadian border. Loggers there were involved in the spring river drive, using spring-swollen rivers to move logs felled the previous winter. A company spy estimated that 70 percent of the loggers around the towns of Eureka and Fortine were "members of the IWW and that they were going to make it hot for the Eureka Lumber Company this spring."[31]

Before the rivers swelled from the melting snow, however, a horrific, violent incident on Puget Sound in late 1916 showed just how polarized attitudes had become in the lumber industry and how hatred pervaded the atmosphere.

The scene of the violence was in Everett, a small lumber town on Puget Sound north of Seattle. It was ideally situated for receiving raw logs rafted in from around the sound, then milling them into boards, posts, shingles, and other finished wood items. Cedar shingles were the dominant product. "A perfume of cedar hung permanently over the city."[32]

While many aspects of the lumber business were risky, the work of the shingle weavers, who cut the cedar shakes, seemed insane. A reporter wrote this description of a shingle mill in the first decade of the twentieth century: "Shingle-weaving is not a trade, it is a battle. For ten hours a day the sawyer faces two teethed steel disks whirling around 200 times a minute. To the one on the left he feeds the heavy blocks of cedar, reaching over with his left hand to remove the heavy shingles it rips off. Hour after hour the shingle-weaver's hands and arms, plain, unarmored flesh and blood, are staked against the screeching steel that cares not what it severs. If 'cedar asthma,' the shingle weaver's occupational disease, does not get him, the steel will. Sooner or later he reaches over a little too far, the whirling blade tosses drops of deep red into the air, a finger, a hand, or part of an arm comes sliding down the slick chute."[33]

Shingle weavers had organized in 1890 and affiliated with the AF of L in 1903. A long strike over wages that had started in the spring of 1916 was headed for defeat. Wobbly organizer James Rowan showed up in August. The next three months were filled with the kind of guerilla warfare Wobblies relished and were so experienced in. Their determined foe was the fulminating sheriff of Snohomish County, Donald McRae, backed by the businessmen and lumber plutocrats who comprised the town's aristocracy.

What happened in Everett has been described as the IWW's last free speech fight.[34] It certainly had all the elements—agitating soap boxers singing Wobbly songs and reciting the Declaration of Independence at street meetings, filling the jail, demanding jury trials and representation by counsel, city officials being condemned for suppressing free speech, a building wave of public support. But Sheriff McRae's furious reaction made it darker, and in the end, tragic.

McRae and deputies stormed the IWW hall on several occasions, determined to rid the city of "the Wobbly nuisance." IWW members were arrested on sight and deported. In late October, McRae and his men arrested forty-one Wobblies attempting to enter the city on a passenger boat from Seattle. Adopting the violent tactics used by anti-IWW forces in San Diego in 1912, they beat them with clubs and revolvers. Then they herded the men into waiting vehicles and drove them to a deserted park.

"They were armed with every kind of cudgel imaginable," Jack Miller, one of the victims, said later, "sawed billiard cues, billy clubs, small base-ball bats, brass knuckles, pistol butts . . . I tried . . . ducking and weaving . . . someone grabbed me by the necktie. Then I felt a blow on my head and another under my eye. . . . One of the IWWs was crippled for life . . . there were lots of concussions and fractures . . ."[35]

The brutal gauntlet raised the public's wrath and aroused the Wobblies. A protest rally was publicized for Sunday, November 5, in the Everett city park. The director of the Employers' Association of Washington urged McRae's deputies to repel the radical union army. The next morning, three hundred Wobblies paraded four abreast through Seattle to the docks, where most of them boarded a small passenger boat, the *Verona*, for the trip up Puget Sound. As the boat eased in to the dock in Everett, Wobblies on the main deck were singing a union song. McRae and his deputies were waiting. Gunfire broke out. At least five Wobblies were killed; half a dozen others may have fallen into the Sound and drowned. Two deputies died. Sheriff McRae was shot in his left leg.

The Everett massacre, said historian Robert L. Tyler, "summed up in a few moments of history—illumined as if by a flash of lightning—all the IWW's exhortations, all its rowdy hymn singing under the street lights of small Western towns, all its picaresque militancy, all its 'martyrdoms,' and also all the righteous indignation and violence of authorities and respectable burghers."[36]

The aftermath was predictable: National publicity in the afterglow of martyrdom, mass protest meetings, mass arrests for the murder of the deputies, and a show trial that put the IWW's philosophy and tactics on trial. IWW lawyers George Vanderveer and Fred H. Moore defended Thomas Tracy, the first defendant. The jury acquitted him on May 5, after a two-month legal battle. Charges against seventy-three other Wobbly defendants were dropped.

Although Tracy and his cohorts were vindicated, the IWW was not. In a country that was now at war, a radical labor organization that despised capitalism, preached sabotage, and was practically synonymous in the public's mind with violence simply had no chance of being viewed dispassionately. All the evidence brought out at the trial about vigilante action and the sheriff's abuse of law and order in Everett had no effect. Americans stood ready to defend their freedoms—including their freedom to round up troublemakers and send them packing.

If anything, the Everett debacle hardened industry employers' intransigence. The Anaconda's Kenneth Ross argued for a nine-hour workday, but his peers in the Western Pine Association rebuffed him. "I am convinced," Ross wrote to the secretary of the Western Pine Association in October 1917, three months after a massive Northwest lumber strike had begun, that "useful work can not be altogether regulated by the mill whistle, but depends more largely upon the satisfied mental attitude of the employee. . . . I would much rather make [labor conditions] fair by voluntary action of the employer than subject the industry to all the harassments which the professional agitator and walking delegate will subject it to in his effort to provide himself a job . . ."[37]

Ross would eventually be proven right. His fellow operators' intransigence eliminated any possibility of company reforms or even more-moderate trade union organizing, and precipitated long and damaging IWW strikes in 1917. Several government reports in the wake of the strikes would make this point. "The IWW is seeking results by dramatizing evils and by romantic promises of relief," noted the President's Mediation Commission in 1918. "The hold of the IWW is riveted instead of weakened by unimaginative opposition on the part of employers to the correction of real grievances."[38]

The first strike in the Northwest began on April 12, 1917, six days after Congress had declared war against the Central Powers. From there, strikes spread throughout the Inland Empire, tying up logging in scores of camps in Montana, Idaho, and Washington.

The strikes compounded the messy stalemate that already existed between the unyielding employers and the agitating IWW. Bitter feelings had intensified in Everett. Now, a long strike in the lumber industry threatened to debilitate the United States as it was frantically trying to accelerate its war effort. Once more, the IWW would be the bogeyman, but in wartime, everything it did would be in the spotlight, including its opposition to the war itself. ✦

FOUR
The Hymn of Hate

Attitudes Polarize with America's Entry into World War I, 1914–1917

"GENERAL SHERMAN SAID 'War is Hell,'" an early IWW pamphlet exhorted. "Don't go to Hell in order to give a bunch of piratical plutocratic parasites a bigger slice of Heaven." Published in 1911, the colorful anti-war screed by Walker C. Smith reminded workers that they were mere pawns in the geo-political conflicts into which the United States was being drawn by the greed of oligarchs. Smith evidently interpreted Taft's ham-handed show of force on the Mexican border in 1911, at the start of the Mexican revolution, as a prelude to an invasion (Taft was acting to protect American property and oil interests in Mexico but had no intention of invading the country). Similarly, Smith condemned American support of Japan's control over Korea after 1905 (Closer to the mark perhaps, as such support allowed the U.S. to assert hegemony over the Philippines). "Don't make yourself a target in order to fatten Rockefeller, Morgan, Carnegie, the Rothschilds, Guggenheim, and the other industrial pirates," the pamphlet said. "Don't become hired murderers. Don't join the army or navy."[1]

The Smith pamphlet was exactly the kind of rhetoric that just a few years later, with the United States involved in a declared war, would be punishable with long prison terms. In fact, this very pamphlet would send one Wobbly to prison in Montana for seven to fifteen years.[2] But it was also just one in a stack of IWW literature speaking out against war since the organization's inception in 1905, framing it as had revolutionists and radicals before, in terms of the class struggle.

Implicit in the Smith pamphlet was the IWW's jaundiced view of patriotism. Its leaders saw it as a device for manipulating the emotions of the workers and enlisting them in the mechanisms that would bind them even tighter in wage-slavery. That view was made explicit in 1912, when the IWW republished French syndicalist Gustave Herve's essay, "Patriotism and the Worker." Predicated on the European class struggle, the pamphlet was based on a courtroom defense by him in 1911. It read, in part, "For you, the country is a mother; for us, it is a cruel stepmother, a shrew whom we detest. For you, patriotism is a sentiment which is natural and profitable; for us, it is a snare. . . . For us there are only two countries in the world: that of the privileged and that of the disinherited . . . whatever language they may speak, or whatever the land may be which chanced to give them birth."

To IWW leaders, it may have seemed only natural that Herve's antipatriotic sentiments, framed in the European industrial conflicts of the nineteenth century, would resonate in the early twentieth century industrial strife in the United States. The fat-bellied plutocrats on both sides of the Atlantic were blood brothers; the chains that bound the workers were forged from the same capitalist steel. In fact, one Wobbly interviewed by the socialist writer Carleton Parker would almost perfectly translate Herve into classic American terms in 1917: "You ask me why the IWW is not patriotic. . . . If you were a bum without a blanket . . . if your job never kept you long enough in a place to qualify you to vote; if you slept in a lousy, sour bunk-house and ate food just as rotten as they could give you and get by with it; if deputy sheriffs shot your cooking cans full of holes and spilled your grub on the ground . . . if every person who represented law and order and the nation beat you up, railroaded you to jail, and the good Christian people cheered and told them to go to it, how in the hell do you expect a man to be patriotic? This war is a business man's war and we don't see why we should go out and get shot in order to save the lovely state of affairs that we now enjoy."[3]

Despite such rhetoric, Wobblies may also have grasped that patriotism in America was a deeply rooted idea not easily killed off. Attitudes about nationhood—shaped in a Revolutionary War then not much more than a century distant and sharpened more recently in a Civil War—were different from attitudes shaped in continental Europe with millennia of changing boundaries and shifting loyalties. It had also become painfully apparent that Herve's proletarian pamphlet was a long ways short of reality. His dream of working-class solidarity in Europe had been shattered in 1914 by the guns of August. Workers-turned-soldiers were slaughtering each other by the millions, cannon fodder for bloody nationalism, sacrificed for Herve's "cruel stepmother."

To most Americans, the war in Europe had come up very suddenly, like white thunderclouds on the horizon of a summer day. Their attention had been focused south of the border. The United States' principle foreign policy problem that year was how to protect American oil and other business interests in Mexico.

When war broke out in August 1914, pacifists commanded the American stage. Wilson, resolutely opposed to entanglement in a European war, nourished a grand vision of being the world's peacemaker. His famous Secretary of State, William Jennings Bryan, shared that idealism, believing the United States could maintain friendly relations with all belligerents and bring them together to resolve their differences. Politicians such as Senator Robert La Follette, a progressive from Wisconsin, spoke out vigorously against American involvement. Feminists, believing war glorified male martialism and magnified sexual differences, were among the first to oppose a military buildup.[4] Others believed the regimentation of war was bad for democracy's freedoms; still others that it undercut social and political reform and strengthened the hand of industrial monopolists. The Socialist Party under Eugene Debs, which had become a force to be reckoned with in the 1912 national elections when it garnered 6 percent of the presidential vote, opposed war for essentially the same reason that the Wobblies did: it was a tool of the ruling elite that had been and would be used to enslave workers and enrich capitalists through war contracts.

The neutrality of the early Wilson administration reflected the prevailing sentiment among newspaper editors, according to a poll conducted in November 1914 by *Literary Digest* magazine. Of four hundred editors surveyed, more than half—80 percent in the West and Midwest—said they were impartial. Those who took sides favored the Allies by a 5-to-1 ratio. Western and Midwestern editors favored the Allies by less than a 2-to-1 ratio.[5]

Manufacturing Consent

As they were exposed to the scale and horror of the fighting in Europe—and as their perceptions of the war came to be shaped by censorship and propaganda—American attitudes about the war became more polarized.

Events in Europe rapidly unfolded on a grand scale that seemed to dwarf even the tales grandfathers had told about the Civil War. Within the first week of August, less than six weeks after the assassination of Archduke Francis Ferdinand in Sarajevo, more than 2.5 million men were mobilized and propelled to the front on thousands of trains after rousing, patriotic sendoffs. Neutral Belgium fell early. Within a month, the Germans had advanced to within thirty miles of Paris. The initial success of Germany's Schlieffen plan for a six-week war—a huge wheeling movement through Belgium, then overrunning fortresses in northern France—seemed to be complemented by success against the Russians in the East. But heavy artillery and machine guns proved their potency against the men and cavalry that the German plan depended on so heavily. Lengthening supply lines for vast bodies of foot soldiers, as well as a brilliant defense of Paris by its military commander, General Gallieni, stalled the German advance.[6]

By the end of 1914, the toll was already staggering. The French, who had mobilized two million men, had suffered 306,000 fatalities, Germany 241,000, Belgium and Great Britain 30,000 each.[7] Worse was yet to come as the opposing forces settled into ghastly, grinding trench warfare on a 900-mile Western front, where they and those called up to replace them would dig in for almost the next three years.

The scale of the war was soon matched by its brutal tenor. German troops early on massacred scores of civilians, including women and children, in Belgian villages.[8] In the venerable university town of Louvain (modern-day Leuven) where the Renaissance scholar Erasmus had once taught, soldiers panicked by rumors of snipers set fire to architectural masterpieces housing priceless paintings, destroyed a library of 280,000 books and medieval manuscripts and forced the populace to evacuate.[9]

The Germans' brutish treatment of civilians and civilization's precious artifacts—not to mention its violation of Belgian neutrality—provided plenty of grist for Allied propaganda efforts intended to sway America to its defense. In the next two years, the British would do a masterful job on the hearts and minds of Americans, complemented by "preparedness" efforts led by those who stood to gain from American participation in the war. Newspapers, particularly in the east, helped promote the pro-Allies sentiment—an effort that Senator George Norris, a Republican from Nebraska, would term "the greatest propaganda the world has ever known, to manufacture sentiment in favor of the war."[10]

That sentiment would also be helped along by the blundering efforts of German spies and propagandists and by the Germans' candid introduction of modern war methods, horrifying in their effectiveness: poison gas, flame-throwers, Zeppelin bombardment, and, especially, large-scale submarine warfare. Well before American domestic propaganda efforts geared up in the spring of 1917, many Americans' minds would have been made up. The image of the "bestial Hun" would be firmly planted in the American consciousness. Whipping people into a patriotic frenzy would be that much easier.

From August 1914 to April 1917, pro-Allies sentiment in the United States was cultivated through classic propaganda techniques. The British government filtered virtually all the news that Americans received of the war, whether from newspapers and magazines or from private letters.[11] Its first act of censorship, on August 5, 1914, was to cut the transatlantic cables between Germany and the United States. That left American newspapers even more reliant than they had been on the advance sheets of London newspapers for the latest war news, which was already filtered through British military censors.[12] American war correspondents were able to gather some news on their own, but had to submit their dispatches to censors. An Associated Press official in 1915 estimated that British censors were spiking three-fourths of American correspondents' dispatches.[13] As most mail between Europe and the United States also flowed through London and Liverpool, it too was censored, giving the British two advantages—the suppression of information favorable to the enemy and the gathering of information valuable to its own intelligence. Adding to Great Britain's success was its ability to intercept and decipher coded wireless messages to and from Germany.[14]

Propaganda techniques pioneered by the British would be emulated by the United States' own highly successful propaganda agency, the Committee on Public Information. Many of these same arts of persuasion would be adopted in the emerging field of public relations. They recruited distinguished writers and academics to contribute materials, whose output was distributed in every medium available. They exploited existing Anglo-American friendships, cultural connections, and their common language. And they persuaded American opinion leaders such as intellectuals, preachers, and journalists to act as volunteer propagandists.

According to historian H. C. Peterson, the British War Propaganda Bureau successfully co-opted many American reporters, editors, and syndicated columnists with unusual access to military commanders and cabinet members, tours of the front, billeting at chateaux with haute cuisine, and a liberal dose of genteel British solicitude by well-mannered chaperones. The same gracious treatment was accorded to "statesmen, university presidents, and men of importance in all walks of life."[15]

The purpose of such methods was always to create a favorable climate of opinion for Great Britain and its allies (unfailingly portrayed as courageous and admirable), in order to make it easier for Americans to recognize that the Allies' cause was their cause—and one ultimately worth sacrificing lives for. Just as important was the goal of painting Germany and its culture as alien, brutal, autocratic, and inhuman, with sole responsibility for starting a war that it was prosecuting for militaristic, unholy ends. Germany, the line went, was attacking democracy itself. It was ruled autocratically by a delusional kaiser who thought he had been appointed by God Himself and who ran roughshod over any elected representatives to fulfill Germany's divine destiny to dominate Europe. Germany's victory would end democracy everywhere. A war that had arisen from a continental power struggle was turned into a titanic battle between the forces of good and evil—Armageddon, as in fact it was frequently described.

The very same propaganda themes introduced by the British during the neutrality years would persist after America's entry into the war—most famously in the phrase "make the world safe for democracy"—through to the Armistice and beyond. For example, a bulletin prepared by the Committee on Public Information for its "Four-Minute Men," its national corps of speakers and propagandists, was titled "Why We Are Fighting." First issued about mid-July 1917, the paper said Americans were fighting: ". . . for an honest world in which nations keep their word, for a world in which nations do not live by swagger or by threat . . . for a world in which the ambition or the philosophy of a few shall not make miserable all mankind, for a world in which the man is held more precious than the machine, the system, or the state."[16]

Neatly encapsulated in that statement were several classic propaganda techniques: the use of half-truths and exaggeration to exalt the Allies and damn the enemy; exploitation of emotions and ideals; over-simplification to a black-and-white world with no grays, and endless repetition. The reference to the "horrible cruelties" was exploited in both the neutrality and the war years, first by the British to recruit "fair-minded" Americans to their cause and later by Americans themselves to help justify being in the war.

Stories of German atrocities surfaced within the first week of the war, based in part on real cruelties, such as the execution of unarmed civilians in Belgium, including women and children. But whatever nuances there were in such incidents—differences in attitudes about civilians in war zones, resistance by Belgians—were completely ignored in the propaganda-driven telling and retelling of atrocity stories.

Instead, the half-truths were exaggerated in atrocity tales and attributed to the official German policy of *Schrecklichkeit* (literally, frightfulness). Civilians bayoneted by German soldiers were "mutilated." Emotions were inflamed by stories of horrible fates for the helpless victims of war: Girls were burned alive. Women were gang-raped in public by smirking soldiers. Babies' heads or limbs were cut off. Babies were impaled on bayonets. Dead babies were hoisted on the shoulders of swaggering German soldiers and carried off as war booty.

Like a ghastly global parlor game, some atrocity stories grew grimmer with each retelling. One such story, reportedly traced by a British Foreign Office official, started with a Cologne newspaper item that church bells in Germany rang when Antwerp was invaded. *Le Matin* in Paris interpreted it to say priests in Antwerp had been compelled to ring their own church bells. In the *London Times*, the priests refused to ring the bells and were fired. A Rome newspaper had the unfortunate clerics sentenced to hard labor. Finally, the report circled back to *Le Matin*, which finished them off in grisly fashion, saying it was confirmed that "the barbaric conquerors of Antwerp punished the unfortunate Belgian priests for their heroic refusal to ring the church bells by hanging them as living clappers to the bells with their heads down."[17]

An even more outlandish atrocity story surfaced repeatedly in newspapers: that of the corpse factory. It was a complete fabrication that, like any good myth or urban legend, took on a life of its own. Essentially, it involved "proof" that the Germans were extracting, in special factories, the last full measure of devotion from their own dead soldiers by rendering their bodies for soap, oil, pig food, manure, and nitroglycerine.

News stories purported to give the facts about the corpse factories as "incontestably borne out by the latest information."[18] A nine-inch story from the *New York Sun* gave authoritative details: the name of the German company contracted to do the job and its capitalization; the location and size of the main factory near the Belgian frontier; how workers in assembly-line fashion conveyed bundles of bodies to a great cauldron, and, supervised by a chief chemist, refined the corpses. "The case seems completely established by American, Belgian, Dutch, and finally by German testimony," the article concluded. "The London and Paris newspapers all accept the story after careful investigation . . ."[19]

The corpse factory was not fully discredited until after the war. According to one account, Brigadier General J. V. Charteris, the chief of the British Army of Intelligence, concocted the tale in the spring of 1917 when he saw two photographs captured from the Germans. One photo showed dead German soldiers being hauled off for burial, the other dead horses on their way to the glue factory. "Bring me a pair of shears and a paste pot," the general told an orderly, according to the account. Soon the deed was done. Charteris took the caption from the horse picture, pasted it under the picture of the dead soldiers, and ordered it dispatched. The story spread swiftly, surfacing on April 16 in the *Times* of London. With every telling, the story grew more fantastic and remained a part of the popular literature until well after the war. Although Charteris later denied his paste-pot story, the corpse factory story lingered until it was denounced as a lie by the British government in late 1925.[20]

German propagandists, too, vied for Americans' hearts and minds, but were overshadowed. Invasion of neutral Belgium had prompted international sympathy and relief efforts for "poor Belgium" led by Herbert Hoover. Further evidence of German inhumanity came with the partial destruction of Rheims Cathedral, the execution by firing squad of British nurse Edith Cavell for spying, the first use of poison gas, all-out submarine warfare and the sinking of the *Lusitania* by a German U-boat on May 7, 1915, resulting in the loss of 1,201 lives, including 128 Americans. All these actions—and their exploitation by Allied propagandists and American interventionists—helped persuade Americans that the "Huns" were indeed alien to all the United States stood for and that they must be fought to the death.

A War Against Barbarism

Woodrow Wilson underlined the accumulating sentiment of a moral crusade to rid the world of evil in his war message to Congress on the evening of April 2. American entry into the war, he said, had been made inevitable by continuing German submarine depredations on American ships as well as brusque diplomatic provocations such as the infamous Zimmerman telegram. The message threatened to breach the Monroe Doctrine of American influence in Latin America by appearing to promise Mexico the return of her former territories in Texas, New Mexico, and Arizona if she would join Germany against the United States.

With Germany having declared "warfare against mankind" with its unrestricted submarine campaign and "civilization itself seeming to be in the balance," the United States had no choice but to declare war, "to make the world safe for democracy," Wilson declared.[21] "[R]ight is more precious than peace, and we shall fight for the things which we have always carried nearest our hearts—for democracy, for the right of those who submit to authority to have a voice in their own governments . . . for a universal dominion of right by such a concert of free peoples as shall bring peace and safety to all nations and make the world itself at last free. To such a task we can dedicate our lives and our fortune . . ."[22] A United States with newfound international zeal would lead the Federation of the World in a sort of global purification ritual, an avenging angel slaying the demons of autocracy.

This Messianic theme would be repeated endlessly, preached from pulpits by progressive ministers, editorialized in countless publications. On Easter Sunday, two days after Congress declared war, The Reverend Ernest Stires, rector of St. Thomas's Church on Fifth Avenue in New York, preached that God's "call summons us to the service of mercy and truth, of righteousness and honest peace. To-day our Easter faith goes into action."[23] A few blocks from the White House, The Reverend Randolph McKim told his flock at the Church of the Epiphany on Thanksgiving Day in 1917 that the war was "the . . . holiest . . . Crusade . . . in history" to "rescue civilization, humanity, and Christianity" from "the armies of Antichrist."[24]

The *Christian Science Monitor* noted a few days after war was declared, "It is no mere freak of princes which has brought about the present war. What has caused it is the crashing together of the thunder clouds of autocracy and democracy in the political heavens."[25]

In Congress, many who favored war echoed the theme of the grand crusade, "when the peoples of Europe may be freed from the tyranny of crowns and scepters and come from the darkness of bondage into the light of freedom," as Senator William S. Kenyon of Iowa declared.[26] "The democracy, the civilization, the Christianization of the world are at stake," cried Senator Henry L. Myers of Montana.[27] Even Republican Senator Henry Cabot Lodge Sr. of Massachusetts, Wilson's political nemesis, agreed: "We enter this war . . . in order to preserve human freedom, democracy, and modern civilization. . . . This war is a war against barbarism. . . . We are resisting an effort to thrust mankind back to forms of government . . . which we had hoped had disappeared forever from the world."[28]

With emotions inflamed, attitudes polarized rapidly. Vocal opponents of war in Congress were attacked as traitors. When Senator George Norris of Nebraska condemned what he saw as Wall Street's eagerness for war profits and shouted, "We are going into war upon the command of gold . . . I feel that we are about to put the dollar sign upon the American flag," he was hectored by other senators. "If that be not giving aid and comfort to the enemy . . . then I do not know what would bring aid and comfort to the heart of a Hapsburg or a Hohenzollern," declared Senator James A. Reed of Missouri.[29]

Fifty representatives (including the first woman in Congress, Montana's Jeannette Rankin) and six senators voted against war. Others had grave doubts. Yet opposition to the war had already been considerably whittled down. Pacifist Bryan had resigned after the sinking of the *Lusitania*, realizing he could not prevail against the preparedness campaign. Many socialists, including Debs, still opposed the war, but an influential minority backed it. Progressives, too, were split. Those who decided to support the war were beguiled by Wilson's crusade to save democracy. They convinced themselves that the sacrifices and hard choices dictated by war also provided a unique opportunity for social reform. Again, the purification theme emerged, as in the same *Christian Science Monitor* article. In this "land of milk and honey . . . the richest country in the world," wealth had been unequally distributed. The country was in danger of having its vitality sapped by the "class antagonism between an unpatriotic and greedy army of workers and an enervated, sensual, and equally selfish body of capitalists." Now, war has come "to rouse the two [classes] out of the sleep of the senses into the vigor of a common sacrifice for the sake of humanity."[30]

Pragmatism vs. Symbolism

Even the Wobblies decided not to mount any concerted opposition to the war, such as a general strike. The IWW wasn't about to endorse Wilson's crusade but it was in no position to stop the American war juggernaut. It had bigger battles to fight at home. Just before Congress declared war, *Solidarity* editor Ben Williams wrote, "Why should we sacrifice working class interests for the sake of a few noisy and impotent parades or antiwar demonstrations? Let us rather get on the job of organizing the working class to take over the industries, war or no war, and stop all future capitalist aggression that leads to war and other forms of barbarism."[31] By concentrating on organizing workers in vital war industries such as timber, agriculture, and copper mining, at a time when labor demand was surging, the IWW's leaders believed they held the winning cards. The federal government could not afford lengthy strikes, and would persuade business leaders to make concessions.

Militants such as Frank Little argued that the IWW faced extinction with rising war fever, and thus had little to lose with a general strike. Better to take the moral high ground against war. Members from ethnic groups antagonistic toward the Allies, such as the Irish, Finns, Germans, and Austrians, tended to agree. To Little, IWW executive secretary Haywood wrote, "Keep a cool head. Do not talk. A good many feel as you do but the world war is of small importance compared to the great class war."[32]

Nonetheless, the IWW was on the blame list for anti-war and anti-draft activity across the country. The "Green Corn Rebellion" in Oklahoma in the summer of 1917, for example, was blamed partly on the IWW. In fact, there was only an indirect connection with it, but the facts seemed so alarming that the Wobblies were tarred with the brush of insurrection. Sharecroppers and tenant farmers in the southeastern part of the state who had joined radical agrarian groups planned to cut telegraph wires to hinder the draft, and perhaps to destroy a bridge. Alarmed citizens formed posses and arrested 450 persons, holding them in the state penitentiary and demanding the death penalty. Eventually, the leaders of the revolt were convicted of violating the federal espionage law and sentenced to three to ten years in prison.[33]

The reaction was typical of the inflamed passions as America launched its all-out effort to "make the world safe for democracy." In this atmosphere, the IWW, which had so often used rhetoric so brilliantly to its advantage, would be assailed by its own words, proof positive that it was as depraved and dangerous as the kaiser himself.

Christians at War

Although the IWW had backed off from any massive anti-war protest, its various organs were still printing anti-war literature. Two of those items would now be pounced on by its opponents. Just before Congress declared war, *Solidarity* had published "The Deadly Parallel," ridiculing the patriotic statement of support by the American Federation of Labor, headed by Samuel Gompers.

After expressing "an unswerving desire for peace, the AF of L's resolution stated, "But, despite all our endeavors and hopes, should our country be drawn into the maelstrom of the European conflict, we . . . offer our services to our country in every field of activity to defend, safeguard, and preserve the republic of the United States of America against its enemies, whomsoever they may be . . ."

The "deadly parallel" lay in the comparison of the trade unions' stance with the ghastly toll of the European war to date: "Ten million human lives stand as a monument to the national patriotic stupidity of the working class of Europe! Who will be to blame if the workers of America are betrayed and led into the bloodiest slaughter of history? Who?"

The "deadly parallel" may have seemed patently obvious to the IWW, but editorialists and politicians seized on the publication as proof of the IWW's disloyalty. "In the wartime hysteria of 1917," wrote William Preston Jr., "Americans were in no mood to accept reasonable interpretations of the inflammatory and incendiary prose by which the IWW had lived."[34] The article would be introduced at the trial of IWW leaders in Chicago in 1918 as evidence of their opposition to the war.

Much darker in tone was the song "Christians at War." First printed in 1915 in the thirteenth edition of the Little Red Song Book ("to Fan the Flames of Discontent," as the booklet's cover noted), the song, to the tune of "Onward, Christian Soldiers," parodied the "holy war" being waged by *both* sides. Ironically, it was penned by a U.S. Army captain, John F. Kendrick, formerly a Chicago newspaperman. The first verse (there were at least five) went:

> *Onward, Christian soldiers! Duty's way is plain:*
> *Slay your Christian neighbors, or by them be slain.*
> *Pulpiteers are spouting effervescent swill,*
> *God above is calling you to rob and rape and kill,*
> *All your acts are sanctified by the lamb on high;*
> *If you love the Holy Ghost, go murder, pray and die.*

The song, labeled the "Hymn of Hate," was widely reprinted by IWW foes as damning evidence of the organization's vicious, godless nature.[35] They used it to great effect, knowing it could push buttons. The words were introduced as evidence in several state and federal trials against IWW members. Montana's Senator Henry Myers would present it, as reprinted on the front page of the *Helena Independent*,[36] to each of his colleagues in August 1917 when he first pressed his case for a sedition law. The *Independent* would reprint it twice more while the Montana legislature was in special session the following February to pass the state sedition and criminal syndicalism laws.[37] Reprints were placed on the desks of all Idaho legislators in 1917 before they passed the nation's first criminal syndicalism law. The song's words threw Washington legislators "into a frenzy."[38]

The IWW was hardly the only organization to borrow the battle hymn's title for propaganda. One patriotic poster published in 1918, for example, used it for its headline, adding, "Onward, Christian Soldiers, for the very angels of Heaven might envy you this supreme opportunity to sacrifice that you may save civilization from barbarism, Christianity from atheism, women and children from brutish beasts . . ."[39] In fact, "Onward, Christian Soldiers" and "The Battle Hymn of the Republic" were enlisted any number of times "as an emotional explanation and justification of total, redemptive war," notes historian Richard Gamble.[40]

The over-used battle hymns' symbolic weight helps explain the emotional punch that a parody triggered. Repeated again and again by the IWW's enemies, the parody's lugubrious lyrics may well have played a role in shaping Congress' decision to pass a sedition bill the following spring to silence dissenters. In this period of churning emotions and accelerated nationalism, the IWW's general opposition to the war on ideological grounds—"bums without blankets" inveigled into a rich man's war—clearly challenged Wilson's notion, supported by a vast majority of the populace, that the war was a popular democratic struggle against a cruel autocracy.

In the hysteria engendered by the war, the IWW's lack of any concerted opposition to the war was ignored. As had happened when the IWW leadership tried to disavow Flynn's *Sabotage*, its enemies chose to discount any evidence of moderation and instead to focus on the easily exploitable. They seized on two things: the IWW's colorful messages—its media and its songs—that gave a much more radical impression of its anti-militarism and on the IWW's targeting of vital industries, such as copper. Both seemed to furnish prima facie evidence of its lack of patriotism and thus its disloyalty. ❖

FIVE
Fire in the Mountain

Labor Strife in Butte Provokes Violent Reaction, 1917

JUST BEFORE MIDNIGHT ON FRIDAY, JUNE 8, 1917, Ernest Sallau, a shift boss in the Speculator Mine in Butte, was attempting to retrieve a damaged electrical cable from the Granite Mountain shaft. Extending his carbide torch to peer at the cable, Sallau accidentally set its tarry insulation afire. Instantly, flames swept up the shaft, propelled by the mine's modern ventilation system. The inferno ignited thousands of feet of dry shaft timbers and forced smoke and gas into every level. Within a few minutes, scores of miners were trapped.[1] Others formed human chains and felt their way to safety through crosscuts. They battered their way through to adjacent mines, punching holes in concrete bulkheads with sledgehammers and heavy timbers. The four-deck cages used to lift men out of the shafts couldn't be lowered because the signaling system had burned out.

In front of a horrified crowd that had rushed to the disaster, a "mighty geyser" of flames shot out of the adjacent Speculator shaft. It incinerated two miners trapped in a hoist cage twenty feet above the collar of the shaft.[2] Gases killed more than a dozen rescue volunteers, including Sallau, who had gone back to try to save men from the inferno he had touched off.[3] Twenty-five men were found alive on Sunday at the 2,400-foot level, but for many others, the frantic search and rescue scramble was too late. Four out of every ten men on the night shift died. Just two burned to death; 166 more suffocated from the deadly gases. Many victims were found piled behind concrete bulkheads that were missing the iron escape doors called for by state law. The victims' fingers were worn to the knuckles from frantically clawing for safety.

Accidental deaths were a common occurrence in Butte. In the "Big Explosion" on January 15, 1895, a burning warehouse in uptown Butte containing 350 boxes of dynamite blew up. Scores were killed, including fourteen of the seventeen men in the Butte fire department and all the fire

Figure 5. A crowd gathers outside the Speculator Mine in Butte on June 9, 1917, the day after a disastrous fire took the lives of 168 miners. Butte-Silver Bow Public Archives.

Figure 6. Mules were used to pull rail carts filled with ore in some of the Butte mines. This train was at the 1,100-foot level of the Rarus Mine. N. A. Forsyth, Montana Historical Society.

horses save one, Old Jim.[4] Mining deaths were the result of cave-ins, falls, blasts, electrocutions, fires, and asphyxiation.[5]

Unfortunately, fatalities were becoming even more common in Butte because of a deadly combination of war-production speed-ups and more inexperienced workers. Seventeen miners working for the same North Butte Company were blown to bits at the collar of the same Granite Mountain shaft twenty months earlier, when a mine car filled with five hundred pounds of dynamite exploded.[6] Fingers with rings attached were found a mile from the scene.[7] Another twenty-one men had been gassed to death in the Pennsylvania Mine on February 14, 1916.[8] Forty-one more miners were killed in 1917 in the five months prior to the Speculator fire.[9]

The Speculator disaster, however, was the worst. It highlighted not only the dangers of working in "The Richest Hill on Earth," but the companies that so ruthlessly controlled the mines, the miners who had flocked there from all corners of the earth and the social and economic conditions that bound them together even as they drove them apart. War brought boom times to Butte, but it also brought inflation and work pressures, inflamed emotions, and caused simmering resentments and hatreds to bubble to the surface.

The Richest Hill on Earth

Butte bore many monikers: Copper Metropolis, perch of the devil, the Gibraltar of Unionism, even "Center of the Montana Wonderland," according to a wildly optimistic chamber of commerce brochure.[10] Beautiful it was not, as the names of some of its districts suggest: Nanny Goat Hill, Dogtown, the Cabbage Patch, and Butchertown. Colorful, without question: its denizens sported nicknames like Fat Jack, Take-Five Annie, Paddie the Pig, Filthy McNabb, Lutey the Box Thief, and Jesus Christ, a dray horse belonging to a Jewish expressman.[11] In *Montana, High, Wide and Handsome*, Joseph Kinsey Howard would later pin another label on Butte: "the black heart of Montana." He left no doubt as to why: "From the sixth floor of one of its office buildings go forth the corporate commands to politicians, preachers, and press, all the pensioners and servile penny-liners of corporate capitalism. Butte is a sooty memorial to personal heroism, to courage and vigor even in rascality; and it is a monument to a wasted land."[12]

Howard was referring to the sixth floor of the Hennessy Building, the executive floor of the all-powerful Anaconda Copper Mining Company. Mining, first for gold and silver, then for copper and zinc, had built Butte into Montana's largest city, by far, with a population in 1917 of about 85,000. The late-nineteenth-century war of the copper kings for control of the vast mineral wealth had resulted in control by New York financiers. By 1910, the Anaconda had a stranglehold on the state's economy, politics, and press. But working-class discontent was swelling, aided by the middle-class progressive movement and fueled by growing numbers of immigrants. The same industrial machinery that had pulled vast riches from the earth and refined them had wreaked enormous damage on the air and water, and on the human cogs in the vast enterprise.

Boom Time

Round-the-clock production for the Great War had brought boom times to the Anaconda and to the other copper producers in Montana, Arizona, and Utah. Prices for electrolytic copper had soared from 13.5 cents a pound in 1914 to a high of 36.3 cents in March 1917 and stood at 32.5 cents that June. In 1916, Montana copper mines and smelters had produced nearly 1.8 million tons[13] of copper (about one-fourth of all U.S. copper), worth almost $100 million.[14] The Anaconda's high profits, higher than any other company in the nation in 1916 except for U.S. Steel, Bethlehem Steel, and duPont, were reflected in fat wartime dividends.[15]

Miners' wages, however, hadn't risen in step with the latest increases in the copper prices, although wage scales had supposedly been tied to copper prices since 1915. The basic wage of $4.75 a day per eight-hour day for all underground miners was tied to a copper price of 27 cents a pound. Although copper had been selling above 31 cents since February, wages hadn't been adjusted.[16]

In a period of prosperity driven by supplying war materiel to the European allies, miners' annual wages, averaging $1,215 in 1917, were 37 percent higher than the average manufacturing wage. They had risen by more than a third since 1914 from $894—far higher than the average wage increase.[17] Inflation, however, had eaten up all those wage increases and more. It was a problem shared by workers throughout the country, but the rise in the cost of living in Butte was extreme. Miners with families did not make enough to maintain a "minimum comfort level" at any time during the war period.[18] Food costs alone had gone up 41 percent from

January 1915—potatoes from 14 cents a pound to 48 cents; beans from 8 cents to 20 cents.[19] Wholesalers were responsible for at least part of the gouging, according to testimony gathered after the war's end.[20]

Merchants and landlords were riding the inflation wave. "Every time the Anaconda Copper Company raises the wages of its men 25 cents a day the Butte property owner raises the rent of the house in which the miner lives from $5 to $8 a month," the *Helena Independent* editorialized in mid-July.[21] "The crux of the Butte trouble is not with a lot of loud-mouthed IWW's nor with the operators of the mining companies," observed newspaperman W.W. Fisher in the same issue. "The trouble is with the actions of the local pirates who are not happy with less than 14 percent net on their investments in shaky, poorly ventilated, brick-veneer rooming houses, and so-called hotels."[22] When a dentist bought the building where Fisher was rooming, the rent shot up from $17.50 a month to $25 ("pay in advance, stand the increase or move in two hours," the dentist had told tenants). Hotel food, Fisher observed, had jumped from 60 cents for a "good meal, meat, potatoes, one vegetable" in 1915 to "$1 to $1.25 at cheap places, where the preparation is poor and the food is sickening."[23]

Rock in the Box

Charred bodies found under knee-deep soot were being brought up from the Speculator shafts when a circular—the *Butte and Anaconda Joint Strike Bulletin*—appeared on Sunday with miner's demands.[24] The copper companies' lust for war profits was the root cause of the disaster, the leaflets claimed: "In order to make this profit there must be 'rock in the box' every minute, and inevitably some deaths must result."[25]

Wartime production demands had quickened the tempo of mining and changed the nature of the work force. "Rock in the box" increasingly came to mean speeded-up output quotas set by remote managers. Technology such as steam-powered hoists and "buzzies," hand-held, two-man air drills, speeded up production but did nothing to improve working conditions. The buzzies, in fact, produced so much fine dust that they led to a higher rate of silicosis, a debilitating respiratory disease, and were soon dubbed "widowmakers."[26]

Mining technology advances had also created more lower-paid unskilled jobs, at the expense of skilled miners.[27] Companies had turned to southern European, Asian, and South American immigrants to fill the unskilled jobs. Many were unmarried and illiterate. The percentage of jobs held by the more experienced Irish, Cornish, Finnish, Austrian, and German miners with families had shrunk. Ethnic tensions had grown. More unskilled jobs led to greater turnover. In 1914, an average of two and a half men worked each full-time job in the Butte mines in the course of a year. By 1917, that ratio had soared to seven men per job per year. The workforce was becoming disposable.[28]

As America entered the war, companies would demand more unmarried, unskilled, immigrant workers. They couldn't be drafted, they could be paid less and they were easier to fire. There was one more advantage to hiring this class of men, the *Strike Bulletin* alleged: There would be fewer worker's compensation claims to pay under Montana's 1915 law, which barred claims for aliens and their families. In more than one-third of fatal accidents, no claims were filed, the *Strike Bulletin* noted.[29] Indeed, that percentage may have been generous in the case of the Speculator fire. An estimated five hundred dependents, the survivors of three-fourths of the men burned and gassed to death, would receive no benefits under the law.[30]

All of these factors would have created major discord in any mining community. But there was a strong historical dimension to labor in Butte that helps explain the bitterness and violence that would unfold there over the next three years.[31] In a nutshell, miners felt resentment for being abused, spied on, manipulated, and controlled for years by the Anaconda and the other operating companies. And they felt betrayed by previous union leaders who had sold out to the bosses.

A mutuality of interest underlay early mining in Butte. In the "war" between Marcus Daly, William A. Clark, and Augustus Heinze, the Butte Miners Union held the balance of power. Butte was spared the labor violence of the Coeur d'Alenes in northern Idaho. In 1900, the copper barons in their carriage led the BMU Miners' Day parade. But that peaceful and paternalistic era unraveled as local owners gave way to New York financiers connected to Standard Oil, such as William Rockefeller and William Rogers. The eastern capitalists formed the Amalgamated Copper Company, which cruelly shut down the mines in order to squeeze out Heinze. The company exercised naked power to force the state legislature to write favorable laws. By 1915, the Amalgamated holding company had been dissolved, leaving the Anaconda Copper Mining Co. as an independent corporation.

By then, the old, conservative BMU had already begun to split apart. Socialists and Wobblies attracted workers hungry for change. In 1912, miners were earning $3.50 a day, the same as their fathers had earned in 1878.[32] About the same time, the Western Federation of Miners moved in a more conservative direction. Within a few years, the WFM, led by Charles Moyer, had parted company with the IWW and opposed its radical rhetoric and tactics.

Union conservatives in Butte—the trade unions affiliated with the American Federation of Labor as well as the WFM—collaborated with the Anaconda when it instituted the "rustling card" system, a blacklist of "troublesome" workers. To guard against further radical influences, the company used spies and informers. Resentments against the company and the union conservatives boiled over in 1914. Rebel miners led by Muckie McDonald sacked, then dynamited, the Miners' Union Hall. The crackdown was swift and brutal. Gov. Stewart declared martial law. McDonald and others went to jail. ACM banned all unions and declared an open shop. For the next three years, Butte simmered.

Rustling Cards

The Butte miners' resentment boiled over on June 11, the third day after the Speculator fire. Angry miners began walking out of William A. Clark's Elm Orlu mine, known as the Ella-ma-loo. At a mass meeting the next day, the dissidents breathed life into the Metal Mine Workers Union.[33] While six more men had been found alive in the Speculator mine the same morning, ample past experience told miners not to expect any more hoist signals.[34] With cremated corpses creating a "Ghastly Sight at the Morgue," as the *Butte Post* noted,[35] demands spilled forth: Recognition of the MMWU by the operating companies; a minimum of $6 a day for all men employed underground and commensurate raises for surface men; increased safety measures including more inspections and manholes in all bulkheads; restrictions on compulsory layoffs for safety violations, and an end to the rustling card system.

A mining company issued a rustling card after checking a man's background and character. Without one, a man could not "rustle" or look for a job in almost any of the mines. When the Anaconda and other companies instituted the system in December 1912, they explained that they simply needed to keep track of what was becoming a much more transient

Figure 7. The dynamiting of the Butte Miner's Hall on June 23, 1914, marked a period of acute labor unrest on "The Richest Hill on Earth." Westphal photograph, Montana Historical Society.

work force. Union conservatives went along with the card because it helped preserve their status as trusted employees and kept out radical hotheads, whom they mistrusted.

By 1917, however, Anaconda officials admitted that screening out radical troublemakers, particularly IWWs, had been the main purpose all along. Anaconda's chief counsel, L. O. Evans, told the Missoula Chamber of Commerce that the IWW "and its disciples and methods . . . have been and are the direct and sole cause of our industrial difficulties in Butte." He explained that the rustling card was instituted after an IWW local was organized in Butte and "soap box orators" began preaching "characteristic IWW methods, including direct action and sabotage . . ." After the serious trouble in 1914, "when the ugliness of the [IWW] men behind the movement became apparent . . . it [became clear] that something must be done towards keeping the avowed wrecker out of the mines." The rustling card system had not been abused, said Evans. "[T]he only men who have been refused cards are men as to whom we had the most indisputable evidence as to their vicious and criminal character."

To the Anaconda Company, keeping "vicious and criminal characters" and "avowed wreckers" out of the mines was not only their right but also their duty. Beginning in 1915, however, the company had expanded its definition of troublemakers to include some of the older, more established miners who were merely pushing for a closed shop and who were beginning to criticize the companies for their rigid control of the work force.[36] For these veteran workers, it became forcefully apparent that the rustling card rules had changed. Now they realized that the card was increasingly being used to suffocate their own freedom of speech (even though it may not have bothered them that the agitators' freedom of speech had also been stifled). Whatever legitimacy the rustling card may have had in the eyes of such men dissolved. The card is "like slavery," the MMWU cried. Its abuse broke down any lingering feeling of cooperation and trust.[37]

Electricians led by William F. Dunn joined the MMWU in striking. Conservative metal trades unions also walked out in sympathy with the electricians. Copper production was decimated. "The miners of Butte went on strike," explained Dunn, "because they could no longer endure the impositions and insults heaped upon them, and because they believe that a man is entitled to decent treatment at all times."[38]

The companies' response to the miners' demands was characteristically tough. They blamed the IWW and waved the flag: "The attack upon Butte's industries is engineered in the main by the same element that was responsible for Butte's serious trouble in 1914," a company official said. "It is well known that recently there has been a large influx into Butte of IWW's and other unpatriotic and seditious persons, whose aim it is to paralyze our industries, and particularly those upon which the government is depending for its arms and ammunition . . ."[39]

Insisting that everything was just fine, the companies pointed to the high average wages in the mines and asserted that they knew of no grievances. And they stonewalled: "As far as I am concerned, I will close them down, flood them, and not raise a pound of copper before I will recognize the anarchist leaders of the union," declared William A. Clark, the multimillionaire mining baron at whose mine the strike began.[40]

The companies may have had a point about Butte wages—if they had made it a decade earlier. Industrial wages in Montana *had* led the nation in 1900, but by 1920 the state's ranking had fallen to twentieth.[41] Conveniently, the companies had chosen to ignore inflation's ravaging effect on miners' wages.

Figure 8. Copper baron and erstwhile U.S. Senator William A. Clark controlled his properties tightly and had no use for unions. Butte-Silver Bow Public Archives.

The companies were also off-target when they blamed the IWW for fomenting the strike, just as they had been off the mark in 1914. Back then, miners who held the IWW red card played a leading role in the labor insurgency against the conservative Butte Miners Union, hoping that the IWW would attract more members. But students of the era say there is no proof that the IWW plotted to destroy the BMU. It simply wasn't a very effective organization then, and it had its hands full trying to maintain any forward momentum.[42]

In 1917, the IWW was a handy scapegoat once more, but the fact is that the core of strikers was the older, more established miners, the mining elite, many of them Irish, who distrusted the IWW. It was these men who felt a deep sense of betrayal at being subjected to the rustling card. "The companies were blacklisting the men who built the city," stripping them of rank and privilege, notes historian David Emmons.[43]

Revolt Against the Trade Unions

In Butte in the summer of 1917, it was the recent memory of bodies piled up behind bulkheads of mines and the stonewalling attitude of mine operators that were energizing radical labor groups and widening the rift between them and the more conservative trade unions.

Solidarity between the trade unions and the MMWU had only lasted six weeks. Water used on the Speculator fire was still being pumped out of the Granite Mountain mine shaft and flowers were still on the men's graves when the members of the trade unions voted to return to work.

The trades rejected an appeal for funds by the MMWU, whose members were still on strike and needed money to feed their families.[44] The cruel snub was hardly a surprise. The MMWU was led by dissidents such as Tom Campbell with close ties to the Wobblies, whom the conservative trade union members despised. The fact that the MMWU offices were in the same building as those of the IWW—not to mention the radical-leaning Finns and the Pearse-Connolly Irish Independence Club—didn't help cure this perception.[45] The old-timers and the new miners' union were grappling for control of the mines.

While Butte history and politics undoubtedly played a large role in the animosity between the unions, the snub was also a good example of the attitude of the trade unions toward radical labor. AF of L president Samuel Gompers, a pragmatic chunk of a man who resembled the stubs of cigars he smoked and once made, had despised the Wobblies since their formation in 1905. As the war approached, he saw radicals as a major obstacle to his dreams of achieving lasting, practical gains for his union members. He feared that their anti-war and "disloyal" attitudes would bring the government down on all of labor. When offered a seat by President Wilson on the prestigious Advisory Committee of the Council of National Defense, Gompers jumped at the chance to achieve an eight-hour day, equal pay for women and guaranteed wages on government contracts. In return, he refrained from insisting on the closed shop (union-only labor) and helped the government discredit radical labor unions.[46]

Now, even as officials in Washington were drawing the war's first draft number (Number 258) on July 20, radicals in Butte were demonstrating just the kind of uncooperative behavior and unpatriotic talk that management—and conservative trade unions—were poised to attack. To complicate matters further, Dunn's electricians, who had precipitated the month-long walkout after the Speculator fire, were on strike again, just a week after voting to go back to work.[47]

In the last month, Dunn had become a new target of both the companies and the conservative trade unions. He had tangled with Gompers' personal representative, International Brotherhood of Electrical Workers president F. J. McNulty, brought in to break the strike. Dunn had hoped to bring the MMWU into the AF of L fold, in order to cement labor solidarity and assure support for the new union, but that had failed when McNulty insisted that the men go back to work immediately.[48]

Now the "copper press" was condemning Dunn as an agitator and IWW sympathizer. Two days later, Dunn would appear on stage at a mass miners' meeting that drew two thousand men. "This strike is an expression against a form of society which allows a few to control the wealth of the nation," Dunn told the miners. "This is also an expression against the system of government which allows a few men who want war to send our boys to the trenches while they profit from their life blood."[49]

From Bisbee to Butte

Butte was not the only copper district where industrial strife was roiling the surface. Strikes over wages and working conditions had started earlier in the year in the southern Arizona copper district around Bisbee. IWW recruiting thrived. Frank Little had helped direct the strike from a miner's cabin in nearby Miami, Arizona, unknown to local peace officers. An auto accident on the way from Phoenix to the district had broken his ankle and prevented him from taking his customary place on the front lines.

Companies refused union demands, emphasizing the need to produce more copper for the war. News of the Butte strike after the Speculator accident added impetus to the strikes. Mining companies organized the Jerome Loyalty League. On July 10, "hundreds of [non-IWW] miners and other citizens, some with rifles and some with pick handles, cleared the town of the agitators . . ."[50]

When federal authorities failed to respond to the lawless action, emboldened vigilantes turned on striking IWW miners in Bisbee. On the morning of July 12, a well-armed *posse comitatus* rousted nearly twelve hundred miners from their beds and houses. Many were Mexicans and southern Europeans, whom the IWW had been particularly successful in recruiting. The posse herded the men into waiting cattle cars with manure-strewn floors. A train dumped the men in the Sonoran desert near Hermanas, New Mexico, 173 miles to the east. Food and water rations were brought but the men had no shelter until July 14, when they were taken to a nearby army base in Columbus.

Little had left the Bisbee area after the deportation, unable to reach the men roasting in the desert. He fired off a telegram from Salt Lake City to Arizona Governor Thomas E. Campbell. According to the *Anaconda Standard*, the telegram read: "Understand that the mine owners' mob will take same action at Globe-Miami [mining district] as was taken at Bisbee. The membership of the IWW is getting tired of the lawlessness of the capitalist class and will no longer stand for such action. If you, as governor, cannot uphold the law, we will take same into our own hands. Will you act or must we?"

In reply, Campbell "said he felt sure no deportations could occur with federal troops stationed in the district and that he was using his best efforts to protect the rights of all citizens. Concluding, he said, 'I resent your disloyal and untimely threats in view of my earnest efforts to bring law and order and such forces as will maintain same . . . '"[51]

As Little "vagged" his way north to Butte to do what he could to inflame the copper strike, the lumber strikes, which had been spreading westward from the Inland Empire, blanketed the Northwest. On July 16, IWW and AF of L lumber unions in western Washington struck, shutting down 90 percent of the lumber operations in that part of the state. Strikers demanded an eight-hour day, a minimum wage of $60 a month, as well as better living conditions for loggers, union-controlled hiring and an end to the rustling card system. "The workers are in rebellion against conditions that reduce them in many cases to the level of degradation and physical misery," George H. Sands of Wallace, Idaho, wrote to President Wilson.[52]

Employers weren't listening. The urgency and patriotism of the war now informed every move. The War Department needed 625 million feet of spruce, lightweight and splinter-free, for a crash construction program to produce thousands of aircraft (only a handful would be produced before the armistice). Even under normal conditions, the Northwest could only provide 325 million feet and that wood needed six months' seasoning before it could be used for airplane frames.[53] Billions more board feet of pine were needed for army cantonments, crating, and normal industrial and agricultural purposes. With the strike, the production outlook was exactly zero board feet.

Thus, as Little approached Montana, enormous strikes had brought two industries vital to the war effort to a halt. As many as forty thousand loggers and lumber workers had walked off the job. In Butte, no more than 10 percent of the twelve thousand or so miners were at work.[54] Cracks, however, were starting to show in the miners' resolve. What they needed was some old-fashioned revival. There was no better "preacher" than Frank Little. ✤

SIX
Patriotism and Propaganda

America's Own Propaganda Machine Dries Up Dissent, 1917

THERE'S NOT MUCH DOUBT WHAT THE OFFICIALS on the sixth floor of the Hennessy Building thought of Frank Little and the organization he represented. "Our western country has been infested by their organizers and leaders, Anaconda chief counsel L. O. Evans said in August 1917. "They have come among us with venom in their hearts and treason on their lips, snarling their blasphemies in filthy and profane language. . . . They have invariably shown themselves to be bullies, anarchists, and terrorists. There can be no doubt in anyone's mind that in this organization the kaiser has found one of his most effective allies."[1]

In its righteous anger at the IWW, the Anaconda reacted in much the same way that most of American industry reacted. It called attention to the organization's radical "un-American" nature, and appealed to patriotic emotions with charges of treason and sedition. A more "sensible and fair" approach to the Butte strike, reasoned Abraham Glasser in his report to the Labor Department in the 1930s, would have been "from the standpoint of finding out what the workers wanted, and whether they were entitled to what they wanted; this attitude would have been further affected, and rightly so, by the vital consideration of keeping up the output of the war industries machine, but it would not have used that factor as an excuse for ignoring the workers' demands and for obscuring these demands beneath a smokescreen of alleged radical aims."[2]

But in 1917 the bosses at the Anaconda, and their counterparts in other industries, saw a major threat to their business. And as the tide of war washed all around, things were passing well beyond "sensible and fair." Business and industry, which the IWW had angered beyond redemption, would exploit public feelings of anger, resentment, and fear. The middle class, which by and large shared the same values and whose very belief system was threatened by the IWW, adopted these emotions. And the press published and reaffirmed those fears and hatreds.

Most Americans also found the Wobblies' ideological baggage unsettling; it overshadowed the organization's bread-and-butter objectives that it was beginning to achieve. Terms such as direct action, the general strike, and syndicalism smelled of anarchy and revolution. So did the idea of sabotage, even if the IWW definition focused on work withdrawal, rather than the spikes and fires they were constantly blamed for. The IWW's radical, long-term Marxist goals, such as abolishing the wage system and seizing the means of production, were no less disturbing.

Within the next decade, syndicalism—the notion that unions were the vanguard of the revolution and represented the larval forms of future political organization of society—would be criminalized, burdened with a much more sinister definition—advocacy of force or violence to accomplish industrial or political reform—in twenty-one states plus Alaska and Hawaii.[3] These laws were aimed directly at the IWW.

The outlawing of syndicalism would be helped along by the pervasive anti-union sentiment in most of the country, in an era when most people considered the process of organizing workers to press for better pay and working conditions to be a hostile act. Unions threatened American ideals of the self-made man and the sanctity of property.

David M. Parry, president of the National Association of Manufacturers in 1903, said unions knew only "one law, and that is the law of physical force—the law of the Huns and the Vandals, the law of the savage."[4] Employers' associations, noted labor historian Robert Hoxie, believed that employers had an absolute right to manage their business without interference. Therefore they could not be compelled to bargain with outsiders concerning the welfare of their workers, whose interests they considered to be identical with their own. Opposition to management's pay scale or working conditions betokened both unscrupulous leaders and ungrateful workers.[5]

Add in the radical elements of the IWW's brand of unionism, and the reaction of organizations like NAM were predictably over the top: "Now we see a new menace completely alien to our history, traditions, laws and institutions . . . a world-wide labor movement which finds its expression in that erratic mass called the [IWW]," warned NAM general counsel A. Parker Nevin in 1914. ". . . It is an angry sea surging against established bulkheads of society. It is utterly repugnant to Americanism; sneers at socialism and smiles at anarchy. Lawlessness is its law . . ."[6]

Putting Down the "I Won't Works"

The rootless migrant laborers with whom the IWW was so closely identified represented a fundamental challenge to the American work ethic and the very identity of most middle-class Americans. Rootless workers became bums and hobos with both sub-human qualities and the super-human capacity to destroy. The IWW's in-your-face combativeness served to intensify such feelings.

The IWW threat to capitalist American society, according to sociologist John Clendenin Townsend, triggered a psychological response that transformed the Wobbly into a one-dimensional devil (mirroring the way in which the German soldier was perceived). Doing so, "it denies him his humanity and thus any sympathy for whatever suffering he might endure . . . it attributes a single-minded malevolence to him, justifying ruthless suppression . . . [and] finally it robs him of his individuality, seeing him only as an interchangeable part of a larger mass."[7]

Those who were not Wobblies but merely expressed their dissatisfaction with working conditions were tarred with the same brush. As Dunn's *Strike Bulletin* editorialized: "Taking the papers' view of the matter, every man who demands better wages automatically becomes an IWW. If such is the case, the 'woods are full' of IWW's, because no union man in Butte is satisfied with present conditions . . ."[8]

Townsend analyzes the psychological dimension: "The extreme vilification of the IWW is a consequence of the necessity to gain power over one's enemies. One must create an image of the enemy that inspires fear (to motivate action) and contempt (to facilitate continued persecution), but has no sympathetic human qualities."[9]

When its archenemies spoke their fears of the IWW, they also revealed an elemental fear almost as old as America itself. Essentially, the Wobblies were viewed as invaders—not only in the physical sense, as in the free speech fights when they often flooded towns with boxcars full of tramps and floating workers—but more fundamentally as invaders of the American psyche, challenging beliefs that underlay the very identity of most Americans.

Robert Tyler, author of *Rebels of the Woods*, a study of the IWW in the Northwest, calls this phenomenon "The Hobo in the Garden." The garden was the mythical place, Jeffersonian in its ideals, where hard work, enterprise, thrift, self-reliance, and independence bloomed and flourished. These concepts were linked with capitalism and the primacy of private property (as they had been for centuries previously with mercantilism in Europe). Work offered the opportunity for those with enterprise to accumulate capital, with which to buy property and thus gain independence and a certain measure of power. Those who failed to accumulate property and remained poor were seen as morally weak.

Over generations, these concepts had become internalized, forming not only a belief system but also an American identity. "[The IWW] entered an American garden as outsiders and outcasts . . ." Tyler writes. "Their very existence as hoboes and aliens, as well as the rude and heathenish doctrine of class division they shouted so loudly, made them a rebuke to and a denial of the cherished myth."[10] Thus the popular label, "I Won't Work," attached to IWW members by their enemies, wasn't merely a humorous word play.[11] It also neatly mirrored prevailing, deeply held beliefs.

Of course, the Wobblies were hardly the only rude challenge to the myth in an era of mind-boggling social and economic change, a period that might be termed the Age of Disorder. Urbanization had jerked millions of Americans out of the garden of self-reliant agricultural pursuits. Industrialization had introduced the strain of impersonal workplaces, labor-saving technology, remote management, the monopolistic excesses of big business, and the large-scale corporate exploitation of natural resources such as minerals, timber, and water. Economic depressions, inflation, deteriorating health and living conditions, and waves of immigration—all had added to the angst, triggering the decades-long labor unrest that had spawned the Wobblies among others.

In a nation under tremendous social stress, it was perhaps only natural for businessmen—and the vast majority of their employees—psychologically invested in the myth of the garden, to romanticize industrialism and its foundation virtue, the work ethic, as the moral path to independence. By the same token, they tended to see the ills of industrialism—the bread lines, the poverty, the dangerous working conditions—as well as efforts to cure them—such as labor unions and the progressive reform movement—as noxious weeds that had floated in from some strange place and that needed to be yanked out. For industry, business, merchants, and the middle class, it was almost impossible to acknowledge that the IWW was merely a symptom of the iniquities and inequalities of the era.

The "I Won't Work" slogan stuck as an epithet with deep moral significance. As one contributor to *American Industry*, the NAM house organ, wrote: "The genius of success is work! Supreme effort only achieves supreme success. . . . The socialistic, demagogic penalizing and punishment of thrift, honesty, industry, and all that is good in men, is for the benefit of the 'I won't work' folks and all those who are vile and vicious. . . . 'Opportunity' comes to everyone who is willing to work and wait, and never has and never will come to the 'I won't workers.'"[12]

Sadly, opportunities for even the most highly motivated self-made man were shrinking fast. Specialization of tasks, large-scale mechanization and new technologies were making training and education much more important, if not vital. Remote corporations guided by faceless directors made the big decisions. But deeply held beliefs did not fade easily in the minds of businessmen and bosses who were convinced beyond the shadow of a doubt that the world was an oyster ready to be harvested by self-made men.[13]

The Newspapers' Role

Among those self-made men, publishers and editors played a vital role in shaping and mirroring attitudes about the IWW and radical dissent. Eldridge Foster Dowell, a political scientist who in the 1930s studied criminal syndicalism laws aimed at the IWW, summarized what he found: "Throughout the whole period from 1917 to 1919, we find the press the great motivating power which created through its news and editorial columns a distorted and vicious picture of the IWW. This stereotype provided the psychological stimulus necessary for the acts of violence against the IWW, their legal persecution and prosecution by the Federal Government, and the enactment of the state criminal syndicalism laws against them. . . . A deliberate policy of distortion and suppression of the news and misrepresentation of the facts would be difficult to prove, but a more unreal picture of the IWW could scarcely have been presented had such a policy been deliberately and maliciously employed."[14]

Newspapers almost always adopted law enforcement's point of view. Equally noteworthy is the virtual absence of any examination by the daily press of the physical abuse Wobblies endured at the hands of law enforcement or vigilante groups—or any editorial comment questioning such violence. The *Spokane Spokesman-Review* reported that jailed Wobblies objected to weekly baths, Elizabeth Gurley Flynn later related, but what they did not report was the nature of the "baths" (described, she wrote, by a man who endured it): "'First they strip your clothes off by force, then turn a stream of hot water over your head and shoulders scalding and blinding you at once, and then a stream of ice cold water.'"[15]

Press attention to the IWW took a sudden leap nationally as the United States entered the war, superheated by propaganda and the stirring up of patriotic emotions. In February 1917, *Sunset* magazine writer Walter V. Woehlke wrote, "The IWW is not an immediate menace." By September, he would write, "During the last seven or eight years the Industrial Workers of the World . . . have become a major problem in the United States [and have] taken up the cudgels for the 'wops' and the 'bohunks.'"[16]

Nationally syndicated columnists whipped up their own stew of hatred. James W. Gerard, the U.S. ambassador to Germany until war was declared (and the son-in-law of Montana copper king Marcus Daly), wrote in the *New York Tribune*, "[W]e should hog-tie every disloyal German-American, feed every pacifist raw meat, and hang every traitor to a lamppost to insure success in this war."[17] Gertrude Atherton, who made a career out of crucifying "pro-Germans," declared: "The IWW, the most pestiferous growth that ever menaced the stable and cultivated products of any country . . . were allowed to shoot forth their sticky, miasmic tendrils from one end of the country to the other. Their purpose is civil war," she asserted, leaving no doubt as to her solution: "When a farmer finds a nest of rattlesnakes on his place, does he wait for them to bite his family or does he exterminate them at once? The words of the IWW's against whom a conspiracy can be proved should be shot, and the rest deported en masse to a desert island . . ."[18]

Even in an era when most newspapers did not hesitate to employ invective, the bias against the IWW was remarkable. It was displayed in almost every imaginable journalistic form: one-sided reporting, slanted language and sensational focus in articles and headlines, undue focus on the Wobbly threat as reflected in the placement and frequency of news, and omission of news that might tend to show the IWW in a positive light. With the advent of Germany as America's enemy and international foe of democracy, it was a simple matter to tie it to the "disloyal" IWW.

In Montana, hostility to IWW by newspapers in the thrall of the Anaconda Copper Mining Co. was unrelenting. Newspapers owned, controlled, or heavily influenced by the Anaconda, including the *Butte Post* and *Butte Miner*, the *Anaconda Standard* (really a Butte newspaper) the *Daily Missoulian*, the *Helena Independent*, and the *Billings Gazette* wore the "copper collar," and cooperated with and supported the Anaconda's hegemony over Montana.[19] As one student of the situation wrote, "The Anaconda Company used the tactics of an authoritarian state to quash a legitimate labor movement within its corporate fiefdom. That the press, an elemental part of democracy, was used in the assault marks a black period in the history of American journalism."[20]

After the Metal Mine Workers Union led the miners out on strike in mid-June following the Speculator disaster, a *Butte Miner* headline proclaimed, "Attempt to Stop Copper Production," followed by the subhead, "IWW, Finns and Old Time Agitators In a New Movement, Their So Called Union Conceived Under Pro German Influences."[21]

Later that month, an *Anaconda Standard* editorial asked, "Vast sums of money have been provided by Germany to stir up trouble in all the copper camps of the West. . . . Who has the money?"[22] No proof of German funding of the IWW was ever made. The following week, the *Evening Capital News* in Boise attributed the German connection to U.S. District Attorney Clarence Reams in Portland, then decided to hedge its bets: "If German agents or not, they might as well be on the Kaiser's payroll as anybody now interfering with U.S. industry is lending comfort to Germany."[23]

Newspaper editorials were often strident and harsh in their judgments. During the Butte strike, anti-IWW editorials appeared on almost a daily basis in one Montana newspaper or another. On July 17, the *Anaconda Standard* declared: "It is certain that the IWW will have to go. The American people and the American government have trifled with that organization long enough, and the days of trifling are over."[24]

The *Butte Miner*, owned by mining magnate W. A. Clark, scolded the government for not doing enough to stop the IWW: "The longer the government postpones handling disloyal movements without gloves, the more difficult it will become to suppress it when it makes up its mind that it must be stopped."[25]

Bias in the Butte papers was so transparent that the printers who printed the *Post*, *Miner*, and *Standard* passed a resolution accusing the newspapers of "persistently and willfully distorted news happenings in an effort to confuse and mislead the public."[26] A few weeks later, churches in Butte and Anaconda spoke out: "The daily press of Butte and Anaconda, controlled by the corporations . . . libelled [sic] the actions of the miners by attributing all the trouble to the Industrial Workers of the World. . . . The

Figure 9. *Helena Independent* editor Will Campbell savaged political and labor dissenters during and after World War I with vicious editorials and biased news stories. Montana Historical Society.

local press has disgusted and alienated the people of Butte and Anaconda, whose intelligence it has insulted, by its stupidity and manifest one-sidedness. . . . Christian people . . . should fearlessly protest against this prostitution of the influence of the press."[27]

Butte's clergy probably would have reached their limit of disgust far earlier had they been regular readers of the *Helena Independent.* So reactionary as to be almost a cartoon character, editor Will Campbell nonetheless was extremely influential, and counted Gov. Sam Stewart, a conservative Democrat, among his closest friends. In early 1918, Stewart would appoint himself and Campbell to the Montana Council of Defense, where they were in a position of extraordinary power to deal with the enemies of the state.

Whether the Anaconda Company owned a controlling interest in the *Independent* in 1917 is not certain.[28] But it's a moot point. Campbell was a "Company man" who lent enthusiastic support to the Anaconda.

Campbell's hatred of the IWW was such a consistent feature in the *Independent* that it became the newspaper's hallmark, along with his knee-jerk super-patriotism. In the first seven weeks after the miners' walkout on June 12, Campbell's *Independent* published at least fifty-seven articles and editorials about the IWW, not to mention many others in which the IWW was mentioned. Typical headlines included "IWW Wrecking Butte Admits Official Organ" (June 22); "Northwest Industries Menaced by Agitators" (June 30); "IWW to Try to Burn Crops, Farmers Warned" (July 4) and "Western Montana Lies in Grip of IWW Hoodlums" (July 8).

Campbell's editorials about the IWW were venomous, provocative harangues. On June 14 ("Turn On The Light"), he said, "Down at the bottom of the threatened trouble in Butte, if search is made, the authorities will find Prussian money—that, and the usual riff-raff of IWW's who, like hyenas, hang in the rear of an army to pick up what may be thrown aside in the conflict . . ." On July 10 ("Declare an Open Season on IWW"), Campbell wrote, "If the government trifles with the traitors in the country much longer . . . it need not be a matter of surprise if the people rise up and declare an open season on the IWW and start a series of hanging bees and shootings which will reduce the visible supply of criminals appreciably. It is high time that IWWism was taken by the throat and choked to death."

Campbell's fixation on the IWW might be dismissed as the ravings of a nut case but for the facts that the *Independent* was the capital's major daily and that Campbell had tremendous influence with Governor Stewart and the political and industrial establishment. His remarkable level of animosity and his reactionary politics buttressed and perhaps influenced like-minded editors, publishers, opinion leaders, and the general public.

The IWW's institutional weakness and unruly membership also made it vulnerable to attacks by the press. Any number of detectives and provocateurs were able to infiltrate IWW locals and quickly become leaders. These moles directly or indirectly used the press to whip up public and press animosity against the IWW.

Wobbly Henry McGuckin was among those who had taken notice of infiltration by agents as war approached. He wrote in his memoir: "I began to notice new faces in the IWW halls. Talk began of the kind that could only mean an attempt was being made to discredit old-timers, men who had been in the thick of things and had proven themselves. . . . It was hard to put your finger on what was happening, but we began to uncover the finks a few at a time. There were Pinkerton men as well as government secret service men, and they were past masters of divide and rule. Old-timers began to look at each other with suspicion. Men turned up missing and were never heard from again . . ."[29]

Quite a few IWW scholars have remarked on its self-destructive nature. "The Wobblies failed to reject [the invective aimed at them], almost seeming to wallow in their notoriety," Professor James Byrkit wrote. "Important, illusory, the tiny IWW struggled toward a piteous affirmation of an image that assured its complete defeat. Proud and romantic, the Wobblies refused to admit, or even see, that they were being manipulated to effect the permanence of all the conditions they so desperately sought to change."[30]

In a sharply polarized climate where one was either for America or against it, the IWW was now Public Enemy Number One. On August 1, 1917, W. A. Clark's *Miner* editorialized: "In a general sort of way, it was thought that the IWW indicated a lot of more-or-less happy-go-lucky individuals who beat their way on freight trains from place to place, annoyed farmers, and used up jail space. . . . In recent weeks, the nation has awakened to the real sinister purpose back of the IWW. It is acting as if it were determined to do everything to advance the German cause by interfering with industrial peace and progress in this country . . ."[31]

The Committee on Public Information

Hatred of the "I Won't Works," which rumbled in the subconscious like a deep bass chord, would be further reinforced by an ebullient new federal agency, whose cheerleading support for the war effort at first seemed so positive, so American.

"No hymn of hate accompanies our message," crowed an early newsletter from the Committee on Public Information.[32] This was undoubtedly true on the surface, for the prodigious output of the CPI was dedicated to channeling public opinion about America's war aims—or as its director George Creel, a former Denver newspaperman and well-known muckraker, phrased it, fusing the American people into "one white-hot mass."[33]

Well intentioned and bursting with energy, Creel sincerely believed, as did all good progressives, in the power of informed public opinion to achieve consensus—in this case support for America's war aims. Instead of promulgating new thoughts from the top down, the CPI took popular ideas about America's role in the war ("make the world safe for democracy"), simplified and homogenized them, and invested them with emotion and moral righteousness. It disseminated its messages energetically, through almost every means imaginable, from cartoons, posters, and leaflets to editorials, speeches, and expositions. "Channels of communication were literally choked with officially approved news and opinion, leaving little freeway for rumor or disloyal reports," observed the CPI's first historians, James Mock and Cedric Larson.[34] Other agencies, from Herbert Hoover's Food Administration to Bernard Baruch's War Industries Board, borrowed CPI techniques to get their particular message across.

However the progressive approach of "substituting aroused passion for political authority," argues historian David M. Kennedy, would also spawn a hysterical brand of patriotism that in turn would lead to the eager repression of minority groups like the socialists and the IWW, who didn't subscribe to the same set of values.[35] Ultimately, the CPI, which more than any other entity set the tone for wartime America, would write its own "Hymn of Hate." If it didn't sing the words, it filled the music hall with a populace eager to act in concert and shout down evil no matter what its form.

The CPI was born just one week after Wilson signed the war declaration, amidst an explosion of patriotism as citizens rallied 'round the flag in parades and mass meetings. Public support for the war was pushed along almost at breakneck speed by a brilliant domestic campaign of propaganda and censorship. Practically all news of the war had the CPI stamp of approval on it (and was doubly filtered at this point, for the British still had a chokehold on European news). News was either distributed to the news media in the form of press releases, bulletins, and documents, or it was vetted by the CPI in a system of "voluntary censorship." Creel and his former journalistic colleagues knew that the censorship scheme had several sticks behind it: As of mid-June 1917, the Espionage Act presented the vague but potent threat of prosecution for making false reports or false statements to obstruct the military forces.[36] Mailing privileges could be revoked under the same law as well as under the October 1917 Trading-with-the-Enemy Act, which also established a Board of Censorship.

In an almost Orwellian manner, the CPI bulletin explaining the press censorship regulations was prefaced by a quotation from President

Wilson, which read in part, "I can imagine no greater disservice to the country than to establish a system of censorship that would deny to the people of a free republic like our own their indisputable right to criticize their own public officials." Wilson evidently envisioned only a certain kind of criticism, as he made clear in the next sentence: "I would regret in a crisis like the one we are now passing through to lose the benefit of patriotic and intelligent criticism."[37]

Teddy Roosevelt and Senator La Follette could rant and rave all they wanted (and no Wilsonian mechanism would ever get T. R. to shut up). But disloyal dissenters and rabble-rousers need not apply. Discriminating between certain kinds or classes of speakers was a widely held sentiment. The right to speak freely was regarded as a privilege not available to those who abjured commonly held moral standards such as the work ethic and the preeminence of private property. Rootless bums or anyone whose ideology challenged sociopolitical norms—descriptive of the Wobblies among others—were deemed not to have earned the privilege of free speech.[38]

In much the same way as the British propaganda office had done, Creel's committee recruited well-known writers, artists, educators, and speakers to its cause. Popular authors such as Booth Tarkington popularized "story lines" the CPI wanted to promote—that the Germans started the war, that morale in the military cantonments was high, that it was not "a rich man's war."[39] Charles Dana Gibson, creator of the stylish "Gibson Girls" in *Life* magazine, headed a Who's Who atelier of artists churning out posters, cartoons, lithographs, and etchings for publication in newspapers and magazines. They illustrated slogans and simplified exhortations, urging men to enlist, citizens to beware of spies, women to save food. Hollywood's most glamorous stars—Douglas Fairbanks Sr., Theda Bara, Mary Pickford, and Charlie Chaplin among them—were drafted to hawk Liberty Bonds, while scores of war films were produced. Some, like *The Kaiser, the Beast of Berlin,* appealed to baser emotions of hatred and fear. "Hyphenated-Americans" received special attention to make sure they knew, in their native tongues, the nation's war aims.

A division coordinating civic and educational groups solicited contributions from scholars and distributed more than 75 million pieces of literature from leaflets to a war encyclopedia to lurid advertisements.[40] One ad said in part, "In the vicious guttural language of Kultur, the degree A.B.

Figure 10. The Committee on Public Information employed every means of mass communication, including patriotic movies, to enlist public support for the war. The Library of Congress.

means Bachelor of Atrocities. Are you going to let the Prussian Python strike at your Alma Mater, as it struck at the University of Louvain?"[41]

School lesson plans across the country were reshaped by CPI propaganda. In Montana, the prescribed eighth grade history curriculum for 1918 included sections on "Why America entered the War," "The German Autocracy," and "The War Message and Facts Behind It." Each section's source was a CPI Bulletin.[42] In pamphlets published by private groups that also used CPI sources, lesson plans outlined patriotism. Albert Bushnell Hart, professor of government at Harvard, suggested that among the hallmarks of patriotism were "undivided love of country," "electing and holding in office men who intelligently serve America first and at all times" and "patriotic talk to neighbors and friends."[43]

The amazing extent to which the CPI fed the superheated patriotic climate in which dissent was enthusiastically suppressed is probably best shown by the Four-Minute Men. Before the spread of commercial radio, the CPI created its own broadcast network—with the vocal chords of tens of thousands of speakers. This ubiquitous corps of amateur orators, "carrying the flaming arrow into every corner of America," rallied public sentiment with short, punchy talks at movie houses, theaters, churches, social clubs—even on trains and streetcars—on pre-selected subjects.[44] By the end of the war, Creel estimated, as many as 75,000 Four-Minute Men had given a million speeches to 400 million people.[45]

Speakers "unabashedly went for the jugular," simplifying the government's message within a strict four-minute time limit.[46] Bloviators were not welcome. "Use short sentences," they were exhorted. "Avoid fine phrases. . . . Talk to the simplest intelligence in your audience."[47] Feelings of pride were manipulated: "The man who stands back now is lost; lost to the ranks of citizenship; lost to the mother who bore him . . . lost to the Flag that protects him . . ."[48] So were feelings of fear: "Are you going to look timidly at long processions of conquering troops tramping down our streets?"[49] Guilt was invoked: "While we are sitting here . . . in comfortable chairs enjoying a good picture show . . . our boys are standing in the trenches down in the mud. Shells are bursting over their heads—roaring cannon—poisonous gases creeping through the trenches."[50]

Unlike many private patriotic organizations, such as the National Security League and Sons of the Revolution, the CPI did take pains to discourage outright expressions of hatred. One four-minute man's sentiment,

"We must keep these goose-stepping, baby-killing, educated gorillas from our shores," was deplored in a speakers' bulletin.[51] Still, the brutish nature of the Germans was hammered home. In one bulletin, a sample speech stated: "Prussian *Schrecklichkeit* (the deliberate policy of terrorism) leads to almost unbelievable besotten brutality. The German soldiers were often forced against their wills, they themselves weeping, to carry out unspeakable orders against defenseless old men, women, and children . . ."[52] A CPI publication, *German War Practices*, quoted German war diaries to detail massacres and other German frightfulness.[53]

The CPI also encouraged speakers to spread the idea that Germany was behind any "disloyal" expression, such as that the draft law was unconstitutional or that America should not be sending men, money, or munitions to Europe.[54] Time and again, in newspapers and magazines stories about IWW's or other dissenters, and in Espionage Act and sedition cases themselves, the same connection would be made as if it were a fact. As *Helena Independent* editor Will Campbell had said of IWW organizer Frank Little, his statements "demonstrat[ed] beyond doubt that [the IWW's] leaders are in the service of Prussia and therefore in its pay . . ."[55]

The end result of George Creel's zeal to "hold fast the inner lines" was an extraordinary monument to the American tendency toward uniformity that de Tocqueville had first described back in the 1830s. In the malign stress of wartime, a thousand ardent fingers had woven a stifling blanket of uniform thought and opinion across America.[56] "One of the most appalling conclusions about the war was the ease with which modern techniques and mass suggestion enables a government to make even a reasonably intelligent people, with an individualistic, democratic background, believe anything it likes," observed historians Samuel Eliot Morison and Henry Steele Commager in 1933.[57] "The Committee on Public Information," noted historians Mock and Larson, "had done its job so well that there was a burning eagerness to believe, to conform, to feel the exaltation of joining in a great and selfless enterprise."[58] For most people, the authors observed, no laws against expressing dissent were even necessary.

But laws to stifle dissent were already being enacted. The Espionage Act, among other things, severely punished "false reports or false statements with intent to interfere with the operation or success of the military or naval forces." While newspapers whipped up a storm of criticism about another provision that would have imposed direct censorship on them (ultimately dropped from the bill), only a few critics saw the dangers of the "false reports" provision, especially in the frenzied climate whipped up by the CPI and patriotic organizations.

"The administration of such laws . . . may easily lend itself to the suppression of free speech, free assemblage, popular discussion, and criticism," a group of well-known liberals and progressives (including Lillian Wald, Jane Addams, Amos Pinchot, Oswaldo Garrison Villard, Herbert Croly, and Max Eastman) wrote to the President on April 17: "Even by this time, we have seen evidence of the breaking down of immemorial rights and privileges. Halls have been refused for public discussion; meetings have been broken up; speakers have been arrested and censorship exercised, not to prevent the transmission of information to enemy countries, but to prevent the free discussion by American citizens of our own problems and policies. As we go on, the inevitable psychology of war will manifest itself with increasing danger, not only to individuals but to our cherished institutions. It is possible that the moral damage to our democracy in this war may become more serious than the physical or national losses incurred."[59]

Warnings such as these turned out to be sharply prophetic. Like acid, the war would eat deeply into Americans' rights and privileges. ❖

SEVEN
Up in Smoke

Frank Little Lynched; Mounting Calls to Squelch the IWW, 1917

THE SUMMER OF 1917 WAS HOT AND EXTREMELY DRY. Drought gripped Montana—the worst in twenty-five years. The weather bureau in Missoula reported six-tenths of an inch of rain in June, less than one-third of normal.[1] Grasshoppers swept like a slow grass fire through the fields. Real fires charred the forests of western Montana. In the Yaak, in the northwest corner, six fires were reportedly started within twenty-four hours, most likely by Wobblies.[2] In Butte, Frank Little was igniting a different kind of fire.

Outraged by the death of 168 men in the Speculator Mine six weeks earlier, thousands of striking copper miners were pressing demands for higher wages and better working conditions. Shocked by the brutal boxcar deportation to the New Mexico desert of 1,186 striking copper miners the week before from Bisbee, Arizona, men were flocking into Butte on every freight to support the striking miners in Butte. What better climate for preaching the radical gospel of the IWW, for recruiting disaffected workers?

A few people may have recognized the slight, one-eyed man on crutches, with a cast on his right leg, as he hobbled up the Butte hill on July 18, 1917—perhaps some Wobblies and maybe a sharp-eyed detective. Little, thirty-eight, was now a central figure in the IWW, as the chairman of its General Executive Board. He was no armchair director. He had earned his position through long, tough years since Missoula, traveling constantly through the West to agitate and direct IWW strikes. He had been nearly lynched a year earlier, taken out of a jail in Iron River, Michigan, beaten and left for dead in a ditch.[3]

Over the next two weeks, Little would castigate the mining bosses and denounce America's entry in the war. His abrasive speeches would give his enemies ample reason to strike back.

The stage had already been set. That very day, a directive was on its way from Attorney General Thomas W. Gregory to U.S. district attorneys and special agents across the country.[4] Gregory, who called the IWW a "grave menace to the nation," asked the local prosecutors to make "special efforts" to gather information about IWW members, leaders, income, literature [to determine] what action may be taken . . ."[5]

One of Little's first stops in Butte was to attend a meeting of the Metal Mine Workers Union in Finlander Hall. Men in the new union had led the wildcat strike two days after the Speculator disaster had burned its way deep into the Butte psyche. But the miners' strike was threatening to collapse, as trade unions initially sympathetic were being lured back to work. Little spoke confidently of the IWW's plans to recruit all metal mine workers, then call on all industrial unions to support a general strike.[6]

A much larger crowd (estimated at between three thousand and six thousand) gathered at the Butte ballpark the next day to hear Little speak. The audience consisted of striking miners, curious townspeople, more than a few detectives, company operatives, and newspaper reporters. Little extolled the virtues of "the one big union" and the organization of the mines. But the *Anaconda Standard* and other newspapers focused instead on what had been a minor feature of his speech. The *Standard's* headline and subhead were typical: "To Keep Army From France," "That is Part of the IWW Plan In This Country it Appears."

Quoting Little as saying "we will give the soldiers of the United States so much to do at home that they will have no chance to go to France," the *Standard* pronounced Little's remarks "the most inflammatory of any made in Butte since the troubles of three years ago." His words "were wildly applauded by the radical element that was in the majority apparently . . ."[7] The article tells as much, of course, about the company-controlled *Standard* and its focus on the most sensational "news": the IWW's "unpatriotic plans" to tie up production of vital industries with strikes, so as to directly inhibit the flow of U.S. troops to France.

Little was as hard on the miners as he was on the mining companies. At a closed-door meeting on July 25, Little blasted them for their caution, for sending resolutions to Congress protesting the Bisbee deportations.[8] "The thing you want to do is organize and then tell Wilson to release those men or by God we will start a revolution and release them ourselves," he reportedly said.[9]

The next day, at another closed meeting with the MMWU, Little was even blunter. "Go take them men off the hill," he exhorted the miners. "Use any means necessary, but take them off the hill!" As for the union's peaceful strike, Little's words dripped with scorn. "What would Uncle Sam say to the soldiers he is sending over to Europe to meet the German army if they laid down their arms and said we are conducting a peaceful war?"[10]

Little even tried to shame the men into action. He told them that a committee of women—wives, mothers, and sisters of the miners—had come to him to see what they could do to help. "The women will do a damned sight more fighting than you fellows have done," he said.[11] Talking to IWW members at Finlander Hall the next day, Little stepped up the rhetoric. "Go out and put on a picket," he shouted. "Send 20 men to jail the first day if they arrest the pickets and then send 40 and then 100 and fill the jails and refuse bonds and pay no fines." Little exhorted the miners, "Look the city daddies in the face and tell them to go to hell, also their city ordinances and laws. A city ordinance is only a scrap of paper, which can be torn up. The same can be said of the Constitution of the United States."[12]

Little's incendiary comments continued to make banner headlines. "In a Treasonable Tirade Little Says Constitution Is Mere Scrap of Paper," declared the next day's *Butte Daily Post*.[13] The *Anaconda Standard*'s main story also signaled what an uphill fight Little had in rallying the troops: The metal trades had voted, eleven to seven, to sign the contract offered to them by the companies with a slightly higher wage scale, meaning that the miners could no longer count on them to support their strike.

The press drumbeat quickened. "How Long is It [Butte] Going to Stand for the Seditious Talk of the IWW Agitator?" the *Butte Daily Post* asked the same day.[14] On July 30, the *Anaconda Standard* issued an ultimatum to the "IWW agitator":

> The American people are patient; the government is patient; the officers of the law are patient. The time is coming, and is nearly here, when patience will have been exhausted. . . . It is a good guess that in American communities treasonable and lawless utterances will not much longer be tolerated.[15]

In the issue that rolled off the presses early on the morning of August 1, 1917, the *Helena Independent* reprinted an even more explicit editorial from *The Western News*, a weekly in Libby, Montana. It characterized the IWW as a "wolf masked in sheep's clothing," an "ignoble and traitorous union of anarchists" masquerading as a workingman's organization to avoid prosecution. "But it will not be for long," the editorial concluded:

> There is a law greater than that of the state of Montana, greater even than that of the United States of America. It is the law of self-preservation. If the national government does not soon uncover and punish this enemy to humanity . . . then the people of the communities threatened must for the occasion make their own law. The days of the wooly sheep are numbered.[16]

While editorial writers seemed to have no doubts that Little should be punished, those in charge of punishment had strong reservations about whether he could be. Just the day before, in a meeting with Anaconda's chief counsel Lewis O. Evans, U.S. District Attorney Burton K. Wheeler had concluded that Little could not be successfully prosecuted under the 1917 Espionage Act. Evans had to agree that nothing Little had said was an indictable offense under the narrow provisions of that law. And even if he could be indicted, he would not be convicted, not in Montana with Federal District Judge George M. Bourquin Jr. on the bench. His legal fundamentalism and refusal to bend the law to conform to public sentiment were well known.

Wheeler and Evans had probably read the judge's comments that very morning in the *Anaconda Standard*. Bourquin had dealt very leniently with a Butte man named John Lennon, a member of the radical Irish Pearce-Connolly Club. Lennon had been jailed for passing out anti-registration circulars on Registration Day, June 5. In jail he refused to register for the draft and was charged with violating the Selective Service law. After a guilty plea, the judge had sentenced Lennon to one day in jail.[17] What the judge wrote obviously applied with equal force to Frank Little:

> In the strenuous times of war, especially when passions are more or less aroused, the accused person charged with offenses which seem to militate against the country's good and their rights must be protected at all times by the court, but more zealously at a time like this . . . no case at such times as these which appeal greatly to the patriotism of all men, should go to the jury to try your patriotism, perhaps rather than your judgment . . .[18]

Figure 11. This placard was displayed at Duggan's Funeral Home, where Frank Little's mutilated body was viewed after his murder on Aug. 1, 1917. Butte-Silver Bow Public Archives.

Few laymen probably appreciated the fine points of the federal law that prevented Wheeler from successfully prosecuting Little or understood what clout Montana's sole federal judge had. But by sunrise on Wednesday, August 1, by the time the newsboys were hawking the morning newspapers with their ultimatums, the lawyers' calculations and judges' admonitions were worthless. The people had made their own law. Beneath the Milwaukee trestle at the edge of town dangled Frank Little's lifeless body.

At about three that morning, six masked men had burst into Little's room—Number 32—on the ground floor of the Steele rooming house, next door to Finlander Hall. They hustled Little, dressed in his underclothes, into a large black car and sped south on Wyoming Street. No one except the perpetrators—who were never identified—saw Little alive after that.

Little's knees, toes, and fingers were pulp from being dragged behind a car. Bruises on his skull testified to a severe beating, possibly from a rifle butt. His neck was not broken, meaning he was probably dead or close to it before he was hung from the rope. On a pasteboard placard pinned to his shorts was an inscription in red crayon: "Others take notice, first and last warning, 3–7-77." Underneath were penciled the letters "L. D. C. S.

Figure 12. The arrow shows the location of Frank Little's rooming house, from which his killers abducted him. Next door was Finlander Hall, where the IWW and the Metal Mine Workers Union (MMWU) were headquartered. Butte-Silver Bow Public Archives.

S. W. T." The "L" was circled. The numbers were the traditional "signature" of Montana vigilantes dating back to territorial days. The letters prompted several theories, the most popular being that they stood for the last names of other potential targets, such as Bill Dunn of the electricians' union and the *Strike Bulletin* and MMWU chief Tom Campbell. The message, however, was clear.

While the city simmered, officials immediately condemned the murder. U.S. Attorney Wheeler termed it "a damnable outrage, a blot on the city and state."[19] His deputy, James Baldwin, said, "It was not a case of lynching by a mob, but a case of cold-blooded and deliberate murder."[20] Rep. Jeannette Rankin vowed to launch an investigation—and seek federal management of the copper mines. She blamed the strike in Butte on Anaconda Copper Company president John D. Ryan and his intransigence on the rustling card issue.[21] Radical union leaders urged caution, fearing immediate reprisal should union members lash out. Gov. Stewart and Attorney General Sam Ford hurried to Butte. Neither stayed long. Stewart traveled to Portland to attend a special western governors' meeting on the IWW situation. Ford found the city quiet. Perhaps guessing the killers would not be found, he was back in Helena by August 3, then went fishing in the Madison River country.[22]

Most newspapers abhorred the act but blamed the government. Declared the *Anaconda Standard*, "The lynching, first that has ever disgraced the city of Butte and brought shame to its good name, a travesty on law and order, followed the failure of . . . authorities to properly deal with the case of Little and his fellow agitators."[23] The leftist *Strike Bulletin* condemned the killers as a "gang of the most cowardly degenerates who ever disgraced this earth" but of course came to a different conclusion: "[I]t is time to demand that Company rule in Butte be broken. Every working man must feel that it is now time to back us to the last ditch."[24]

Other newspapers called the murder foreseeable: "The treason-spreading lawless vagabonds who have been infesting Montana in the name of the IWW have . . . had the inevitable effect of breeding lawlessness among those whose patience has been strained beyond the breaking point," noted the *Bozeman Chronicle*.[25]

Will Campbell of the *Helena Independent* proposed a final solution: "[T]he opinion prevails that it would be better for the United States army to lead the IWW leaders out to a convenient mountain side and with one volley from the rifles of a picked company, end the agitation in Montana."[26] A few days later, he ran a front-page cartoon suggesting that Little's killers were patriots. Illuminated by moonlight, a corpulent mustachioed figure hung from a tree limb. The caption read, "If the Butte Committee Could Call on the Kaiser."[27]

Little's funeral on August 5 was a massive and ponderous affair that gave Butte labor a chance to demonstrate solidarity and to express its members outrage peacefully. More than three thousand mourners marched in the silent procession, taking two hours to travel the four miles down the Butte hill from Duggan's Mortuary to Mountain View Cemetery. At the front marched Bill Dunn and MMWU president Tom Campbell, flanking an American flag. Members of the Pearce-Connolly club, wearing green, joined MMWU and electrical union members and Finnish women. At the rear, IWW members wearing huge red sashes took turns bearing the grey casket on their shoulders. It bore the words, "Martyr for Solidarity." The procession drew more than ten thousand onlookers.[28]

At the graveside, with the mourners down to one hundred or so, a fellow Wobbly delivered a brief eulogy. Little's casket was lowered into the ground. A dozen red silk handkerchiefs and some red carnations were tossed in before the dirt was spaded over.[29] Frank Little had joined the pantheon of IWW martyrs.

The inscription on Little's polished granite headstone reads: "1879—1917. Slain By Capitalist Interests For Organizing and Inspiring His Fellow Men." That he was murdered by his enemies and that they were employed by capitalists is a safe enough bet. That his tough defiance inspired others to fight for labor's cause is beyond dispute. So signal was Little's impassioned rhetoric against the bosses at such a crucial juncture that some have wondered whether he was a mole and a provocateur. Whether that was true or not, Little did as much as anyone to energize business and industry to wipe out the IWW and to crack down severely on all forms of political dissent. Certainly his death did nothing to mollify those offended by his flaming revolutionary talk. Instead, his killing was like the incendiary flame his fellow Wobblies had been accused of using to torch the forests of western Montana. Instead of larch, fir, and pine, it was reason, understanding, and patience that went up in smoke.

The First Casualty

The horoscope in the August 1 *Anaconda Standard* had read, "Beginning with this month, many remarkable and unprecedented things will follow."[30] That prophecy had already proved to be on the mark but more was yet to come. Little's murder accelerated the calls for action against the IWW. A counter-current to this insistent torrent, urging a more measured response and pointing out that the IWW "menace" was exaggerated, was hardly noticed. Before the summer was over, repressive measures by state and federal governments would stagger the organization. Before a year had passed, the IWW would be all but crushed.

Hiram Johnson, the progressive governor of California in the World War I period, is credited with having said, "In wartime, truth is the first casualty."[31] The epigram could as well be applied to the war against the IWW. Its efforts to force reform were seen as a treasonous blow against the nation's war effort. Observed historian Robert L. Tyler, "The 1917 lumber strike, the first and last real display of power by the IWW in the Pacific Northwest, produced an angry and determined manhunt that ended only years after the war."[32] The same could be said of the copper strikes. In that poisoned and desperate atmosphere, Johnson's maxim proved itself over and over. Using hyperbolic claims about its danger, those determined to end the IWW menace pulled out all the stops in a smear campaign aimed at getting the federal government to take decisive action in what they claimed was a dire national emergency.

Advocates for suppressing the IWW repeatedly made several claims, according to Robert Evans in a 1964 thesis: "[That] the IWW was a seditious and unpatriotic organization; it was a destructive organization that openly practiced sabotage; [it] was a revolutionary conspiracy to overthrow the U.S. Government; that conspiracy was financed by the Imperial German Government to undermine the American war effort and . . . if the IWW was not legislatively suppressed, the American people would take the law into their own hands."[33] Employing all of these arguments, key figures in this campaign created a clamor that the federal government could not ignore.

The clamor began just hours after Little's body was discovered. According to the *Helena Independent*, the state's congressional delegation was "deluged with appeals for troops" to steady what promised to be an explosive situation.[34] Gov. Stewart also started receiving telegrams expressing outrage and demanding an immediate investigation.[35]

On August 2, five influential men in Missoula sent a telegram to Montana's senior senator, Henry L. Myers, in Washington. It read in part:

> The conditions in Missoula and adjoining counties call for immediate action on the part of the federal government to make secure the lives and property of the people. . . . The IWW agitators are openly preaching treason and threatening reprisals for the death of Little. They are insulting the flag, belittling the authority of the government and are increasing in numbers. For weeks they have terrorized the lumber camps and are openly threatening the destruction of crops.[36]

The men demanded that federal officers be dispatched immediately "to disperse or arrest these disturbers of peace and traitors."[37]

Myers had been a virtual unknown, a district judge in Hamilton, when elected as a compromise candidate on the eightieth ballot by the Democratic-controlled legislature in 1911. He was soon considered to be solidly in the Anaconda's camp. In 1916, Myers was re-elected, this time by popular vote, to what would be his last term in a mediocre political career.[38]

Myers forwarded a copy of the telegram to Attorney General Gregory. "Matters in Montana are in a very critical condition," he stressed. "Unless more vigorous action is taken by the Federal officials in Montana, I fear there will be other lynchings in that State."[39] In an interview the same day, Myers termed the Little lynching "inevitable" given the government's inaction and added, "I suppose some of the people of Butte became so exasperated by continual defiant talk and threats and abuse of the government and the army that their patience got beyond control."[40]

Assistant Attorney General William C. Fitts, on loan from a Wall Street firm, responded immediately.[41] Well known for his anti-IWW notions—his pet theory was that IWW secretary Big Bill Haywood had Little killed because he was getting too powerful—he assured Myers the Missoula situation would be looked into right away.[42] He telegraphed special agent E. W. Byrn Jr. in Butte, requesting a careful investigation.[43]

Byrn's report, mailed three days later, was thorough and scathing. After talking to Missoula's chief of police, mayor, county attorney, and postmaster and to other leading citizens, he wrote, "This survey failed to disclose any disorder or disturbance or undue activity whatsoever on the part of the IWW or others. The streets of the town are quiet. . . . There is absolutely no evidence to warrant the statement that treasonable and seditious utterances are being made . . . or that the flag is being desecrated."[44] Striking lumberjacks who had been camping outside of town had left— many to fight the forest fires.[45]

Byrn had also interviewed two of the five men who had signed the telegram. Kenneth Ross, the manager of the Big Blackfoot Milling Co. in Bonner, an Anaconda subsidiary, told him no one was interfering with the mill's operation there, although the lumber strike was curtailing the mill's output. C. H. McLeod, president of the Missoula Mercantile Co., told Byrn that his own knowledge of IWW activities was limited and admitted that the statements in the telegram were possibly exaggerated.[46]

Without waiting for an answer on the Missoula "crisis," Senator Myers continued to badger the Justice Department. He passed on more calls for action, including one from the Montana Bankers' Association demanding that the military be empowered to deal "expeditiously and summarily" with the IWW. In fact, troops were already on their way and by August 11 would be patrolling the streets of Butte—where they would remain garrisoned until January 1921.

Myers again wrote Asst. Atty. Gen. Fitts. "The state has been invaded by a horde of IWW agitators," he said. "They are openly preaching strikes and advising workingmen to quit their jobs and denouncing the prosecution of the war. Every sawmill in the state is closed down and the mines are all seriously handicapped in their workings . . ."[47] In an exasperated tone, he added, "I have laid a number of complaints, such as this, before the Department of Justice, but, so far, without any results . . ." He added that he would gladly introduce any legislation the department would draw up.[48] Justice would be happy to cooperate, Fitts replied, but legislation should originate in Congress.[49] It was a misleading statement at best, as a fellow high-ranking official at Justice, Charles Warren, had been the principle author of the Espionage Act, enacted less than two months earlier.[50] But it was enough to get Myers off his case for the time being.

The very next day, Myers and four other western senators attacked the IWW on the Senate floor. "[T]heir official utterances, their printed literature, their speakers, advocate murder . . . and dynamite," charged Senator Miles Poindexter of Washington.[51] "The trouble in Montana," said Myers, "has been not so much open violence but mostly incendiary and inflammatory talk, seditious talk, threats, abuse of the government . . . denunciation of the war, fomenting strikes, and inciting disturbances." Federal legislation was needed. "If there is no law to punish such talk, some should be provided," Myers added.[52]

On August 15, Myers introduced Senate Bill 2789, "for the better safety and welfare of the United States." His bill was a sedition law, pure and simple. Its language bore a remarkable similarity to the despised sedition law of 1798, which punished, "any person [who] shall write, print, utter, or publish . . . any false, scandalous and malicious writing . . . against the government [Congress or President] of the United States . . . with intent to defame them . . . or to bring them into . . . contempt or disrepute; or to excite against them . . . the hatred of the good people of the United States . . ."[53]

Criminal punishment for seditious libel, for impugning the authority of government by lowering it in the public esteem, or by stirring up discontent, had long been used by the Crown to suppress dissident political thought. American colonists had felt its sting, and, on its face, the First Amendment seemed to repudiate the concept as an abridgement of the right to free speech or a free press. Nonetheless, the Alien and Sedition Acts passed just seven years later in the Adams administration gave the president extraordinary powers to deport non-citizen residents and prosecutors the power to punish false, scandalous, and malicious publications against the U.S. government. The laws were never held to be unconstitutional. Still, the raw political use of the law in punishing Adams' critics had backfired against the majority party. Prison sentences for anti-Federalist newspaper editors undoubtedly contributed to Jefferson's election in 1800, and the bad taste of the Alien and Sedition Acts lingered for decades.

Yet the notion of punishment for sedition had never been completely discarded. Now, energized by industry's extreme alarm at the IWW's "incendiary" threat, Senator Myers and his cohorts were urging Congress to unsheathe a crude but powerful weapon. Wartime, they argued, had made it necessary. Montana's senior senator was dusting off a rusty, mighty broadsword whose heft and sweep, whose potential impact on American constitutional liberties, he clearly did not appreciate.

Four days later, the junior senator from Montana, Thomas J. Walsh, announced that he was drafting criminal syndicalism legislation "to curb the violence of agitators who oppose the constituted government of the country" and "to suppress agitators who, in the name of labor, are treasonably trying to tie up industries of the country."[54] Several states had already passed such laws, Idaho doing so first on March 14.

Myers' bill had plenty of popular support. Patriotic organizations had begun passing resolutions supporting it.[55] Petitions circulated through state defense councils by the American Defense Society urged passage of a national sedition law.[56] Editorials expressed impatience at federal inaction, some making even Myers look moderate. The *New York World* accused "many of the socialist, Sinn Fein, IWW, and Jewish radical publications" of giving aid and comfort to the enemy: "If there was ever a time in American history when treason deserved to be punished as treason, that time has come, and the longer the delay the deeper this cancer will eat into the vitals of the republic."[57]

To fan his own flames of discontent, Myers provided each of his colleagues with copies of the August 19 edition of the *Helena Independent*. On the front page was the "Hymn of Hate," the IWW's "Onward, Christian Soldiers" parody that could be counted on to raise tempers. The main headline on page one trumpeted the "Three-fold Conspiracy of the IWW," over several anti-IWW articles and an editorial in Campbell's typical, inflammatory style.

Myers assured his colleagues that the *Independent* was a "highly rep-utable and independent daily newspaper" and was "in a position to speak advisedly and disinterestedly" about the IWW situation.[58] No lawmaker challenged his mendacious assertion. Campbell would boast later that that particular issue had enormous influence on Congress and thus had helped put away the IWW.[59]

Even as Myers lauded the not-so-independent *Independent*, a stinging rebuke of the "copper press" by U.S. District Attorney B. K. Wheeler was in the mail to Attorney General Gregory. "It is a fact," wrote Wheeler, "that the Press of Montana generally have published reports of labor con-ditions which are . . . unfounded; these reports have magnified the activi-ty of the IWW element; have reported doings by this element which never happened and business men . . . have circulated reports about the existing conditions which upon investigation have proven to be wholly without foundation in fact."

Wheeler added, "The press of Montana is acting at the request of the employers to create an impression . . . that the IWW element is creating a lawless situation and by high-handed methods destroying the industries of the state, whereas in truth . . . any strikes which are now on are being conducted in the most orderly manner, no violence or public disturbances are had . . ."[60]

Two county prosecutors backed up Wheeler's remarks in letters to U.S. Attorney General Thomas Gregory.[61] T. H. MacDonald, county attorney of Flathead County, wrote that lumbermen had launched an inflammato-ry newspaper campaign against the IWW but his office had protested because there is "no excitement and no reason for such reports." After the lumber strike in northwest Montana was declared, detectives employed by both the lumber companies and MacDonald had turned up "not a single report of force on the part of the strikers" or even the threat of force except by one employer. Despite the union's lawful conduct of the strike, MacDonald added, army troops had been ordered in, had raided IWW headquarters in Whitefish, and held Wobblies in jail for several weeks without filing charges against them. The men were finally released after fil-ing habeas corpus proceedings.[62]

Wade Parks, Sanders County attorney, also blasted the press for giving a "wholly misleading" impression. Fires in the area blamed on the IWW had been caused by campers, sparks from locomotives, and ranchers burning slash—facts he had already reported to Gov. Stewart. Farmers in need of harvest hands had turned to the local IWW with excellent results. Striking lumberjacks who turned to haying made the best crew he had ever employed, a rancher told Parks.[63]

It was the lumbermen, Parks told Gregory, who were provoking the strikes through their intransigence. "I think that if the employing class of the West would meet the IWW's and other wage employees half way on a common ground that there would be no general discontent and that the IWW aggitation [sic] would die."[64]

The "employing class" was not about to seek common ground. On the same day that Parks sent his letter, Anaconda general counsel L. O. Evans was attacking the IWW:

> "It is nothing more or less than a rebellion against our government and its laws," Evans told the Missoula Chamber of Commerce. "The remedy will be hastened by an appeal from each of us . . . to our constituted authority to handle these . . . anarchists and allies of the Kaiser. . . . There can be recognized but two classes, the American and the traitor . . . If Montana fails in its duty . . . the members of this pernicious organization, unable to remain in our neighboring states, will find their haven with us."[65]

While Montana's two senators were pushing hard for laws to suppress the IWW, Gov. Stewart was pushing as hard for force to do the same thing. Earlier, Stewart had met with other Northwest governors in Portland, anxious to placate powerful business constituencies howling for decisive federal action against the IWW. The Justice Department, they agreed, was not being forceful enough.

Justice had already rejected the governors' bold (and illegal) plan just before the war to intern IWW members for the duration of the war and to require federal censors to excise all mentions of the IWW from all publications.[66] Instead, the department had urged the states to step up their vigilance, counter IWW propaganda and do more to improve lumber workers' conditions.[67] Now, with the United States at war, the IWW had become a pressing political problem that required a faster solution. Attorney General Gregory found such a solution in a blueprint drawn by John Lind, a former governor of Minnesota, in dealing with the IWW there. Lind's solution was a coordinated attack by three cabinet departments: Justice to prosecute for violations of wartime statutes; the Post Office to withhold mailing privileges from the IWW; and Labor to deport illegal immigrant Wobblies.[68]

In Portland, Stewart advocated a harsher crackdown, if only to prevent the kind of lawlessness that had resulted in Little's lynching. He advocated "direct action in putting down IWW invasions. . . . It is fatal to let these exponents of destruction get a foothold. Experience has taught us that determined action rather than procrastination is what is effective."[69] And determined action had a uniform: Federal troops should be used as strikebreakers, said Stewart.

There was precedent. In mid-July, authorized by Secretary of War Newton Baker to suppress "civilian acts of seditious intent" under the federal government's constitutional obligation to protect states against domestic violence, National Guard troops had arrested scores of IWW men in Washington, Idaho, and Oregon. However, many were arrested merely because they held the red card of IWW membership. They were interrogated on their social and economic views; only those who promised to "work without agitating strikes" were released.[70] The remaining prisoners were held in military stockades without any formal charges and barred from talking to attorneys.[71] The regional army commander assured Stewart and his colleagues that troops were standing by if the states encountered any difficulty.[72]

By great good luck, a situation presented itself within days that offered the governors a chance to test their Portland strategy. James Rowan, IWW secretary in the Spokane region, threatened a general strike on August 20 by men in the harvest fields and fruit orchards and in construction work in the Northwest unless all IWW prisoners arrested by Guard troops were released from prison.

Rowan may have had right on his side—the arrests and detentions were almost certainly unconstitutional—but not might. On August 19, the area troop commander placed Spokane under martial law, raided the IWW hall and arrested Rowan and twenty-six other IWW leaders.[73] The Washington Supreme Court refused to intervene because it had no jurisdiction over military prisoners.[74]

Delegated by his colleagues to go to Washington, Gov. Stewart left immediately for the capital. The Spokane action played right into his

Washington agenda: To convey the urgency of the situation, to ask for immediate federal assistance and to inform the federal government of the governors' plan to establish special state constabularies to deal with the Wobbly menace.

Montana's elected officials were thus pursuing a pincers movement on Washington. Myers and Walsh were advocating federal laws to punish seditious speech; Stewart was urging force. Stewart and Myers met briefly with President Wilson. The situation, they warned, was dire.[75]

Whether Wilson apprised Stewart and Myers of the massive, national raid being planned on IWW offices for the following week is not clear. Wilson had approved the plan, for he despised the IWW.[76] "Instinctively and philosophically, the President detested the Marxist, anarchist, or class-war theories of society," historian William Preston Jr. observed. "To Wilson, the IWW was 'a menace to organized society and the right conduct of industry.'"[77]

The Justice Department's plans for the raids had fallen into place despite the fact that district attorneys or special investigators had uncovered no incriminating evidence.[78] Members of the American Protective League, the largest of the wartime "patriot" organizations, had also worked on the case for months, "shadowing the suspects, intercepting their mail, watching all their comings and goings, transcribing and indexing the reports," as APL historian Emerson Hough later proudly recalled, then feeding information to the Justice Department.[79]

Assistant Attorney General Fitts could not contain his enthusiasm for the upcoming raids. "Something quite effective is under way," he confided to New Mexico Senator Albert Fall on August 30.[80]

At 2:00 p.m. Central time on September 5, in a nationwide action coordinated by Fitts in the Justice Department and Chicago U.S. Attorney Frank Nebeker, federal marshals operating under broad search warrants raided sixty-four IWW halls from New York to Seattle. They confiscated mountains of records—five tons from the Chicago headquarters alone.[81] Agents seized correspondence, minutes, financial records, and membership lists as well as literature and recruiting material—even *Ladies Home Journal* dress patterns, suspecting code messages in the perforations.[82]

Although agents found no evidence of spying or of German gold or other financial backing—a connection Gregory believed existed—the evidence would soon be used to arrest hundreds of IWW leaders on charges of violating the Espionage Act and other federal laws.[83] In the view of the reactionary APL, the evidence included "more proof of the depravity of the human mind than any like assemblage of written and printed material known to man."[84] More than a few newspapers agreed. "Throttle Him!" the *Sacramento Bee* exhorted on September 8. A cartoon showed Uncle Sam gagging a figure labeled "IWW."[85]

Ironically, the massive punch against the IWW probably hurt Myers' chances of pushing his sedition bill through Congress that session. His bill languished in a judiciary subcommittee—"put to sleep with the slumber that knows no awakening," he later complained.[86] Perhaps it was thought that convictions under the Espionage Act would take care of the problem. The Justice Department had not been terribly enthusiastic.[87] Myers had his own theory on why his bill stalled: "In the closing days of a session it is almost impossible to get an independent bill of *a minor nature* through Congress," he said (emphasis added).[88]

Myers seemed nearly desperate to have his "minor" bill adopted. "Surely there is no good American citizen who is in favor of the things which are forbidden in this amendment. If we are not in favor of them, we must be against them; and if we are against them, we ought to enact a law against them," he babbled.[89]

Myers' bill was not reported out of committee. But the groundwork was laid. Virtually the same bill would resurface a few months later—first in Helena and then back in Washington—on the desks of anxious politicians representing a frenzied state and nation desperate to root out the "enemy within." ✤

EIGHT
Standing Against the Mob

Montana's Federal Judge and U.S Attorney Resist Popular Passions, 1917–1918

THREE WEEKS AFTER THE NATIONWIDE RAIDS on IWW halls, federal marshals started arresting Wobblies, from Big Bill Haywood down. Armed with
what they considered to be persuasive evidence of massive violations of a
half dozen criminal laws, the Justice Department had no trouble persuading
a Chicago grand jury to indict 166 IWW leaders on September 28.[1] Other
grand juries would soon indict IWW members in Sacramento, Fresno,
Omaha, and Wichita. The Wobblies tried in Chicago would include the
executive board, the general organizers, the editors, and the heads of the
lumber, mining, and agricultural subdivisions. Historian William Preston Jr.
noted, "More than any other single event, the Chicago case helped turn the
IWW from the aggressive, organizing menace it had been that summer into
the defending and then ex-champion of the radical world."[2]

The IWW could not even effectively rally others to its defense, thanks
to an overreaching enforcement of postal censorship laws. A 1911 amendment of the Comstock Act declared non-mailable any "indecent" matter,
including "matter . . . tending to incite arson, murder, or assassination." The
recently enacted Espionage Act added "any matter advocating . . . treason,
insurrection, or forcible resistance to any law of the United States."[3] Under
these gaping provisions, Postmaster General Albert Burleson was able to
stop the mailing of most Wobbly literature and to revoke the second-class
mailing privileges of several leading IWW newspapers.[4]

As far as the Post Office was concerned, Wobbly logos that appeared
commonly on IWW literature, such as the black sab cat, fit the 1911 law.
So did mottoes identified with the IWW, such as "An injury to one is an
injury to all." Even mailings containing verbatim reports of the Chicago
trial, assertions of the impossibility of getting a fair trial and "any anti-capitalist remarks" were banned.[5]

"No Pope during the Inquisition, no absolute monarch at any stage of the world's history, ever displayed more high-handed tyranny in his actions toward a subject than the mediocre monarch now mismanaging the post office displays in mistreating the mail of a citizen," the socialist *New York Call* complained. Burleson retaliated by lifting the *Call's* mailing privileges.[6]

Prosecutions under the Espionage Act, signed into law on June 15, 1917, appeared to bode well for the big IWW show trials. Section Three of Title I comprised perhaps five percent of the law's wording, but was the focus of almost all prosecutions under the act. It dealt with deliberate obstruction of military forces by making false reports or false statements (see Appendix I).[7]

The Justice Department's intent, in drawing up the legislation in this section, had been to shut down political agitation and "disloyal propaganda" aimed at disrupting the operation of the armed forces.[8] It was clearly directed at the IWW, as well as other radical groups and anarchists.

Consequently, much of the government's case against the IWW in the mass trials would hinge on proving—based on the IWW's own words—"a conspiracy to persuade individuals to hamper the war effort by resisting registration for the draft and through insubordination."[9] The government would do this by taking all the ideology published by the IWW since 1905, all the angry class-struggle and anti-capitalist rhetoric, all the outrageous statements about sabotage, all the anti-war rants, then combine them with the IWW's conduct of strikes during wartime, to make its conspiracy case.

The cumulative effect of this speech and action, the government would argue, was intent to obstruct the war effort. Just because many of the statements were made before the war and before the Espionage Act was passed didn't pose any great obstacle, as long as the judge agreed that they showed the IWW's intent and preparation to obstruct the war. Such a line of reasoning squared with the prevailing legal theory of the time, the "bad tendency" test. Dating back before the eighteenth century and explicated by legal philosopher William Blackstone, the test allowed speech to be punished where it could be shown that it had even a remote tendency to produce an illegal action. Therefore, prosecutors did not have a heavy burden of proof to persuade juries that some comment or writing was punishable. The result in the IWW prosecutions, noted historian Preston, was that "[T]he administration equated an attack on capitalism as hostility to a government at war . . . the Department of Justice indicted radicals for their political and economic views and their labor agitation."[10]

With the IWW in the Justice Department's sights, it soon became clear that its weapon of choice, the Espionage Act, worked more like a shotgun, hitting a broad target, than a rifle. The way judges and juries were interpreting the law made it clear that it would be easy to obtain convictions even for casually uttered disloyal statements. In fact, that may be what the Justice Department intended. "The [Justice] department believes that this section should be interpreted broadly," wrote special assistant John Lord O'Brian to the American Protective League in December 1917, after the Act had been in operation for six months. "[I]t is not necessary, in order to secure a conviction, to . . . prove that the acts . . . actually accomplished the results intended, but only that they had a natural and reasonable tendency to bring about these results."[11]

Two other things were also becoming clear: One, enforcement of the law was going far beyond a ban on criticism of the military. Williams College professor Alfred Dame, among others, had warned President Wilson that the law "may bring undeserved punishment upon many patriotic citizens whose conscience would not allow them to remain silent in the face of wrongs that might conceivably be committed by the military."[12] Two, pure statements of opinion were being regarded as "false reports or false statements" within the reach of the Espionage Act.

Two cases illustrate the cruel and misguided reach of this law:

Clarence Waldron, a Pentecostal minister in Windsor, Vermont, was convicted of violating the Espionage Act in the fall of 1917 by allegedly telling his Bible class that "a Christian can take no part in the war," and "Don't shed your precious blood for your country." He also distributed a pamphlet preaching the same pacifist message. Despite evidence that Waldron had also sung the "Star-Spangled Banner" on Liberty Loan Sunday with a flag draped around his shoulders, the jury found that his anti-war remarks showed an intent to "cause insubordination, disloyalty, or refusal of duty." Waldron was sentenced to fifteen years in the Federal Penitentiary in Atlanta.[13]

In another case, H. E. Kirchner, an elderly shopkeeper in Elizabeth, West Virginia, was sentenced to two years for saying, both before and after the passage of the Espionage Act, "that the United States in the prosecution of the war with Germany was corrupt and controlled by the moneyed interests . . ."[14] A federal appeals court affirmed the conviction, holding that Kirchner's statement could be intended as a statement of fact, not opinion.[15]

Figure 13. Burton K. Wheeler, Montana's U.S. District Attorney in the WWI period, refused to kow-tow to reactionaries. Prior to WWII, he was an isolationist U.S. Senator. Montana Historical Society.

Cases such as these proved exactly what opponents of Section Three of the "Spy Bill" had pointed out before its passage. "Do not let us get into the position where . . . pacifists will be put in jail, or where the whole country can be regimented a la Kaiser, and marched to the jingoistic music that is becoming popular," wrote New York businessman Charles H. Ingersoll. "It is easier to put across legislation of this sort at a time like this, than to recover from the effects of it. It is easier to have a lot of vague fears of unseen things, than a sublime faith in substantial things."[16]

Such cases also illustrate why there was a 97 percent conviction rate in Espionage Act cases brought to trial before January 1, 1918—just six acquittals in 180 trials.[17] And another pattern was becoming apparent as well: The Espionage Act was being most vigorously applied in western states, especially in districts where the IWW had a significant presence.[18]

Bourquin and Wheeler

One exception stood out like the proverbial sore thumb: The federal district of Montana, where there were *no* successful Espionage Act prosecutions.[19] Eight persons—seven men and one woman—were indicted on Espionage

Figure 14. An abstemious legal purist, George M. Bourquin, Montana's sole federal district judge, was a constant thorn in the side of the state's political and industrial establishment. Butte-Silver Bow County. Photograph copied by Derek Pruitt, *Montana Standard.*

Act charges. Three men were acquitted; the rest had their cases dismissed.[20]

Why would Montana, a hotbed of IWW activity, not have seen any Espionage Act convictions? For one thing, the state had its own sedition law after March 1918. But more importantly, two men—U.S. District Attorney Burton K. Wheeler and U.S. District Judge Bourquin—stood in the way. For their principled stands against the mob sentiment of the war, both men endured years of vilification and even threats to their lives.

A losing hand in a poker game in Butte had been Wheeler's entrée to law practice in Montana. Born in 1882 in Massachusetts, the son of a Quaker cobbler and a Yankee Methodist, Wheeler completed his law degree at the University of Michigan before heading west. Stranded in Butte thanks to an ill-advised game with a couple of card sharks, Wheeler found a job with a local attorney and made a reputation representing organized labor against the Anaconda Copper Mining Co. He soon found his way into local and state politics. At thirty-one he became the nation's youngest U.S. district attorney.

Bourquin was about twenty years older, born in Pennsylvania in 1863 to the French wife of a Swiss blacksmith. He arrived in Butte in 1884, finding work as a miner and hoisting engineer. In his spare time, he read the law and was admitted to practice in 1894. In 1904, his election as district court judge in Silver Bow County helped break copper baron Fritz Heinze's stranglehold on the local legal system.[21] In 1912, President Taft appointed him the state's only U.S. district judge.

Described as "austere and caustic-tongued" but also as "handsome and distinguished looking," and as "vain, arrogant, and irascible," Bourquin kept others at a distance. He never permitted anyone to discuss a case pending before him and always dined alone, with the other chairs at the table turned up to dissuade conversation. He was a legal purist, devoted to the Constitution. His Puritanical roots instilled in him a loathing for the mob. "The consistent theme of Bourquin's career," wrote historian Arnon Gutfeld, "was the protection of the individual encountering the power of the state."[22]

America's entry into the war—and the simultaneous gearing up of its war propaganda machine through the Committee on Public Information—had opened the tap on reports of disloyalty. Reports of allegedly disloyal persons poured into Wheeler's office—ten a day, he wrote Senator Walsh in June.[23] Most smelled of gossip and grudges and saloon talk, or simmering resentment against the strikers. Wheeler refused to take the cases to the grand jury for indictment.[24] "A great many well-meaning people who do not understand Federal law and think that the government of the United States is all-powerful and that it is able to prosecute every one who makes a statement derogatory to the . . . United States feel that all they have to do is to report the matter to me and I will immediately prosecute the guilty party," he complained to Walsh.[25] The real solution, he suggested to businessmen in Butte is "to get the copper companies and the labor men together upon some plan that will work equal justice to all."[26]

Criticism of Wheeler's inaction started to surface. The *Helena Independent* commented, "In Iowa and Illinois, in New York and Nebraska, we find judges, attorneys, and court officers who can find a way to deal with the men who abuse the freedom of speech. . . . Out here in Montana everyone pleads 'There is no law against it.'"[27]

Bourquin told Wheeler to go ahead and seek indictments. "Send some of those sedition cases up to me and I'll take care of them. I have more standing in the state than you do," he advised Wheeler.[28] A grand jury returned the first indictment in September, against a dry land farmer near Wolf Point, in the northeast corner of the state. A local chamber of commerce official had sworn out a complaint, alleging the man had said he would resist the draft and if called, would desert and join the German army. Bourquin dismissed the case.[29]

Some months later, Wheeler and Bourquin persuaded a grand jury in Great Falls *not* to indict (out of fifty cases presented) forty-eight persons who had been arrested on picayune sedition allegations. This was a brave act by the grand jurors, as their names were printed and they risked being branded as unpatriotic. To explain their decision, the panel issued a statement (drafted by Wheeler) exposing the true nature of the so-called crimes:

> In many cases . . . it has been found by us that reports of so-called "seditious utterances" and "disloyal statements" were highly colored and greatly exaggerated. . . . The testimony disclosed complaints of words of a most trivial character showing a specie of hysteria prevalent in the minds of people in many communities. . . . Some cases, it appears . . . have been instituted by persons who have ulterior purposes in mind, either desiring personal revenge for some grievance, real or fancied, or are desirous of obtaining some pecuniary advantage for personal benefit as a result of the prosecution and the odium resulting therefrom."[30]

The grand jury suggested that state officials could prosecute under existing laws "persons who indulge in indiscreet statements and criticisms which are of such a character as might naturally lead to breaches of the peace."

The jury's remarkable statement received hardly any public attention, not only because it contradicted what many of the newspapers were screaming about, but also because it came while the state legislature was in special session, busy enacting the reactionary laws that the papers had been urging.

The two cases on which the Great Falls grand jury did hand down true bills showed that people were being held for trial merely for expressing their opinion. In one case, the grand jury indicted Dr. Gus Pitkanen, a well-known abortionist in the Butte area who had been jailed under a complaint lodged by members of a "Liberty Committee" in Deer Lodge. Pitkanen had allegedly said, "This is a rich man's war brought about by the politicians and the munitions makers and the capitalists for the purpose of making money profits . . ."[31] But Pitkanen was never tried.

At the end of March, newspaper accounts told of forty Finnish men jailed in Butte on sedition charges. Their wives stormed the office of the [U.S.] attorney and announced their intention of remaining in his office until given food and clothing while their husbands languished in jail charged with sedition. The women declared they have had nothing to eat and dragged in twenty half-clad children as Exhibit A. The men were released after being forced to kiss the flag.[32]

Bourquin's strict interpretation of the Espionage Act blocked the prosecution of several cases. In November 1917, for example, a Butte grand jury indicted the editors of the *Strike Bulletin* for printing a sarcastic reaction to a suggestion by Elihu Root—the prominent Republican statesman who had been secretary of war and secretary of state in the Theodore Roosevelt administration—that conscripts be sent to France and regulars billeted at home to keep law and order. The *Strike Bulletin's* bitter response to the 1912 Nobel Peace Prize winner: "Let us send off to France where they can be killed by a foreign foe the young men of the people; let us keep here the men who . . . will put down our revolution without a qualm." Bourquin dismissed the case.[33]

"We have to put away the fiction about the missing laws and enforce the laws of WAR . . ." the fed-up editor of the *Helena Independent* remarked in November. "Every day we delay means that many more of our boys have to die in France and their blood will be on the stupid courts and stupid public prosecutors."[34]

A Montana Village

Whether Wheeler had balked at prosecuting "ridiculous" cases under the Espionage Act hardly mattered after January 26, 1918—the day Bourquin directed an acquittal in the prosecution of rancher Ves Hall of Ashland.

Early twentieth-century photos of Ashland, in southeastern Montana, show a handful of two-story wooden buildings, log barns, and corrals in a treeless, sagebrush-dotted valley. At the junction of Otter Creek and the Tongue River, just east of the Northern Cheyenne Indian Reservation in the southern panhandle of Rosebud County, this dusty, somnolent little settlement and its environs was where Hall allegedly made seditious remarks between July and October of 1917.

"In badinage with the landlady in a . . . kitchen" [of the hotel where Hall boarded], as well as at a picnic, on the street, "in hot and furious saloon argument," and at times in the presence of a young man who had registered for the draft, Hall allegedly declared that if the United States wanted him as a soldier to fight the Germans they would have to kill him first; that Germany would whip the United States, that men who were drafted and crossed the water were damn fools, and that it had the right to sink the *Lusitania* and kill Americans without warning.[35]

Hall had some choice things to say about President Wilson. He allegedly called him a "Wall Street tool," a "British tool," "the richest man in the United States" and "the crookedest son of a bitch that ever sat in the President's chair."[36]

Neighbors reported Hall and a banker named A. J. Just, who they said had also made seditious remarks. Both were arrested and indicted in Butte under the Espionage Act. Wheeler, who had been in Washington meeting with Justice Department officials, let Rosebud County Attorney Felkner "Fritz" Haynes argue the case against Hall "because there had been a lot of agitation in [the county] for immediate trial," he later recalled.[37] Wheeler's former law partner, Matt Canning, represented the defendant.

Haynes decided to release the men while they awaited trial, but warned them not to leave the Alexander Hotel in Forsyth.[38] They went to see State District Judge Charles L. Crum for advice. He suggested that they immediately visit Wheeler, who had just returned to Butte. When Haynes discovered that the men had left town, he wired the Butte sheriff to pick the men up as they stepped off the train.[39]

The trial was originally scheduled for Billings, 120 miles west of Ashland, but was changed to Helena, 240 miles farther west. Canning had moved for a change of venue, arguing that Hall could not be fairly tried on pro-German charges in Yellowstone County.[40] Two months earlier, a "third-degree committee" hunting bond slackers in Billings had forced the resignation of an architect and a city alderman, and made the latter carry an American flag through the streets. A butcher who allegedly tore up a Liberty Loan subscription blank was forced to kiss the flag.[41]

After the testimony in the three-day trial ended, including that of Judge Crum as a character witness for Hall, Canning moved that Bourquin direct a verdict of acquittal.[42] Bourquin did so, hurriedly issuing a written opinion "because of the grave issues involved, and the necessity for interpretation of the Espionage Act."[43] He also dismissed the case against Just.

The Espionage Act, Bourquin noted, "is not intended to suppress criticism or denunciation, truth or slander, oratory or gossip, argument or loose talk . . . nor any slander . . . of the President . . . but only false facts, willfully put forward as true." Even if Hall's "unspeakable" slanders of the president and nation could be considered false reports and statements, Bourquin added, their natural consequence would be "a broken head for the slanderer," not interference with military forces.

In this case, when "the declarations were made at a Montana village of some sixty people, sixty miles from the railway, and none of the armies or navies within hundreds of miles . . ." convicting Hall of attempting to interfere with the American war effort was "absurd," Bourquin concluded. "It is as if A. shot with a .22 pistol with intent to kill B., two or three miles away," he explained. "The impossibility would prevent public fear or alarm of homicide, and A. could not be convicted of attempted murder."[44]

It's a mistake to believe that "any slanderous or disloyal remark . . . can be prosecuted" under the Espionage Act, he advised. If the remarks lead to a breach of the peace, they can be punished under state laws. However, Bourquin warned, laws that punish seditious remarks lead to greater evils than benefits, as the Acts of 1798 had proved.[45]

Bourquin's opinion provoked a passionate reaction. As he stepped to the bar of the Placer Hotel in Helena after the acquittal, Canning was punched in the nose by a sixty-year-old deputy sheriff from Rosebud County.[46] And Judge Crum and County Attorney Haynes had a near-fatal confrontation.

Separately, Crum and Haynes had gone to visit Attorney General Sam C. Ford at his capitol office, perhaps to get his take on Bourquin's surprise ruling. According to the men's accounts to the *Helena Independent*, Haynes accosted Crum in the library adjacent to Ford's office. Angry about the Hall acquittal, Haynes told Crum there would soon be a killing in Rosebud County. He accused the judge of being pro-German.

Expecting to be assaulted, Crum took his small revolver from his overcoat pocket and shouted, "Goddamn you, I'll kill you like a dog! You have published me in eastern Montana as a traitor . . . [You are] an infamous liar!" Then, Haynes recalled, "I lifted both hands to the lapels of my coat, flung the coat open and said: "Shoot, you miserable Hun. I'm unarmed but my father lost his right arm at Shiloh; I had two brothers in the Spanish-American war, and I have a brother in the trenches in France. I'm ready, you cowardly ___ __ _ ____."[47] Neither man fired.

The dustup was reported prominently on the front page of the *Independent*, under a banner headline, GUNPLAY AT MONTANA CAPI-TOL.[48] Editor Will Campbell wrote to Senator Myers the following day. "The cause of this trouble is the absolute inability to secure punishment for slackers or preachers of sedition and creators of false reports in the federal district court for this state. [The Hall decision] is the last one of a series which has made the people of this state plan violence, and I tell you honestly there will be some blood-shed, some hanging and unheard of physical violence when the lists of Montana boys killed in action begin to reach this state . . . there is going to be trouble, deep, wide, and serious . . ."[49]

Gov. Stewart was of the same opinion. Senator Myers passed the letters on to Attorney General Gregory, asking, more politely this time, that "any relief which may be possible be granted."[50] A state official, less temperately, wrote Gregory, "Montana is fed up with Bourquin. If there is a speck of an island somewhere in the seven seas over which the United States has jurisdiction and a second hand federal judge may be exiled, without giving the country the worst of it during wartime, there by all means should Bourquin be sent to remain until peace is declared."[51]

Justice officials were concerned about Bourquin.[52] Summarizing the judge's contrarian rulings, John Lord O'Brian, special assistant for War Work in the Justice Department, called them "a source of serious embarrassment to government prosecutions in Montana." Bourquin's "strictest possible interpretation" of the Espionage Act was "squarely in conflict with the rulings elsewhere." If Bourquin was correct, "[the law] would be practically useless for suppressing sedition."[53]

Hewing to a strict interpretation of the Constitution and laws, Bourquin would continue to stubbornly resist the passions of the mob. In granting the habeas corpus petition of the assistant secretary of the Butte IWW in 1920, arrested in a raid on IWW offices and being held for deportation, Bourquin issued a fierce defense of the Fourth Amendment protections against search and seizure.[54]

In his later years on the bench, Bourquin developed a national reputation for his speedy handling of Prohibition cases, which were clogging the courts. In Butte, he tried thirteen jury cases in one day.[55] On loan to the bench in Trenton, New Jersey, he "sent hundreds of dry-law breakers to jails at the rate of two per minute and fined a half-dozen attorneys for contempt of court.[56] He would remain the sole federal district judge in

Montana until his retirement in 1934, on the twenty-second anniversary of his confirmation by the Senate.

The official who had suggested an island exile for Bourquin had also noted, "There is slight chance of his death for he is an exceedingly healthy specimen of whatever he is." Indeed. Bourquin walked five to twenty-five miles a day and lived to the age of ninety-five.[57] He ran as the Republican candidate against Wheeler for a Senate seat in 1934 but committed a huge political blunder by calling the new Fort Peck dam a "mud pond." Montana farmers thirsting for the huge irrigation project in the northeast part of the state voted against him in droves. He moved back to his native state and died in Wilkes-Barre, Pennsylvania, on November 15, 1958. He is buried in a family plot in Holy Cross Cemetery in Butte.

Along with Wheeler, Bourquin did his best to stem the tide of hysterical hyper-patriotism that swept Montana from 1917 to 1920. At the end of that period, at his acerbic best, he commented on a case involving a Forsyth man who refused to kiss the American flag and was convicted of sedition under the state law. Although Bourquin found he could not grant the man's petition for habeas corpus, he had some strong opinions on the excesses of patriotism:

> Like religion, patriotism is a virtue so indispensable and exalted, its excesses pass with little censure. But when . . . it descends to fanaticism, it is of the reprehensible quality of the religion that incited the massacre of St. Bartholomew, the tortures of the Inquisition, the fires of Smithfield, the scaffolds of Salem, and is equally cruel and murderous. In its name, as in that of Liberty, what crimes have been committed! In every age it, too, furnishes its heresy hunters and its witch burners, and it, too, is a favorite mask for hypocrisy, assuming a virtue which it haveth not.[58]

Fanatical patriotism was about to be written into Montana law. Gov. Stewart was determined to put an end to disloyal talk. On February 3, he called a special session of the state legislature. ✤

NINE

On the Wings of a Snowstorm

Montana's Legislature Passes a Harsh Sedition Law, 1918

IN HIS OFFICE IN THE NORTHEAST CORNER OF THE CAPITOL, Governor Sam V. Stewart fiddled with the latest draft of his speech. He still wanted to make a few changes before meeting with the leadership. He was set to address the lawmakers in joint session that afternoon. Only twice before had Montana governors called a special session, but there was no avoiding this one. Congress had declared war a month after the last regular session adjourned. It was a different world now. The agenda was pretty pared-down. It should take just a few days. Per diem and travel expenses for 123 legislators plus staff costs would add up to more than $20,000.[1] But an amazing thing had happened. Clerks, janitors, pages, stenographers— even a legislator or two—wrote to the governor and volunteered to work at this extraordinary session for no remuneration.[2] Of course not paying these patriotic citizens was out of the question, but it made him feel proud. That was the kind of spirit that would win the war, the kind of spirit he wanted to talk about.

Stewart examined the latest typed draft, double-spaced on nine legal-length pages.[3] It had already been circulated to editors, and embargoed until his delivery that afternoon.[4] When the war had come to America, he noted, loyal citizens had sprung to their duty: " . . . with a promptness that evidenced the spirit of patriotic devotion which has ever impelled and inspired the men and women of the great West."[5] But new laws, predicated on this great struggle, were now needed.

The farmers needed relief. He had dozens of letters from them, crying for help.[6] It was another of those painful cycles. Farmers had planted "on the cuff." They had pledged not only their land but also their crops against the bankers' credit. Bankers, fearing non-payment in the drought, were going to court to satisfy judgments. Farmers were losing their animals, their machinery, their seed grain, anything that moved.[7] Many of those who planted didn't even bother to harvest. The best yields in north central Montana were coming in at half a bushel to the acre. A sick shadow of just two years before, when yields hit fifty bushels.[8] The irony was that grain prices were higher than ever. The European war spurred demand. Wheat was very close to two dollars—if you could grow it.[9]

The state Council of Defense, of which he was ex-officio chairman, had been doing patriotic work. It had helped farmers through the drought, promoted garden plots and food conservation, aided in the military mobilization, and acted as a patriotic booster organization through a statewide network of county and community councils. But the Council needed to be officially constituted and funded by the state.[10] Also for the sake of national defense, firearms would have to be registered and a home guard set up.[11]

It was the business about disloyal talk, though, that captured Stewart's interest. The Frank Little lynching had demonstrated tragically that the IWW's seditious talk would end in a hangman's noose unless tougher laws were enacted. If Little's talk wasn't seditious, what was? Yet U.S. Attorney Wheeler had refused to prosecute him!

The Ves Hall acquittal by U.S. District Judge George Bourquin just three weeks earlier had also shown the pressing need for a state sedition law that would get him out of the picture. Bourquin had been a thorn in the side of the political establishment for years, especially since the start of the war.[12] He had thrown out federal attempts to draft aliens in the state, granted habeas corpus petitions and embarrassed the state's war effort. While the U.S. Department of Justice was beginning to take the kind of action that Stewart and other western governors had long sought, with the mass arrests of IWW leaders across the country, the Espionage Act was clearly a dead letter in the state as long as Bourquin was the sole federal judge in Montana.

For the same reason, a state law would also get around the U.S. District Attorney for Montana. Burton K. Wheeler was a fellow Democrat, but in Stewart's estimation was a socialist sympathizer. Finally, state Attorney General Sam Ford, a liberal Republican and former assistant to Wheeler, would be obligated to enforce a state sedition law.

The same laws could also help cool the Non-partisan League, a radical farmers' organization started in North Dakota. The NPL was beginning to engage the attention of Montana farmers—who felt poorly served by the railroads and grain elevator operators with their questionable weighing and grading standards and who felt the Anaconda Copper Mining Company was not paying its fair share of taxes.[13]

With the nation at war, positions hardened. Farmers assailed the monopolistic trusts that had already profited immensely from the war and stood to gain even more. They stepped up their demands for reform, including state-owned grain elevators and fairer taxes. Industrial interests led by Anaconda called the farmers disloyal pro-Bolsheviks.[14] In a sardonic counter-measure, a handful of legislators had cheerfully adopted "bolsheviki" as their nicknam just weeks after the Russian Revolution.[15]

The NPL had even helped stir opposition to the idea of a state sedition bill. When Stewart had addressed a farmers' congress in Great Falls at the beginning of the month, he drew applause for his patriotic homilies and his attack on the IWW, but the delegates turned down his sedition bill. That action had aroused suspicion by the Company press that NPL sympathizers would try to gut the bill. As the *Daily Missoulian* had growled:

> There is unfortunately in Montana, a class interested in confiscating the property of others, one that has been interested in conducting a war within our own borders while the nation is beset with the enemy outside. . . . Under the camouflage of the right of free speech, the foul hand of treator [sic] will seek to throttle such legislation . . .[16]

Public sentiment was on the governor's side. His mail enthusiastically endorsed measures to halt seditious talk. Just that morning, Stewart had responded to the cashier of the Bank of Twin Bridges. A. J. Wilcomb had written: "I hope that this special legislature will pass a law that will enable the authorities to deal with unamerican utterances, and kindred acts, without too much 'red tape.'" Stewart had assured him, "The Legislature will start off today and I am hoping they will deliver the goods."[17] That same morning he had received a resolution from the Missoula Chamber of Commerce expressing the hope that any obstacles "to [bringing] the prosecution of the war to a speedy and successful conclusion be dealt with summarily and decisively and in a manner commensurate with the gravity of the offense." The resolution was signed by its president, Arthur L. Stone, former editor of the *Daily Missoulian* and now dean of the new School of Journalism at the University of Montana.[18]

The Fifteenth Legislative Assembly

The weather was bad as the legislators gathered in Helena. "On the wings of a snowstorm sweeping across the Prickly Pear and up Last Chance Gulch," wrote a correspondent for the *Daily Missoulian*, "Montana's legislators arrived today to attend the opening session of the special assembly . . ."[19] In the exigencies of the war, its members were unusually unified and single-minded. Yet it was in many ways a classic legislature of the still-raw mountain West. The members of the fifteenth Legislative Assembly were shallow-rooted in Montana, inexperienced, rural, and relatively young. They represented small populations and huge territories. Some legislators had traveled close to five hundred miles. By the time they returned home, the eighty-five members of the Montana House and thirty-eight members of the Senate who attended the special session would have traveled a total of 35,682 miles, almost one-and-a-half times around the earth.[20] One legislator, Arthur U. Sand of Valley County, had ridden eighty miles on horseback overnight through a snowstorm, from his ranch near Opheim, close to the Saskatchewan border, to Glasgow, where he caught the Great Northern train to Helena.[21]

Considering that the state was only twenty-eight years old, it's not surprising that in this session just four of sixty-four members of the House of Representatives and two of thirty-six members of the Senate for whom such biographical information is available were born in Montana—state or territory.[22] Three times as many representatives and twice as many senators were foreign born, mostly in England, Ireland, and Canada. All born outside the state had arrived in Montana between 1878 and 1914. About one-fourth were farmers and stockmen, one-eighth lawyers, one-half professionals and merchants. A few represented labor. A handful worked for mining and lumber interests, the state's dominant industries.

The newness and mobility of the state's population was also evident in the number of prior sessions the average legislator in 1917–18 had served—just one.[23] This legislative greenness was compounded by the fact that Montana was in the throes of county splitting, supposedly in the name of better government. Between 1912 and 1923, the number of counties would more than double from twenty-seven to fifty-five. More counties meant more legislators, especially those representing agriculture. The size of the legislative assembly had jumped from 102 in 1911 to 136 in 1917.[24]

The previous night, Republicans, who held a slim majority in the

Senate, had held a night caucus at the Placer Hotel. They gave unqualified support to Democratic Gov. Stewart's agenda. "'It's a question now of patriotism and not of politics' was the sentiment of the meeting," the *Daily Missoulian* reported.[25] In fact, conservative Stewart's politics were closer to the Republicans' than to that of Democrats. Speaking for the caucus, two senators predicted they could wrap up the session in three days.[26]

The House Chamber, Thursday, February 14, 1918

Escorted by three House members, Gov. Stewart arrived at the bar of the House chamber at 2:00 p.m. He stepped up to the platform with its ornate carved rail.[27] Behind him, the great Charles M. Russell mural, "Lewis and Clark Meeting the Indians at Ross' Hole," reminded the assembled legislators of their heritage, while the marble columns and ornate copper fixtures assured them of the state's wealth.

As the applause receded, Stewart put on his reading glasses and unfolded his text. Recognized as a commanding orator, the governor already had a silver head of hair at forty-five. His tall, muscular frame belied his farm youth in southeastern Kansas, where the family had moved to from Ohio when he was ten. Earning a law degree in 1898, Stewart struck out at age twenty-six for the new state of Montana. Soon he became city attorney of Virginia City. He quickly ascended the political ladder to chairman of the Democratic State Central Committee. He was elected governor in 1912 and re-elected in 1916. "High destinies doubtless are reserved for him," puffed a contemporary reference work.[28] Indeed, Stewart would go on to a rare trifecta as a one-term state legislator and then as an associate justice on the state Supreme Court for seven years before his death in 1939.[29] But it was Stewart's fate to preside over a troubled state in desperate times and it was his destiny to propose, as he was just about to do, one of the most repressive pieces of anti-speech legislation in American history.

The governor probably had read the lead editorial that day in the *Anaconda Standard,* owned by the Anaconda Copper Mining Co. and one of the most influential newspapers in the state:

> Let not this state be made a place of refuge for those who wish in safety to desecrate the flag of our country, for those who would revile our president and our government, who would slander the boys who are fighting the battles of this nation. . . . They are not

Figure 15. Governor Samuel V. Stewart signed Montana's sedition bill into law in 1918. He later served terms in the legislature and on the state supreme court. Montana Historical Society.

wanted in Montana, and if they utter seditious expressions in this state, they should be punished with utmost severity.[30]

Stewart also would not have missed that day's headlines. Five Montana soldiers, including a sophomore at the University of Montana, had been killed off the coast of Scotland when a German U-boat had sunk their transport, the *Tuscania*, on February 6. Ten months into American participation in the war, American casualties were still very light, with only 136 men killed in combat and 134 more in accidents.[31] So the news of five Montana boys dead must have been shocking news indeed. "Torpedoed," wrote *Daily Missoulian* editor Martin Hutchens, "by one of the Hun pirates of the underseas, and their torn and lifeless bodies were driven against the rocks of a Scottish coast. Now they rest in foreign soil, gallant sacrifices of their home state to the cause of human liberty . . ."[32]

Stewart went Hutchens' rhetorical flourishes a few turns better. Delivering a speech that drew enthusiastic applause again and again, Stewart

Figure 16. The sixth floor of the Hennessy Building in Butte housed the executive and legal offices of the Anaconda Copper Mining Co., the power center of Montana. Clemens P. Work.

honed in on his message. Germany's defeat, "no matter what may be the sacrifice of treasure and of blood," can never come while we have "vipers circulating the propaganda of the junkers," he warned. Germany's spy system, which "reaches its poisoned tentacles into every part of the world," would surely carry "every disloyal utterance and every treasonable act . . . in exaggerated form" back to German soldiers, thereby causing "some certain company or unit to make just one more stand for the Kaiser and autocracy."

The orator twisted the knife deeper: "Who knows but that [some Montana] mother, wakened from her troubled sleep by some occult influence wafted clear across the ocean by a medium unseen, unheard, and little understood, may in reality be recoiling from the terrible pain of the smothering gas, or the sharp point of a bayonet, directed at her boy, her own flesh and blood, by the relentless barbarians, spurred on, strengthened, and emboldened to make just one more stand by the stories that America is disunited, that the timber of her manhood has decayed, that the luster of her womanhood has tarnished."[33]

The only thing to do, "to make strong the good right arm of America's offensive and defensive," Stewart boomed, is to "enact a law here in Montana that will make available a mighty means of throttling the traitor and choking the traducer."[34]

Then Stewart played his trump card: "The free air of Montana is too pure, too sacred, and too precious a heritage here in this mountain region to be used as a medium by the vicious, the traitorous, and the treasonable to breathe forth sentiments of disloyalty against our cause and to extend comfort to the enemies of the country."[35]

With applause ringing the chamber, and "tears running down the cheeks of many legislators,"[36] the governor added a cautionary note: ". . . [C]are should be taken that no machine be created for the oppression of the innocent."[37]

Had dead silence gripped the chamber at that moment, Stewart's warning might have been heard. But the legislators were buzzing from the governor's exhortation against the "Huns" and their treasonous, loose-lipped allies here at home. They were in no mood for due process.

The Legislature Does Its Work

The House and Senate set up abridged rules for the special session. The leadership created four committees in the House rather than the usual forty-five and just two in the Senate. To determine membership on each House committee, Speaker James F. O'Connor assigned the two female members of the House, Mrs. Emma A. Ingalls of Kalispell and Mrs. Maggie Smith Hathaway of Stevensville, to pass two hats filled with numbered slips among the members.[38]

O'Connor assigned the sedition bill to Committee No. Three, composed of twenty-one Democrats and Republicans. Carrying the bill for Stewart was wealthy fruit grower William J. Crismas, a third-term Democrat from Joliet with a grade school education. But the language had come from the bill introduced in Congress the previous August by Senator Henry Myers. Considering Myers' close connection with the Anaconda Copper Mining Co., it is possible that the language for his sedition bill in April 1917 had been drafted on the sixth floor of the Hennessy Building in Butte, the company's executive and legal offices. Myers' bill had failed to clear the Senate Judiciary Committee.[39] So it was recycled and put in the hands of the obliging Rep. Crismas.

The heart of the bill was a single-sentence, 376-word legal godzilla that boiled down to less than two dozen words: Anyone who during wartime criticized the government or communicated an intent to incite resistance to the war effort was guilty of sedition.[40] The crime was punishable by a fine of up to $20,000 and imprisonment for up to twenty years (see Appendix I).

The kind of language to be prohibited was "any disloyal, profane, violent, scurrilous, contemptuous, slurring, or abusive language" and "language calculated to bring . . . into contempt, scorn, contumely, or disrepute." To be protected from such vile language were the U.S. form of government as well as its Constitution, flag, soldiers, and sailors, and military uniforms.

The terms in the bill were subjective, vague, and imprecise. What was "disloyal" language? What language would bring the government into disrepute? What exactly did "calculated" mean and was it the same as "intended"? Could anyone who criticized the government or its sacred objects be punished, or only those who were viewed as disreputable enemies of the state? Where was the line between honest opinion and "abusive language"? What about the right to oppose the government and to advocate change? Did wartime provide a legitimate excuse for abridging such rights?

While the bad taste of the Alien and Sedition Acts of 1798 had lingered, it clearly was not bitter enough to have rendered a new sedition law entirely unpalatable in 1918. For one thing, public debate about the rights of free expression had long been muted. Such rights did not seem to enjoy any special position with the public and least of all with the U.S. Supreme Court, which had never considered whether punishment for seditious libel violated the First Amendment. Anarchists and radical labor union leaders had been effectively censored in the latter half of the nineteenth century through enforcement of state and city laws aimed at blocking "dangerous" political dissent.[41] But these laws were not thought to be covered by the First Amendment.

The fact that the nation was engaged in the Herculean task of making the world safe for democracy had pushed any semblance of calm reason from the minds of most people. As the *Great Falls Tribune* confidently noted: "While we are in the death grapple of war we can not be too squeamish about the personal rights of men who are insisting in abusing these rights to the detriment of all the rest of us. Under existing conditions no real American is in any danger from any law that the Montana legislature is likely to pass . . ."[42]

The "bolsheviki" of the House doubtless considered themselves "real Americans." But they feared that a state sedition law might be used against them. Lacking the political strength to derail the bill, they proposed an alternative—a joint memorial to Congress calling for a stronger federal law. The resolution was approved by the legislature but not before the conservatives amended it.[43] Aimed straight at Federal Judge Bourquin, the wording was changed from "Whereas . . . successful prosecutions of persons *cannot be maintained*" to "has not been maintained in the Federal District of Montana."[44] The opposition's impotence was underscored when all of its members ended up voting for the sedition bill anyway.[45]

But not before the legislators had a little fun with the press. Retaliating against the Company-controlled newspapers for the charges of disloyalty they had hurled against farmers, Rep. Clarence C. Davis, a Democrat from Conrad, offered an amendment making the sedition bill applicable to "the editor or manager of any newspaper who shall publish or cause to be published untruthful statements that any citizen of the country is disloyal to the United States."

The amendment failed, as its supporters undoubtedly realized it would.[46] The only amendment that passed was one offered by Rep. Ronald Higgins of Missoula, doubling the prison term for sedition to twenty years. Within forty-eight hours of its introduction, the House had approved a sedition law by a vote of 76–0.[47]

The Senate voted to reduce the maximum prison term in the bill from twenty years back to ten.[48] This may have been done to mollify the president of the Montana Federation of Labor, Mortimer M. Donoghue, who was also a member of the state Council of Defense. Saying its provisions "reach to the very vitals of unionism," Donoghue vowed to fight the sedition bill "to the last ditch."[49]

Donoghue's ditch proved a shallow one. A conference committee not only reinstated the twenty-year term, but also doubled the maximum fine to $20,000.[50] The Senate concurred unanimously, and Gov. Stewart signed House Bill 1 into law on the morning of Saturday, February 23, 1918.[51] As an emergency measure, it took effect immediately.[52]

The criminal syndicalism bill received similar express treatment. It defined and criminalized "the doctrine which advocates crime, violence, force, arson, destruction of property, sabotage, or other unlawful acts or methods . . . as a means of accomplishing . . . industrial or political ends

. . ." Whoever advocated such a doctrine, "by word of mouth or writing," would be in violation of the law.[53] Senator C. S. Muffly, a mine manager from Winston,[54] southeast of Helena, carried the bill, copied almost exactly from an Idaho statute passed in 1917.[55]

Once more, the "bolsheviki" farmer-legislators' misgivings dissipated. At the Great Falls convention of the Equity Society, a populist farmers' organization, just before the special session, delegates had snidely acknowledged the "vast amount" of criminal syndicalism as evident in the "activities and operations of the Flour, Milling, and Grain Gambling trust, the Packing trust, the Sugar trust, the Usury trust . . ." But not a single member of the House or Senate voted against Muffly's bill.[56]

Organized labor proved powerless as well. After three days of hearings with union representatives, a joint committee inserted an amendment shielding labor from prosecution for "peaceable assemblage to advocate means toward their industrial and political betterment . . ."[57] The next day, the House stripped out the amendment.[58] Gov. Stewart signed the measure on Washington's Birthday.[59]

With both the sedition and criminal syndicalism bills passed, Gov. Stewart and the legislators of the special war session must have believed that the IWW, the NPL and all other "disloyal" persons had been dealt with. The governor's agenda had been passed. The session was set to adjourn. But they were not finished yet. The bad feelings from the Ves Hall acquittal had erupted on February 19. In a coda far crueler than the below-zero temperatures that gripped the capital that day, a judge's life would be ripped apart. The patriotic sentiments of the lawmakers would transmogrify from the polished legal phrase to the ugly face of hatred.

The Tragedy of Judge Crum

In September 1917, three Wobblies sat in the Rosebud County jail, awaiting trial on charges that they had burned a railroad bridge on the Milwaukee Line.[60] County Attorney Fritz Haynes had no evidence but later said he "knew these fellows to be bad actors."[61] To wile away the time, the men wrote Wobbly slogans on the wall. It seemed to be a Wobbly tradition. Old jail cells in Utah, Washington, and Montana still bear evidence of this "art form." Jailer C. A. Klingle wasn't amused. He locked the men in solitary confinement, pulled out everything moveable from their cells, including the bedclothes, and put them on a bread-and-water diet.[62]

When District Judge Charles L. Crum heard about the treatment of the men awaiting trial in his court, he was irate. He ordered Sheriff Henry Grierson to give the men back their sheets and blankets, and to feed them regular rations.[63] Crum could hardly have realized that this humane action would form the basis for one count in an article of impeachment against him just five months later. By all accounts, Crum was a respected and popular jurist until Congress declared war against the Central Powers. With judicial experience in Oklahoma already under his belt, Crum had moved his family to the Yellowstone Valley in 1906. He was elected Rosebud county attorney in 1910. Two years later, running as a Republican, he was elected to the bench. In 1916 he was re-elected, endorsed by the Forsyth *Times-Journal*, which enthused, "There is no judge on the bench today that is held in higher esteem . . ."[64] But Crum was outspoken and given to fustian phrases. "Most of what he said," recalled his grandchildren, "was delivered pompously, deliberately . . . in capital letters."[65] In the West of the early twentieth century, a strong will and oratorical skills had helped assure Crum's success in his chosen profession. But when war came to Montana, Crum's character traits began to betray him.

In September, according to testimony later given by his court stenographer, the judge had told a jury panel in a trial that "this was a rich man's war," and that the Allies were in the war to acquire more territory.[66] The deputy clerk of the district court would testify to the Senate that she overheard Crum say that if the United States entered the war "we would go to the Fiji Islands, where there was civilization," and that he would rather have his son dead than in the trenches. She also said the judge "was overjoyed at German victories" and spoke German with visitors.[67] A sheepman would tell of an encounter with Crum at the Forsyth post office, where the judge said, "I consider Kaiser Wilhelm the greatest man in the world."[68] Crum refused to meet with the Belgian commission touring the country, saying the stories of the atrocities committed upon them were not true, the Forsyth superintendent of schools would allege.[69] Haynes would label Crum "the most dangerous man in Montana."[70]

Given the super-patriotic zeitgeist and the opinionated nature of his statements, Crum would probably have received some sort of censure, and would likely have been voted off the bench at the next election. But it was Crum's double misfortune to have a German surname and also to have been involved in one of the most sensational cases of the day, the Ves Hall sedition trial. That caustic combination gave his enemies, as well as politicians and newspapers eager for a sacrifice, the opening they needed. Crum's fate was sealed.

The gunplay incident at the capital following Hall's acquittal had not only crystallized Haynes' enmity of Crum, it was also a dream come true for *Independent* editor Will Campbell. In subsequent articles, Haynes came across as courageous; Crum was described as "villainous," "disloyal," and "un-American."[71] He was the Hun within the gate.

With the newspapers stirring the pot, Crum was haled before the Forsyth County Committee of 100 in early February. The committee was an extra-legal body of citizens formed to "promote patriotic endeavor and deal with sedition."[72] The Forsyth committee heard Crum out for two hours, and then demanded his resignation. He refused.[73] But the special session provided another way to get Crum, through impeachment. On February 19, fifteen affidavits by Rosebud County residents were presented to Gov. Stewart, who forwarded them to the House leadership.

Within four days, a special House committee had taken testimony. Crum was unable to attend. He was in Miles City, at the hospital bedside of his son Claude, who was dying of cancer. The judge asked for a delay. The House went ahead. Seeing as how the judge's honor is at stake, observed Rep. Higgins of Missoula, that consideration should be more important to him than remaining at his son's bedside.[74]

On February 25, the House impeached Judge Crum in six different articles. Most of the counts in the articles referred to his allegedly seditious remarks. The remainder recalled incidents such as the Wobbly prisoners on bread and water.[75]

Meanwhile, the legislature and the newspapers lashed out at two of the other principal actors in the Hall case. A House resolution calling for Judge Bourquin's resignation received enthusiastic support, but eventually was tabled.[76] A resolution calling for Burton K. Wheeler's resignation barely lost, 30–29.[77]

The House's articles of impeachment were served on Crum at his son's bedside. With his personal and professional life in tatters, the judge suffered a nervous breakdown. Only a resolution of support from residents of Roundup, part of his district, broke the torrent of bad news—and that turned into a liability. The judge decided to resign his seat, in a last-ditch effort to forestall his Senate trial. He submitted his letter to the governor, who accepted it. But the Senate plowed ahead, partly in reaction to the Roundup resolution, in order to quell any latent support for the disloyal jurist.

The Senate convened for trial on March 20, 1918. Three times the clerk called the absent defendant. Three times the pathetic echo of Crum's name went unanswered. He was said to be in Costa Rica, but was probably in Kansas and Oklahoma with relatives.[78] Wild charges surfaced in the Senate trial. A Forsyth attorney testified that Crum had related details of Allied ships sunk a week before the government released the data, prima facie evidence of espionage. In a climactic frenzy, a newspaper headline blared CRUM GERMAN SPY.[79]

Crum's resignation letter was read. "My action simply means that there is a limit to human endurance," Crum wrote. "I also feel that a trial of my case would simply provide an opportunity for certain people to pose before the public as super-patriots . . ."[80] Senator Fred Whiteside of Kalispell raised the point that Crum had no lawyer. No matter.[81] The die was cast.

On March 22, the Senate found Judge Crum guilty on all six articles of impeachment and thus disqualified to "hold any office of honor, trust, or profit under the state of Montana."[82]

Seventy-three years later, on January 26, 1991, the Montana Senate exonerated Judge Crum. His grandchildren had approached historian Dave Walter of the Montana Historical Society to clear his name. Senator Harry Fritz, D-Missoula, a history professor at the University of Montana, offered the motion of exoneration. Judge Crum's grandchildren were in the gallery when the senators voted unanimously to approve the motion. The legislators rose in unison to applaud them.[83] It was a touching and sincere note of apology, but for Crum it came too late. "He should never have been convicted," Fritz later reflected. "It was a time of super-patriotic hysteria. It wouldn't have happened any other time."[84] ✤

TEN

The Pot Boils Over

War Hysteria Paralyzes the State, 1918

"WAR GIVES THE CONGENITAL LIAR AN EXTRAORDINARY OPPORTUNITY," the *Saturday Evening Post* advised its readers six months into the war. "Newspapers and newsgathering associations receive grotesque tips of happenings that would be sensational in the superlative degree if they really happened. The newspaper man is able to spot the fake at sight. . . . But a great many credulous people . . . swallow inventions whose falsity would be apparent to their simple horse sense if they would exercise that faculty."[1]

The magazine was half right. Citizens in wartime were indeed susceptible to rumors, half-truths and bald-faced lies, but more often than not their fears were manipulated—by the press, by private "patriotic" organizations, and by public officials.

If Montana editors were able to spot a fake, they also knew how to take something less than accurate and run with it. Newspapers and popular magazines in the state and across the country whipped up the frenzy with sensational stories on German spies and fantastic tales of German plots. Lurid cartoons demonizing the enemy and lionizing the "sammees" drove home the point, along with less-than-subtle advertisements for Liberty Bonds and other war measures. Newspapers blared headlines such as "Huns Plan Bestial Fight on Sammees" and "Hello! Heaven? Vat? Yes? Dis is Vilhe'm, Kaiser of Chermans" and the like.[2]

In an era when airplanes were exotic, they seemed to blossom in the Big Sky. Two women swore they saw an airplane spin into a Bitterroot valley swamp in early August but it was never found.[3] Flathead valley residents told of airships flying south. "Are the Germans about to bomb the capital of Montana?" asked master manipulator Will Campbell, editor of the *Helena Independent.* "Have they spies in the mountain fastnesses equipped with wireless stations and aeroplanes? Do the enemies fly around over our high mountains where formerly only the shadow of the eagle swept?"[4] Several weeks later, he announced that Helena citizens "incensed by recent visits" had become the first to fire shots at an enemy aircraft. Gov. Stewart vowed to follow the next airplane and hinted he would take an expert rifleman with him.[5]

Tainted produce, toxic substances and mysterious diseases were blamed on German spies—often accompanied by editorials. Two liters of toxic bee pollen were in the hands of German agents in California, ready to destroy Montana's wheat crop, the *Daily Missoulian* reported. "We need not picture the disaster that will follow, affecting the most vital welfare of all the population in this great and prosperous territory and acting in the most deadly way to lose the war for us and win it for Germany," the newspaper warned.[6] Ground glass in a sack of flour was "apparently unmistakable evidence that enemy agents in the state are poisoning flour," the same paper declared.[7] "Poisonous" Burma beans, akin to navy beans, had been shipped into Pacific ports in a "diabolical plot to murder Americans," the *Independent* reported.[8] "How would you like it, Mr. Ordinary Citizen, if one of your children or your wife lay dead in your home as the result of using tetanus court plaster or poisoned beans?" the editor asked.[9]

The "pro-German" Wobblies were, of course, often blamed. According to one study, "Federal detectives could supposedly prove that IWW saboteurs had attempted to poison the water supply of Denver; had poisoned fruit shipped from California; and had poisoned horses throughout Idaho by pouring lye and other chemicals into the animals' food. . . . According to rumors, the IWW even had a widespread plot to murder government officials. Envelope flaps were coated with cyanide of potassium, officials would die of 'heart failure' seconds after licking the poisoned flaps."[10]

Whatever "proof" federal agents had of such activities never surfaced. No IWW was ever charged with such crimes and the "evidence" was never used at any trial, including that of the IWW leaders in Chicago in the summer of 1918.

In addition to regularly published tales of German brutality, newspapers and magazines indulged in a favorite pseudo-science of the time: phrenology, the analysis of skull shape and facial features to read personality characteristics. Side-by-side photos of Allied and German generals' eyes, for example, revealed remarkable differences. The "wide-open clear eyes of [British commanding General Douglas] Haig, are the eyes which picture no hate, no lust, no greed. They are the eyes of a commander who would not countenance wanton slaughter of foe nor inhuman sacrifice of his own soldiers." The eyes of German commander-in-chief von Hindenburg "see no further than the accomplishment of his own brutal will. They are the eyes which believe in neither man nor God. They are suspicious, searching eyes. . . . They are the eyes who sicken not at needless bloodshed, ruined homes, and murdered babies."[11]

One-Hundred Percent Patriotic

The suspicions and jealousies that pervaded the state and nation were also the lifeblood of the shadowy, quasi-legal organizations that dominated life in Montana in 1918—the state, county, and community councils of defense. They formed the lower and broader tiers of a vast pyramid with the Council of National Defense at the apex. The councils' original purpose had been to help the war effort. Until 1918, the focus of the state and local councils in Montana had been increased food production.

Their focus changed dramatically—Montana's in February 1918 after the special legislative session. A reorganized and funded state council, with authority equal to that of the legislature, began to concentrate on boosting patriotism and ferreting out anybody perceived as disloyal. To back up the councils' power, a new law provided that any person who violated or refused to obey their orders would be guilty of a misdemeanor, punishable by up to a year in jail.[12]

Gov. Stewart chaired the state council, while its guiding spirit and most active appointee was his ally, archconservative Will Campbell of the *Helena Independent.* Another newspaperman, Charles D. Greenfield, was the executive secretary. Other appointees represented business, farm, and labor interests.[13]

After the state council gave itself the power to investigate people "in all matters pertaining to the public safety and the protection of life and property," councils at the grassroots level assumed the same powers. County councils in Montana, composed of prominent men in the community, began squelching "pro-Germanism" and rooting out suspected spies and "slackers."[14] Mass-membership liberty committees, third-degree committees, loyalty committees, war leagues, and the like, which included almost every adult in the community, had already been harassing Liberty Bond slackers since the previous year. Now, more committees formed and their energies redoubled.

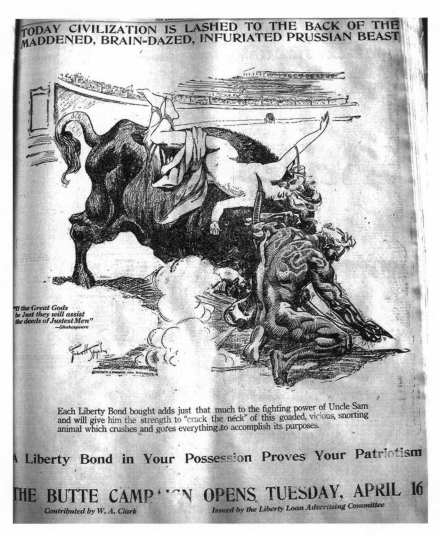

Figure 17. This allegorical cartoon, published in the *Butte Miner* in 1918, typifies the symbolism used in advertisements to promote the sale of Liberty Bonds and other public war financing. Butte-Silver Bow Public Archives.

[facing page] Figure 18. The members of the
Montana Council of Defense had wide-ranging
powers in World War I. Council orders banned
German books and preaching in German.
Montana Historical Society.

Montana Council of Defense.

Pressure to join these grassroots groups, to "make Montana 100 percent patriotic," was strong.[15] The Jefferson County council of defense organized citizens as War League No. 1, making it clear that "any man who refuses to sign the membership card and pledge of the War League is open to suspicion. The membership certificate is placed in the window, and is an incentive to patriotic endeavor by the neighbors."[16]

In Montana, conditions for repression seemed particularly ripe. With the vast economic and political power of the Anaconda and the copper press influencing public opinion to rally against the demonic forces of labor unrest and radicalism, there was no effective check on hyper-patriotism. Now, with Montana's sedition law on the books, a national sedition law in the works in the spring of 1918, and loyalty organizations behind every bush, citizens could get to work. Local councils and loyalty groups plunged into the job of investigating cases of "pro-Germanism."

Lewistown mayor Lewis C. Clark organized a Loyalty Committee composed of himself, the fire and police chiefs, the sheriff and the city clerk "because . . . there were so many complaints about people making seditious talks" and because "[we] know what is going on."[17] His committee illustrated the common blurring of lines between the functions of elected city officials and defense and loyalty groups—the latter often gave orders to the former and greatly reduced the chance of any impartiality by law enforcement officers. It also increased the risk that overzealous acts by loyalty groups would not be stopped before harm was done.

Clark also shed light on the pressure put on citizens to conform: "[I]f a man is in business and is found disloyal we suggest that the public stop buying from him. If he has a job, we suggest to the employer, that he lets the man go," he wrote.[18] The committee asked persons working on war bond and Red Cross drives to report "any person who failed to support these movements without good reason in order that these cases might be investigated."[19]

Whipped up by such exhortations, the citizens of Fergus County threw themselves into a roundup of pro-Germans that exploded on March 27 in Lewistown, the county seat. A real estate man named Edward Foster, an officer in the Montana Regiment in the Spanish-American War, was accused of making a disloyal remark.[20] He was found "guilty" of sedition by a "committee of loyal citizens" meeting in a pool hall, then forced to march up and down the street carrying the American flag before he was officially arrested. The crowd that had gathered then swept to the high school and demanded all the German textbooks. They were carried to the street and burned as the mob sang "America" and the "Star Spangled Banner." The citizens made nine more "disloyal" men kiss the flag and take the Oath of Allegiance, then nearly lynched another man who had refused to buy Liberty Bonds or War Savings Thrift Stamps on conscientious grounds.

Anna Zellick, who wrote about this incident, interviewed an eyewitness, a high school girl at the time, who recalled:

> They nearly hung a man, and he was going to be thrown into the Spring Creek. When my sister and I came upon the scene, they were calling for the ropes. I can still remember how I felt in my bosom. I was just a kid then, but I felt this was so wrong because this was our United States which was supposed to be free, and we could do as we wished as far as buying bonds were concerned.[21]

As a finale, two thousand people marched in a parade that evening and "cheered lustily" at patriotic speeches. It was, the *Fergus County Argus* crowed, a "Big Day in America and the City of Lewistown."[22]

Somewhat chastened by the mob violence, and perhaps by a mysterious blaze that burned the now-thoroughly-loyal high school to the ground a month later, a re-organized county-wide committee continued to report suspected instances of disloyalty.[23] Eventually, at least ten men would be charged with sedition in Fergus County, giving it one of the highest tallies of sedition cases in the state (a statistic not incongruent with the fact that it surpassed its April bond drive quota of $241,000 by more than 100 percent).

In district court, Foster was found guilty for having remarked, "Because I don't buy Liberty Bonds and don't carry the God-damn flag they call me pro-German." He received a $500 fine.[24] A sheep rancher, Anton Schaffer, accused of sedition by tenants he had been trying to evict, received a $12,000 fine.[25] Four other men were convicted of sedition.

"Not engaging in . . . rituals of patriotism was tantamount to being a traitor, 'un-American,'" Bonnie Christensen observed in a recent book about Red Lodge, Montana, where Finnish miners were beaten up in the name of patriotism.[26]

A leading coal-mining town since the 1880s, Red Lodge was a smaller version of Butte, subject to all the social and economic phenomena of the era, including the emergence of the IWW and the Socialist Party. Finns, the biggest ethnic group among the miners, were never big flag-wavers, and when some of them joined the IWW and publicly denounced the war, they became targets for the town jingoes. In the fall and winter of 1917, the local Liberty Committee, headed by a retired publisher and a former sheriff, brutalized the Finns. One miner who refused to give the names of other IWWs was taken to the basement of the Elks Lodge and strung up by his neck until he did so. The attacks culminated in the accidental death of a Finnish woman. The terrorized Finnish community then publicly embraced loyalty, aiming to show that its members were 110 percent Americans.[27]

There was practically no limit to the number of patriotic organizations a person could join. The Montana Loyalty League was formed in July 1918, with editor Will Campbell as its executive secretary.[28] "Get behind the boys 'over there' with every ounce of power, every atom of strength and every dollar to help crush autocracy," Campbell exhorted citizens. "Thousands of eyes will watch and thousands of ears will listen for the Hun spy or agent or sympathizer within our gates . . ."[29] The group claimed sixty thousand members.[30] It spent much of its money and energy exposing the Non-Partisan League, influencing politics, and attempting to "curb the treacherous alien" and "exterminate the Industrial Workers of the World."[31]

Other large private loyalty organizations included the National Security League and the American Defense Society (with its American Vigilante Patrol, "formed to put an end to seditious street oratory").[32] Largest of all was the American Protective League, with a claimed 1918 national membership of two hundred and fifty thousand, which took spying on one's neighbors to a new level.[33]

The League "constituted a rambunctious, unruly posse comitatus," historian David Kennedy observed.[34] With offers of well-heeled volunteers and free transportation with fleets of automobiles, the APL worked out a quasi-official relationship with the Justice Department. Members spied on suspected pro-Germans in all sorts of illegal ways—phone taps, burglary, mail and telegram intercepts—which the Justice Department overlooked. The APL "brought to judgment three million cases of disloyalty," boasted author Emerson Hough.[35] Among its chief prizes, Hough claimed, was the arrest of Eugene Debs for sedition, based on a speech in Canton, Ohio, on June 16, 1918. The speech, recorded by APL operatives and stenographers, was the principal evidence at his trial.[36]

Even young boys were recruited to ferret out disloyalty. The Anti-Yellow Dog Club, founded by writer Henry Irving Dodge, brought to life the fictional plot of Dodge's story, "The Yellow Dog," published in the *Saturday Evening Post* in May 1918.[37] The club trained Boy Detectives to challenge "yellow dogs"—anyone who "knocked" the government. The boys would hand offenders a "summons" to "the court of your conscience" and report them to the authorities. The club's motto: "Free speech, yes! Free lies, no!"

By mid-1918, the Department of Justice was receiving fifteen hundred letters a day related to loyalty charges.[38] Attorney General Gregory boasted that, "Never in its history has this country been so thoroughly policed."[39] To which CPI director George Creel added, "Not a pin dropped in the home of anyone with a foreign name but that it rang like thunder on the inner ear of some listening sleuth."[40]

Smoldering Suspicions

Countless other suspicions smoldered. In western Fergus County, a farmer named VandenBerg complained to Gov. Stewart about a neighboring farmer, Vander Giessen, and his family. "I am sorry thad I have to write this letter, but I tink it to be my duty, when I drove from town Saturday, I seen 3 big boys playing in the yard, two of military age and their father was loafing in town . . . I have not heard of iny of them being drafted. Maybe they have not registered at all. Of course I don't know but one ting I do know that I work 640 acres all alone [whereas all of them together] do not work iny more than 640 in all." The previous summer, he related, "the old fellow said give me a Kaiser and you can have Wilson, one of the boys said if he had to fight for the U.S. he rather be in jail."[41] The Fergus county council investigated and found it to be "a personal feeling" between the families.[42]

Those who balked at financial contributions to the war were often punished. Alma J. Swift, a store manager in Butte, had bought a Liberty Bond earlier but refused to pitch in during a bond campaign in October 1918. "Nothing doing!" she said. "Let the profiteers pay for that!" After her boss threatened to fire her and to have her sister, principal of a local grade school, investigated, Miss Swift evidently had second thoughts over her lunch hour. She subscribed for a $50 Liberty Bond, instead of the winter clothing she had planned to buy. When she came back to the store, her time card had been removed.

Miss Swift tried to fight back. "An American citizen has the right of personal security, of personal liberty, of . . . freedom of speech and of the press," she told the county council. "This girl is being black-listed all over this town," a defender from the Good Government Club protested. "If this girl is allowed to be dismissed without protest, you can imagine the rest of them not being able to open their mouths. She has not committed any crime."

The council members were obdurate. A person's duty, she was reminded, is "not to knock publicly in these times. If a person should come out and say, 'I cannot afford to subscribe' . . . that would be all right. If you came out and made a slurring remark as to the reason the Liberty Bonds were sold, I would say you are to the bad."[43]

Loafers, vagrants, slackers, and IWWs came under special scrutiny. Although the state's vagrancy law already applied to "every person (except an Indian) without visible means of living," the state council in April ordered every able adult "to work and engage in some legitimate occupation for at least five days during each calendar week for the period of the existing war."[44] A similar "work or fight" order issued by Gen. Crowder, the Provost

Marshal General, required that men be drafted regardless of their draft number if they could not show they were engaged in useful work.

The state's order raised all kinds of questions. The Granite County attorney in Philipsburg inquired whether real estate agents and saloon owners were "engaged in some useful occupation."[45] The Big Horn County Council of Defense had questions about "merry-go-round men" in Hardin.[46] Should clerks and moving picture managers do farm work, even if they are unsuited for it, asked the Custer County chairman. "Shall such men just quit what they are doing, and wait till they are called for some productive work?" No, as long as they work five days a week, state council secretary Greenfield advised.[47]

H. A. Simmons, county attorney in Red Lodge, took a tougher stance. He prosecuted eight men arrested after soliciting orders for enlarged portraits. A colorful account appeared in the *Helena Independent*, reporting that the men "started with a loud crashing of cymbals and beating of tomtoms to canvass the town for pictures of departed relatives and photographs of Pa and Ma when they were married years ago, with ears pinched between the forks of a photographer's head steadier."[48] Seven of the portrait men pled guilty and were fined $25 each.[49]

Most city officials were eager to cooperate in squelching dissent. The state council asked all municipalities to ban public speaking without permission. A separate order prohibited all parades, processions, or other public demonstrations without a permit.[50] In Butte, "the talker and the subject matter is first made known to this office and to the chief of police," reported the mayor. "We have absolutely prohibited such for some months past, except for the Salvation Army," the mayor of Missoula noted. Frank Conley, warden of the state penitentiary in Deer Lodge, and the town's mayor as well, said no street speaking had been allowed "since the trouble in Butte in 1914." Banned in Bozeman was "talk in any public place . . . that was not for the betterment, or for the good of the great conflict that is being waged."[51]

Ford's Burlesque

In such a climate, unpopular speakers and radical organizers were not likely to get permits, but rather a clear signal they were not welcome, an escort to the next train, or worse. Rep. Jeannette Rankin, who had voted against declaring war with Germany and was frequently charged by the newspapers with being associated with Wobblies, socialists, and Nonpartisans, was refused permission to speak in Butte, Deer Lodge, and Missoula, even though she was making Liberty Loan addresses.[52]

But the unwelcome mat was out particularly for organizers for the IWW and the Non-Partisan League. On the same day that Frank Little arrived in Butte, the *Anaconda Standard* related the reception for an IWW organizer named Blomkvist. The man arrived in Anaconda on the two o'clock train. Police had been tipped off to his arrival, but didn't show their hand when they met him at the train. Thinking the men were his Wobbly welcoming committee, the unwitting Blomkvist chatted away as he was escorted—right to the courthouse and jail.

"Noticing bars on the county jail, he was suddenly afflicted with a severe attack of cold feet," the *Standard* reported, "and he suddenly realized he had said a trifle too much." The detectives confiscated socialistic and IWW literature in Blomkvist's bag. "Seeing the authorities had the goods on him, Blomkvist formed the opinion that Anaconda was a mighty poor place to deliver a speech . . . and was more than willing to accept the proposition that he leave the city on the next train. In order that his memory might not fail him, two of the officers accompanied him as far as Silver Bow, where they saw him safely aboard the southbound short line train [to Butte]."[53]

The policemen's attitude (and the newspaper's as well) was a manifestation of a widespread public attitude that contemporary journalist John Fitch had noticed back in 1915: "Baiting the IWW has become a pastime in nearly every place in the United States where that organization has made its appearance. Members and leaders have had their constitutional rights atrociously invaded by officials and by 'good' citizens."[54]

Similarly targeted were organizers for the Non-Partisan League, whose endorsement of greater state regulation through state-owned elevators, cooperatives, and extended farm credit branded them as socialists, and whose opposition to the state sedition bill had labeled them as pro-German sympathizers. In March, the NPL's two top leaders, A. C. Townley and Joseph Gilbert, were indicted by a Minnesota grand jury for sedition.[55]

Crowds of several hundred persons awaited NPL organizer Robert Martin at the Big Timber and Columbus train stations in March 1918. Although he was accompanied by State Attorney General Sam Ford, he decided not to alight.[56] Even Gov. Stewart issued a plea for tolerance, saying, "It is highly essential that the right of free assemblage and free speech should not be denied to anyone in . . . Montana so long as they keep within lawful bounds."[57]

His plea was ignored. In mid-April, Martin was scheduled to speak at the University of Montana in Missoula, this time escorted by U.S. District Attorney B. K. Wheeler and bearing accreditation as a Liberty Loan speaker. But as they approached the theater where Martin was to speak, a member of the Missoula County Defense Society stepped from the shadows—a prominent lawyer in town, Wheeler recalled—and told Martin that if he went ahead, he'd be tarred and feathered. "If it must travel into the twilight zone to clean the city of disloyalty," the *Daily Missoulian* said of the local council, "it will be because our citizens, individually, are not in co-operation . . . Missoula is to be cured of the last trace of kaiseritis. Don't forget that.[58]

J. A. "Mickey" McGlynn, a young farmer from Sidney who became an organizer with the NPL, paid for his courage against the mob. In early April he survived a close call near Mizpah, where ranchers had planned to drag him down a creek at the end of a rope.[59] Then, on the night of April 7, a loyalty committee in Miles City hustled McGlynn down to the basement of the Elks Club, beat him up and "persuaded" him to hop the next train west.[60]

Saying the Miles City incident was "setting a flagrant example of the very kaiserism against which the U.S. is warring today," State Attorney General Ford vowed to prosecute the men who mistreated McGlynn.[61]

County Attorney Frank Hunter brought kidnapping charges against not only the men named by McGlynn but also against the county's leading lights, some of whom weren't even in Miles City at the time of the McGlynn incident. The action prompted a letter of congratulations to McGlynn from the NPL's state superintendent, saying, "If we can get a few of these self-styled super-patriots up against a dose of their own medicine, they may hesitate to use their political prejudice under the guise of patriotism."[62] But the man had badly misread the county attorney's true intent: to embarrass Ford by stirring citizens to rally in defense of their "patriotic" leaders.

The *Daily Star* bought into Hunter's ploy: "Take a good look at . . . the 21 'kidnappers.' . . . Has there been a patriotic movement of any kind at any time in . . . which these gentlemen have not been conspicuous? . . . [Then] turn your eyes in the direction of the witnesses for the prosecution. . . . How many Liberty bonds have [they] purchased? . . . How many patriotic movements have they fathered . . . at this particularly critical time when your son is in the trenches [prepared to give] his life in sacrifice for the flag we love?"[63]

On Monday, May 13, all twenty-one defendants met Ford at the train station and escorted him to the courthouse.[64] People flocked from Terry, Forsyth, Roundup, Mizpah, and surrounding communities to attend the proceeding. "Sweet Red Cross nurses" sold tickets to the hearing, which they billed as "Ford's Burlesque, or the Thrilling Adventures of the Kidnapper Kid." They collected more than $250. The spacious courtroom was packed "almost to suffocation" as the hearing began.[65]

Hunter cross-examined McGlynn about the April 7 incident in Miles City, but also questioned him about his loyalty. McGlynn denied having said that maimed Belgian children being shown around the country to raise money for war relief had actually been injured in Chicago. But Hunter had already prepared a warrant for his arrest on sedition charges based on those remarks.

As McGlynn left the witness chair, slouch hat in hand, the county sheriff served him with the warrant. At the courtroom door, a supporter of McGlynn accosted the sheriff, who punched him. The man ran back into the courtroom. McGlynn made a run for it (officials later claimed an escape plot); the sheriff drew his gun, shouting at his prisoner to stop. McGlynn skidded to a halt. The courtroom erupted in pandemonium. "Bailiffs pounded for order, women screamed, and for a moment a tragedy threatened, for hundreds were struggling to get to the man who had attempted interference," according to one report. "Then officers charged the crowd and after a short struggle succeeded in getting [the supporter] away."[66]

With McGlynn and the other man in jail cells, Ford did his best to press his kidnapping case against the men who had actually confronted McGlynn in the Elks Club basement. Defense attorney Sharpless Walker delivered an impassioned patriotic oration in support of his twenty-one clients and moved for dismissal of the charges. The judge agreed, declaring, "This is certainly not a case of kidnapping. Miles City has been able to handle its own problems, and handle them to a queen's taste and has never needed any help from the western end of the state . . ."[67]

"The thunderous applause that followed . . . shook the walls of the courtroom and the demonstration continued for nearly five minutes," the *Daily Star* reported. "The 21 defendants were surrounded by a veritable mob of men and women, each trying to shake the hands of one of the 'kidnapers.'"[68]

"More dramatic and patriotic scenes were never witnessed in a Montana courtroom," the newspaper exulted. The defendants had been acquitted and the witness for the prosecution was in jail for sedition along with "his IWW bodyguard." Ford had "made a serious blunder," the newspaper editorialized.[69] "The swollen head of our little attorney general hit a solid, concrete wall of American patriotism at Miles City," said the *Daily Missoulian*.[70] The *Terry Tribune* was blunter: "Ford is dead, damned, delivered politically, so why waste valuable space for an obituary?"[71]

Ford (who later achieved his ambitions for higher office when he served as governor from 1941 to 1949) did not back down. Three weeks after his humiliation in Miles City, he sent a letter to the Montana Council of Defense warning that in "numerous" cases involving county councils of defense and other patriotic bodies, "the right of free speech and the right to make public addresses have been denied individuals . . . by violence . . . intimidation and forcible coercion."[72]

Ford continued: "A cloud has arisen upon Montana's horizon that threatens dire consequences to the people of the state. Class is being arrayed against class and bitterness is being engendered; and if the lawlessness cited is not put down, and the right of free speech is not rescued from the disrepute thrown upon it, in my opinion, conditions may follow that will do the people and the fair name of the state incalculable injury . . . precedents in lawlessness and violence extremely dangerous to the conservative and law-abiding people of this state are being established, and a civil and social evil is rearing its head that may bring down upon them appalling penalties . . ."[73]

Few newspapers in the state even took note of Ford's letter. The *Daily Missoulian* called it "a rather wearisome communication . . . much of which is pointless."[74] Nor did the newspapers give any play to similar cautions issued by the national Committee on National Defense. "In the past few months there has been a tendency toward lawless treatment of those suspected of disloyalty," the Committee's bulletin said. "However patriotic may have been the motives which prompted these outbursts, their effect is deplorable. They are blots upon the war record of a nation which has declared itself to be fighting for a universal reign of law; they furnish ammunition to those makers of enemy propaganda who are trying to make the world believe that the enemies of Germany, too, are capable of atrocities . . ."[75]

President Wilson weighed in on "the mob spirit," taking his characteristic high road: "No man who loves America, no man who really cares for her fame and honor and character, or who is truly loyal to her institutions, can justify mob action while the courts of justice are open . . ."[76]

Despite his high-minded language, Wilson could only blame himself. He had set the tone with his policy choices. The launching of Creel's Committee on Public Information had done an extraordinary job of shaping public opinion about the war and energizing the hyper-patriotism that followed. His appointment of reactionaries like Attorney General Gregory and Postmaster General Burleson and his hands-off attitude toward their excesses had added to the strength and velocity of the hatred. "Without meaning to," noted Meirion and Susie Harries in *The Last Days of Innocence*, "by working on the fears and prejudices already latent in society, Wilson and Creel had helped to shape a divided, fearful, intolerant nation."[77] ✢

ELEVEN
Liberty Can Wait

Newspapers Approve as Germans and Dissenters Are Persecuted, 1918

"THOSE WERE THE SWEETLESS, WHEATLESS, MEATLESS, HEATLESS, and perfectly brainless days when your fathers broke Beethoven's records, boycotted Wagner's music, burned German books, painted German Lutheran churches, and Goethe's monument in Chicago the color of Shell filling stations," recalled American socialist Oscar Ameringer after the war.[1]

In this mindless frenzy, Montana's cruel jingoism stood out. The government's foolish, obstinate attempt to root out what was not only the language of its enemy but also the native language of one of its largest immigrant populations etched a black stain on its history.

On April 22, 1918, the Montana Council of Defense issued Order Number Three, decreeing "the use of the German language in public and private schools and in the pulpits of the state be . . . forbidden." It ordered all librarians to withdraw from circulation a dozen named books dealing with German history, language, and music. Where the list of banned books came from is not certain but the Lewistown book burning about four weeks earlier would have raised public consciousness about German books (and encouraged other burnings). The Helena school board had already been screening German textbooks and the placement of the first book on the list was undoubtedly the work of John G. Brown, a moss-backed Helena attorney.

Ancient World, an ancient history text by Willis Mason West, was being used in forty-two high schools in the state. But it was "most insidious in its propaganda," because it presented history in a light favorable to the kaiser's claims of hegemony, Brown declared in a letter to the governor four days before Order Number Three. For example, the book taught that in "early Roman times, 'the German Rhine, not the Italian Tiber, was the center of their State' . . . that 'the great contributions to modern civilization were the Roman contributions and the Teutonic contributions' and it emphasizes the present ruler's claim for 'Mitteleuropa.'"

Until the war, German had been the most popular foreign language in Montana schools, probably because of the state's large German immigrant population. Out of the fifty-six high schools offering modern foreign language instruction in 1916–17, forty-two taught German, three Spanish, and two French, according to Henry Haxo, an education professor at the state university. After the council's order, all German courses were immediately suspended. University students majoring in German were allowed to substitute French or English so that they could graduate.[2]

With the war, German culture became the hated *Kultur*, a code word for the cultural underpinnings of a strutting kaiser's mad ravings and dreams of world domination. The hyphen in German-American loomed large as nativist feelings built, reaching a fever pitch in the spring of 1918. National magazines and newspapers published articles calling for the abolition of the German language in America.[3] Any evidence of the greatness of the German civilization, even going back two thousand years, had to be erased. "It is a natural outcome and lies in the very fundamentals of American craving for freedom from all pernicious and meddlesome influence," said Professor Haxo.[4]

Attorney Brown suggested to the governor that a committee of "plain business or professional men . . . other than teachers" be appointed to screen the state's schoolbooks. Educators would engage in "naught but academic discussions as to the truthfulness of various paragraphs" whereas "plain men" would be better at smelling propaganda.[5]

Brown got the job—and plunged into his newfound career. Those who tangled with the irascible patriot-in-chief had their ears pinned back. A high school principal in Brockway, northwest of Terry, had the temerity to suggest that the charges against West's ancient history text were biased and wrong. Brown replied:

> [Y]our letter is quite astonishing to me; its poor writing, its lack of date, and its mis-spelling, but confirm the ignorance behind it, which fails to appreciate that this is the time when your Country needs your assistance rather than your asinine and mistaken criticism. . . . It is . . . remarkable that, in as big and fine a State as our's [sic], with the remarkable educators that we have, practically the only criticism . . . should come from a country teacher forty or fifty miles off of a railroad, whose location shows his ability, confirmed by his penmanship . . .[6]

Brown's pompous fulminating hit the wrong target. Principal Ward, it turned out, was highly critical of a half-dozen other German texts, and had in fact done a much more thorough analysis. Ward concluded that "In no book can one find a word of praise of the free institutions of England or America; military officers . . . play the part of ideal heroes . . . and . . . all the sentiments expressed run counter to American ideals." He had his students burn the books.[7]

To a teacher in Martinsdale who put a copy of "German School System" in the stove, and had written to ask whether she would get into trouble with the trustees, Brown replied, "Where a mother has laid so costly a sacrifice as you have [her only son was in France] to the cause of the extermination of German systems of every kind from the face of the earth, you are entitled to all of the protection that can be given you . . . both the Governor and myself would be very glad indeed to know the names of anyone who give you any trouble [sic]."[8]

Brown would probably have lent the same aid to the citizens of Miles City, who torched all their German books on April 17.[9] West's offending texts were also burned in Hilger in May. Citizens "'weeded' out all german texts in the school library, clipped out all german songs in our books of national songs, blotted out the coats of arms and german flags in the dictionaries . . . [sic]"[10]

The university librarian in Missoula dutifully reported compliance with the order and listed nine other books pulled "because in the judgment of the librarian and members of the faculty they contain German Propaganda."[11] Other librarians did likewise. No one apparently objected to the legality of the order. The only hint even of sarcasm came from the superintendent of schools in Anaconda. "My duty is to obey your body blindly," he wrote. West's texts were under lock and key, "but the copies which the pupils themselves have paid for they have taken home and are reading with a view to discover why the Council of Defense condemned the book." The teachers, W. K. Dwyer added "are anxious that I get for them a text in ancient history, but I tell them that it may happen that the text I choose would be condemned in a few weeks."[12]

"A Sobbing and Trembling Heart"

The state's ban on German in "the pulpits of the state" caused the most contention and heartbreak of any of the Council's seventeen orders, but no one

ever challenged it in court. Churches undoubtedly felt intimidated. To challenge the orders would appear unpatriotic. Besides, First Amendment guarantees of religion and speech were not thought to apply to action by the
state, while the state's constitution afforded little protection either. Only one
minister ever raised the argument of the free exercise of religion to the
Council of Defense, and that was after the Armistice had been signed.[13]

While other states banning German in the pulpit usually made an exception, such as one service a week, Montana's order was absolute.[14] The order
hit hard in German churches in eastern Montana, primarily
Congregationalist, Lutheran, Mennonite, and Hutterite. German was used
for services and was the only language that many of the older parishioners
spoke and could understand. Ancestors of the Congregationalists had emigrated from Germany to Russia in the 1700s, but eventually fled tightening
restrictions under the czar and pursued freedom in the United States.

Mennonites and Hutterites had a history of persecution, also coming
to the United States via Russia. Determined to exclude worldly influences,
these separatist denominations invited special attention because they
refused to buy Liberty Bonds or to salute the flag—a form of idolatry to
them. All emphasized German language and culture to shape their religious identity. In the hysterical climate of 1918, their focus on the fatherland seemed to signal their support of its political goals.[15] In fact, they had
a history of anti-Prussian sentiment. Nonetheless, Mennonites and
Hutterites became special targets of patriotic zealots. At least one
Mennonite pastor, John M. Franz of Bloomfield, was abducted and almost
lynched by a mob for preaching in German.[16]

Thousands of Russian Germans settled on farms in Montana around
1912–14. The huge sugar beet industry around Billings depended on them.
Clustered in communal settings, Mennonites and Hutterites worked the
land as model farmers throughout eastern and north central Montana. For
them, the state's ban on preaching in German was devastating. Their pastors beseeched the Council of Defense to rescind or modify the order.
"Most of the people were crying as they could not understand the word of
God, which they love and enjoy after their hard week's work," wrote Rev.
Fred Oscar Brose, pastor of the Congregational Church in Billings.[17]

"I can not believe," wrote the Rev. D. Bergstedt of Jordan, "that it is
the intention of the government to leave the people in these sad times of
war without any consolation from the word of God, while their sons are

offering their lifes for the country [sic]. That is the worst, when a sobbing and trembling heart must go without consolation in the language that it understands. . . . We had no services since 4 weeks, but it was the loneliest and bitterest time we ever met. . . . Please inform me whether we may use the German language or not."[18]

No, council secretary Charles D. Greenfield replied.

Community supporters of the Russian Germans vouched for their loyalty. A Big Horn County commissioner attached a list of parishioners' Liberty Bond contributions: "Bauer, George, 2 Liberty Bonds, $50; Flegler, John, 1 Liberty Bond, $50 . . ." and so forth. "I am somewhat in doubt whether we will be able to hold these beet workers here without a church; they seem to be quite church-going people," he wrote.[19] "These older people . . . have shown every response to our appeals to be good patriots in that they have . . . responded to the requests of the Food Administration to grow beets and produce sugar in a greater measure than many of the real American farmers have done," wrote the assistant general manager for Great Western Sugar Co., requesting leniency.[20]

No, responded Greenfield.

Others appealed to the Governor's patriotism. "It is an evident fact that these immigrants . . . need a religious and patriotic message," wrote the Rev. Walter Henry North, pastor of the First Congregational Church in Billings. "They need that there should be interpreted to them the high purposes and ideals of the American government that they may the more admire and love it . . . the only approach to them is in the only language they understand."[21]

"It was decided the order should stand," came the answer.

Various requests for modification of the order were floated: Just the sermons in German. One service a week in German. Let the pastor preach the sermon in German, and translate it into English sentence by sentence. Issue licenses to ministers who furnish evidence of their loyalty.

"It was decided the order should neither be abrogated or amended," Greenfield replied.

Confronted with such intransigence, some German pastors adopted a sly form of disobedience. In response to a sharp note from Greenfield that he had been reported using German on Christmas Day, Pastor Brose wrote:

I have all my services in English, only that I sometimes forget myself or cannot express my thoughts and use here and there German. I

always read the Bible first in English than in German, so that the
people know what I am talking about. On Christmasday I gived the
Lord Supper in german after the ritual . . . this was the only time, I
remember, when I use german . . . I try to learn English every day. . . .
How could I comfort the mothers of our dear boys that we give 17 to
the great army and sacrifid some on the fields of France, when I not
can speak to them in the language that they understand . . . our great
Service Flag found a special place on Christmasday by the tree and
the pictures of our boys with evergreen Decoration and electric
illumanation equel to any church in the City . . .[22]

Another pastor in Billings, Rev. Seil of the German Congregational
Church, also pleaded absent-mindedness—and kept on using German. "It
is certainly exasperating to have the little devil act this way," fumed
Billings Gazette editor Leon Shaw, a member of the Yellowstone County
Council of Defense.[23]

Seil's disobedience provoked a turf war with Lutheran pastor H. E.
Vomhof in Laurel, who saw his German-speaking congregation slipping
away to hear Seil's German sermons.[24] "It must be cut short," Vomhof
demanded in April 1919. "Justice demands it. If it is not done, I must take
up German . . . they go there, sent their children to that [Sunday School]
because of the German. We will no longer bear it."[25]

But it was not changed. In fact, the state council recommended to
Stewart in 1919 that Order Number Three be made state law.[26] Even harsher legislation was introduced, making it "unlawful for any person in any
meeting to speak, preach a sermon, express any sentiment or opinion or
judgment on any question, public or private, in any except a dead language or English."[27] The bill's sponsor argued "70 percent of the mine
accidents are caused by foreigners failing to understand signs printed in
English."[28] Fortunately, despite his assertion that "this is not even a debat-
able question," the bill did not pass.[29]

Council members kept holding out for the peace treaty with Germany
to be ratified before lifting the ban on German in the pulpit. Finally, in
April 1920, Greenfield suggested that treaty or no, it was time. The
Lutherans, he noted, were behaving. Employing the same argument earlier made in vain by the churches, he noted that ministers were getting out
of touch with the older members of their flocks.[30]

"Okeh with me, Anything you do," editor Will Campbell replied in the margin of Greenfield's letter.[31] The other council members agreed.

For the Mennonites, the postwar stubbornness of the Council of Defense was a moot point. Many had fled Montana for British Columbia in 1918, unable to endure the German bans and the ostracism for their pacifist nature. The angry words of Charles Greenfield (sounding more like attorney Brown) may have been ringing in their ears:

> It is a great pity that these Mennonites, who came to this country and settled . . . a majority of them getting without cost from Uncle Sam from 160 to 320 acres of land, have not had the first idea of loyalty to this country. . . . Your Mennonites appear to be under the impression that they cannot serve God and Jesus Christ unless they can do it in the German language. They are so dense in this particular that they are willing to move and make "this great sacrifice for their religion's sake and their history." . . . Under the circumstances I think it is just as well that Montana and all other states loose [sic] a class of people who are selfish and as absolutely self centered and as lacking in love of country as these Mennonites.[32]

The Montana Council of Defense was not abolished until August 25, 1921, one day after the peace treaty with Germany was signed. In 1920, J. M. Kennedy, a member of the Lincoln County Council of Defense, blasted Campbell's Montana Loyalty League. But his words could just as well apply to the state and county Councils of Defense: "Thousands and thousands of dollars have been wasted . . . and what is the harvest? Hatred, contempt, ignominy! For the great fortune spent, the returns are exclusively statewide discord, hand against hand, class against class, injury to farmers, injury to business, injury to finance, injury to everybody and not one dollar's worth of good done—all in the name of loyalty."[33]

Liberty Can Wait

In the wartime climate of super-patriotism, editors and publishers waved the flag and showed themselves to be remarkably willing to limit the free speech of others, particularly that of the dissident minority. Reflecting a narrow but prevalent concept of free expression, dissenters' speech was labeled "disloyal" and thus undeserving of any protection—in fact, quite the opposite. And the lengths to which most Montana newspapers were willing to go to silence disloyalty is well illustrated by this: They even favored their own licensing by the state, in order to certify that they did not carry propaganda or print news detrimental to the execution of the war. Ultimately the state Council of Defense decided not to implement a licensing order because newspapers had "demonstrated their loyalty."[34]

In addition to lavish coverage of loyalty news, such as sedition arrests and trials, and "kiss the flag" and other mob events, news managers often led the patriotic charge. At the Associated Press annual meeting in 1917, days after war was declared, publishers pledged their "hearty support" for the president in carrying out the people's war mandate. "Soon after the guests were seated at the luncheon, the lights were turned off while four marines hoisted the flags of the United States, Great Britain, and France to masts so constructed that compressed air kept the colors of the three allies waving."[35]

In Montana, newspaper publishers sponsored loyalty parades and waved the flag in print. *Lewistown News-Democrat* publisher Tom Stout, a member of the three-man county council of defense, organized an enormous loyalty parade and warned his fellow citizens: "We are done with the days of a divided allegiance in this broad land of liberty. With our sacred honor and our liberties at stake, there can be but two classes of American citizens, patriots and traitors. Choose you the banner beneath which you will stand in this hour of trial."[36]

Given this mindset, which most Montana newspapermen shared, they had no trouble discriminating between loyal and disloyal speech. "Offenses to the flag, slurring remarks as to our government or the gallant men who have gone to the front to fight our battles are abuses of liberty which cannot be tolerated," the *Anaconda Standard* had proclaimed ten days before Frank Little's murder. "An individual who thinks that because he lives in free America he has the right to say what he pleases about the country, government, man in uniform, or flag is in for a rude awakening. When it comes to a question between liberty and patriotism then let liberty go by the board. There is no right which is unpatriotic. Liberty can wait until we are at peace again. In these times there can be no freedom of speech which is not patriotic." The editor went on to warn of a "sudden and certain awakening" for those who failed to keep their mouths shut.[37]

That same week, the *Daily Missoulian* may have been the first newspaper in the state to suggest a sedition law.[38] After the state law was enacted, it editorialized, "We limit speech today that it may live free forever. . . . Whenever a free and self-governing people fights for more freedom, it must momentarily restrict its own liberties. But liberties so self-repressed are never lost. They are only laid aside where they can easily be reached."[39] In a war to end war, such doublespeak was perfectly logical. As the newspaper explained it, "only those who secretly distrust democracy and freedom find inconsistency in such action."[40]

The state and nation must protect themselves from "enemies within" by squelching sparks before they burst into flame, the *Great Falls Tribune* argued. "It is absurd to say that the man who slanders the government on account of . . . the carrying on of the war is harmless in his utterances. . . . No man says these things nowadays without having bitterness in his soul towards this country. The bitterness must be curbed through law or there is danger that it may arouse violence."[41]

The *Tribune* was also one of many newspapers that apparently saw no inconsistency in distinguishing free speech for itself or for other respectable elements of society from speech for speakers with an unpopular viewpoint. In editorials one week apart, the *Tribune* protested wartime censorship then advocated severe punishment for "soapbox orators." Nine days before Congress declared war, the *Tribune* agreed not to print "rumors about government policies with relation to the war."[42] But it noted that "[T]he silence . . . imposed on the press . . . prevents the masses of people from taking as great an interest in national affairs with relation to the war as they would do if they were more fully acquainted with all the facts."[43]

On the eve of the declaration of war, the *Tribune* called for ". . . the utter suppression of the soap box orator who stands on street corners and preaches treason to the government. In time of war, he should be crushed like a wasp. . . . We have no time to be bothered with traitors at home, or fools who preach treason and call it liberty of opinion and free speech. . . . The easy going American way with cranks and citizens who abuse freedom of speech and freedom of action should end when war is declared."[44]

Arthur Stone, dean of the University of Montana School of Journalism, took issue with that idea. In a talk at the Missoula Public Forum (before it was shut down by the local loyalty committee), he said, "You cannot blame the IWW for feeling sore when he is raided, suppressed, and jailed for making speeches as treasonable as those which a member of the national Senate makes with impunity. The same law ought to hold for the IWW and Robert

La Follette."[45] A liberal from Wisconsin, Senator La Follette was the favorite whipping boy for his long-standing opposition to the war.

This dichotomy in perceived free speech rights between citizens who took a sincere interest in the nation's war effort and those who preached "treason" was highlighted that same month when Senator William J. Stone of Missouri, a Wilson loyalist, assailed Theodore Roosevelt. Stone objected to Roosevelt's attacks on the government for various delays and scandals in the war buildup. Roosevelt had charged that 110 warships bound for Europe had been lying to in New York harbor for six weeks because of a coal shortage. Stone said that Roosevelt's criticisms, made by a less powerful citizen, would subject him to charges of disloyalty, and insinuated that T. R.'s statements made him, in effect, an agent for the kaiser.

The sensational charges touched off a debate about wartime criticism. Louis Marshall, a constitutional lawyer, advocated in the *New York Times* a wide scope for criticism of government operations. Indeed, "to discourage debate would be disastrous," for only debate could bring out all sides, thus enabling Congress and other decision-makers to make fully informed opinions.[46] But Marshall, too, distinguished between "the bitter and carping critic" and "criticism of the men of reasonable minds who approach the subject patriotically, who have the welfare of the country at heart."[47]

President Wilson's own beliefs seemed to fit right in line. "The advocacy of political change, however fundamental," was acceptable, but "passion and malevolence tending to incite crime and insurrection under guise of political evolution," he wrote, was sedition.[48]

Charles Evans Hughes (who had narrowly lost the presidency to Wilson in 1916, between two terms on the U.S. Supreme Court) told the American Publishers Association in May that "War demands fighting men, who see straight and shoot straight. It also demands fighting critics, who see straight and are honest and candid in criticism."[49] But in the same speech he said, "It is vitally important that the wells of public opinion should be kept free from the poison of treasonable or seditious propaganda."[50]

As reflected in the *Literary Digest*, by the end of August 1917, editors in all parts of the country were demanding suppression of all "treasonable, seditious, and disloyal" activity.[51] Many advocated extreme measures. "A man who by speech or action endeavors to impede America's efficiency in this righteous war should be judged by law, and if convicted, promptly executed," said Henry Van Dyke in *The New Republic*.[52] "A public execution by the guillotine is a revolting, repulsive sight, but if nothing else will serve to stop the work of the treacherous thousands with which this country is honeycombed, we might better set up the gleaming blade in our public places and . . . put it to use," wrote H. H. Windsor in the April 1917 *Popular Mechanics.*[53] Diagrams were not included.

Whatever free speech the minority possessed was considered a "technical" right, unavailing in times of national stress. "[I]n a democracy trained to believe that the will of the majority is the law of the land, [a man] cannot express sentiments that run counter to the will of the majority in a matter so close to their hearts . . . without results that are likely to be both dangerous and disagreeable to him, statutes and court decisions notwithstanding," the *Great Falls Tribune* warned. "[T]hose citizens who claim and exercise the technical right of free speech in a way obnoxious to the will of the patriotic majority had better change their ways for their own good . . ."[54]

In the aggregate, statements such as these reflected beliefs about the freedom of speech that were widely held, but contradictory and inconsistent, if not downright hypocritical. Liberty of speech could be suspended in wartime, but would not really be harmed, for the cause was good. Citizens with "honest" motives could criticize the government; radicals "preaching sedition" or powerless store clerks like Miss Swift, fired for refusing to buy a Liberty Bond, could not. Teddy Roosevelt had opinions; Robert La Follette made "erroneous statements of fact." The "patriotic majority" rules; those in the minority who technically have the right of free speech had better shut up.

These statements reflected beliefs not only about constitutional rights, but also about class and status. They reflected a certain knowledge about the law as it then stood, such as the "bad tendency" test, which set a low bar to the punishment of "disloyal" speech, but which also was irrationally colored by the war. To grant the same speech rights to Wobblies as to Teddy Roosevelt would have seemed absurd and unpatriotic to most. All these conflicting, confusing thoughts about free speech would soon be dumped in the black-robed laps of the U.S. Supreme Court.

The Open Light of Day

Few newspapermen in Montana championed freedom of speech during this difficult period. Bill Dunn of the Socialist *Butte Bulletin,* the leading

Figure 19. Socialist newsman and Butte labor leader William F. Dunn was convicted of sedition in Helena in 1919 after questioning the legality of the Montana Council of Defense. His conviction was reversed by the state supreme court in 1920. Montana Historical Society. Photo from *Butte Daily Bulletin*, March 27, 1919.

spokesman for a decidedly unpopular viewpoint, spoke out frequently against attempts by the state to shut him down. Eventually, his bold declaration that the state Council of Defense had no legal authority led to his conviction for sedition (See Chapter 15).

J. R. Faulds, editor of the *Northwest Tribune* in Stevensville, criticized the local council's harassment of "slackers" and was also put on the griddle. Faulds editorialized against the extreme actions of the Ravalli County Council of Defense in harassing alleged "bond slackers." Six ranchers who had "absolutely refused to buy Liberty Bonds or War Savings Stamps" through a Stevensville War Service League had been subpoenaed to appear before the county council. Faulds called league members "kaisers" and "accused them of furthering the ends of autocracy." The state council summoned Faulds and the county council members to a hearing in Helena. It censured him but did not order him to cease publication, as some members had favored.[55]

Edwin Craighead, a former college president turned editor, stood out for championing free speech and for taking on the Montana Council of Defense, the Anaconda and the "copper collar" press. As editor of the *New Northwest* in Missoula during the war years, Craighead exhibited uncommon courage and intellect.

After three years as president of the University of Montana, Craighead was fired in 1915 for leading a campaign to consolidate the state institutions of higher education. At the time there were four; Craighead favored one larger institution in Missoula (where there were 568 students). A voter initiative to consolidate failed in 1914, but Craighead had made enemies, including businessmen and Gov. Stewart, who came from the Bozeman area and who had feared the loss of Montana State College (now Montana State University).

After his dismissal, Craighead worked in North Dakota as the state commissioner of education for two years until the Nonpartisan League, in political control, abolished his position.

Craighead and his two sons started the *New Northwest* in September 1915 with about a thousand subscribers, $100 and an old typewriter. When he returned from North Dakota in 1917, he took over the day-to-day operations, although he had already been contributing editorials.[56]

Despite his experience in North Dakota, Craighead was a strong supporter of the NPL. The nasty treatment given its speakers and organizers in Montana was one of the main points of friction between him and the loyalty groups in the state. When organizer James Martin was prevented from speaking in Missoula, Craighead wrote, "There is nothing that free men value more highly than open speech in the open light of day. Unfair, unjust, and crooked men fear the light and seek the retreats of darkness."[57]

When William A. Clark's *Butte Miner* labeled the NPL "more dangerous than the Russian Bolsheviks," Craighead shot back, "Are the Nonpartisans of Montana, who are fighting to rescue themselves and this nation from the thralldom of profiteers, disloyal? Or are the men who are collecting vast sums of money to fight this farmers' movement, disloyal? Are the men who are fighting for freedom of speech under the law and the right to public assemblage disloyal? Or are the men who resort to mob law and violence, to dragging good men into jails, to tarring and feathering patriotic men, to terrifying whole communities, disloyal?"[58]

Craighead thought the German language ban was just plain foolish.

"How are we going to keep abreast of German science, of German war inventions, of German propaganda . . . ? If other states follow [our] example, we shall be even more foolish than the men who 'bite off their noses to spite their faces.' We become back numbers, provincials, out of touch with the world's progress . . ."[59]

In "A Plea for Tolerance," published four days after the state council had promulgated Order Number Three, Craighead wrote, "Intolerance has wrought more woe to the human race than all the wars of the world; than all the plagues and pestilences. . . . God save America, the refuge of the oppressed, from the anarchy of the mob and the intolerance and anarchy of impudent plunderers and rapacious multimillionaires. . . . Tolerance is the greatest word in human speech."[60]

In 1919, Craighead called for the abolition of the Montana Council of Defense. Tragically, he never saw his wish come true. He died of apoplexy in 1920 at the age of fifty-nine.

Guilty as Charged

For all his admiration of the Nonpartisan League, Craighead had contempt for the IWW, calling them "thugs with thick skulls [who] ought to be pitied, not persecuted."[61] By the time he wrote that, the Wobblies had endured years of attacks, legal and otherwise, intended to suppress them and their radical ideas. The great IWW trial of 1918 in Chicago, like other show trials, was conducted for political effect. To ultimately secure the convictions of ninety-six IWW leaders, including Big Bill Haywood and Elizabeth Gurley Flynn, prosecutors were aided by favorable law, favorable rulings by the judge and a jury that was later described as "frightened, jingoistic, and vindictive, all in all thoroughly sympathetic to the government's aims."[62] Following nearly seven months of pre-trial motions and evidence gathering, the Chicago trial began on April 1, 1918. After a month of jury selection, the prosecution began presenting its case on May 1. "How fitting," remarked labor historian Melvyn Dubofsky, "that a trial that was to become a judicial farce, if not a circus, should commence on April Fool's Day, and that presentation of evidence against a radical, allegedly revolutionary labor organization should begin on May Day!"[63]

Fresh from covering the Russian Revolution and its aftermath, journalist John Reed described Judge Kenesaw Mountain Landis: "Small on the huge bench sits a wasted man with untidy white hair, an emaciated face in which two burning eyes are set like jewels, parchment-like skin split by a crack for a mouth; the face of Andrew Jackson three years dead."[64]

The 113 defendants were indicted in multiple counts under the Espionage Act and the Selective Service law, charged with conspiring to hamper the recruitment and enlistment services and to stir up insubordination. They were also charged with conspiring to hamper the country's war production effort with strikes and sabotage.[65] Evidence of specific illegal overt acts by the defendants came almost exclusively in the form of speech—what defendants and the IWW as an organization had said about capitalism, sabotage, the war, general strikes, and so forth. And they had said a lot, from their infamous preamble in 1905 to Flynn's *Sabotage* to their anti-war statements and songs. For a month and a half, the prosecution had witnesses (144 in all) testify on various points of IWW philosophy. Chief defense counsel George F. Vanderveer objected over and over to the relevance of the statements, but Judge Landis let it all in, to show the defendants' intent—the words' tendency to lead to illegal actions.

Vanderveer conducted a vigorous defense, putting on 184 witnesses over three months, including many of the defendants. They testified as to their individual loyalty, including military service for many. IWW strikes, experts testified, came in response to industries exploiting their workers, not a general hatred of capitalism. As the case wound up, many defendants felt optimistic about their chances because of the lack of specific evidence about actual crimes presented by the government.

On August 17, more than ten thousand counts against the defendants went to the jury. Fifty-five minutes later, the men were back. All guilty on all counts. "It was a great surprise," Haywood was quoted as saying. "I can't understand how some of us were not acquitted at a moment's notice."[66]

Judge Landis (who went on to greater fame as Commissioner of Baseball after the Black Sox scandal of 1919) sentenced fifteen men, including Haywood, to twenty years in the federal penitentiary in Atlanta and levied fines totaling more than $2 million. "In times of peace you have the legal right to oppose, by free speech, preparations for war," Landis told the convicted. "But when once war is declared, that right ceases."

Most newspapers hailed the decision. "Hey, Bill! Your Old Pal, Big Bill Haywood, Has Been Drafted; He's Going to Lead a Contingent to Camp de Penitentiary," the *Helena Independent* headline read.[67] The *Los Angeles Times* declared that "the free speech guaranteed by the Constitution is not the free speech demanded by these miscreants." The *Kansas City Journal* said the IWW "stands revealed in all its 'hellish character as the Bolsheviki of America."[68]

Later in 1918 and 1919, other lower-level IWW leaders were tried in Sacramento and Kansas City, resulting in seventy-two more convictions. Another sixty-four Wobblies arrested in Omaha in November 1917 were jailed for more than a year before charges were dismissed.[69]

"The law had clearly proved to be an effective instrument of repression," IWW historian Melvyn Dubofsky reflected. "When vigilantes had deported miners from Bisbee or had lynched Little in Butte, the American conscience had been troubled." But when IWW leaders were tried under legal due process, "the American conscience rested easier."[70] Another historian, William Preston Jr., was even more pessimistic. "The Justice Department was in effect eliminating mob violence against IWW's and other nonconformists by removing the enraged citizen from the mob and placing him in the jury box."[71] The convictions proved the IWW had no free speech rights—or had forfeited them in time of war. Their confrontational attitude and their rebellious spirit made them easy to dislike, but they were convicted for their radical beliefs.[72] ❖

TWELVE
No Possible Means of Escape

Montana's Senators Help Push Sedition onto the National Stage, 1918

As the IWW courtroom drama in Chicago was beginning, a different drama was unfolding in Congress—the debate over the sedition bill. Like so many other bills, the legislation reflected far less wisdom and light than the emotion and heat of the moment, far less a rational meeting of the minds than an opportunistic jab at the enemy. And, as with other bills, enacted in emergency circumstances, the eloquent warnings of its outnumbered opponents echoed louder after the damage had been inflicted—in this case on thousands of men and women.

The bill debated and passed by Congress was never an attempt to cure widespread deficiencies in the Espionage Act, for the law had been very effective in prosecuting wartime dissenters, as shown by the 97 percent conviction rate in Espionage Act cases brought to trial before January 1, 1918. The bill was a well-timed, fear-biting attack on the IWW, the nation's principal "Hun within the gates," and on the near-anarchy that it represented. To squelch the IWW rabble who heaped contempt upon the nation's institutions and its war aims was a goal around which consensus could easily be built—regardless of the collateral damage it might inflict on constitutional liberties of free expression.

How and why did Congress pass a sedition law in 1918 when a similar bill couldn't get out of committee in 1917? Quite simply, the timing was right. The desires of Attorney General Gregory coincided with those of a majority in Congress at a high tide of wartime passions. Gregory's philosophy—suppressing crime regardless of its toll on due process or civil liberties—naturally led to greater suppression of disloyal talk.[1] In addition, Montana's senators struck when the iron was hot. With the alarming Ves Hall acquittal in hand, Senator Walsh began discussing with Gregory and his chief lieutenant, John Lord O'Brian, the possibility of amending the Espionage Act.[2]

Figure 20. U.S. Attorney General Thomas W. Gregory oversaw the prosecution of nearly two thousand men and women for sedition crimes in the World War I period. The Library of Congress.

O'Brian was concerned that the opinion in the Hall case could end up "practically nullifying prosecutions."[3] In Judge Bourquin's opinion, prosecutors would have to show actual obstruction of military recruiting. Mere attempts to do so would not meet the legal litmus test for conviction under the Espionage Act. Gregory suggested that the Espionage Act be amended to get around Bourquin's ruling.

Historian David Kennedy points out that Gregory and Wilson regarded a sedition law as a compromise to head off an even-worse court-martial bill submitted by Senator George Chamberlain of Oregon. The bill, pending before the Senate Committee on Military Affairs, would have put the army in charge of prosecuting disloyalty. Wilson also saw a way to neutralize congressional critics who were accusing him of being soft on pro-Germans.[4]

With Gregory anxious to protect his turf and Wilson eager to protect his administration, the Justice Department wrote an amendment to the Espionage Act, covering *attempts* to obstruct the recruiting services. The vehicle for this amendment was a minor bill, initiated by the Justice Department, to "protect liberty loan flotations against false and malicious mis-statements."[5] Rep. Edwin Y. Webb of North Carolina, chairman of the House Judiciary Committee, was the obliging sponsor. After it passed the House with virtually no debate, the Senate Judiciary Committee added the attempt language. But the same committee, which had ignored Senator Myers' sedition bill just eight months before, went a great deal further. At Senator Walsh's insistence, the committee pounced on the Webb bill and drastically altered it by importing most of the language from Myers' "minor bill."

The bill would now severely punish persons who in wartime used "disloyal" or "abusive" language about the United States form of government, its Constitution, flag, soldiers, sailors, and their uniform, or employed any language that might hinder the war effort (See Appendix I).

The attorney general did nothing to dissuade the senators from, in effect, hijacking his bill, for they were carrying it in the right direction. He must have applauded Senator Walsh's rationale for the changes when the senator addressed his colleagues on April 4. Walsh charged that judges like Bourquin in Montana, through their "strained construction" of the Espionage Act, had made it easier for agents of German propaganda "unmolested to disseminate the poison with which they have become infected."[6] Walsh had the Ves Hall opinion read into the record. While many convictions had been obtained under the Espionage Act for offenses "much less grave and heinous," the sedition amendment was needed so that "no possible means of escape would present themselves to those who might be disposed to assist the cause of our enemies in this war by disloyal and seditious utterances."[7]

In the six days of Senate debate on the sedition bill, comprising perhaps twenty-five hours of floor discussion, westerners dominated. The politicians were reacting to the pounding pressure from their business and industrial constituencies to do something about the IWW and the NPL. In a nutshell, their argument was that in a desperate struggle to defend democracy, disloyal talk from IWWs and others must be squelched before enraged citizens take the law into their own hands.

Utah Senator William King's description of the IWW typified the tenor of the debate. "That organization," he said, "aims at the destruction

Figure 21. U.S. Sen. Henry L. Myers represented Montana's industrial powers from
1911–23. His insistent calls for action against
the IWW resulted in Congress' adoption in
1918 of a near copy of the Montana sedition
law. Montana Historical Society.

Figure 22. U.S. Sen. Thomas Walsh helped
push anti-dissent legislation in Congress in
the WWI period. He later led the investigation of the Teapot Dome scandal. Photo
by Clinedinst, Washington, D.C.
Montana Historical Society.

of all government, the dislocation and destruction of our industrial and
economic system. Its members do not strike for higher wages or improved
conditions of labor; they strike for the purpose of absolutely destroying
government. It is an anarchistical . . . murderous, wicked, destructive
organization. . . . It is high time that the federal government did something to protect itself . . ."[8]

To the objection that the legislation was not limited to the IWW,
Senator Myers had a glib answer: "If people adopt the practices of anarchists and IWW's, then they ought to be punished the same as anarchists
and IWW's. This language was intended to apply to people who get up on
street corners or in logging camps or in the halls of cities and towns and
advocate resistance to all authority . . ."[9]

Proponents of the sedition measure seized on a lynching in Illinois on
April 5, in the predawn hours of the second day of the Senate debate, to

underline their argument that mob violence could be averted only by strong laws. A drunken mob of about 350 men and boys in Collinsville, a rough suburb of a rough town, East St. Louis, had grabbed Robert Paul Prager, a thirty-year-old German baker with socialist leanings. He was said to have made disloyal utterances in a speech to local coal miners. The mob wrapped Prager in a flag and made him kiss it while waving more flags, parading up and down the street. Police rescued the man and hid him under some tiling in the basement of the local jail. The mob broke in, hauled him beyond the city limits and strung him up from a tree just after midnight. Before the rope was placed around his neck, Prager scribbled a note to his parents in Dresden. It read: "Dear Parents: I must on this the 4th day of April, 1918, die. Pray for me, my dear parents."[10]

The lynching made the front page of newspapers across the country. A letter from Collinsville's mayor, read into the Senate record the next morning, called the murder "the direct result of a widespread feeling in this community that the Government will not punish disloyalty."[11] Atty. Gen. Gregory leapt on the issue. "Until the federal government is given the power to punish persons making disloyal utterances, Department of Justice officials fear more lynchings . . ."[12]

By coincidence, Gov. Stewart, in town to support the bill's passage and to attend a conference on "Americanization," had warned his fellow governors the previous day that more lynchings like those of Frank Little would occur unless the government cracked down.[13]

Myers was quick to take the cue, declaring, "The principal object of this bill is to prevent mob law."[14] "[T]he people of this country will [not] tolerate disloyalty and treason, and if Congress does not afford the remedy they will take the remedy into their own hands. . . . Conditions demand it. Necessity demands it. Loyalty to our . . . soldier boys on the firing line demands it. . . . Let us give it to them and not be squeamish or timorous about it."[15]

Prager's murder resonated strongly in a nation where lynching, mostly motivated by racial hatred, had reached a high-water mark.[16] In fact, the worst example had been in East St. Louis where race riots in 1917 had resulted in the deaths of more than one hundred blacks. Between 1912 and November 1917, 671 persons had been lynched, not including those in the East St. Louis riots.[17]

More mobs, proponents warned, were ready to rampage. "I want to tell you, there is dynamite all over the Mississippi Valley," said Senator Lawrence Y. Sherman of Illinois. He said he was referring to the IWWs, and their hobo ilk, which he described as "these bronzed, blistered, odoriferous knights of the tomato can."

Wartime necessity was argued throughout the debate. Echoing Judge Landis in the Chicago IWW trial, Senator Miles Poindexter of Washington noted, "Many of the things that are proposed to be punished . . . might be . . . of trivial public importance in time of peace, but the bill ought to be judged by its application to the emergency that confronts the country. . . . Everything that the country stands for is in the balance . . ."[18]

Thus, the need to sacrifice even the liberty of speech: "[I]s it too much to ask," wondered Senator William E. Borah of Idaho, "that those who are not making the supreme sacrifice, but are here enjoying the protection of our form of government to refrain from the use of such language as is profane or abusive or calculated to bring these objects into contempt?"[19]

In wartime, even the requirement of intent to speak or write contemptuously about the government wasn't necessary, some senators argued. "[I]n the crisis with which we are confronted carelessness or ignorance may bring about as disastrous effect as any willful intent might bring about," said Senator Albert Fall of New Mexico.[20] In the end, the Senate decided intent was necessary, voting to substitute the word "intended" for "calculated" as in the Montana language.

The fine points batted about among the many lawyers in the Senate so exasperated Senator John Williams of Mississippi that he burst out: "You have chosen rather to waste time talking, fooling, camouflaging, tweedleduming, and tweedledeeing, splitting hairs at a time when the whole cause of liberty of the world is at stake. . . . Who cares a cent which one of the two words you put into the statute?"[21] Williams was right. The change had no discernible effect on subsequent prosecutions.

Hours more were spent debating the difference between legitimate criticism and "profane" or "scurrilous" language. "A person would be perfectly free under this bill . . . to discuss the incompetency of any officer or the policy of any office . . . or of the administration or the inefficiency of any department," noted Borah. But "if he advocated it in disloyal, profane, scurrilous, or abusive language I think he would [come under the law]."[22] Myers had an even stronger position. Even if people spoke the truth, he said, they could be punished if they did so in such language.[23]

To Myers and his colleagues in this post-Victorian era, the form of the language was at least as important as the substance. Gentlemanly discourse or academic treatises could freely discuss anarchy or revolution but a disrespectful curse could fetch one twenty years at Leavenworth. Reading from a small item in that day's *Washington Post* about a cotton-press watchman in Memphis who cursed high officials during a liberty loan parade, Myers remarked, "Think of that, please! In time of war, when a liberty-loan parade is in progress, a man publicly curses the President of the United States, the Commander in Chief of our Army and Navy, and no law to punish such vile and reprehensible, such disloyal utterances!"[24]

But there was also a deeper significance to such terms as abusive, profane, and scurrilous: Used as synonyms for indecent speech, which was widely recognized to be beyond the pale of the free speech guarantee, these terms were also labels for unpopular opinions, such as criticisms of political or community leaders or "unpatriotic" sentiments. The use of such wildly subjective terms in the sedition law, particularly in the minds of jurors who almost uniformly conformed to middle-class values, would spell a great deal of trouble for defendants.[25]

An erroneous AP story reporting that contemptuous comments about the president were punishable under the bill caused a predictable eruption by Teddy Roosevelt, Wilson's volcanic Critic-in-Chief. In an editorial published April 6, 1918, in the *Kansas City Star*, Roosevelt condemned "the foolish or traitorous persons who endeavor to make it a crime to tell the truth about the administration when [it] is guilty of incompetence and other shortcomings . . ." Calling it a "proposal to make Americans subjects instead of citizens," T. R. promised to give the Justice Department an opportunity to test the bill should it become law.[26]

Roosevelt's blast threw the Senate into an uproar. Senators lined up to demand an apology. But his wider point about the legitimate role of criticism in a democracy stung because it was true. The bill's opponents, mainly conservative Republicans critical of the administration's war effort, embraced T. R.'s words.

"From the gush of this human Vesuvius has fallen, perhaps accidentally, some jewels of truth," remarked Senator James K. Vardaman of Mississippi.[27] "[T]here is much fundamentally un-American, and many of the elements of potential despotism, in the pending measure." Citizens and officials with an ax to grind would find the law "a convenient engine of oppression . . . there is always some groveling politicaster to do the little dirty things to please the anointed one and punish the disobedient." And "the times are all out of joint," he argued. "The fevered state of the public mind prevents calm, dispassionate discussion and fearless reasoning. Men are not permitted, be they ever so honest and patriotic, to express their honest thoughts, if . . . those thoughts should be in discord with the wave of popular passion."[28]

Fellow opponents—a dozen or so senators participated in the debate—argued that the bill was a drastic, unnecessary overreaction that endangered basic freedoms. "Unjust and repressive acts are the food of anarchy," warned Senator James A. Reed of Missouri. The Sedition Act of 1798, with its strikingly similar language, led to oppressive prosecutions and the popular fury that effectively ended the power of the Federalists. In fact, he said, the present measure was worse, "because the old law required that everything that was done should be done maliciously and falsely, whereas the proposed act omits both of those important qualifying terms."[29] The bill's language would make it far easier for juries to convict, because defendants could not assert that their words were true and had a justifiable purpose.[30]

"It is not necessary to destroy the freedom of the press of a whole people because there may be some miserable wretch who prints an obscene or an indecent or a disloyal thing," added Reed. "We need not grow alarmed and lose our heads. This whole Republic still stands and it will stand, though the storms and tempests of a world war may beat about it."[31]

The real object of the bill, Senator Thomas W. Hardwick of Georgia noted, "is to get some men called IWW's operating in a few of the Northwestern states. . . . In the name of patriotism we are being asked to jeopardize the fundamental rights and liberties of 100 million American people in order to meet a situation in a few . . . states, [yet] senators from those states admit to me freely that they have ample . . . statutes to deal with most of the things these IWW's are doing or are threatening. Why do they not enforce them instead of coming and asking us to pass a statute that is much worse than the sedition act of 1798 . . . ?"[32]

"It is not only a bill that seeks to throttle honest and legitimate discussion and criticism," declared Senator Hiram W. Johnson of California, "but it even purports to prevent one from thinking as he wishes to think."[33] Picking up on that thought, Senator Thomas P. Gore of Oklahoma added, "This bill . . . undertakes to turn an X ray into hearts and minds of men . . . but I know of no means of scrutinizing the inner thoughts of men. . . . The guarantees in favor of freedom of thought and freedom of speech are the fruits of immemorial centuries of experience. They were embodied in our Constitution because experience had demonstrated that [such freedoms] did not work as much mischief as the intolerance and the despotism which undertook to cut the tongues out of the throats of men who sought to give utterance to honest convictions."[34]

Opponents, with help from otherwise loyal supporters of the bill, sought to defeat an amendment that gave Postmaster General Sidney Burleson unlimited power to stop material sent to any group or person who in his judgment was using the mails in violation of the act. Such a provision was not only subject to abuse, but it would also cut off any money mailed to anyone arrested under the law and thus cripple their ability to mount a defense. But the bill as enacted included the provision, despite even Gregory's misgivings. The amended law thus broadened what was already a wide-open postal law under the 1917 Espionage Act. That law authorized the stripping of second-class mailing privileges for any material violating the Act—or which in the sole judgment of the postmaster general advocated treason, insurrection, or forcible resistance to any law of the United States.

On April 10, the Senate approved the amended bill without even a recorded vote. Attorney General Gregory assured the American Bar Association that judges would no longer be able to thwart the punishment of disloyalty, reciting the facts of the celebrated Ves Hall case.[35]

Prager's murder was still fresh. "Lynch law is the most cowardly of crimes," Gregory declared. "No greater wrong can be done to our soldiers in France than that of lynching Germans in America . . ." But now, he assured the officers of the court, "laws [will soon be] upon the statute books, which will reasonably protect the interior defenses of our country."[36]

Comments historian Kennedy: "In a remarkable revelation of the crime-control mentality, with its favorable regard for night-riders and lynch law, Gregory proposed not to prosecute the mobs but to pre-empt them, to replace crude vigilantes with trained government agents armed with the new sedition statutes! Here was an inventiveness in the art of subverting free speech that rivaled the considerable accomplishments of Burleson."[37]

The rationale of a prophylactic against lynch law also struck Harvard law professor Zechariah Chafee Jr. as peculiar: "Doubtless some governmental action was required to protect pacifists and extreme radicals from mob violence, but incarceration for a period of twenty years seems a very queer kind of protection."[38]

Debate in the House was a one-sided affair consisting chiefly of patriotic orations. The single dissent came from Socialist Congressman Meyer London of New York City, who called the bill "one of the most mischievous pieces of legislation ever imposed upon a free people." From his perspective, the fate of sedition defendants seemed clear: "[W]hen an ignorant judge or a grand jury composed of butchers and shopkeepers and retired businessmen is to decide whether the advocacy of a new economic or social theory is a violation of law, then God save the country."[39] As almost no other member of Congress had, London suggested that it was the unhealthy economic conditions leading to the rise of the IWW that needed addressing.[40] But London was alone. The House approved the bill on May 7 by a vote of 293 to 1.[41]

The bill "establishes a vicious precedent which will be utilized to the full by the reactionary forces of this country," a lawyer from Philadelphia named Harold Evans wrote to Wilson on May 9, urging him to veto the bill. "It seems inevitable that at the close of the war," Evans presciently observed, "there is going to be in this country a titanic struggle between the forces of liberalism and of reaction." The latter, he warned, "under the cloak of patriotism and the cry of 'support the President' [are] using the present crisis to further their own ends by fastening upon this country instruments of autocracy, such as suppression of free speech, and free press. . . . These things strike at the men and women who will be your supporters in the battle for democracy at home as well as abroad, who are now bending every effort to keep us from descending to 'the level of the very people we are fighting . . . '"[42]

It was a good argument, using the President's own words, but powerless in the face of the Justice Department's recommendation. In a memo to Gregory, Justice Department lawyer Alfred Bettman advised that the sedition bill would "have the advantage of calming [the public] clamor [for a tougher law]. If administered with some discretion . . . the act ought to have no consequences detrimental to the best interests of the country."[43] Gregory passed those sentiments on to Wilson.

Wilson, who habitually deferred to the judgment of his cabinet officers, concurred. On May 16, he signed the bill into law. It took effect immediately.

The *Anaconda Standard* explained the new law. If its interpretation of free speech was warped, its reading of the sedition law's intent was accurate:

> A man can talk all he pleases if he talks right. He can say what he thinks if he thinks the war is just. . . . The loyal people of this country have and will have all the freedom of speech and freedom of the press that they want. For the disloyal free expressions are over. Nor is it sufficient that one may claim that his disloyal expressions are his honest sentiments. . . . The man with disloyal sentiments must keep them to himself or take his punishment.[44]

"To Work Their Extermination"

The harsh wording of the federal sedition law did not satiate Congress in its war on radicals. Even as the sedition bill was being debated in Congress, another bill was aimed directly at the IWW. Once again, a Montana senator played a leading role. The Unlawful Associations bill submitted by Senator Walsh on May 2 was a federal version of the criminal syndicalism law passed by the Montana legislature in February, with roots in anarchy laws such as New York's, passed in 1902 soon after the assassination of President William McKinley.[45]

Walsh's bill did not specify the IWW but it was plain from his remarks and those of other senators which organization was being targeted. The bill was far-reaching. It would outlaw any organization "whose purpose . . . is to bring about any governmental, social, industrial, or economic change within the United States by the use [or threats] of force, violence or physical injury to person or property or which teaches, advocates, advises or defends [such methods] . . ." The bill also made criminal mere membership in such organizations, as well as "communicating by any written means or knowingly housing or permitting advocates of such doctrines."[46]

To pound home the point, Senator Charles S. Thomas of Colorado had the clerk read that tried-and-true conversation starter, "Christians at War," the IWW "Hymn of Hate." The song's lyrics, he advised, "gives a graphic idea and mental picture of the infernal activities and criminal characteristics of this . . . foul nest of thieves and murderers."[47]

Even the senators who opposed the sedition bill endorsed Walsh's bill. "[D]isloyal organizations like the IWW which are going about at a time like this seeking to stir up dissension in the land and which commit acts of sabotage and other criminal offenses, get no sympathy from me," declared Senator Reed. "I am willing to go almost to any extent to work their extermination."[48] But he was concerned that the bill reached too far, including in their scope people who simply paid dues to an organization later found to come within the scope of the act. "I presume we shall repeat the old experience—that is, because some outrageous . . . organization has come into existence, we at once proceed to pass laws so broad and sweeping that scores of objects we do not want to penalize will nevertheless be declared felonies."[49]

Idaho's Senator Borah, too, sounded a note of caution. A strong-arm measure like this, he advised, may be acceptable in wartime, but "the time may come when we will have to choose our methods and our remedy with greater wisdom. . . . We must remove some of the causes before we expect trouble to disappear."[50]

Still, these were relatively minor cautions in a bill designed to outlaw Public Enemy Number One. The Senate passed the measure on an unrecorded voice vote.[51] After the House Judiciary Committee reported out an amended version, the bill was placed on the House calendar. The Armistice on November 11, however, erased the justification of a wartime measure. Walsh's bill was never debated in the House. Had the war continued, the law almost surely would have been enacted, and Wilson would not have vetoed it.

After the Armistice, the business of outlawing the IWW remained with the states. In the postwar period of industrial strife and anti-Bolshevik hysteria, the tempo increased. By 1922, twenty-one states plus Hawaii and Alaska—including every western state except North Dakota and New Mexico—had criminal syndicalism laws.[52]

"Oh, Adjectives!"

In the debate on the sedition law, Senator Hardwick of Georgia honed in on that string of words that lay at its heart—disloyal, profane, scurrilous, contemptuous, or abusive language. "Oh, adjectives!" he cried. "God save us from the adjective lawyers and the adjective courts! I do not know what they will say is 'abusive'; I do not know what they will say is 'disloyal.'"[53]

Hardwick had put his finger on one of the most disquieting aspects of the new law. Its vagueness made it subject to a multitude of interpretations.[54] Gregory had recognized it in his memo to Wilson recommending that he sign the legislation. He admitted that the law was "vague and broad" but justified it on the grounds that it dealt with an inherently difficult area, "namely the legitimate limits of free speech."[55]

His assistant, Alfred Bettman, suggested "a word of warning" to the U.S. Attorneys. The Justice Department circular that would be sent out a week after Wilson's signature, read in part: "It is also of the highest importance that this statute be administered with discretion. It should not be permitted to become the medium whereby the government attempts to suppress honest, legitimate criticism of the administration, or discussion of governmental policies. Nor should it be permitted to become the medium for personal feuds or oppression or persecution of persons of German extraction or birth. The protection of loyal persons from unjust suspicion or prosecution is as important as the suppression of actual disloyalty . . ."[56]

While the caution memo was intended to clarify the scope of the law and qualify its breadth, it raised more problems. What exactly was "honest legitimate criticism"? The law gave enormous discretion to U.S. Attorneys. As Judge Amidon in North Dakota observed, the circular "converts every United States Attorney into an angel of life and death clothed with the power to walk up and down his district, saying, 'This one will I spare, and that one will I smite.'" As a result, "[H]ow is a citizen to know when he is exercising his constitutional right, and when he is committing a crime?" asked Harvard Professor Zechariah Chafee Jr., a leading critic of the Wilson administration's attempts to suppress political dissent.[57]

One very natural response in the face of uncertainty of the reach of a speech law was self-censorship. People steered clear of saying anything the least bit controversial. The extent of that behavior of course cannot be measured. There were plenty of other "keep quiet" signals emanating from America at war—the pervasive propaganda, the constant patriotic messages, the continuing prosecutions under the Espionage Act, the vast undercurrent of citizen patriotism.

The broad scope of the sedition law created another problem. Because it "covered all degrees of conduct and speech, serious and trifling alike, [it] gave the dignity of treason to what were often neighborhood quarrels or bar-room brawls" and it "fanned animosities into flame, vastly increasing the amount of suspicion and complaints across the country," O'Brian later commented.[58] U.S. Attorneys came under enormous pressure from citizens to bring charges.

"It was almost impossible for the United States district attorneys to keep abreast of the complaints," recalled Professor Chafee.[59] "It is obvious that a country full of would-be spies chasing imaginary spies and finding only pro-Germans and pacifists is a very unfit place for the decision of those psychological questions which . . . inevitably arise from the prosecution of utterances."[60]

In this atmosphere, the number of prosecutions went up.[61] But no statistics were kept on prosecutions or convictions under the amended language as opposed to those under the original language or those under both. Altogether, 1,956 cases were brought under the Espionage Act (including cases under the Sedition Act amendment). A total of 877 persons were convicted—45 percent. Figures show a 10–15 percent increase in Espionage Act cases in the fiscal year starting July 1, 1918, but a sharp decrease—almost by half—in the *rate* of convictions.[62] More cases were being weeded out, most likely via dismissals rather than acquittals.

The numbers also show wide disparity in prosecutorial zeal among the U.S. Attorneys. Nearly half the cases under the Espionage Act (both old and new) were brought in just thirteen of the eighty-seven districts, mostly in the West.[63]

Once sedition cases reached the trial stage, there were other grave difficulties—the passions of the jury, the prevalent legal standards that set a very low bar to convictions in free speech cases, and the possible prejudice of the judge, as well as the often-palpable bias of the newspapers covering the proceedings and their influence on jurors and judges.

Of the juries, Professor Chafee commented: "It is only in times of popular panic and indignation that freedom of speech becomes important as an institution, and it is precisely in those times that the protection of a jury proves illusory."[64] Men (in almost all cases) imbued with the patriotic spirit of the times, in an economic class not likely to sympathize with radicals who hated capitalism, were probably not going to parse the meaning of disloyalty or consider the vast economic inequalities that may have impelled such speech. A defendant, perhaps with a foreign-sounding name, accused of saying an unpopular thing or two, especially if voiced in a crude way, was not likely to receive the benefit of the doubt. Commenting on the well-to-do jurors in the sedition trial of Eugene Debs, journalist Max Eastman described "faces . . . bitterly worn and wearied out of all sympathy with a struggle they had individually surmounted."[65]

Nor were jurors likely to ponder long over fine questions of intent, which they, as triers of fact, played a central role in determining. The basic principle was that one is presumed to intend the natural and usual consequences of his acts. If two men get into a brawl and one man is knocked down, hits his head on the curb and dies, the other man can be prosecuted for manslaughter because his opponent's death could reasonably be seen as a consequence of his act, even though he didn't subjectively intend to kill the man. Translated to the free speech arena, the law at the time interpreted "natural and usual consequences" very loosely under the prevalent "bad tendency" test. If speech had even a remote tendency to lead to an illegal act, to spark what might eventually become a conflagration, it fit the intent test.

Although jurors were supposedly screened for bias, they still were susceptible to the one-sided views they read in the papers, and tended to see danger in every utterance. As Walter Nelles, counsel to the newfound National Civil Liberties Bureau put it, "The very ideals of socialism and communism in their most pacifist forms shock an average jury to such an extent that they mistake the shock itself for force and violence."[66] Therefore, juries did what Gilbert Roe, a leading constitutional lawyer and representative of the Free Speech League had predicted when Congress was debating the original Espionage Act: During wartime, "you are going to get a conviction any time the United States district attorney asks for it."[67]

Judges, too, were not immune from partisanship in their conduct of sedition trials. Some allowed prosecutors wide latitude in bringing in evidence of intent—even, as in the case of the IWW leaders, words spoken or published long before the law went into effect. Judges often regarded the requirement of intent as a mere formality. "Since most of the courts took the attitude that anything which tended to dampen the war enthusiasm was a violation of law, and that success was not necessary to constitute a violation, the question of intent became a mere formula," social scientist O. A. Hilton noted.[68]

Some judges succumbed to the temptation to lecture the jury on economic or political facts—as they understood them to be—and on patriotism and love of country. "The courts were simply reflecting in a large measure the intolerance of an aroused public opinion which refused to permit any questioning of the purity of American motives," Hilton noted.[69] Their views of free speech were usually cramped. "[W]henever a charge [to the jury] did mention freedom of speech, it was almost sure to say or imply that this right had nothing to do with opposition to war and put such opposition in the same class with extreme utterances like the advocacy of a natural right to kill men or outrage women," Chafee noted. "Almost no emphasis was laid on the desirability of wide discussion . . ."[70]

Finally, the sentences imposed were often draconian and unprecedented. Judges in eighteenth-century English sedition trials never imposed a sentence longer than four years; in the United States, at least twenty-four persons were sentenced to twenty-year terms, not including the sixteen IWWs in the Chicago trial (who were tried on other counts as well).[71] O'Brian later conceded, when Wilson was granting clemency to dozens of men, that some sentences were excessive. "In some cases, the judges deliberately made the sentences high as a wartime policy expecting a reduction after the cessation of hostilities," he explained in a 1919 letter.[72] In other words, judges piled on prison time to express support for the war.

The continuing clamor for sedition prosecutions in 1918, combined with an emerging pattern of wildly uneven treatment of such cases in the various districts, compelled the Justice Department to issue another circular two weeks before the Armistice. The department ordered all U.S. Attorneys to submit all new cases for approval before sending them to grand juries for indictment.[73]

The circular did not necessarily solve any problem, however. From hundreds or thousands of miles away, the Justice Department was giving the thumbs up or down based on a brief description of the facts, examining fine distinctions in language and attempting to divine intent. For example, one Justice Department lawyer recommended no prosecution in the case of a man who allegedly said, "Our government is a hypocritical government; we had no business sticking our noses into the war; it was England's war and England ought to fight it out; Germans can sink our soldiers as fast as we could send them over."[74]

Yet in the case of another man, described as "some sort of preacher who travels through the country," the lawyer gave the go ahead. The man had allegedly said, "President Wilson was the cause of this war and could stop it if he would; that the President is a murderer; that the uniform is a disgrace to any man; and one with religion in his heart would not fight . . . Jesus Christ wouldn't fight if he was here on earth . . ."[75]

Thus, more heated or specific language about a protected object like the military uniform made the case viable, although it seems clear that the man was being punished for his opinion, not for a "false statement of fact." Unfortunately, in the eighteen months prior, many persons had gone to prison for a range of utterances that encompassed both cases. The distinction was meaningless and the vetting of the cases came too late to make much of a difference.

In Montana, the nuances in the federal sedition law didn't make any difference, as no one ever went to jail under it, thanks to Judge Bourquin and U.S. District Attorney Burton K. Wheeler. But the state had been busy with its own sedition law, the progenitor of the U.S. law. It was subject to the same calamitous flaws in the "human machinery" as was the federal law. Overzealous prosecutors, super-patriotic juries fired up by the copper press, and biased judges combined to punish scores of people for opening their mouths in the wrong place and at the wrong time. ✦

THIRTEEN
"Good Night with Mr. Damned Wilson"

Prosecution of "Beer Hall Germans," 1918–1919

COMMENTING ON THE CASE OF A MAN imprisoned for ten to twenty years under the Montana state sedition law, Montana Federal District Judge George M. Bourquin cited George Bernard Shaw: "During the war the courts in France, bleeding under German guns, were very severe; the courts in England, hearing but the echoes of those guns, were grossly unjust; but the courts of the United States, knowing naught save censored news of those guns, were stark, staring, raving mad."[1]

The stories of the 130 or so sedition cases in Montana in 1918 and 1919 are a frightening example of what can happen when freedom of speech is taken hostage by war hysteria. Citizens saw themselves engaged in a titanic struggle for the future of mankind, their foe the brutal, despotic, barbaric Huns. Rights of free expression were consistently trumped by the question of loyalty to one's country. The sedition law (see Appendix I) was essentially a loyalty law. Those who spoke against the country—its president, military, war aims, flag, even its uniform—were disloyal, and therefore guilty of sedition.

The cases illustrate the trivial nature of Montana's loyalty crimes. Virtually all sedition convictions in the state were based on offhand outbursts, often in saloons. Most defendants worked at menial, blue-collar, or rural jobs. More than half were farmers or ranchers. Others worked as butchers, carpenters, cooks, teamsters, bartenders, and saloon janitors. At a time when xenophobia was near its zenith, it's not surprising that more than half of the men sent to prison had been born in Europe, many in Germany or Austria. Only three trials involved the printed word.

While connections to the IWW carried 2-to-1 odds favoring a sedition conviction, almost as dangerous was the statement, repeated countless times in a nation reluctantly drawn into a war on another continent, that "we have no business being there." Liberty Bonds and other war measures such as savings stamps and food rationing occupied a hallowed niche; those who denigrated them risked prison terms. A wine and brandy salesman visiting Red Lodge received a seven-and-a-half– to twenty-year sentence for saying that the wartime food regulations were a joke.

Foul language, the kind that still is represented by dashes in mainstream newspapers, figured in many cases and probably contributed to convictions and sentences. Statements that questioned the chastity of women or the morality of the nation's soldiers were dangerous. A Rosebud County farmer got eight to sixteen years for making the curious remark that, "These free taxi rides given to the soldiers at Miles City were just for the purpose of getting them into private houses, so that they may have intercourse with [the wives, sisters, and daughters of the town's citizens] and get war babies."

By setting stiff criminal penalties—a maximum of twenty years in prison and a $20,000 fine—the legislature had conveyed the seriousness of the crime. So, too, did prosecutors. Sedition, deputy Lewis and Clark County Attorney J. R. Wine told one jury, "is the most heinous act that a citizen of this country can commit."[2] His boss, County Attorney Lester H. Loble, later a district court judge, told another jury, "I believe that this man tomorrow morning at dawn should be led out into the jail yard and forced to face a firing squad."[3]

That may have been hyperbole for the benefit of the jury, but at least one death can be linked to the sedition cases. Charles Zastrow of Clancy, implicated in the pages of the *Helena Independent* as a ringleader of loyal Germans, shot himself to death while out on bail after his arrest, the day before formal charges were to be filed against him.[4] He would almost certainly have been convicted.

Forty men and one woman, whose average age was forty-five, would collectively be sentenced to more than 164 years in the state penitentiary at Deer Lodge. They would end up serving more than sixty-three years at hard labor, an average of nineteen months apiece, for criticizing or bad-mouthing the government. Of the seventy-four persons convicted of sedition, twenty-nine received fines of as much as $20,000 (equal to $265,000 in 2005 dollars). Four were handed both fines and prison sentences. Just eleven men were acquitted, twenty-four cases were formally dismissed, and a score or more other cases were not accounted for. Newspaper articles suggest that eighty to one hundred more persons were arrested for sedition in Montana in 1918 and 1919, but were not formally charged.

The number of state sedition cases in Montana may have been affected by Judge Bourquin's roadblock to prosecution of federal sedition cases under the Espionage Act. Bourquin's acquittal of Ves Hall and Wheeler's position as U.S. Attorney effectively froze federal prosecutions in Montana, even after passage of the federal sedition law in 1918.

State sedition cases were concentrated along a great south-bending arc across the state, corresponding roughly to what is now the Interstate 90 and 94 corridors, extending from Thompson Falls in the northwest to Sidney in the far east. The biggest cluster of sedition cases was located in the southeast. Thirteen cases were tried in Miles City, seat of Custer County, and another four in Forsyth, seat of neighboring Rosebud County, resulting in a total of fourteen convictions. The next biggest cluster was in Helena, where eleven cases resulted in ten convictions.

The clusters of cases reinforce the impression that successful sedition prosecutions depended more on the zeal of the county attorneys and the local press and the prevailing political conditions (which affected jury attitudes) than on any organized or coherent political dissent which might give rise to seditious utterances. Butte and Silver Bow County, then the state's most populous city and county, had long been wracked by labor strife and were probably the biggest pocket of strength in the state for the IWW. Yet they had only seven sedition cases, resulting in two convictions.[5] The county certainly had stridently conservative newspapers in the *Butte Miner* and to a lesser extent in the *Anaconda Standard* but its prosecutors knew from experience it was hard to get a Butte jury to convict on a charge like sedition.

Drinking While German

The sedition trials in Helena may collectively have had the greatest impact. Eight Germans, most of them associated with German beer halls in the capital, were convicted largely on the word of a former German army officer turned stool pigeon, who himself had done time at the state prison. A bartender and a short-order cook in a saloon each received the maximum sentence of ten to twenty years at hard labor for offhand remarks in German to the informer.

In Helena, as in many other communities, Germans ran many of the saloons. They knew beer, they did their job efficiently, they worked hard and therefore prospered in the hard-drinking, blue-collar towns. But after

America declared war against the Central Powers, and especially after February 1918, when the state sedition law was passed, being a vocal German became a dangerous exercise. Perhaps recognizing this, German beer hall operators in Helena had "put the kibosh," as one bartender put it, on all war talk in their establishments. All meant all, neither boosting the U.S. nor cheering the kaiser. Not in English, not in German, not in any language.

As war hysteria tightened its grip on Montana in the spring of 1918, rumors and articles about German spies were common. Curiously, some persons chose to employ Germans to ferret out "pro-German" disloyalty, despite the obvious risks. Lewis and Clark County Attorney Lester Loble decided to employ this stratagem to trap seditionists. To make this work involved some high-stakes maneuvering at the highest levels of state government.

The story begins in Butte. Oscar Rohn, proprietor of the South Butte Mining Company and president of the Butte Employers Association, had employed a man named Carl von Pohl, ostensibly to find good men to work his mine, but really as a spy to make sure the men he hired were not IWWs or other scum.[6] For that service, Rohn paid von Pohl more than $5,000. Von Pohl was like a dime-store novel caricature of a German spy. He had a pointed goatee, wore green-gray suits that only foreigners wore, told fantastic tales of intrigue of "portable wireless equipment relaying messages through Mexico and Paraguay to Berlin," and was said to have a "svelte, elusive and dark-eyed"[7] woman associate who would from time to time mysteriously vanish from dinner parties "with a swish of silken skirts and a flash of lingerie into the darkness of a closed automobile."[8]

But was von Pohl using Rohn for cover, to spy for Germany? Many folks in Butte thought so. In the fall of 1917, Campbell of the *Independent* had accused von Pohl of transmitting information to Berlin via a secret wireless station in the forest west of Missoula. He labeled von Pohl a "pretty important wheel in the kaiser's spy machine"[9] and called for his arrest. Even Rohn hadn't been positive of von Pohl's allegiance, yet was satisfied with his work, so had kept him on. With America in the war, however, von Pohl's passport and pro-German statements were impossible to ignore. In October, U.S. Attorney B. K. Wheeler had von Pohl arrested and interned as an enemy alien.

Some months later, another "von" came along—Eberhard von Waldru—and was given the same job von Pohl had had. Von Waldru, thirty-one, said he had experience in the German army and a German passport—exactly the kind of person who should have been on the German side of the trenches. But his wits and charm had allowed him to navigate many a ticklish situation. Now he was able to convince his handlers that he was just the right man to root out German spies.

To spy on disloyal pro-Germans, von Waldru joined the IWW and the MMWU. He dropped the "von" and obtained a "rustling card" for working in the mines. He set about gathering information, his base a fake real estate office. There, he and another operative would hang out with the likes of Bill Dunn, then just an electrician, and with radical miners, presumably collecting tidbits of information. The office had a good view of Finlander Hall, where the Wobblies and the MMWU had their headquarters.

In April, von Waldru moved his spying operation to Helena under the aegis of Thomas A. Marlow, president of the National Bank of Montana. Marlow was also on the board of directors of the Anaconda and headed the Lewis and Clark County Council of Defense. Within a few weeks of his arrival in Helena, von Waldru had the goods on a bunch of beer hall Germans, and was waiting to testify against them. The men were about to be arrested.

But there was a problem. Rohn, the Butte mine operator, was concerned that his links to the first German spy, von Pohl, were poisoning his own reputation. Despite the man's internment, rumors of his duplicity had continued to swirl and intensify with the growing war hysteria.[10] Those who were privy to von Waldru's mission, probably including Campbell and Gov. Stewart and high officials at Anaconda, worried that his connection to Rohn would damage his credibility at the upcoming sedition trials. Surely the defense would question his allegiance. The state Council of Defense had von Waldru cleared by the Department of Justice and the immigration service in Washington, and now would add its own imprimatur.

With Gov. Sam Stewart as ex-officio chairman and the *Independent's* Will Campbell and other archconservatives as members, the Council was the patriotic nerve center of Montana. Given new blood, greater authority and a budget in the February 1918 special session, the Council was eager to step into the quasi-official shoes supplied it by the legislature—and even to stretch the shoes a size or two. It was the perfect vehicle for sanitizing both Rohn and von Waldru.

The fact that the Council lacked authority to hold hearings was easily countered: At its monthly meeting on May 28, 1918, the council issued orders arrogating the power to hold "hearings and investigations in all matters pertaining to the public safety and the protection of life and property," along with the power to issue subpoenas.

A second problem surfaced. U.S. Attorney Wheeler—no fan of the Council of Defense—had von Waldru arrested as an enemy alien. If the German was interned and not allowed to testify, the sedition trials could never take place because he was the star witness. In fact, his enemies believed, that was why Wheeler had the German arrested. Wheeler denied it, blaming the arrest on a lack of communication between him and his investigator while he was out of town. If Wheeler did try to throw a wrench into the sedition trials, if for no other reason than his sincere doubts about von Waldru's credibility, he could not have admitted it, for such a "pro-German" move would have been political suicide.

The council's hearings began almost immediately, on June 1. In the closed-door session (thoroughly leaked by the *Independent*), Gov. Stewart, County Attorney Loble and Campbell himself reviewed in detail Rohn's dealings with von Pohl.[11] They also brought out von Waldru's curious background.

According to von Waldru, he was educated in law and history, and then became a socialist. He had served a year as a private in the German army, and had been a commissioned officer for twenty-four hours. He told the Council that he had been kicked out for gambling, although he had earlier told employers that he left the army because his politics were in danger of getting him in trouble.

He had come to America in 1913 with $45 in his pocket, he said. After working as a reporter for German-language newspapers in New York, Charleston, and Chicago for about three years, he found work on a ranch near Fort Benton. There, he forged a $20 check and drew a prison sentence. On the way to the penitentiary, the deputy sheriff taking him was called back—so von Waldru continued faithfully on his own and turned himself in. In prison, he single-handedly thwarted a riot plot, turning over notes written with invisible ink to Warden Frank Conley, thus earning a shortened sentence. He washed up in Butte and found an even better way to capitalize on his newfound talent for stool-pigeonry.

The end result of five days of hearings came as no surprise. Rohn and von Waldru were both exonerated. Rohn received a slap on the wrist. He was cleared of any disloyalty, but also called "indiscreet in employing Carl von Pohl, alien enemy, to do detective work for him." Von Waldru was cleared to testify. The only condition: He would have to sleep in the county jail. His deportation would be on hold.

On May 31, Sheriff Ed Majors had arrested seven Helena men for sedition, based solely on von Waldru's evidence. Adam Steck was a night bartender at the Trocadero Saloon.[12] Tony Diedtman was trained as a baker but worked as a swamper—a janitor—at the Central beer hall.[13] Frank Heil was a swamper at the Milwaukee saloon.[14] John Milch, his boss, was the owner of the saloon.[15] John's brother, Joe Milch, was a tailor and part-time bartender.[16] August Lembrecht, also a former German army officer, was a blacksmith.[17] Leo Reno was a short-order cook at the lunch counter in the Black Eagle saloon.[18] An eighth man, Richard Lohe, would be arrested later.

Bond for each man was set at $5,000; none made bail immediately. All were housed in the county jail, along with von Waldru and another stool pigeon planted there to overhear their conversations.

All the suspects, while engaged in conversation with von Waldru, had supposedly said disloyal things within a ten-day period between the end of April and the beginning of May, according to the charges prepared by County Attorney Loble.

As recounted by von Waldru, the men's remarks were strikingly similar. They heatedly expressed their anger about the United States and the war.

"This damn country is not worth a damn and as soon as Germany gets here, me for the old country," Tony Diedtman was reported to have said while in the Central beer hall.

John Milch, the saloon proprietor, allegedly said, "What did this country ever do for us except take taxes . . . and don't give a damn thing in return. . . . This is supposed to be a free country but I be damned if it is. They tell you what to eat and what to drink. . . . They are [be]ing so God damn foolish they will tell you what name you have got to wear, but I be damned if I change my name. My name is Milch and I am German and I am damn proud of it."

Others allegedly expressed pride in and loyalty to Germany. "I know I would die for our kaiser and Fatherland the same as the boys in the trenches," Adam Steck was quoted as saying. "All they need is a good licking and they are going to get it before William gets through with them," predicted Frank Heil. "I know this damn government is getting nutty but it won't last long," said August Lembrecht.

Joe Milch was said to be distressed at the "damn lies" in the newspapers. "The damn sonofabitch French, American, and English aeroplanes bombarded some of the towns in Germany," he allegedly said. "You don't see a sonofabitch thing about that in the paper but when the German aeroplanes bombarded places in England and France, you always hear they kill women and children. They never kill men. They call the Germans Huns!"

And, as damaging as anything else, the men allegedly laced their remarks with expletives and contempt for the flag and for the president. "I wish they would come after me some night to take me out to kiss the dirty rug what they call the American flag," said Steck. "This president should go fuck himself and Uncle Sam too," said Joe Milch.

Reno topped them all: "I be damned if I would kiss this rotten flag. I would take it to the shithouse. . . . To hell with them. . . . I would fuck them all. I am an Austrian and they can all kiss my ass. Just wait until the Germans bring the black, white, and red over here, then we will get even with them and then some. Then good night with the Stars and Stripes, Army, Navy and Mister damned Wilson."

Expressed openly to "red-blooded Americans," every one of those statements would have invited a punch in the nose, or worse. But all of these statements were made *in German*, to a German stool pigeon sent into beer halls to engage German men in incriminating conversations. Nevertheless, such tawdry crumbs were considered prima facie evidence of sedition.

Tony Diedtman drew the short straw. His was the first trial—and the second, for the first ended in a hung jury. The two trials set the tone for the subsequent sedition trials in the state. Diedtman's conviction was critical to the prosecution, for it would make it easier for Von Waldru to testify in the trials of the other German beer hall men.

Diedtman's alleged remarks, ("this damn country is not worth a damn" and "me for the old country") received little attention during the trial. The bartender simply denied having made any of the statements to von Waldru. Instead, the case was largely a battle over von Waldru's credibility.

More details of von Waldru's curious past came to light. The witness said his father was a member of the Reichstag and that their estate in Prussia had been in the family since 1155—a date that must have boggled a jury in a state settled by white men only eighty years earlier. Unfortunately, von Waldru added, his entire distinguished family had perished in the Great War.

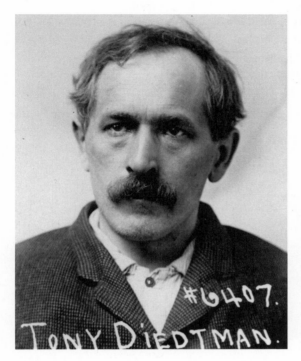

Figure 23. It took two trials to convict Helena beer hall swamper Tony Diedtman of sedition. He was sentenced to ten to twenty years in prison, but the state Supreme Court reversed his conviction twenty-two months later. Montana Historical Society.

Prosecutor Loble's job (other than to keep a straight face) was to convince the jury that this man's evidence was worth believing, for there were no other witnesses to the remarks. His job became even harder when it developed that von Waldru had torn up the notes he had made, and relied on typewritten "transcripts" he had made later.

Von Waldru testified that his investigative method had been fairly straightforward. On a tip from a federal immigration inspector, he had gone out to Clancy to talk, as one loyal German to another, to a man named Charles Zastrow, who gave him a list of more than one hundred other "loyal" Germans in the Helena area. That had led him to some of the German saloons. His MO, under the alias Charles Stone, was to stand around and listen to incriminating conversations and to engage those involved in further discussions.

As there was no other direct evidence of Diedtman's disloyalty, other than perhaps an Iron Cross ring he wore, most of the evidence went to the character of the defendant and the bona fides of the star witness. Loble did what he could to cast doubt on Diedtman's loyalty, getting him to admit that he thought the United States wrong for shipping arms and ammunition to the

Allies, and that he believed that some of the reports about German atrocities in Belgium were false. To bolster von Waldru, Loble emphasized that he had been checked out by the Justice Department and the immigration service.

Judge Smith, Diedtman's lawyer, hammered at von Waldru's credibility. In his closing argument, he pulled out the long guns, or, as the *Independent* reported "viciously attacked the state's chief witness, heaping upon him abuse and villification [sic], characterizing him as a Hun, a spy, an informer, and even asserting that . . . he was working here in the interests of the German government and had deceived federal, state, and county officials."[19]

Von Waldru was simply unbelievable, Smith declared: "Are our courts to be trifled with and our juries fooled by the high state of public feeling in this time of war? Why, you wouldn't convict a dog of stealing a bone on such evidence as this!"

Smith reminded the jurors of their duty. Von Waldru was counting, he said, on a jury not having the guts to render a verdict of not guilty in the face of public opinion. "I would like to be able to say to our boys, if they come back," Smith added, "that we not only supported them in the trenches but have kept the Constitution for them inviolate."[20]

Loble, too, appealed to the juror's patriotism, asking them to help "uproot the insidious German activities in this country." Upon their heads, he told the jurymen, rested the question of whether sedition in this county would go unpunished. The Hun was in the room, he said. "As our boys went away to war they need not have waited to reach Germany to see the Iron Cross—they could have looked at the hand of some fat German bartender over the curtain of some saloon . . ."

After more than twenty-four hours of deliberations, foreman J. M. Brandt told Judge Lee Word that the jury was hung. The *Independent's* page-one headline read, "Diedtman Jury Unable to Agree, Fired."[21] The newspaper's account of the jury deliberations was typically incendiary. The two factions for and against acquittal had almost come to blows over von Waldru's credibility, the *Independent* reported. Under the subhead "Pidgeon Swallows Smith's Pills," juror E. G. Pidgeon, a railroad agent, was reportedly greatly impressed by Smith's arguments that von Waldru was a German spy. Under the subhead "Verdict Disappointing," the *Independent* stated, "The responsibility for the failure of the jury to reach a verdict is placed by several jurors upon Juror [W. H.] West, whose strenuous and aggressive campaign [succeeded in putting together seven votes for acquittal].

And under the subhead "Lightweight Americanism," the *Independent* related how West and another juror had told fellow panel members they had heard worse sedition than what Diedtman had said but had not reported it. While identifying jurors by name and address was a common practice, implying that they were unpatriotic during a period of jumpy vigilantism and hair-trigger arrests for sedition seemed very close to either an invitation to a necktie party or at least a visit from the sheriff.

To top it off, in an editorial the same day, titled "A Streak of Yellow," Campbell (who had once been convicted of contempt of court for publishing information on a defendant's criminal background that was not part of the trial record[22]) attacked defense counsel Smith. He assailed "men who consciously or unconsciously serve the German kaiser—men who are un-American, selfish, political soldiers of fortune and bankrupts seeking to regain their financial prestige by doing service for the pro-Germans."[23]

Smith objected strenuously to the *Independent's* articles on the hung jury, arguing that they "were published with the object of intimidating jurors (of this and future trials) so that they would not dare vote for acquittal."[24] Evidently, Campbell received no admonition. Loble opted for an immediate retrial.

Much the same evidence was presented at Diedtman's second trial. Four days later, the case went to a new jury. Smith again lambasted von Waldru, asking the jury, "Are you going to convict this man, even if he were born in Germany, on the testimony of a man . . . who still owes allegiance to those hell-hounds over there?" Loble lobbed the patriot card. Recalling schoolmates in the war, he said, "I can see them in their dugouts, waiting with gas masks on, to go over the top into No Man's Land to almost certain death, and I wonder if they are going over the top for the seditionists and others like this defendant. . . . The kaiser laughs because we have spent two weeks time and $1,500 trying to convict one seditionist and we haven't been able to do it yet."[25]

After eighteen hours, the second jury returned a verdict of guilty—with a recommendation of leniency. Judge Word ignored them. He sentenced the beer hall swamper to the maximum term of ten to twenty years. At the sentencing hearing on July 31, attended by many state and county officials, Judge Word told the defendant, "At a time when the United States was at war with Germany and needed the support of every loyal citizen, you saw fit to belittle your own country and praise its enemies."[26]

Diedtman entered prison the same day and was assigned to the bakery. The news he received twenty-two months later, on May 8, 1920, must have made him want to bake a giant celebration cake: The state Supreme Court, in a unanimous opinion, had reversed his conviction. Judge Word had committed reversible error in the examination of jurors, during the trial and in the instructions to the jurors, the high court said.[27]

The high court scored Judge Word in particular on the handling of von Waldru's testimony. Letting in evidence that he had been cleared by the Justice Department before his character was even in issue "violated the most elementary rules of the law of evidence." In a case where jurors had to rely on von Waldru's word alone that the seditious words were spoken, the improperly introduced character evidence undoubtedly influenced the jury to overlook his forgery conviction and other credibility problems. "[I]t would be easily conceivable that a jury of laymen would be impressed profoundly by the favorable findings of the Department of Justice at Washington and the Attorney General, after an investigation into von Waldru's history. . . . [T]he verdict rests largely, if not altogether, upon the support which von Waldru's reputation received from the [improper] hearsay testimony . . ."[28]

Judge Word had also been biased in favor of the prosecution, unduly restricting defense counsel's attempts to cross-examine von Waldru, the court added. This was the defendant's only means of testing the credibility of a "detective employed for hire to ferret out violations of the sedition statute." The errors in this respect, the court said, "are too numerous to be treated separately."[29]

The Supreme Court's opinion was a sharp rebuke to both the prosecution and the judge, but it came too late to forestall other sedition prosecutions in Lewis and Clark County. However, at least one other beer hall defendant benefited. The county attorney dismissed charges against Joe Milch, who received a $3,000 fine and a three to six year prison term but had been out on bail.[30]

It's fair to conclude that prosecutors recognized that Milch's case, as well as those of the other beer hall Germans, may have been fatally infected by Von Waldru's tainted testimony, the only witness testimony in their trials. But none of the other defendants appealed, so the errors attributed to Judge Word may or may not have re-occurred. A different judge had presided over the other trials, which were postponed until 1919 because of the influenza epidemic. Skimpier court and newspaper records of these later cases obscure any thorough examination of the record.

Steck and Lembrecht received one- to three-year sentences. Frank Heil received a one to two year sentence but was placed on probation. John Milch was assessed an $1,800 fine.

Only Leo Reno was still in prison when the Diedtman opinion came down. Like Diedtman, Reno had received a ten to twenty year sentence. The fact he broke out of jail for a few hours before his trial, by sawing a bar in half and sneaking out through the cellar, may have contributed to his long sentence.[31] The saloon cook spent twenty-seven months in Deer Lodge. On April 19, 1921, he was transferred to the state insane asylum at Warm Springs. He died there four days later at age forty, of chronic inflammation of the kidneys.[32] A medical text of the time described his disease as particularly prevalent in middle-aged, male beer-drinkers.[33] ✤

FOURTEEN
The Wine Salesman's Tale

A Closer Look at the State's Sedition Defendants, 1918–1919

AT ABOUT 8:30 A.M. ON MARCH 6, 1918, Ben Kahn sauntered downstairs from his room in the Pollard Hotel in Red Lodge to await breakfast. Kahn, thirty-eight, was a traveling salesman for the Sierra Campo Wine and Brandy Co. in San Francisco. For the past year he had been living in Billings to cover his assigned territory of Montana and Wyoming.

Kahn had grown up in St. Joseph, Missouri, after being brought to the United States as an infant from Russia. He had left home at age seventeen, but now was selling liquor to help support his father, who was in the Old People's Home in St. Paul.[1]

The Pollard was the place to stay in Red Lodge. It was the social and business center of the coal-mining town. Early guests had included such legends as Calamity Jane, Buffalo Bill Cody, and William Jennings Bryan. The proprietor, the eponymous T. F. Pollard, was an influential man in town and the chairman of the county council of defense.[2]

As Kahn stood in the lobby, waiting for his breakfast, he struck up a conversation with Pollard. He griped that Prohibition, set to come soon to the state and nation, would put him and other salesmen out of business.

Perhaps emboldened by seeming agreement from Pollard, Kahn ventured, "Mr. Pollard, this is a rich man's war."

Pollard warned him he could get in trouble for saying things like that.

Kahn turned to the wartime food regulations enacted by the Food Administration under Herbert Hoover. The agency's constant stream of directives and pleas for conservation of foodstuffs was popularly known as Hooverism.

"There's nothing to that," Kahn said. "It's all a big joke."

Pollard got up and walked over toward his office. Kahn followed.

"Well, if you feel that way about it, you must justify the sinking of the *Lusitania*," Pollard countered.

Figure 24. A wine and brandy salesman, Ben Kahn was convicted of sedition and sentenced to seven-and-a-half to twenty years in prison for calling the nation's wartime food regulations a "big joke." The state supreme court affirmed his conviction; he served thirty-four months. Montana Historical Society.

"[The Americans] had no business in that boat," Kahn replied. "They were hauling over munitions and wheat."

That was enough for Pollard. "Anyone who says that is either a pro-German or an IWW or a damn fool," he told the salesman.

Kahn walked out of the hotel and spent the morning visiting saloon-keepers on business. By lunchtime, the sheriff had tracked him down and arrested him for sedition.[3]

In a town where super-patriotism reigned by force and fear, where Finnish IWW's had been savagely attacked by the local Liberty Committee, any intimation of "pro-German" sentiment was bound to get one into trouble. Loyalty became the sine qua non.

In his trial one month later, Kahn tried to explain that what he had said wasn't meant to be disloyal or incite or inflame anyone to resisting lawful authority.

"I did tell Mr. Pollard that Hooverism was a joke," Kahn explained. " But I meant that in large cities rich people and many others were not living up to it. . . . I didn't intend to criticize the Hoover rules . . . and I didn't think Mr. Pollard would stop following the Hoover rules because of what I said."[4]

The trial transcript is filled with protestations of Kahn's loyalty. The U.S. Commissioner in Billings told how Kahn had donated a couple of cases of wine to the soldiers leaving for the war, and had bought them cigars and cigarettes. The lady who ran the Billings hotel where Kahn stayed testified he pledged $5 a month for War Savings and Thrift Stamps. A newspaperman in Billings talked about how Kahn had planned a benefit boxing match for the troops.[5]

Even Judge A. C. Spencer, a political conservative, was skeptical of the charges—but only because he didn't think the law was strong enough. "The law is a disappointment," he said. "I don't think that the testimony in this case is sufficient to justify a conviction [except possibly] on the third count [of inciting or inflaming resistance to a federal authority, in this case the Food Administration], and I am also frank to admit to you that if he is guilty at all that you have got to stretch this language to the limit to cover it."[6] He instructed the jury that they could only find Kahn guilty of that count.[7]

The jury was not troubled; it promptly found Kahn guilty. Judge Spencer sentenced Kahn to seven-and-a-half to twenty years at hard labor. He served thirty-four months, one of the longest times of the state's sedition prisoners. He played in the prison band, a favorite project of Warden Conley's.[8] His appeal, the first heard by the Montana Supreme Court, was turned down on May 20, 1919.[9]

The court rejected the argument that only the federal government could pass a sedition law. It dismissed the inchoate notion that the First Amendment controlled state actions against speech. And it agreed with the high court's recent unanimous rulings affirming sedition convictions of wartime dissenters, including that of Socialist Eugene V. Debs. The court quoted Justice Oliver Wendell Holmes Jr.: "When a nation is at war many things that might be said in time of peace are such a hindrance to its effort that their utterances will not be endured as long as men fight, and that no court could regard them as protected by any constitutional right."[10] Reviewing even the evidence relating to the other counts of Kahn's indictment, which the trial judge had thrown out, the court decided Kahn had had a fair and impartial trial.[11]

Mob Hysteria

Montana's sedition cases arose in an atmosphere of hysteria and inflamed passions, where "justice" was meted out swiftly and sometimes just one step ahead of the mob. Take the case of H. F. "Harry" Lucas, forty-four. He had first arrived in Butte when he was twenty, in 1894, then left to fight in the Spanish-American War, and served four years in the Army. After his discharge, he worked for the government. When America entered World War I, he tried to enlist but was turned down as physically unfit.

By the fall of 1917, Lucas was a widower with two daughters in school in Butte. Drink was clearly taking its toll. In January of 1918, he was arrested for vagrancy in Butte, a common charge for stumbling drunks.

On April Fools Day in 1918, Harry Lucas left Wise River, where he was working as a cook at a lumber camp. As did many fellow camp workers, he would come into Butte every once in a while to hit the saloons and visit houses of prostitution.

In Crowley's Saloon at 39 East Broadway, three city firemen had just ended their shift at the Quartz Street station. One of them remarked that Germany would "not have such an easy mark" now that the U.S. had gotten into the war. The United States was just beginning to station troops in front-line positions in France.

The men heard a voice behind them. It was Lucas—and he was drunk. "Fuck the bloody country. Fuck the flag. I am an IWW and I am proud of it," Lucas exclaimed, according to the firemen.

The trio grabbed Lucas, hustled him out of the saloon and down the street to city hall, a block and a half away. There he was arrested for sedition and thrown in the city jail. He could not make bail.

Nine months later, on December 30, 1918, Lucas' sedition case finally came to trial. The war had ended six weeks earlier with the Armistice. The firemen testified about their encounter with the drunken cook. "He was fucking everything," according to one of them, whose testimony was read to the court because he was on active duty in the army.

Lucas said he didn't remember making the statements. He had been drinking heavily and he didn't recall what had occurred until he awoke in the city jail. He was "never in the habit of saying anything of that kind," he insisted. But full of drink, he allowed, he was "liable to say anything." "Never been a Wobbly," he declared. And not a foreigner either; born in Cincinnati. Both his parents hailed from Kentucky. Daughters were in school. As far as he could recall, what he *did* say was that the country that was good enough to live in was good enough to fight for, and that the man who would not fight for his country ought not to have anything to say about it.

Lucas' trial took less than a day, perhaps just a morning. The jury declared him guilty. On December 31, 1918, the day after his conviction, Prohibition officially took effect. Ultimately, eight other men in Silver Bow County would be charged with sedition.[12] But only one of them would be found guilty and sentenced to prison—the worst batting average for any county in the state, yet not too surprising considering the radical political climate in Butte.

On January 11, 1919, District Court Judge John V. Dwyer sentenced Lucas to five to fifteen years at hard labor at the state penitentiary. He was immediately transported to Deer Lodge and began serving his sentence the next day. Lucas joined thirty-four other persons in prison for violating the state sedition law. By the time he was paroled on July 24, 1921, he was one of the last Montana sedition prisoners remaining in prison. He had served more than thirty months—not counting the nine months he may have been in jail awaiting trial—for his intemperate, drunken outburst. At least fifteen of the men convicted of sedition in Montana were in a saloon when they allegedly made the off-hand remarks that sent them to prison.

Tightening the Noose

Several sedition prisoners were nearly lynched by "patriotic" mobs. For example, Earnest V. Starr of Forsyth was, in the words of the judge who sentenced him, "waited on by [his] neighbors and given an opportunity to demonstrate [his] loyalty" in March 1918.[13]

Told to kiss an American flag, Starr refused. "What is this thing anyway, nothing but a piece of cotton with a little paint on it and some little marks in the corner there. I will not kiss that thing, it might have microbes on it."[14]

Starr, a forty-eight–year-old farmer born in Ohio, was found guilty of sedition in September. In imposing the maximum sentence of ten to twenty years, plus a $500 fine, Judge George P. Jones (who had replaced Judge Charles Crum, impeached by the legislature) waxed patriotic: "That 'piece of red, white, and blue' bunting means five thousand years of struggle upwards. . . . It is the century plant of human hopes in bloom . . . that 'combination of colors' is the hope of the world today. . . . It may have microbes on it but a thousand times more dangerous are the microbes that live under it—the microbes of IWWism, of anarchy, of pro-Germanism, of disloyalty, of sedition."[15]

In Billings, Herman Bausch, a well-to-do farmer who had immigrated from Germany nineteen years earlier, was accosted by the city's "third-degree committee" for his failure to buy Liberty Bonds or aid the Red Cross. Bausch allegedly remarked, "I don't care anything for the Red, White and Blue," and "I would rather see Germany win than France [or] England." He was hustled into the police station on the night of April 18, 1918. After a brief trial, the judge sentenced him to four to eight years.[16]

The *Billings Gazette* congratulated the committee for its "determination" and restraint in not stringing him up to a telephone pole—the nationally publicized lynching of Robert Prager, the "pro-German" in Collinsville, Illinois, having just occurred. "When one considers the real sacrifices true blue Americans are making both in blood and wealth, it is galling indeed to have one who has benefited to such a degree absolutely decline to come to the rescue with a single dollar."[17]

Louis Effinger, a wealthy German rancher in the Rattlesnake valley near Missoula, nearly met mob justice. He allegedly exclaimed to a fellow farmer, upon seeing the headlines in the evening paper regarding the Germans breaking through the British line and taking twenty-five thousand prisoners, "I hope the [Germans] get every sonofabitching one of them." The farmer punched him in the jaw and drew a crowd. A patrolman hustled Effinger to jail, saving him from bystanders who had rushed to a nearby hardware store for a rope.[18] He was convicted of sedition and fined $800.[19]

On the very same day in Bozeman, it was a sheriff's punch that evidently *saved* a barber accused of sedition from a lynch mob. Julius Heuer had allegedly declared in the Hermitage Saloon that, "I hope the Germans will advance each day as much as they have."[20] After hustling him to the county jail for protection, Sheriff Del Gray faced down an angry crowd of about two hundred men.[21]

A newspaper account has the sheriff in his nightclothes, with "biceps . . . like those of a gladiator" telling the crowd to go home:

"You cannot have Heuer, boys," said Gray quietly.
    "Then we will put you out of the way and take him," said the mob leader, as he aimed a blow at the officer.
    The sheriff blocked the blow and stepping to the side, drove his

farmer fist full at the point of the jaw of his assailant. The man went down in a lump, and took no further interest in the proceedings.[22]

The mob directed its fury toward the saloon where Heuer had allegedly made his remarks Two days later, the city council revoked the license of the German owner and closed his establishment permanently, as detrimental to the peace of Bozeman.[23] Heuer was acquitted after a daylong trial that attracted more people than had two recent murder trials. Whole classes of schoolchildren were excused from classes to attend his trial.[24]

Wobblies and Nonpartisans

While fear of the IWW had led to the enactment of the state sedition law, only a dozen or so Wobblies may have been ensnared in the sedition net. Those who were publicly identified in court documents or news accounts as Wobblies tended to be clustered in western Montana—where IWW membership and activities in the state were centered.

So did those who merely voiced pro-IWW sentiments, such as Thomas Burans, sixty-two, an illiterate farmer near Missoula "with a face that would crack a mirror."[25] Burans allegedly told a draft registrant at a saloon, "Get out of the country and the jurisdiction of the draft board. Don't enlist. They are only tin soldiers anyway and they are persecuting the IWW." He was found guilty by a jury that included the Rev. John N. Maclean, the Presbyterian minister later made famous by his son, Norman Maclean, in *A River Runs Through It*.[26]

Wobbly sedition defendants were slightly older on average than the general sedition prisoner population (forty-seven, compared to forty-five). More were convicted and handed prison sentences (55 percent compared to 42 percent of all sedition defendants), and served longer sentences. However, all five of the sedition convictions overturned by the state supreme court were of men associated with radical dissident groups: Two IWW members, an NPL organizer and two socialists.

Like Harry Lucas, John A. "Jack" Griffith was arrested and convicted for making a foul-mouthed remark in a saloon. Griffith, a forty-seven–year-old laborer and IWW organizer, had just come into Billings from Livingston, where he had worked on a ranch for thirty-seven days. He was on his way to the North Dakota harvest. On the morning of July 8, Griffith and a sidekick walked in to the Blue Front Saloon. In a conversation related at trial

by the proprietor, L. W. Lamb, Griffith allegedly told him he was an officer in the IWW, "and I am proud of that. I am not like the rest of the
IWWs. If an officer would stop me, I would show him my card. I would
not . . . swallow it or throw it away."

The conversation turned to the trial of the IWW leaders in Chicago.

"What do you think of the trial . . . ?" Griffith asked Lamb.

"I don't know," Lamb replied.

"I can tell you," Griffith said. "We are going to give this God-damned
government a good fucking," Griffith allegedly said.

To check up on Griffith and his pal, Lamb testified, he supplied a
friend of his with an old IWW card lying under the counter and asked
him to get acquainted with Griffith. The card trick worked; the three men
had a few beers, bought some more bottles and took them to the Star
rooming house where the two visitors were staying. There, Lamb's friend
testified, Griffith showed him IWW literature and the men discussed the
miserable working conditions in the lumber camps in Washington.
Griffith repeated his remark about the Chicago trial (except the adjective
modifying "government" became "cock-sucking," and it was this language
that was used in the charges against Griffith).

As a job delegate, Griffith was defended by one of the IWW's best
lawyers—George W. Vanderveer. An 1896 graduate of Stanford University,
Vanderveer had gained renown for his defense of seventy-four IWWs in
Everett, Washington, following the *Verona* massacre in November 1916, and
of the IWW leaders in Chicago. In his closing argument, Vanderveer argued
that nothing Griffith had said was calculated to bring the U.S. form of government or its Constitution "into contempt, contumely, scorn or disrepute."[27] Therefore, he argued, Griffith had not violated the sedition statute.

For the jury, however, it was enough that he had said the slurring and
contemptuous words. They found Griffith guilty on December 7, 1918.
Judge A. C. Spencer sentenced him to eight to sixteen years.

Vanderveer appealed his client's conviction to the state supreme court.
Atty. Gen. Sam Ford conceded that Griffith would not have been prosecuted had he used "chaste English." On September 22, 1919, the five-man state
high court unanimously reversed Griffith's conviction. Justice Holloway did
not repeat Griffith's earthy remark, calling it "too vile and vulgar."
Nonetheless, said Holloway, "it was never the intent of the lawmakers to
establish rigorous censorship over the common conversation of individuals

or to require the citizen to refine his speech to conform to the standard of belles-lettres."

Griffith's pungent comment, the high court said, violated no law. It "doesn't even rise to the dignity of criticism" and was merely the expression of an opinion as to the outcome of a trial fifteen hundred miles away. "It does not attack our form of government."[28] Nine days later Griffith was a free man.

The Supreme Court also reversed the conviction of IWW organizer Albert Brooks, because of juror prejudice. Brooks, twenty-nine, was arrested near Dillon after making a street-corner speech criticizing the United States' participation in the war. He had distributed the IWW anti-war pamphlet titled "War and the Workers."[29] What made matters worse was that when sheriff's deputies went to the cabin where Brooks was living, they found an unusual amount of firepower: "15 pounds of military powder, 3,000 primers, 500 military bullets, 160 loaded rifle cartridges and 450 revolver cartridges," according to the *Anaconda Standard.*[30]

Brooks, who had an American flag tattooed on his right arm, was found guilty of sedition and sentenced to seven to fifteen years in prison.[31] Almost two years later, the state supreme court unanimously reversed his conviction. Unlike Griffith's case, the court found no problem with the sedition evidence, the IWW pamphlet. Even though it had been published in 1911, well before America entered the war, "it does contain some statements the natural and probable effect of which would be to obstruct the draft . . ." the court wrote, quoting this passage: "Let those who own the country do the fighting! Put the wealthiest in the front ranks; the middle class next; follow these with judges, lawyers, preachers, and politicians. Let the workers remain at home and enjoy what they produce . . ."[32]

Under the recent guidance provided by the U.S. Supreme Court in the first World War I speech cases, the Montana justices applied the so-called "bad tendency" test—whether a statement had even some remote tendency toward sedition—without taking into account the immediacy of the threat.

The reversible error committed by the trial judge had been in seating a juror who "entertained a bitter prejudice against the [IWW]."[33] The juror had testified that he would require less evidence to convict Brooks than if he were not an IWW. Therefore, his assertion that he would remain impartial was worthless. To overlook such an error even with sufficient evidence to find Brooks guilty "would destroy every right guaranteed by the

Constitution, lead to anarchy and defeat the very purpose for which courts are created, viz: to administer justice according to law, said the court."[34]

Brooks was never retried. According to an affidavit filed by his attorney, articles in at least three newspapers about Brooks and his IWW affiliation had created substantial prejudice. The stories had caused many persons in the community to make statements "to the effect that members of said organization were not entitled to a fair trial, should be taken out without trial and shot . . . accompanied by epithets of hatred and condemnation." Even if an unprejudiced jury could be found, its members would feel intimidated by the hostile demeanor of trial spectators and by the fear of being injured in their business should they acquit Brooks.[35]

Whether prosecutors found Brooks' affidavit persuasive or whether it was the changing temper of the times by 1920 will never be known. But the lawyer had accurately described the atmosphere that prevailed before and during many, if not most, of the state's sedition trials.

One sedition defendant who certainly experienced more than his share of community hatred was Mickey McGlynn, the young NPL recruiter whose beating in Miles City had led to "Ford's burlesque" at the county courthouse.[36] He was tried for sedition in neighboring Carter County, found guilty and fined $500.[37] But in June 1921, the state supreme court reversed his conviction. In the charges against him, the prosecutor had in effect put words in McGlynn's mouth, using brackets to add seditious meaning to what McGlynn actually said. For example, McGlynn was charged with having said, "I suppose you heard about those Belgian kids that were sent to this country. The Germans never done that [meaning that the injuries and mutilations received by the Belgian children were not caused by the German soldiers] . . . it was done in Chicago [meaning that the injuries received by the Belgian children were caused . . . in factories in the city of Chicago by American citizens for the purpose of creating false and untrue sentiment and feeling among the people of the United States]."

"It is elementary," the high court said, "that the ultimate facts constituting the crime, and not conclusions, must be stated. . . ."[38]

The court added another interesting observation: The circumstances under which the remarks were made should have been set forth, "as it is obvious, if uttered in private conversation to a single person, it would have a radically different complexion than if spoken from a public platform or disseminated through . . . written articles."[39]

The court's opinion could have applied to almost all of the sedition cases brought in Montana. In dozens of charges in sedition cases, prosecutors added similar inferences in brackets. And in most sedition cases, the seditious utterances had been made in private conversations. But of course it was too late for appeals, for by then, all but five of the sedition prisoners had been paroled.

German Homesteaders

While men like Griffith, Brooks, and McGlynn encountered prejudice because of their radical beliefs, others suffered because of their enemy ancestry. A typical case was that of Herman Rohde. A seventy-four–year-old rancher near Miles City, Rohde had emigrated from Pomerania in northern Germany in 1893 and had become a naturalized citizen in 1898.[40]

An eleven-year veteran of the German army, and a sergeant in the German cavalry in the Franco-Prussian War of 1870–1871, Rohde was a fan of German military tactics. He used his own experiences in France to back up his opinions—in German—in beer-and-politics sessions with other German immigrants at the cribbage tables in Miles City saloons. Despite his having lived in the United States for twenty-five years, Rohde's command of English was so limited that the court appointed two interpreters for him at the trial.[41]

Rohde was portrayed in newspaper accounts as obtuse, naïve, arrogant, proud of his ancestry and language, and eager to help the enemy. According to the *Miles City Daily Star*, Rohde smiled as witnesses reported barroom conversations in which he predicted German success in the war.[42] The chief prosecution witness, a local plumber, said that when he asked Rohde if he would help the kaiser whip the United States, the farmer had answered, "Ja! Ja!"[43] Should the German army invade the United States, the same witness testified, "he would have no fear of it nor would any true German, as all they would have to do is give certain signs, which would convince the invaders that they were all right." In reference to his broken English, Rohde reportedly declared at trial, "I did not want to speak English, as German will be the universal language some day."

The prosecutor, too, played on the jury's patriotism, in an atmosphere in which, the *Star* reported, "Spectators could scarcely hide their emotions." County Attorney Frank Hunter criticized Defense Attorney Sharpless Walker's closing argument to the jury, saying, "Walker, if you will write out that address which you made to the jury and mail a copy to the kaiser, I will guarantee that he will send over two iron crosses, one for you and one for Rohde."[44]

The jury was out thirty-five minutes—and may have taken as few as twelve, according to the *Star*, to reach a guilty verdict. In an editorial the same day, editor Joseph Scanlon jumped on Rohde's testimony about "certain signs," which of course ignited already impassioned fears:

[T]o subject all nations to his iron will . . . [the kaiser] has subtly planted thousands of his servile subjects all over the earth. They lie like snakes in the grass stealthily watching their chance. They do not, like the brave rattlesnake, give the unintended intruder a warning that he may take heed to his steps, but silently watch like a spider for the victim to be helplessly enmeshed in their net and then pounce on him.

They work and plan in secret ways and wait for a signal which shall mean the surrender of their country to the enemy who would murder and enslave their fellow countrymen, mutilate and outrage their women and make them beasts of burden and propagation, crucify their soldiers, bayonet their babies, bomb their wounded, sink their hospital ships, steal their possessions, and lay tribute of billions on their labor forever.[45]

Only Rohde's age may have saved him from a more severe sentence; as it was, Judge Word handed the elderly farmer with four children a four to eight year prison sentence. Rohde ended up serving thirty-four months in Deer Lodge. Along with Ben Kahn's, it was one of the longest prison times for any of the Montana sedition prisoners.

A neighboring rancher, Martin Wehinger, born in Austria, received three to six years for allegedly expressing his opinion to some freighters passing through that "[W]e had no business sticking our nose in there and we should get licked for doing so" and that "one German soldier could kill five or six American soldiers without any trouble, because we didn't have any experience and were not trained and didn't know anything about war and we ought to get licked."[46]

Born in 1860, Wehinger had followed his older brother Michael to the United States and landed in Miles City in 1883. In his prime he himself

Figure 25. Intrigued by freighter Martin Wehinger's story of killing a bear with an axe, pioneer photographer L. A. Huffman took this studio portrait of him in the 1890s. Wehinger died, toothless, in 1920, four months after his release from prison. L. A. Huffman, Courtesy of Coffrin's Old West Gallery, Bozeman, Montana.

Figure 26. Fred Rodewald and his bride, Pearl, on their wedding day in 1903. After Fred was released from prison in 1920, the family moved to Minnesota, where Fred farmed until his death in 1960. Courtesy of Phyllis Rolf.

was a freighter, a man who handled wagon trains with long strings of horses. He once told the photographer L. A. Huffman that he had had to use an ax to kill a bear pawing through his wagon.

"'Luckl for me dot I get one good chop in de side py his head vitch is kinder stunted hem til I give him two more vitch preak his pack close to der heat by his neck,'" Huffman quoted him in his diary. "'Zay! py got tammit, if I ever get some hell of a times dese is ven I round up dose horses unt try to hitch oop again . . . '"[47]

Huffman's studio portrait shows a muscular man with a firm set to his jaw and enormous hands. In time, as the wagon train business gave way to the railroads, Martin became a farmer and homesteaded land near his brother. He never married.

Wehinger was released from prison just before Christmas in 1919. After serving 18 months, his teeth were all gone. He died four months later, not

Figure 27. Martin Wehinger emigrated from Austria to Miles City in 1883. He worked as a freighter before joining his brother in ranching. He was handed a three- to six-year sentence for sedition for saying "we had no business sticking our nose in [the war] and we should get licked for doing so." Montana Historical Society.

Figure 28. Fred Rodewald, trained as a carpenter in Germany, homesteaded 320 acres near Sumatra in Rosebud County. When he went to prison for two to five years for sedition, he left behind his pregnant wife and eight children. Montana Historical Society.

yet sixty, on April 12, 1920. The man who once killed a bear with an ax died a toothless felon for having spoken his mind.

Fred Rodewald had eight children and a ninth on the way when he was sent to prison. Born in Germany and trained there as a carpenter, Rodewald had immigrated at the turn of the century. He married his wife, Pearl, in Charter Oak, Iowa, in 1903. They farmed and raised a "first family" of five children there before heading west in 1912 to homestead 320 acres north of Sumatra, in Rosebud County. On April 23, 1918, Rodewald was accused of having said, according to the court record, "in substance as follows: that we (meaning the people and citizens of the United States) would have hard times unless the kaiser didn't get over here and rule this country."[48]

For that, Rodewald received two to five years in Deer Lodge, leaving his pregnant wife and a shack full of children to manage the homestead in one of the worst drought years in living memory. Ethel, the ninth child, was born while her father toiled in Deer Lodge as a carpenter. After he walked out of prison in April 1920, Rodewald sold the homestead and moved his family to Minnesota to farm, where Raymond, their last child, was born. Rodewald lived until 1960, almost to age eighty-five. Said Phyllis Rolf of Atwater, Minnesota, a granddaughter, "They just put that all behind them when they moved here, and no one ever spoke about it." Raymond Rodewald died on October 5, 2004, according to his family. If he ever knew of his father's imprisonment, he never spoke of it.

Theodore Klippstein, farming with his wife (pregnant with a seventh child) in Richland County near the Missouri River, also got crossways with the law. Born in Pomerania, Germany, in 1878, he had arrived in Ellis Island on the steamship *Polynesia* with his parents, five siblings, and one piece of luggage. Although he was almost forty on Registration Day— September 12, 1918—Klippstein had recently been made eligible for the draft. But he wasn't happy about it. At the Lone Ridge Schoolhouse where the registration was taking place, Klippstein allegedly said, "It is a wonder our government didn't send us some papers before we got in the war so we could have had something to say about it and then we wouldn't have had war. We have no business to be in war as the people don't want it; it was only the officials we sent to Washington that got us in war; only the big moneyed men [who] wanted war."[49]

That emotional outburst earned him four to ten years in prison, of which he served more than twenty-five months. Paroled, Klippstein took his family to Portland, Oregon, where he worked for many years as a laborer for the electric company. He died there in 1966 at the age of eighty-seven.

Unsympathetic Defendants

Further south in Custer County, stockman William K. Smith and his wife, Janet, did not have German ancestry, but if anything, they came across as even more unsympathetic.[50] W. K., forty-nine, originally from Ohio, was a well-known rancher in the Moorhead area, not far from the Wyoming line in what is now Powder River County. He had homesteaded 320 acres a dozen miles west of Moorhead and later purchased a like amount. He had three hundred head of cattle, about thirty-five horses, and "a full set of machinery and implements."[51]

Smith and his second wife, Janet, forty-two, from Iowa, also ran the post office in the outpost of Sayle, more than 130 miles south of Miles City. It was there, witnesses said, that the couple sounded off about the war and refused to contribute to the war effort. The isolated Smiths may not have realized that the shadow of fear darkened even one of the most remote settlements in the country.

After being relieved of the postmaster's job (an action taken immediately after the charges against them were quietly filed on May 22), the Smiths gathered a few friends and rode up to Miles City to see if they could settle the matter. But the matter was far beyond palavering. On the same day, the county's first sedition trial had started. The Smiths were arrested and jailed. Their friends posted $5,000 bail bonds but withdrew the bonds less than a week later. The couple was once more thrown into jail.

The Smiths' trials in Miles City in mid-October provided the capstone for a remarkable season of sedition hunting in Custer County. Not only the trials themselves, but also the gavel-to-gavel coverage they received in the *Miles City Daily Star* and the two weeklies in town had kept the town on edge. Before the bar of justice had come a man and woman with few, if any, redeeming qualities—at least in the eyes of a wartime Montana community. The statements and actions attributed to them sound hard-bitten and distrustful, the kind made by tough, taciturn, misanthropic loners—in other words, the kind of people that might be expected to survive in the desolate buttes and coulees of southeast Montana. But in 1918, what was skeptical became unpatriotic, what was thrifty became miserly, what was opinion became sedition.

One witness against W. K. testified that the stockman said to him, "President Wilson got $60 a head for American soldiers delivered to France," and that he "would not be surprised to see a revolution and would take his gun and help the revolt when it occurred." Another witness said he grumbled that this was the worst government in the world and "we would be better off under German rule."

When he heard that a delegation of patriots from Powderville would call on him to escort him to a Red Cross meeting, the dour Scotsman allegedly said he would see that an undertaker was required. When Smith heard of a telegram announcing the death of a local boy in a training camp, said a third witness, he called out from bed, "Hell, what do you expect? That's what you sent him away for, to get slaughtered." Smith had even hoped the Germans would cut his own soldier son, Jim, "square in two in the middle," another witness swore.

Inexplicably, Smith's lawyer, Sharpless Walker, presented no rebuttal evidence other than putting Smith on the stand to deny making the alleged statements. He did not even make a closing argument to the jury. The prosecutor asked for the maximum punishment—ten to twenty years and a $20,000 fine. Just twenty-three minutes after the jury room door had swung shut, the jury summoned the bailiff. The verdict, as the *Star* noted, "was never in doubt."

The scene in Janet Smith's trial the next day "was one of the most gripping things ever staged here," the *Star* noted. It described the defendant as "a woman well along in age, gray faced, her iron visage determinedly set, defiant under examination by counsel . . ." Later in the trial she was described as "obviously ill at ease, her face white and set, wary to the utmost," who "did not remember most of the conversations alleged to have been made by her."

If her husband came off as a hard-boiled grouch, Janet Smith came off as a hard-boiled shrew. Witnesses said she "advocated turning the stock into the crops to prevent helping the government" and "killing off all cripples, insane, and convicts in order to save food instead of making all the food restrictions." The Red Cross she declared to be a "fake," and "while she didn't mind helping the Belgians with the relief work, the trouble was that the damned soldiers would get it." She allegedly sent back War Savings Stamps supplied by the Post Office Department.

At least defense counsel Walker presented a more vigorous defense, impeaching the credibility of one key witness. Still, one rebuttal witness he called (a man who had worked at the Smith ranch and who himself was convicted of sedition later that week[52]) "effectively clinched the case for the state," as the *Star* reporter observed, when he declared "there was no liberty in a state which was at war." The all-male jury did its duty and found Janet Smith guilty of sedition after deliberating from 9:00 to 9:50 p.m.

Attorney Walker may have rued his more vigorous defense of Janet Smith. A witness whom he had criticized attacked him after court, striking him twice in the face before they retired to the corner saloon to repair what he called "the scars of battle."

The denouement of the Miles City trials came with the sentencing of the Smiths. Janet, "leaning on the arm of her counsel . . . buried her face in her handkerchief, completely unnerved." Judge Taylor handed her a sentence of five to ten years for "one of the most serious offenses which can be perpetrated at this time."

"Shaken with sobs, the woman was taken in charge by the sheriff and escorted back to her cell," the *Star* observed.

W. K.'s sentencing the next day, October 19, prompted a wrathful sermon from Judge A. C. Spencer of Billings. It was "an address," *Star* editor Joseph Scanlon gushed, "the like of which has rarely been heard in Custer County and will live long in the minds of the fortunate ones who heard it."[53]

"If I could follow the dictates of my own judgement," thundered the judge, "I would either sentence you to a term in the state prison for your natural life, or I would order you banished entirely from the country. . . . I would send you straight to Germany, where you would flourish and glory among the savages and barbarous people the Germans have shown themselves to be."[54]

Referring to the testimony that Smith wished his own son would be killed in the war, the judge told him, "You are inhuman. You are as near a human brute as I have seen. You have violated every provision of the sedition laws . . . openly, flagrantly, boastfully, in a spirit of braggadocio . . ."

Saying he could find not "one single extenuating circumstance," Judge Spencer sentenced Smith, "pale but composed," to the maximum: ten to twenty years in Deer Lodge, as well as the maximum $20,000 fine (which was satisfied with a sheriff's sale of half a quarter-section, eighty acres, of Smith's land).

The Smiths ultimately spent about two years as Warden Conley's guests—he working as a weaver, she one of only two women incarcerated at Deer Lodge at the time.[55] Both were paroled in late 1920. ✦

FIFTEEN
A Contest of Wills

The Sedition Trials of Butte's Socialist Editors, 1919

SHORTLY AFTER MIDNIGHT ON SEPTEMBER 15, 1918, the headlights of a high-powered automobile knifed through the night as the vehicle sped north from Butte over the Continental Divide at Elk Park Pass. It was heading for the Boulder River, thence north along Prickly Pear Creek. The waxing gibbous moon had already set. On one side of the back seat sat Lewis and Clark County Sheriff Ed Majors; to the other, one of Majors' deputies. Wedged between them sat a large, stocky man, wearing hand-cuffs. William F. Dunn, chief editorial writer for the *Butte Daily Bulletin*, was on his way to Helena to stand trial for sedition.[1]

Of all the persons charged with sedition in Montana, Dunn was the biggest fish. Unsophisticated men had been prosecuted and convicted for blurting out their thoughts in the Helena beer hall cases and in most of the other cases in the state. The sedition case against journalist Dunn (and a parallel case against an associate) stood on a different plane. Their trials were still a crude swipe by the dominant political faction against its ene-mies, but the defendants were well educated and were seen by prosecutors, at least in class terms, as equals. Here, freedom of the press was on trial, as well as the freedom of political dissent.

The sedition cases against Dunn and Bruce Smith (who was tried sep-arately and played a lesser role) assumed greater importance because of the connections to high state officials such as Gov. Sam Stewart and the high-powered legal talent brought to bear. Consequently, the trials received widespread publicity, particularly from the super-patriotic Will Campbell, editor of the *Helena Independent* and an influential member of the power-ful Montana Council of Defense. Campbell was so personally involved in the sedition case against Dunn that it became a contest of wills between two very strong-minded newspapermen with diametrically opposite views.

There were important political ramifications. The *Butte Daily Bulletin*, socialist and pro-labor, was a thorn in the side of the ruling conservatives and the Anaconda Copper Mining Company, the state's dominant economic and political force. The trials and convictions of Dunn and Smith were retribution for their leftist politics and for Dunn's defiance of these powerful forces. In the end, their cases may also have contributed to the bitter gubernatorial campaign of 1920, when both major party candidates were Progressives. One of those, Burton K. Wheeler, who also owned shares in the newspaper, was Dunn's principal trial counsel. His defense of Socialist Dunn and fierce attacks on the Anaconda precipitated a Company-inspired backlash that led to his defeat by the more-moderate Joseph M. Dixon.

By the time Dunn was arrested for sedition, most people would not have been surprised. Dunn had emerged in the previous fifteen months as probably the most outspoken critic of the political-industrial establishment in Montana. He was called "the most dangerous man at large in Montana today."[2] That he wasn't silenced as Frank Little was silenced—a fate he publicly confessed to having feared—may have been just luck. But his survival probably speaks more to his political and mental acuity, a forcefulness of intellect and personality that seemed to demand a certain measure of respect, even from his bitterest enemies. Besides, Dunn would prove more useful alive than dead, as a political foil and as a sedition defendant.

Dunn, who had grown up in Minnesota and attended the College of St. Thomas in St. Paul, burst onto the scene in Butte after the Speculator fire in June 1917 that killed 168 miners. An electrician by trade and a former prize fighter, the barrel-chested Dunn, then just twenty-nine, had emerged as the leader in a fast-spreading series of strikes in which more than fifteen thousand men walked off the job in little more than a week. Dunn managed to accomplish what mine owners had feared most. He aligned the more conservative trade unions, at least for a month or so, behind the more radical striking miners.[3]

But the overwhelming power of the Anaconda, particularly with its war production needs, had exploded any notion of labor solidarity. Dunn had turned to a different weapon to wage his struggle against capitalism—and against what he called the "kept press" that published the companies' lies. A labor newspaper, the *Butte Weekly Bulletin*, was born on December 15, 1917, taking the place of a more irregularly published sheet put out since the Speculator disaster.[4]

Anaconda and other mine operators staunchly opposed the *Bulletin*, even prohibiting business owners from advertising in it.[5] Dunn's criticism of the kid-glove way in which the "kept press" treated mine owner Oscar Rohn for his questionable use of Germans to spy on IWWs raised hackles in Butte. But it was a mild prelude to a Dunn editorial on May 31, "Turn on the Light," which criticized the state and county councils of defense for their closed-door opposition to B. K. Wheeler's re-nomination as U.S. Attorney. The members of the Montana Council of Defense, Dunn charged, had "grown lean and gray, or fat and bald in the service of big business . . . tried and trusty lieutenants of the same old political gang . . . [engaged in] putrid tactics [that] offend the nostrils of every right-minded citizen . . ."[6] It was Dunn's opening salvo in a series of skirmishes with the state's powerful political establishment.

Dunn's editorial was like waving a red flag in front of a bull. It furnished the council a handy excuse for investigating the loyalty of the *Bulletin* staff. A willing accomplice was the Montana Newspaper Publishers Association, whose officers complained that the *Bulletin* was "creating dissension and prejudice at a time when loyalty and unity of purpose is earnestly sought."[7] The publishers also asked the Council to urge U.S. Postmaster General Sidney Burleson to revoke the *Bulletin's* second-class mailing privileges under the Espionage Act.

The newspaper publishers of the state saw no press freedom issue—indeed no irony—in the fact that they themselves were calling for a state investigation into a publication's loyalty. They saw nothing wrong with instigating what amounted to a star-chamber inquiry to squelch the publication of political dissent. And they saw nothing wrong with using the Post Office to censor the *Bulletin*. While Montana newspapers lined up against provisions in the first versions of the 1917 Espionage Act that would have subjected newspapers to government censorship, they seemed to be blind to the fact that this was exactly what they were proposing for a newspaper they regarded as "dangerous."

Montana newspapermen would have been keenly aware that President Wilson had just signed the federal Sedition Act, the amendment to the Espionage Act that copied Montana's sedition law virtually word for word and added another powerful weapon to the war against sedition. Hearings would be an excellent way to question the loyalty of a dissident newspaper, with all the attendant publicity that the *Independent* and other "copper-collar" and company-oriented newspapers in the state could muster. The proceedings would also put additional pressure on Wheeler to enforce the federal law. These events underscore the fact that the vast majority of the Montana press not only endorsed the wartime "need" for suppressing dissent, but also were leaders in legitimizing and drumming up popular support for it.

The council's secretary, Charles D. Greenfield, himself a former newspaperman on the *Helena Independent* and the *Montana Daily Record*, promptly acted on the publishers' suggestion and forwarded files on the *Bulletin* to the postmaster general, without even telling the newspaper's staff.[8]

Over two long days, Council members grilled Dunn (and Smith to a lesser extent) about matters that stretched even the broad investigative powers they had just given themselves. Led by Gov. Stewart and editor Campbell, the Council inquired into Dunn's journalistic practices, his company's stockholders, his affiliations and beliefs, whether he had supported Frank Little's views, his contributions to the war effort, and his editorial stance vis-à-vis the war.[9]

Dunn, ever the pugilist, fought his inquisitors to a verbal standstill. "What I do object to is for the state council of defense to set itself upon a pinnacle," Dunn told the council members. "They are not above criticism."[10] When a council member inquired whether "all citizens, especially at this time, should support the constituted authority, both of states and nations," Dunn caustically retorted, "Oh yes, all *legally* constituted authority undoubtedly."[11]

Dunn's feistiness even earned an accolade from Campbell, who called him "cold as a wedge, keen as a razor, widely informed, personally dispassionate, of ready wit and spontaneous mental action [who] proved more than a match for all those who cross-examined him . . ."[12]

While the hearing gave Dunn a chance to explain his socialist views, they also provided an opportunity for council members to introduce damaging testimony against him. For instance, John H. McIntosh, secretary of the Montana Employers' Association, testified that his conversations with Dunn had led him to believe that "The *Butte Bulletin* is doing more to harm this country than if a whole regiment of Prussian soldiers was turned loose in Silver Bow County." He added, "The minds of the workers and farmers of the state are being poisoned by [its] pro-German propaganda. . . . All these people are doing is to stir up class hatred, to plant the seeds of suspicion of our officials and to circulate the impression that half of our people are profiteering at the expense of the blood of our boys in France . . ."[13]

After a similarly grueling grilling of U.S. Attorney Wheeler (who also gave as good as he got), the inquisition ground to a halt. But the Council would soon test Dunn's loyalty from a different angle. In early August, in the name of wartime conservation, the federal War Industry Board had prohibited the start-up of any new newspaper. Within a week, the Council seized on this mandate to issue a new Order Number 12, which not only carried out the federal directive but also prohibited any newspaper or magazine which published less than six days a week from converting to daily publication during the war.[14] This order was obviously aimed at Dunn's *Bulletin*, which planned to go to daily publication about a week later. Campbell's fingerprints were all over the decree. In his newspaper, he had said the federal order would have "little effect in Montana beyond making impossible certain publications planned by the disloyal newspapers . . ."[15]

Dunn's reaction to "the handpicked gang who masquerade under the title of the State Council of Defense" was predictably fiery:

> Their latest dictum stamps them as . . . the willing, cringing tools of the autocratic forces of the state.
>
> Fortunately, they have no legal status or authority. They can fulminate to their heart's content against anything and everything that menaces their master's interest, but—no one need pay any attention to them.
>
> The *Daily Bulletin* will be on the streets when the plant is ready, and if we are interfered with we will take it to the highest courts of the land . . .[16]

Four days later, on August 20, the first edition of the *Butte Daily Bulletin* rolled off the presses. Dunn had stepped down as editor because he was campaigning for a seat in the state legislature. He was now chief editorial writer but still at the heart of the action.[17] Campbell goaded the Council to take action or resign and "admit they constitute a big bluffing society."[18]

Ostensibly acting on behalf of the War Industries Board to curb Dunn's "illegal" daily newspaper, Campbell and Gov. Stewart led the Council in again grilling Dunn on matters well beyond the publication frequency of the *Bulletin*. Dunn reiterated that the council had no legal authority and could not squelch criticism. "The moment the right of criticism is taken away, right then government ceases to be a democracy. I maintain that I have the right, the *Bulletin* has the right, to criticize the State Council of Defense as a body or as individuals."[19]

Dunn acknowledged that he and the council would never see eye to eye: "It is simply a question of whether or not a paper, or a group or a movement which is opposed to the dominating interests of a state or nation can be persecuted and put out of business by those interests. That is the only thing there is to it."[20]

Dunn had nailed it. He and the council were at loggerheads. Now, the Council would look for any pretext to get Dunn.

The opportunity arose just a few days later. A wildcat miners' strike hit Butte on the morning of Friday, September 13, part of a wave of nation-wide strikes protesting the convictions of Big Bill Haywood and other IWW members in Chicago and the sedition conviction of Eugene Debs in Cleveland. That evening, federal officers led by a six-man army detail commanded by Major Omar Bradley, acting without any search or arrest warrants, raided IWW and Metal Mine Workers Union headquarters in Finlander Hall—and the offices of the *Butte Bulletin*. A total of seventy-four men were arrested. Many were charged with sedition; others were held for investigation by the Department of Justice. All but Dunn were released for lack of evidence.[21]

At the *Bulletin*, officers seized strike posters and a strike circular that they said had been printed there, as well as subscription lists. The sedition charge against Dunn accused him of "printing and publishing to urge and advocate the curtailment of copper production in this country."[22] The charges were brought by Ed Morrissy, chief of detectives—and former bodyguard for Con Kelly, the president of the Anaconda Copper Mining Company.[23]

Wheeler telegrammed Attorney General Gregory about the warrant-less searches, touching off a brisk debate between the Justice and War departments about the use of the military in strike situations and the lim-its of the army's jurisdiction.[24] Later, in ruling on a deportation case involving one of the IWWs arrested, John Jackson, the assistant secretary of the Butte local, Federal Judge Bourquin blasted the raiders:

> There was no disorder save that of the raiders. These, mainly uni-formed and armed, overawed, intimidated, and forcibly entered, broke, and destroyed property, searched [and arrested] persons,

effects, and papers . . . cursed, insulted, beat, dispersed, and bayonet-ed union members by order of the commanding officer. They . . . per-petrated a reign of terror against citizen and alien alike, whose only offense seems to have been peaceable insistence upon and exercise of a clear legal right. . . . No emergency . . . warrants violation [of fun-damental rights of personal security and due process] for, in emer-gency, real or assumed, tyrants in all ages have found excuse for their destruction. . . . Assuming petitioner is of the so-called "Reds," he and his kind are less a danger to America than are those who indorse or use the methods that brought him to deportation. These latter are the mob and the spirit of violence and intolerance incarnate, the most alarming manifestation in America today. Far worse than the imme-diate wrongs to individuals that they do, they undermine the morale of the people, excite the latter's fears, distrust of our institutions, doubts of the sufficiency of law and authority; they incline the people toward arbitrary power, which for protection cowards too often seek, and knaves too readily grant, and subject to which the people cease to be courageous and free, and become timid and enslaved. . . . They and the government by hysteria that they stimulate are more to be feared than all the miserable, baited, bedeviled "Reds" that are their ostensi-ble occasion and whose sins they exaggerate.[25]

Dunn was taken to the city jail and spent the night there before being bailed out the next afternoon. At about the same time in Helena, Lewis and Clark sheriff Ed Majors was obtaining a judge's signature on an arrest warrant for Dunn, Smith, and business manager Leo Daly on sedition charges stemming from the *Bulletin's* defiant editorial casting doubt on the Council of Defense's legality.

Warrant in hand, Majors and a deputy hopped the next Great Northern train to Butte. There they enlisted local police to scour the city for Dunn, who was again arrested about 10:30 p.m., this time on a spuri-ous concealed weapon charge. Dunn had a permit but wasn't carrying it. He was returned to the city jail.

After midnight, as Dunn's lawyer waited in the police station to post bond for him once more, the jailer awoke Dunn, handcuffed him, hustled him down some back stairs, and delivered him to Sheriff Majors, who put Dunn in a car waiting in the alley behind the station. Fearing a lynching like

Little's, Dunn asked that his handcuffs be removed, but Majors refused.[26]

"Before his associates had fairly grasped the situation," the *Independent* crowed later that morning, Dunn was being spirited to Helena by the sheriff and his deputy. It was, in effect, a legal kidnapping of a political prisoner. The objective, of course, was to try Dunn in a jurisdiction where there was no hometown sympathy, in a city where his conviction could be assured.

In a front-page news story that day, readers of the *Helena Independent* (whose editor had recently grilled Dunn for his journalistic ethics in the Council of Defense hearing) were treated to this description of the sedition suspects:

> Dunn is a labor agitator from Seattle, imported by the Wobblies of Butte to conduct their labor troubles.
>
> Smith is a tramp who became president of the Butte typographical union, stockholder in the *Butte Bulletin*.
>
> Daly is a Sinn Feiner whose meal ticket is furnished by Dunn and his Wobbly crew.[27]

All three posted $5,000 bail in Helena. Without missing a beat, Dunn was back at it at the *Daily Bulletin*. In a September 18 editorial, he heaped scorn on Campbell, calling his newspaper's name "sadly inappropriate" and terming him a "'mental pervert' of mediocre talent who sought to advance Prussianism by destroying the *Bulletin* and incarcerating its staff for daring to criticize Campbell and the rest of the company tools on the Council."[28]

In a more considered thirteen-page letter to the editor of the *Missoulian* dated September 19, Dunn lobbed more missiles at the Anaconda's political supremacy and the supine nature of the "kept press." It ended with a pledge "that this condition of affairs shall not exist forever; that at no matter what cost freedom is going to be restored to the people of . . . the state . . . that the Democracy for which we are fighting abroad is realized in [Montana] . . ."[29] His letter was never published.

Seven weeks later, the fighting in Europe had ceased, but the kind of democracy Dunn envisioned was if anything, further off, thanks to the growing Red Scare and the rising labor unrest. The parlous conditions made it certain that the *Butte Bulletin* men would be prosecuted for sedition despite the end of hostilities. Dunn himself was becoming even more strident, as this excerpt from an editorial in support of the Seattle general strike in January 1919 shows: "We must not think, we must not speak; we are dogs to work, to slave, to die, for our Masters' profit. Away with it all. We will speak. Workers of Seattle, the working class of Butte are with you. Demand the freedom of speech. . . . Stand in your power and challenge these lying despots. Unmask these hypocrites. . . . Defy these plutocratic Von Hindenburgs, these uncrowned kaisers. Speak!"[30]

Dunn's treatment at the hands of the establishment certainly explains his radical politics. The climax of his defiance of that power structure in Montana was about to unfold in the courtroom of Judge Lee Word in Helena.

Word's conservative politics were no secret. His conduct of the sedition trials of Tony Diedtman in Helena and of several sedition defendants in Miles City confirmed the fears of Dunn's attorneys that their client could not receive a fair trial. But he rejected a motion to step aside.

Dunn's sedition trial finally got under way in Helena on February 20, 1919. County Attorney Lester Loble, the chief prosecutor, admitted at the outset that he was trying Dunn in Helena because he would not have been able to find a jury in Butte to convict him.[31] Four Butte attorneys formed Dunn's defense team, led by B. K. Wheeler, now in private practice after having failed to win re-appointment as U.S. District Attorney. His feisty liberalism in resisting the repressive agenda of conservatives like Stewart and Campbell had eventually resulted in his ouster, through pressure on Senator Thomas J. Walsh, who was up for re-election.

As was the practice, an all-male jury was seated, composed mainly of working men from Helena—a janitor (and Spanish-American war vet), a fireman, a stonemason, three ranchers, a mine operator, a smelter operator, other company employees, and a "colored employee of International Harvester."[32]

The three-day trial held few surprises, for the main actors in the drama had already shown their hands. Will Campbell was shown to have been the primary instigator of the prosecution. Not only did he call the *Bulletin* editorial to prosecutor Loble's attention, suggesting that "these people were getting dangerously close to the line over there,"[33] but Loble's jurisdiction over the case hung solely on Campbell's own Helena subscription to the *Butte Bulletin*. While denying any personal animus, Campbell told the jury that he believed it was his duty as a member of the State Council of Defense to bring "one of the most dangerous men at large in Montana today" to justice.[34]

Under questioning from Wheeler, Campbell's motives came across as political and ideological. His concern about Dunn's "continual agitation and stirring up of the men engaged in producing copper during the war" and his fear that the resulting rising wage scales in Butte would drive up printers' wages in Helena had nothing to do with Dunn's editorial poke in the eye at the Council of Defense.[35]

Judge Word's bias against Dunn was palpable. He rejected many of Wheeler's attempts to introduce evidence favorable to the defense and other defense motions. One biographer of Dunn notes that a review of the trial transcript shows that Word sustained seventy of the prosecution's seventy-five objections, but only seven of forty-eight defense objections. Even prosecutor Loble recalled, in an interview years later, that he himself had had to intervene to keep the judge from throwing Wheeler in jail for contempt.[36]

As he had in other sedition prosecutions, Loble threw down the patriotism card. He blasted Dunn for being "a Bolshevist and an agitator; one not satisfied with conditions as they exist in this country," who acted "to bring down the fabric of this government" in stark contrast to the boys "over there" who went "over the top."[37] He also compared Dunn to the eight beer-hall Germans he had just finished successfully prosecuting for sedition. These he termed "external" seditionists, while Americans like Dunn were "internal" seditionists "who were sticking knives into the backs of the men, the defenders of this country, and its government." Of the two varieties, he advised the jury, Dunn was the worse.[38]

Dunn's defense team put up a robust defense in the face of long odds. They attempted to show that Dunn did not incite resistance to the Council of Defense, but had only tried to point out that its authority wasn't supreme. Defense counsel also argued that the sedition law required specific intent by Dunn to "publish any language calculated to incite or inflame resistance to any duly constituted Federal or State authority in connection with the prosecution of the War . . ." This point was not yet settled by the state supreme court.

Whether it was wise for Wheeler and company to let Dunn speak in his own defense is a moot point. He probably would have done it anyway, and his views were well known. A Helena jury may not have known as much of Dunn's views as a Butte jury, but as a freshman legislator, he had also made his views known in the capital. On the stand, Dunn railed against the Anaconda, the "copper press," Campbell and "the rottenly corrupt gang of politicians" who had sold out Montana.[39] The sedition law had been passed, he claimed, at the behest of "the corporations of the state." Pointing to a bespectacled man in the gallery, he said, "That is Mr. Roy Alley, who is John D. Ryan's private secretary, and head of the Anaconda Mining Company," who controls the legislature and high state officials, he said.[40] The implication that the Company man was there to see Dunn punished was clear.

Dunn may as well have saved his breath. The jury was out two hours before returning a guilty verdict, having debated most of the time about an appropriate penalty. The jury decided to recommend clemency to Judge Word, who ignored them and fined Dunn $5,000. Before imposing sentence, Word raked Dunn: "Your faith is not in the ballot but in the bullet. . . . I am satisfied that you are against all legal authority. Never before have I seen a man with so little apparent regard for laws, courts, or juries. Your doctrines go back to the cave man, who recognize no authority. You, an intelligent man, should know that in a country where democracy rules the ballot must bring about all reforms and changes."

Dunn, whose faith in the ballot was manifest in his seat in the state legislature and in the fact that he was now running for mayor of Butte, stood impassively as sentence was pronounced. Insult followed injury a few weeks later when his victory in the mayoral primary was nullified by electoral fraud by his Company-backed rival. The Anaconda-controlled *Butte Miner* had called the election a choice between "Americanism and Bolshevism," an early symptom of the Red Scare that was about to blanket the country.[41]

Smith's sedition trial in June was a less passionate proceeding. Loble grilled both Smith and Dunn as to who was responsible for the editorial. Smith, a printer for thirty years, said he had read the allegedly seditious editorial in the type form—backwards and upside-down as any printer could—out of curiosity. Dunn was evasive about who had the final say. Again, it hardly mattered. True to form, Judge Word spurned suggestions of mercy and handed Smith a $4,500 fine.[42] Charges against Leo Daly, the third *Bulletin* employee, were dropped.

E. B. Craighead, editor of the *New Northwest*, was completely disgusted. He editorialized:

> Men who prefer sedition charges against their fellow men, not for the high purpose of protecting the flag, but for the base purpose of punishing their personal enemies, deserve the condemnation of

good men and women. Such men should be punished as traitors to their country. Some good citizens unfortunately hate their enemies, but only a very bad man will prostitute patriotism to the low and dirty work of getting even with enemies in times of war and unrest, when it is easy to fan prejudices and spread suspicions.[43]

While Dunn's and Smith's lawyers were busy perfecting their appeal to the state supreme court, Campbell and Stewart were not resting on their laurels. After all, the *Butte Daily Bulletin* was still in business. They continued to put pressure on the U.S. Justice Department to prosecute Dunn under the federal sedition law. Senator Myers visited the assistant attorney general in late November 1919, to advise the department that the *Butte Bulletin* "does much damage in Butte and the surrounding country in stirring up radicalism."[44]

In a letter to U.S. Attorney General A. Mitchell Palmer, Gov. Stewart asked for a special prosecutor to be assigned to Butte, which he termed one of the national centers for mounting radicalism and eventual revolution. At the epicenter of this unrest, he pointed out, was the *Butte Daily Bulletin*, with its "most revolutionary, seditious, and violent everyday utterances that go forth to other parts of the United States and help to carry its message of sedition and disloyalty to many other communities. . . . Why it is allowed to circulate in the mails is more than I can understand." Stewart also said he had suggested to the U.S. Army commander in Butte that he declare a state of martial law in order to suppress seditious publications.[45]

A week later, on May 3, 1920, the Montana Supreme Court unanimously threw out Smith's conviction, remanding his case for a new trial, and then used it as precedent in Dunn's case to do the same thing. The court cited two principle reasons for its action: Judge Word was biased in making certain rulings erroneously in favor of the prosecution and the state did not make its sedition case against either of the men.

The biggest error committed by the judge, according to the court, was in not letting the defense ask prospective jurors whether they could vote for acquittal if they entertained a reasonable doubt that the editorial in question "was calculated to incite or inflame resistance to the state council of defense." The effect of this ruling, the court said, was to deprive the defendant of his right to a fair trial because it gave the jury the impression that they did not need to determine this fact.[46]

Even if the jury *had* been able to make that determination, there was insufficient proof that the editorial incited or inflamed anyone in Lewis and Clark County. The only person in the county tied by the evidence to the defendants was Will Campbell, "the guiding genius of the *Helena Independent*," who admitted he subscribed to the *Butte Bulletin.* "Who but Mr. Campbell (as member of the state Council of Defense) could be incited or inflamed to resistance," the court asked, "and is it within the range of probabilities that he would be incited to resist the very organization of which he was a member? We think not."

Campbell, in other words, had been hoisted on his own petard. His eagerness to bury his socialist foe by fomenting the sedition charges against Dunn and Smith had blown up in his face. Trying the case in Helena, suggested the high court, was a subterfuge, an attempt to deprive the defendants of their state constitutional guarantee of a "speedy, public trial by an impartial jury of the county or district in which the offense is alleged to have been committed."[47]

It was a stinging rebuke for the state from a court not inclined to favor the likes of Dunn and Smith. In fact, the high court the previous year had refused an appeal by Dunn to be placed on the Butte city election ballot, despite evidence of fraud.[48] Dunn was "fortunate," one observer noted, "to have both a judge and a prosecutor (and a chief witness, he might have added) whose anxiousness to punish him blinded them to numerous legal technicalities."[49]

Campbell buried the story on page four and blamed the reversal on "technical errors."[50] Dunn was hardly more gracious in victory. He called Word the "alleged judge . . . who presided at the witch burning of the *Bulletin* editors."[51]

Five days after the Smith and Dunn decisions, the state supreme court handed down another reversal of a sedition conviction, in the case of Tony Diedtman, the beer hall swamper from Helena. Again, the high court blistered Judge Word for his biased rulings in favor of the prosecution. Although all three reversals were on evidentiary grounds and did not hold the sedition law to be unconstitutional, they were a blow to prosecutors. Their combined weight surely would have given prosecutors pause about further sedition prosecutions.

Epilogue

Bruce Smith's was the last sedition case tried in Montana. Even though Gov. Stewart had signed a peacetime sedition law in March (the same law minus the phrase, "Whenever the United States shall be engaged in war") no one would ever be prosecuted under it. In a delicious irony, the man who led the effort to finally repeal the outdated law in 1973 was the grandson of the lawyer whose case had prompted the sedition law in the first place. Matt Canning had been the lawyer for rancher Ves Hall, whose acquittal on federal sedition charges by Judge Bourquin provoked so much outrage and factored in the adoption of both the federal and state sedition laws in 1918—and a punch in the nose for Canning. Grandson William F. "Duke" Crowley, a lawyer and professor at the University of Montana School of Law in Missoula, sat on the state's criminal law revision commission in the 1970s. "I made it my business to repeal that law, and there was unanimous agreement [in the legislature]," Crowley recalled.[52]

It would be another eighteen months after the state supreme court's ruling in Smith's and Dunn's cases before the last sedition prisoner would be released from Deer Lodge. Martin Ferkovich, a Croatian miner from Roundup sentenced to ten to twenty years,[53] had his sentence commuted on the recommendation of Gov. Joseph M. Dixon.[54] Ferkovich walked out of Deer Lodge on November 16, 1921, after thirty-three months in prison.

Radicalized by his political and legal experiences in Montana, Dunn left the state in 1924 as a member of the American Communist Party. As his biographer wrote, "When Dunne came to Butte, he still believed that social change could occur through the democratic process. By 1921, his personal experiences caused him to reconsider, probably because the Anaconda Company was unwilling to allow democracy to work."[55] While not going so far as to prove Judge Word correct about putting his faith in the bullet, "Communism was an understandable next step, since he had completely lost faith in the existing system."[56]

Dunn's writing and rhetorical skills and his forceful personality helped him rise to influence within the Communist hierarchy. He was a founding editor of the *Daily Worker* in Chicago, ran twice as the party's nominee for governor of New York, and traveled several times to the Soviet Union. He might even have been named head of the American Communist Party by Joseph Stalin had he not drunkenly boasted of his selection before it became public. After the stock market crash, he returned to the United States to recruit party members in various industries. In 1946 he was expelled from the Communist Party for "failing to fight Trotskyism." He died in 1953, a few months after Stalin.[57]

Dunn reportedly returned briefly to post-Depression Montana.[58] He probably did not recognize the deadly pall that hung over almost all of Montana's press, for it had by then become the unwritten policy of Company-controlled newspapers to avoid all controversy. Dunn might even have felt a twinge of pity for his old adversary, Will Campbell, who roared on through the Red Scare but now had overstayed his time.

As historian K. Ross Toole noted, "Gone were the blasting editorials, the diatribes, the big black alliterative headlines. Someone, somehow, even pulled the fangs of Will Campbell. If the vituperation was gone, so was aggressive reporting and imaginative writing. So was the thorough coverage of state and local news, which did not affect the Company. Talent departed along with invective. The Company simply dropped a great, gray blanket over Montana."[59]

Campbell died of heart disease in 1938. Obituary writers glided over the deceased's vicious World War I period. They memorialized him as "courageous, charitable, and intensely human," and the *Independent* under his leadership as "independent at all times in spirit as well as in name."[60] A more levelheaded assessment comes from a 1970 thesis on Campbell by Charles Johnson, now chief political reporter for Lee Newspapers (which bought the Anaconda's newspapers in 1959): "In some ways, Campbell aptly symbolized the wartime years. He was a talented man overtaken, like the nation, by an obsessive hysteria. Instead of using his influential newspaper to help set the country he loved straight, Campbell was at the forefront of the movement to strip away rights that were guaranteed in the Constitution he venerated."[61]

Prosecutor Loble served two terms in the state legislature in the mid-1920s. A bill he introduced and had passed in 1923 to create a publicly funded old-age pension system was one of the models used by President Franklin D. Roosevelt for the Social Security system. Loble was a district court judge in Helena from 1956 to 1968, gaining renown once more when he called for making public the names of juvenile felony defendants. He also wrote a book on rehabilitating juvenile delinquents. He mellowed toward the end of his long life and was a George McGovern delegate at the Democratic National Convention in 1972. He died in 1974.

Wheeler, Dunn's friend and defender and Campbell's other nemesis, was labeled a Bolshevik by the Company in retaliation for his relentless attacks against it as he campaigned for governor, losing to Joseph Dixon in 1920. So nasty was the campaign that Wheeler nearly lost his life to a lynch mob in Dillon, and was forced to hide in a freight car, thus earning the moniker Boxcar Burt. But he went on to a distinguished career in state and national politics. He was elected to the U.S. Senate in 1922 and served four terms.

Wheeler was best known for his role, along with Senator Walsh, in pursuing the Teapot Dome scandal, as well as for his staunch opposition to Franklin Roosevelt's court-packing plan and then for his opposition to American involvement in World War II prior to Pearl Harbor. The isolationist movement he led, often sharing the stage with Charles Lindbergh, was so popular by 1940 that he may well have become the Democratic nominee for president that year had not Roosevelt decided to run for a third term. Wheeler died in 1975 at age ninety-two. In his autobiography, *Yankee from the West*, Wheeler wrote of the World War I period in Montana:

> I was shocked that the American people could be so carried away and lose their sense of right and justice at so critical a time. It was a lesson I never forgot. . . . Twenty years later, when I led the fight against the attempt to pack the United States Supreme Court . . . it was in large part because I recalled how state judges, elected to office, were carried away by the World War I hysteria in their own communities when rendering decisions.[62]

As Wheeler's own experiences show, the hysteria did not fade with the Armistice, but continued almost unabated for another two years. It would not be until the end of that second dark period before the American public came to its senses, fear loosened its grip, and freedom of conscience and liberty of expression began to assume a cherished place in the pantheon of American values. ✦

SIXTEEN
"The Agitation of the Billows"

Excesses of the Postwar Red Scare Provoke Reaction, 1919–1920

ONE MIGHT WISH TO IMAGINE A PAY ENVELOPE or at least a tolerant shrug for those who had been so cruelly caught in the sedition net, but that is, as the Wobblies put it, "pie in the sky." For Martin Ferkovich and his forty co-felons, seeing the outsides of the Montana state penitentiary's high stone walls must have produced relief but little elation. The world into which the sedition prisoners slowly emerged—sixteen straggled out of Deer Lodge by the first anniversary of the Armistice, twenty-four more by the second, and Ferkovich three years and five days after the end of hostilities in Europe—was no friendlier a place than it had been when they entered prison.

Much of the world was reeling from a vicious period of postwar economic and social dysfunction. Jobs were even harder to come by, costs were rising far faster than wages, the state was in a desperate drought, hysteria was still in the air, radicals were still despised, and most newspapers were still the mouthpieces for corporate powers like Anaconda—which were even stronger. The United States was gripped by another cycle of political repression, this time, as a British journalist remarked, "hag-ridden by the spectre of Bolshevism . . . like a sleeper in a nightmare, enveloped by a thousand phantoms of destruction."[1]

Fear of Bolshevism had almost seamlessly begun to replace fear of the kaiser in 1918. The United States could not escape the effects of the Russian Revolution any more than it could shield itself from the French Revolution in the late eighteenth century. As Thomas Jefferson had so aptly put it: "The agonized spasms of infuriated man, seeking through blood and slaughter his long lost liberty, it was . . . wonderful that the agitation of the billows should reach even this distant and peaceful shore: that there should be more felt and feared by some, and less by others, and should divide opinions as to measures of safety."[2] As with the fear of the Jacobin rabble in Paris, fear of the proletariat's fury would rise to a hysterical pitch by the following summer and continue for another year. Bolshevism's implacable foes saw it everywhere. To the man who would become the nation's leading Red hunter, Attorney General A. Mitchell Palmer, the "sharp tongues of revolutionary heat were licking at the altars of the churches, leaping into the belfry of the school bell . . . burning up the foundations of society."[3]

Initial Red victories in Germany and Hungary, though ephemeral, helped encourage communism in the United States. Two factions split from the Socialist Party, the American Communist Party and the Communist Labor Party. Their attendance at the Third Communist International in 1919, Lenin's stern organization of global revolution, ratcheted up postwar fears of a foreign menace. "Every ambitious politician, overzealous veteran, anti-union employer, super-patriotic organizer, defender of white supremacy, and sensational journalist jumped into the fray, using the issue of radicalism as a whipping boy for their own special purposes," wrote historian Robert K. Murray.[4]

Thus, the trajectory of political repression launched with the passage of the Espionage Act in June 1917 was hardly altered by the Armistice. Repression would continue, in even more arbitrary and desperate ways, to try to neutralize or destroy those who threatened political and economic stability. Like the foreign and domestic conflict that preceded it, the Red Scare would scar the nation's soul, in a brief but violent set of events.

The Scare was touched off by an unending series of strikes. Labor historians attribute the thirty-six hundred work stoppages in 1919, involving a record four million workers, to a convergence of economic and social factors, but the principal causes seemed to be these: workers faced a much tighter job market as war contract work wound down; while wages were much higher than in 1914, a soaring cost of living—the Consumer Price Index in 1919 was 77 percent higher than in 1916, and 105 percent higher in 1920—was hammering their buying power[5], and a classic battle over control of the workplace was unfolding. Organized labor was trying to consolidate the membership and wage gains from the prosperous war years—and had become more radical in its determination to realize workers' aspirations. Even some of the leading state branches of the mainstream AFL were calling for nationalization of transportation, communications, and energy.[6] Management was determined to return to the pre-war status quo, keep unions as weak as possible and stave off any move toward socialization.

Labor's struggle for workplace democracy was painted by management, and daily by the news media, as dangerously un-American and disloyal. Moreover, this national battle for the workplace followed a strike that colored red all those that followed—the Seattle general strike in February 1919.

In Seattle's shipyards, which had launched ninety-six ocean-going vessels in 1918, workers loyal to a militant leadership (many of whom were IWWs) had high hopes for wage gains to overcome inflation. Owners met their demands with folded arms, arguing that demand for tonnage was plummeting. A shipyard strike snowballed into a five-day general strike. Although it was entirely peaceful, the fact that close to sixty thousand workers from painters and cooks to machinists and pressmen laid down their tools at once set off all sorts of alarms. A strident editorial in a union newspaper, trumpeting, "we are starting on a road that leads no one knows where," inspired widespread fears of revolution.

The strike collapsed because its leaders had no strategy for extracting realistic concessions from anyone, but it was Mayor "Holy Ole" Hanson who gained national fame for putting it down.[7] "The revolution is at an end," crowed the *Seattle Post-Intelligencer*. "The serpent head of Bolshevism has been crushed under the heels of an onward-marching citizenry led by a fearless mayor."[8]

No other general strike would take place in the United States until the 1930s (although a forty-day general strike in Winnipeg later in 1919 provoked the same sort of fearful response by manufacturers in Manitoba and received heavy U.S. press coverage). Nonetheless, paranoia from Puget Sound echoed through rancorous steel and coal strikes, and through a strike by more than eleven hundred Boston police in September. Boston newspapers denounced the cops as "agents of Lenin" while Gov. Calvin Coolidge's tardy but well publicized opposition helped propel him onto the national stage.

As with the lumber and mining strikes of 1917, the massive postwar labor turmoil was blamed on radical dissidents, with little attention given to the underlying causes of workers' distress. Already at the top of the public enemy list, a resurgent IWW was painted with the brush of Bolshevism as well—not entirely unfounded as leaders like Big Bill Haywood and others joined the Communist Party and IWW delegates had attended the 1919 Comintern. Reckless urging of the general strike—not only by boisterous Wobblies in Seattle but also by the organization's inexperienced national leaders, whose ranks had been depleted by the mass convictions in the Chicago trial—bolstered this image. The IWW's continuing legal tribulations, with another mass trial in Sacramento, kept its negative image in the limelight. So, too, did a pair of sensational, back-to-back investigations that spring, one in the U.S. Senate and one in the New York State Assembly. Larded with evidence of Bolshevik atrocities, not to mention shocking tales of free love, the hearings rolled to their pre-ordained conclusions that Bolsheviks and domestic radicals were marching arm in arm under the red flag of revolution.

When the next big shock of 1919 hit, the Wobblies were again among the first suspects. Package bombs damaged the homes of several prominent figures. In Washington, D.C., one bomb blew both hands off a maid in the household of Senator Thomas W. Hardwick of Georgia on April 29; another splintered the front porch of Attorney General Palmer's house on June 2. Postal workers intercepted three dozen more bombs sent to men such as J. P. Morgan, Oliver Wendell Holmes Jr., and Ole Hanson. The blasts recalled recent assassinations and injuries in Europe. However, the "infernal machine" that killed the Italian anarchist holding the bomb with Palmer's name on it packed the most punch, for it was an immediate cause of the fearsome crackdown that was to follow.

Palmer, who took office near the midpoint of Wilson's second term, had seemed at first intent on putting the war behind him. He had released nearly ten thousand enemy aliens from parole and finished disbanding the xenophobic American Protective League.[9] The bombs pulverized whatever reformist impulses Palmer might have had. Unable to use the wartime sedition laws to go after the "dynamitards," Palmer turned to the federal deportation laws to get rid of radical aliens.

Previous deportations of Wobblies from the Seattle area had provided a precedent of sorts. In February 1919, a "Red Special" train bore thirty-eight Wobbly detainees eastward to Ellis Island—a pathetic and ironic ghost of the rollicking Overalls Brigade that had so optimistically set the IWW's on a Western course in 1908. In Butte, a thousand Wobblies and supporters stormed the train, hoping to set their fellow workers free. But authorities had routed the detainees through Helena instead.[10]

Eventually, only seven Wobblies of that group were deported. Judges reviewing habeas corpus petitions rebuked the Labor Department's Immigration Bureau for its shoddy hearing practices that denied detainees due process and for finding men deportable simply for their membership in the IWW. The slap in the face only increased the Red-hunters' determination to evict Communists from the nation's shores. Although the government by now had a tougher law that did permit deportation of aliens for mere membership in organizations found to advocate anarchy or violent overthrow, Palmer endorsed a scheme of shady legality. The Justice Department's new Red-hunting unit, headed by J. Edgar Hoover, would conduct widespread raids and arrests of suspected communists and hand them over to the Immigration Bureau for deportation hearings. Even as Palmer and his lieutenants were laying their plans, pressure from Congress was mounting. Senator Miles Poindexter of Washington authored a resolution asking Palmer why he hadn't taken action yet against "persons . . . who . . . have attempted to bring about the forcible overthrow of the Government; who have preached anarchy and sedition . . ."[11]

The first set of raids, on the second anniversary of the November 7 Bolshevik Revolution, targeted the Union of Russian Workers, more a social club than a revolutionary cabal. The raid yielded 250 sullen minnows, not the big fish the feds had advertised. Four days later, the shooting deaths of four American Legionnaires outside an IWW hall in the lumber town of Centralia, Washington, during an Armistice Day parade—and the subsequent lynching of a Wobbly—led to demands for wholesale deportations of IWWs and tougher action.[12]

Palmer soon hustled four-fifths of the aliens captured in the November raids aboard an old army transport. The *Buford* steamed out of New York harbor on December 21, bound for a Finnish port to be handed over to the Bolsheviks. Adding infamy to the passenger manifest of the "Soviet Ark" were anarchist Emma Goldman and her lover Alexander Berkman, who had served fourteen years for the attempted slaying of steel tycoon Henry C. Frick during the 1892 Homestead strike near Pittsburgh. Epithets bobbed in the ship's wake: "Cargo of undesirables," "soldiers of disorder," "believers in sabotage," "the ultra-red faction," "this class of cooties."[13]

In much more massive dragnets on January 2, 1920, the Justice Department jailed at least three thousand persons in thirty-three cities and twenty-three states; at least ten thousand persons were initially arrested.[14] Due process went out the window. Innocent citizens were swept up in meeting halls and homes, lined up against the wall and searched without warrants. Raiders found exactly three pistols. Many aliens caught in the web were poor, illiterate, and, as one observer noted, "did not so much as

Figure 29. Assistant Secretary of Labor Louis F. Post, pictured here as a younger man, blocked the deportation of nearly three thousand aliens arrested in the infamous Palmer Raids in 1920. The Library of Congress.

know the difference between bolshevism and rheumatism."[15] But Palmer knew they were guilty. "Out of the sly and crafty eyes of many of them leap cupidity, cruelty, insanity, and crime," he observed to a House committee. "From their lopsided faces, sloping brows, and misshapen features may be recognized the unmistakable criminal type."[16]

Those arrested were often held under disgraceful conditions and subjected to third-degree interrogations, held incommunicado, denied counsel, and incarcerated for months because they couldn't meet bail set as high as $10,000. In Detroit, eight hundred men were held for six days in a small corridor of the Federal Building, sharing one toilet and stale air and sleeping on the floor as they awaited examinations.[17] Another eight hundred were handcuffed in pairs, chained together and perp-walked before the press as they were ferried to Deer Island in Boston Harbor. In that dilapidated and chaotic facility, one alien killed himself by plunging headfirst from the fifth floor and another merely went insane.[18] It was "a collection of lawless precedents which may yet serve more efficiently than reckless mobs to shatter the liberty guarantees of the American Constitution," wrote Assistant Secretary of Labor Louis F. Post.[19]

Like Horatio at the bridge, Post, then seventy, almost single-handedly blocked deportation of nearly three thousand men and women, defeating the shameful rights abuses by the Justice Department and the Bureau of Immigration through a strict adherence to the law and to his conscience.[20] A decade earlier, the *Outlook*, a liberal journal, had been outspoken under his editorship against suppression of speech by anarchists.[21] Now Post was fighting a different method of suppressing dissidents' speech. He knew that the department was the final judge in most deportation cases, for if there were even a scintilla of evidence, the courts would not interfere. Although criminal laws did not apply, Post insisted that constitutional guarantees for criminal suspects be honored.[22] Post also adhered to court precedents. One of the most influential deportation decisions was that of Judge Bourquin in Montana, who held that statements made by a suspect without being afforded the opportunity for counsel could not be used against him or her.[23]

Personally reviewing as many as one hundred files a day, Post found endemic abuse of due process. In one "revolting instance," an alien with no evidence against him was in jail for more than eight weeks before, during, and after a hearing, and then the Bureau of Immigration wanted him held indefinitely while the Justice Department tried to dig up evidence.[24] Other aliens were held more than ninety days and one man in Cleveland 162 days, even though an inspector had recommended release two days after his arrest.[25]

Post's fiery defense of his actions disarmed impeachment proceedings against him in May 1920.[26] The bottom dropped out of deportation futures.[27] Reflecting on the "deportations delirium" in his memoir, Post said, "The popular approval it received lies beyond the range of any reasonable explanation other than that the public mind was under the influence of . . . a monstrous social delirium. Such deliriums cannot continue . . . without disastrous social consequences."[28]

Post's courageous stand prompts the question whether the Palmer raids would have been approved had President Wilson been well. His stroke in September 1919 near the end of his cross-country campaign for the League of Nations had effectively put his wife, Edith, and his private secretary, Joseph P. Tumulty, in control of the White House. Wilson tended to give his cabinet officers carte blanche. And had not Palmer and his subordinate, J. Edgar Hoover merely carried out what he had urged in his 1915 State of the Union address? Wilson had called for the crushing of the "creatures of passion, disloyalty, and anarchy . . . who have poured the poison of disloyalty into the very arteries of our national life; who have sought to bring the authority and good name of our Government into contempt, to destroy our industries wherever they thought it effective for their vindictive purposes to strike at them, and to debase our politics to the uses of foreign intrigue."[29]

The Pendulum Swings

As Harold Evans has noted, "The genius of America has been to avoid pressing any political theory too far or too systematically."[30] The excesses of the Palmer-Hoover raids of 1919–20, along with other reactionary excesses, prompted a potent national backlash that spelled the end of the Red Scare and provoked more liberal ideas about the scope of constitutional liberties. Most prominent in leading the reaction to the raids was a group of twelve noted legal scholars—including Zechariah Chafee Jr., Roscoe Pound, Felix Frankfurter, Ernest Freund, and Frank P. Walsh. In May 1920, the group issued a scathing rebuke of Palmer. "Punishments of the utmost cruelty and heretofore unthinkable in America have become usual," the lawyers reported, referring to "great numbers of persons, both aliens and citizens, [who] have been threatened, beaten with blackjacks, struck with fists, jailed under abominable conditions, or actually tortured." Constitutional protections against search and seizure, self-incrimination, excessive bail, and cruel and unusual punishment had been trampled. Agents provocateurs had been widely employed to ensure that party members were meeting on the night of the raids. The scholars charged Palmer with "deliberate misuse of his office and a deliberate squandering of funds entrusted to him by Congress in carrying on a propaganda against the radicals through the public press."[31]

Palmer apologized for nothing. At legislative hearings early in 1921 instigated by Senator Walsh of Montana but chaired by Senator Thomas Sterling of South Dakota, a Palmer supporter, the attorney general mounted a full-scale defense, saying the raids were justified and that the end justified the means. When you are "trying to protect the community against moral rats you sometimes get to thinking more of your trap's effectiveness than of its lawful construction," he said.[32]

Peacetime Sedition Laws

Brandishing the pamphlet found near Palmer's house after the bombing

("There will have to be murder; we will kill . . . there will have to be destruction; we will destroy . . . *The Anarchist Fighters* . . ."), Montana's Senator Walsh had urged passage of a peacetime sedition law, punishing anyone who urged overthrow of the government, displayed the symbols of international socialism or used the mails to distribute anarchistic literature.[33] The 1917 Espionage Act and the 1918 wartime sedition law that Walsh and colleague Henry Myers had been so instrumental in effecting would expire on the last day of Wilson's presidency.[34]

During the winter of 1919–20, more than seventy anti-sedition bills were introduced in Congress. Palmer and the White House were enthusiastic supporters. A bill introduced by Rep. Martin L. Davey (D-Ohio) would have imposed the death penalty for persons "who shall teach . . . or encourage forcible resistance to or destruction of the Government of the United States . . ." and whose seditious activities caused a death. The same measure proposed to ban all seditious literature from the mails, abrogate the Fifth Amendment self-incrimination protection in sedition cases, deport convicted aliens and imprison convicted citizens for up to twenty years.[35]

Congress did not enact any of the bills, thanks to strong opposition from the AFL, from many newspapers and magazines, and from scholars such as Zechariah Chafee Jr. The AFL's Samuel Gompers warned the measures would breed even more radicals. Under the bill's language, the *New York World* noted sarcastically, the Declaration of Independence "on its face is hideously seditious and about to be banned by law." Others wondered whether Congress had learned anything from the storm over the Alien and Sedition Acts in 1798 (which Woodrow Wilson himself, in his *History of the American People*, said cut "perilously near the roots of freedom of speech and of the press.").[36]

As the debate on peacetime sedition laws continued, there seemed to be more introspection in editorial pages and more awareness of the deeper wounds that further suppression would inflict upon constitutional principles. When the *Literary Digest* queried editors about what provisions a sedition law must have, many gave specific suggestions, but others, like an unnamed Indiana editor, realized the extreme difficulty of the line-drawing task before Congress. How to penalize "an intent to invite forcible revolution against the Government without giving overzealous and incompetent authorities the opportunity to cause suffering to persons whose acts and speech may be wrongly construed as an incitement to revolution?"[37]

That really was the nub of the problem. In their anxiety to get at "the really bad man" who intended violent harm to the United States, Congress was crafting a sledgehammer to swat a horsefly. This blunt weapon would not only hit every form of overt radicalism but also would inhibit inquiry, thought, and expression and "suppress the discussion of public questions at point after point," wrote Zechariah Chafee Jr.[38]

A host of evils, in fact, would follow passage of a sedition law, Chafee predicted. Suppression of radical thought in books, newspapers and periodicals would not only prevent airing of unpopular ideas, it would even allow the government to escape scrutiny for how offenders were punished. Remember, he added, (quoting Wilson), that "The seed of revolution is repression," and that at least some of the violence of 1919–20 was a reaction to the raids and the heavy sentences imposed on many radicals during the war. Better to recall, he said (quoting Oliver Wendell Holmes Jr.), "With effervescing opinions, as with the not yet forgotten champagne, the quickest way to let them go flat is to let them get exposed to the air."

When applied by fallible human beings, sedition laws would reflect the worst of human nature, Chafee warned. "Enforcement will let loose a horde of spies and informers swarming into our private life, stirring up suspicion without end, making all attacks on government either impotent or unsafe." History also teaches, Chafee added, that "persecution of unpopular doctrines is [like] a drug . . . the pleasure of being able to silence [radicals] was so agreeable in 1917 and 1918 that it will be abandoned only with extreme reluctance, and we long for more suppression to satisfy the appetite which has been created . . ."

The United States, whose founders fomented rebellion and triumphed by revolution is "the last place where mere talk about revolution ought to be treated as inherently vicious and intolerable," Chafee lectured. "[W]e cannot honor and praise these men for their courageous onslaughts on established evils, and at the same time pronounce it a heinous crime for any one today to urge the removal of wrongs by force."[39]

Such arguments may have helped stall peacetime sedition laws in Congress but had little effect at the state level, where many legislatures were busy passing criminal syndicalism and red flag laws. Montana's early passage of a criminal syndicalism law in 1918 (Idaho and Minnesota were first in 1917) presaged passage of similarly worded laws in seventeen more states between 1919 and 1920.[40] Each criminalized mere membership in any organization embracing the "doctrine of advocating, teaching, or aiding and abetting the commission of crime, sabotage, or unlawful acts of force or violence or unlawful methods of terrorism as a means of accomplishing a change in industrial ownership or control, or effecting any political change."[41]

Aimed directly at the IWW and the Communist Party, the laws sailed through legislatures often with no opposition and with "a great outburst of oratory characterized more by passion, prejudice, and misinformation than by a reasoned effort to get at the facts . . ." wrote political scientist Eldridge Foster Dowell in his classic 1939 study of such laws. The legislators who passed such laws were "average middle-class Americans, believers in the existing economic and political system, usually uncritical of what they read in their newspapers and endowed with a deep antipathy or distrust for groups or individuals labeled as radical or unpatriotic."[42]

Criminal syndicalism prosecution would flourish in four states: New York, Illinois, Oregon, and particularly in California, where 504 persons were arrested and 264 actually tried between 1919 and 1924.[43] The laws' violation of constitutional guarantees of free expression seemed pretty patent to Chafee. "This is not punishing a man for what he does, or even for what he says, but for what someone else says, which he may possibly not approve."[44]

In 1919, twenty-seven states also outlawed all public displays of the red flag, bringing the total to thirty-two by 1920.[45] Their purpose was to squelch public demonstrations by radical groups that had adopted a red flag, including, of course, the Communists and the IWW. Yet many red flag laws were so vague that the laws criminalized what was perfectly legal. Oklahoma's, for example, banned the display of any banner "indicating disloyalty or a belief in anarchy or other political doctrines."[46] In all, state red flag, sedition, and criminal syndicalism laws were used in 1919–20 to arrest no fewer than fourteen hundred persons, of which approximately three hundred were sent to prison.[47]

Unseated

Overreaction by legislators to the Red Scare extended to the legislators themselves. Refusals to seat socialist representatives in Congress and in the New York Assembly raised the question whether unpopular views would have a voice in the law-making branch of the government.

In the spring of 1919, the U.S. House of Representatives refused to seat Victor L. Berger, a rather conservative leader of the Socialist Party and editor of the *Milwaukee Leader*. The stated reason was that Berger had committed treason by opposing the country's participation in the war, but the underlying reason, it became clear, was his leadership in the Socialist Party. Berger had already encountered plenty of trouble for denouncing the war as an exercise in European imperialism and capitalist profiteering. Postmaster General Burleson had lifted the *Leader's* second-class mailing privileges in 1917. The next year, after his election to Congress, Berger was convicted under the Espionage Act for having "conspired to . . . willfully cause insubordination, disloyalty and refusal of duty in said military and naval forces . . . by persistently dwelling upon the evils and horrors of war." Federal Judge Kenesaw Mountain Landis sentenced him to twenty years in prison.[48]

The Supreme Court's reversal of Berger's conviction in 1921 came far too late to affect his fortunes in the House, which voted 311–1 in November 1919 to deny him the seat he had handily won representing sixty thousand Milwaukee residents. After a second election that Berger won with an even bigger margin, the House again refused to seat him. Berger eventually reclaimed his seat in 1923 after passions had subsided and continued in Congress until his death in 1929.[49]

Historians compared Berger to the English journalist John Wilkes, refused a seat in Parliament four times in the 1760s while in prison for seditious libel, the result of his criticism of King George III and his ministers. After his release, Wilkes became mayor of London and was reelected to Parliament in 1774, this time with no opposition from the Crown. The lesson was lost on both Congress and the New York State Assembly, whose unseating of five Socialists on January 7, 1920, followed.

Unlike Berger, the Albany Socialists had committed no crimes. Four had already served legislative terms. But the Assembly's action occurred at the spring tide of the Red Scare. Just five days earlier, newsboys had hawked the headlines trumpeting Palmer's raids. Anarchist Emma Goldman and her fellow deportees had just disembarked in Hangö, Finland. The 109-day steel strike was still on. And the legislature's radical-hunting Lusk Committee had already raised the temperature to boiling, conducting raids and investigations for the past year, accumulating materials that would lead to the charges against the socialists.

In the ceremonial first hours of the Assembly's opening day, Speaker

Thaddeus C. Sweet had summoned the five Socialists to the bar of the chamber and charged them with "being elected on a platform that is absolutely inimical to the best interests of the State of New York and of the United States." The men were charged with belonging to a "revolutionary party" that preached disloyalty and treason because it had endorsed the Third Communist International, which bound signatories to the violent overthrow of the government.[50]

Just as remarkable as the Assembly's action was the reaction to it—swift, broad, and powerful. If there is proof of their crimes, produce it, challenged Charles Evans Hughes, former Supreme Court justice, former governor of New York, and GOP candidate for president in 1916. "But I count it a most serious mistake to proceed," he warned, "against masses of our citizens combined for political action, by denying them the only resource of peaceful government; that is, action by the ballot box and through duly elected representatives in legislative bodies . . ."

"Is it not clear that government can not be saved at the cost of its own principles?" Hughes asked.[51]

Editorial condemnation poured forth from lawyers, clergymen, and civic organizations across the political spectrum. More harm "has been inflicted upon the principles of political freedom and popular self-government," said the *Pittsburgh Leader*, "than all the blatant mouthings of the reddest of the Red." Voicing a growing sentiment, the *Fresno Republican* called for an end to "the present boisterous campaign against all radicalism and all liberalism."

Not all newspapers agreed. The *New York Times* termed the expulsion "as clearly and demonstrably a measure of national defense as the declaration of war against Germany."[52] But the *Times* was behind the times. The final straw came in September when the Assembly obstinately refused to seat three of the Socialists who had been elected again. "The red terror became ridiculous on the lips of Speaker Sweet," Chafee recalled. "A legislature trembling before five men—the long-lost American sense of humor revived and people began to laugh. That broke the spell."[53]

Besides providing a belly laugh, the State Assembly's overreaction also gave Congress pause about the sedition bills under consideration. Editorial opinion shifted just after the Socialists' initial disbarment. "Many journals [including the *New York Times*] now agreed that in the haste to avoid bolshevism . . . the institutions most in danger were not those attacked by revolutionists but the basic rights of free speech, free press, and free assemblage," observed Red Scare historian James Murray.[54] Congress delayed action and adjourned in June with no sedition bills passed.

Palmer, the chief architect of the Red Scare, left office at the end of the Wilson administration. His reputation was tarnished in the public's mind, however, and his presidential ambitions were in tatters. Palmer's Chicken Little routine about Bolshevism had worn thin. Despite his dire warnings about radical violence on May Day 1920, nothing happened. When he proclaimed that the horrific Wall Street bombing on September 16, 1920, which killed thirty-three and wounded two hundred, was proof positive of an imminent radical takeover, growing segments of the press and public weren't buying it. "Capitalism is untouched," said the *Cleveland Plain Dealer.* "The federal government is not shaken in the slightest degree. The public is merely shocked, not terrorized, much less converted to the merits of anarchism. Business and life as usual . . ."[55]

The report of the subcommittee that investigated Palmer's raids languished until 1923, when Senator Walsh forced the issue and inserted the hearing transcript into the *Congressional Record.* "I find it difficult to conceive of a course more powerfully calculated to excite widespread hatred of our government," Walsh wrote in his minority report. "The indignities and outrages suffered by the victims . . . will rankle in their breasts until their dying day, and their friends and relatives will share with them the conviction that justice 'for a season bade the world farewell' . . ."

"There was a time when it was fondly believed that nothing of the kind could occur in America," Walsh continued, "that the constitutional guaranty of a speedy public trial meant something more than a mere declaration." The Red Scare did not justify illegal measures, Walsh concluded in an oft-quoted passage: "It is only in such times that the guaranties of the Constitution as to personal rights are of any practical value. In seasons of calm no one thinks of denying them; they are accorded as a matter of course . . ."[56]

The words were stirring, but by then Palmer had been out of office for two years. Walsh, a nationally respected constitutional lawyer, undoubtedly felt anguished by Palmer's raid on the Bill of Rights. But it was Walsh who had urged passage of a peacetime sedition law after the bombings and Walsh who had helped his fellow Montana senator, Henry Myers, push the passage of the 1918 wartime Sedition Act. Perhaps wartime or terrorism justified such restrictions to Walsh, even if neither justified invasions of other personal liberties. By mid-1919, practically no one had articulated a legal theory that would give more breathing room for political dissent. That would slowly begin to change as some of Walsh's fellow lawyers, energized as he had been by Palmer's trashing of the Constitution, would fight back.

The Blanket of Repression

The reactionary extremism of the postwar Red Scare era did not turn the nation into a fascist state, unlike Germany and Italy and other nations in Europe, because there were still many avenues for opportunity and for political, social, and economic democratization. Still, the nativist impulses implicit in President Wilson's 1915 speech had hardly been quelled. Conservatives and patriotic societies turned to public education as the pathway to ideological conformity. Twenty states passed teacher-loyalty legislation in the 1920s. At the urging of the American Legion and the Ku Klux Klan, history and civics texts were "purified." Immigrants underwent Americanization, a more subtle form of weeding out radicals and nonconformists. To the same end, industry underwent open shop "reform" that denied unions exclusive bargaining rights. The IWW continued to be repressed, particularly in California where large IWW-led strikes led to numerous criminal syndicalism prosecutions. Immigration was tightened in 1924. Sacco and Vanzetti, the Italian anarchists, were executed in 1927 for the murder of a shoe company paymaster—railroaded, radicals charged, because of their beliefs. And the federal government's regime of security and surveillance first developed in the war was continuing to grow with every stack of file cards in J. Edgar Hoover's office.[57]

Senator Hiram Johnson's prediction had come to pass. In January 1920, the senator from California had said, "The war has set back the people for a generation. They have bowed to a hundred repressive acts. They have become slaves to the government. They are frightened at the excesses in Russia. They are docile; and they will not recover from being so for many years."[58]

The blanket of repression thrown over the nation starting in 1917 would not have been woven had not the press contributed the loom, charged *New York World* editor Frank I. Cobb in a stinging criticism published at the end of 1919. Governments had "conscripted public opinion . . . mobilized it . . . goose-stepped it . . . taught it to stand at attention and salute," and newspapers were its willing tools, passing along government and business propaganda. Without "driving to the heart" of industrial upheavals and the social ferment, newspapers had instead "hunt[ed] out the devil upon whom the responsibility could be laid," faulting the IWW and Communists. In the process, constitutional rights were being eroded, giving way to the tyranny of the majority.[59]

What was needed, Cobb said, was a restoration of the people's belief in the driving principle behind the Bill of Rights that made it "the one guarantee of human freedom to the American people": that its provisions *limited* the powers of the government. Congress shall make *no* law [respecting freedom of religion or freedom of expression]; the right of the people to keep and bear arms shall *not* be infringed; the right of the people to be secure . . . against unreasonable searches and seizures shall *not* be violated, and so forth. "The Bill of Rights," Cobb counseled, "is a born rebel. It reeks of sedition."[60]

So there was the grand irony. A seditious principle at the heart of liberty would safeguard the nation from those who would protect the country from sedition. It was a paradox that the forces of reaction, the self-appointed patriots, would never fathom. Even constitutional lawyers like Thomas Walsh could only half appreciate the power that lay within the First Amendment. And if minds like his could not fully grasp Cobb's point as applied to freedom of expression, what of the justices of the Supreme Court? For 128 years since its ratification, the First Amendment had scarcely been interpreted by the high court. That was about to change, as sedition cases from the war percolated to the top of the judicial pyramid. ❖

SEVENTEEN
The Dawn of Free Speech

U.S. Supreme Court Begins to Rethink Free Speech, 1919–1927

The U.S. Supreme Court rulings immediately after the Armistice were an unmitigated disaster for free speech. Wartime hysteria continued to echo inside the marble halls of the U.S. Supreme Court.

The first three decisions handed down in early March 1919 were all unanimous. In the first, Socialist Party leaders in Philadelphia had been convicted under the Espionage Act, punishing conspiracies to "obstruct the recruiting and enlistment service of the United States." They had mailed a leaflet to draftees attacking the draft as a violation of the anti-slavery Thirteenth Amendment and as "tyrannical power in its worst form." The leaflet asked, "Will you be led astray by a propaganda of jingoism masquerading under the guise of patriotism? . . . Are you with the forces of liberty and light or war and darkness?" and declared, "If you do not assert and support your rights, you are helping to deny or disparage rights which it is the solemn duty of all citizens and residents of the United States to retain."[1]

Attorneys for party general secretary Charles T. Schenck and Dr. Elizabeth Baer, a member of the executive committee, argued that the conviction violated the First Amendment. "If it is criminal to say the draft law is wrong, then it is criminal to say that any law is wrong, for the Constitution, we are told, is not suspended in time of war; but we dare not attack it or our form of government." They quoted from the Ves Hall opinion in Montana for the proposition that actual obstruction and injury must be proven, not mere attempts to obstruct. And they concluded by arguing that "no government and no court and no law can easily afford to take issue with the smallest minority of citizens, if they are . . . steadfastly standing for what they honestly, conscientiously believe."[2]

Justice Oliver Wendell Holmes Jr., writing for the court, noted that the circumstances in which the words were uttered were vital in determining whether they were protected under the First Amendment. Just the previous year, Holmes had expressed beautifully the changing character of words: "A word is not a crystal, transparent and unchanging, it is the skin of a living thought and may vary greatly in color and content according to the circumstances and time in which it is used."[3]

This time, Holmes reached for a more volatile metaphor. "The most stringent protection of free speech would not protect a man in falsely shouting fire in a theatre and causing a panic." In wartime, too, he indicated, constitutional guarantees of free speech are diminished: "The question in every case is whether the words used are used in such circumstances and are of such a nature as to create a clear and present danger that they will bring about the substantive evils that Congress has a right to prevent. It is a question of proximity and degree. When a nation is at war many things that might be said in time of peace are such a hindrance to its effort that their utterance will not be endured so long as men fight and that no Court could regard them as protected by any constitutional right."[4]

To Holmes, the expression "clear and present danger" signaled the degree on a sort of danger thermometer at which the government was justified in suppressing speech because violence would follow. In the case of Schenck, Holmes believed the critical temperature had been exceeded by sending anti-draft leaflets to draftees in wartime—not because they necessarily caused young men to tear up their registration papers, but because a jury had agreed that they had a *tendency* to do so. Speech that *might* lead to violence was so much like violence itself that the government could criminalize it. Holmes was therefore endorsing the "bad tendency" test that judges regularly used to punish dangerous speech.

His "clear and present danger" was therefore a hollow test, at least for Schenck and Baer. And by equating the socialists' anti-draft leaflets in wartime to false cries of fire in a theater, Holmes had characterized their defiant words as either sociopathically mischievous or a vicious and premeditated criminal act. In fact, as law historian Richard Polenberg has pointed out, the leaflet's language was misquoted and mischaracterized by Holmes, turning a strongly worded screed into language that justified punishment.[5]

The full import of Holmes' conservative stance would become clear a week later in two other cases. In the first, Jacob Frohwerk, working at less than a day-laborer's pay for a small German-language newspaper, the *Missouri Staats Zeitung*, had been convicted of violating the Espionage Act for a dozen anti-war articles in the latter half of 1917. The army, he wrote, had been raised illegally, the war was being financed by Wall Street and the great trusts, and resisting the draft was an honorable course. For these crimes of utterance, Frohwerk had been sentenced to ten years on each of twelve counts (compared to six months for Schenck and ninety days for Baer).[6]

Holmes seemed at first to soften his stance on wartime utterances: "We do not lose our right to condemn either measures or men because the country is at war." The newspaper's circulation was tiny and "It does not appear that there was any special effort to reach men who were subject to the draft." Nonetheless, he concluded (although the record was skimpy), the *possibility* that Frohwerk's words were circulated "in quarters where a little breath would be enough to kindle a flame . . ." was enough to sustain a conviction.[7] A poor—and poorly represented—immigrant's commonplace rantings about an unpopular war in a small German-language newspaper in Kansas City were enough, because of the remote possibility they might somehow obstruct the war effort, to strip him of any free speech protection.

Holmes and the high court were no more sympathetic to the famous man whose case was paired with his, whose anti-war speech was widely circulated across the country, and who had the most competent of counsel. Eugene V. Debs, four-time Socialist Party candidate for president and the Wilson administration's most prominent leftist critic, had been convicted of violating the Espionage Act with a speech he gave to a state convention of socialists in a park in Canton, Ohio, on June 16, 1918.

In an emotional three-hour address to the delegates, punctuated 185 times by applause or laughter, the ailing sixty-three–year-old socialist skewered the capitalists, hailed the Bolsheviks, praised comrades convicted under the Espionage Act and other wartime laws and blasted the class apartheid of war: "The master class has always declared the wars; the subject class has always fought the battles. . . . If war is right let it be declared by the people. You who have your lives to lose, you certainly above all others have the right to decide the momentous issue of war or peace." The Socialist Party, he declared, develops the full human potential. "You need at this time especially to know that you are fit for something better than slavery and cannon fodder. You need to know that you were not created to work and produce and impoverish yourself to enrich an idle exploiter . . ."[8]

At trial, Debs had told the jury, "I have been accused of obstructing the war. I admit it. Gentlemen, I abhor war. I would oppose the war if I stood alone."[9] The jury found him guilty as charged of "causing and inciting insubordination, disloyalty, mutiny, and refusal of duty in the military and naval forces of the United States."[10] Condemning those "within our borders who would strike the sword from the hand of this nation while she is engaged in defending herself against a foreign and brutal power," the federal judge sentenced Debs to ten years in prison.[11]

The "vital issue in this case," argued Debs' appellate lawyer, was Debs' First Amendment rights to criticize American participation in the war. The guarantee of free speech would become a mere caricature if the critical national policy questions inherent in declaring and conducting war could only be debated in peacetime. Debs' conviction for military obstruction was a conviction for sedition, for mere words, he emphasized. Gilbert Roe, in a friend-of-the-court brief, pointed out that Debs' conviction was an excellent example of what he had warned when Congress was debating the Espionage Act. Juries given "bad tendency" instructions to [convict if] "the words used had as their natural tendency and reasonably probable effect to obstruct the recruiting service" would almost always convict.[12]

Holmes brushed aside the constitutional objections. The First Amendment issue had been "disposed of in *Schenck*." Without even mentioning "clear and present danger," Holmes declared there was enough evidence "to warrant the jury in finding that one purpose of the speech, *whether incidental or not does not matter,* was to oppose not only war in general but this war, and that the opposition was so expressed that its natural and intended effect would be to obstruct recruiting."[13] (Emphasis added). Debs' rhetoric on that warm spring day in Ohio, the justices said, was so dangerous to America's self-preservation that it had to be stopped.

Fear, indeed, had overcome reason.

On March 10, 1919, when the *Debs* and *Frohwerk* opinions were issued, as far as the U.S. Supreme Court was concerned, there was no First Amendment protection for dissident wartime speech considered dangerous to the nation—and therefore, no free speech for all. The unanimous decisions were a stunning blow to radicals, to libertarians and to a growing number of progressives disgusted by the super-patriotic excesses of the wartime era and the imprisonment of hundreds merely for expressing their criticism of the government. For those who were convinced that the guarantees of free speech in the Bill of Rights protected dissenters from being squelched by the majority, it was an especially bitter day. The highest court in the land had confirmed that repression of political dissent was necessary for national security—and had done it in a brusque and almost cruel way, confirming harsh prison sentences and barely giving the time of day to constitutional concerns.

The U.S. Supreme Court in 1919 was clearly not much concerned about protection of expression. Rather, the Court was characterized by its vigorous protection of an altogether different type of freedom—the laissez-faire notion of economic liberty and liberty of contract. Time and again, it had endorsed the right to use private property as one chose, keeping business and industry free from meddlesome state and federal regulation. The Court's position was crystallized in a 1905 decision that struck down, as an unreasonable exercise of its police power, a state law limiting bakery employees from working more than ten hours a day, and upheld "the right of the individual to labor for such time as he may choose."[14]

A generation later, Harvard law professor Felix Frankfurter would venture this explanation for the court's attitude just after the World War: "That a majority of the Supreme Court which frequently disallowed restraint on economic powers should so consistently have sanctioned restraints of the mind is perhaps only a surface paradox. There is an underlying unity between fear of ample experimentation in economics and fear of the expression of ideas."[15]

While Frankfurter's theory may have explained the mindset of most of the members of the Court, it didn't explain the philosophy of the man to whose opinion in the first free speech cases they had signed on—Oliver Wendell Holmes Jr. He, in fact, thought the economic liberty theory, grounded in the due process clause of the Fourteenth Amendment, was passé and "perverted," in the sense that it no longer represented the majority's will. As a progressive, he took a rational, objective and collective approach to social problems, favoring the will of the majority over the individual.

Holmes' take on "dangerous" speech was neatly encapsulated in his comparison of the speech cases to another case the court had decided in 1905, involving a Cambridge, Massachusetts, law that mandated vaccination to stop a smallpox epidemic. The court, including Holmes, had decided in this case that the law was "for the common good," a necessary health and safety measure. "Upon the principle of self-defense, of paramount necessity, a community has the right to protect itself. . . . Even liberty itself, the greatest of all rights," Justice Harlan had written for the majority, "is not unrestricted license to act according to one's own will."[16]

Similarly, Holmes had reasoned, punishment of speech hostile to the nation's war effort was a necessary measure when it presented a "clear and present danger." Unfortunately, Holmes' view of *when* the danger justified repression—not at the point of incitement but much earlier, when there was even a tendency to touch off a spark—aligned him with the rest of the court. But that was about to change in the next eight months, the period of the much-analyzed "conversion" of Holmes.[17]

In a nutshell, the Civil War veteran, seventy-eight years old in 1919, would be persuaded by some of his intellectual peers—and through his own reading of history, philosophy, and current events that summer—that more breathing room was necessary for dissident speech. Through correspondence, conversation, and published critiques, men such as Federal District Judge Learned Hand (who held in the 1917 *Masses* case that speech could be punished only if there was "direct advocacy of resistance"[18]), University of Chicago law professor Ernst Freund, *The New Republic* editor Herbert Croly, and Harvard law professor Zechariah Chafee Jr., had a profound influence on Holmes' thinking.[19] The result would become obvious in the next free speech opinion the Court issued, on November 10, 1919.

The Dawn of Free Speech

Seven Russian Jewish immigrants in New York City, avowed Bolsheviks and anarchists, were arrested on August 23, 1918, after tossing copies of leaflets printed in English and Yiddish out of a third-floor window of an office building on Second Avenue in Manhattan. The leaflets expressed their outrage that seven thousand American troops were being sent to Siberia to aid anti-Soviet Czech forces, at a time when the new Soviet government had made peace with Germany and thus posed a threat to American interests.

To Jacob Abrams and his fellow radicals, the American action jeopardized the newborn Soviet state. In impassioned language in their leaflets, they assailed President Wilson for his "cowardly silence" about the intervention, "the hypocrisy of the plutocratic gang in Washington" and capitalism as "the enemy of the workers." American "bullets, bayonets, [and] cannon" intended for German soldiers, they pointed out, would be used to murder "your dearest, best, who are in Russia fighting for freedom."[20]

Unlike the previous cases that had involved violations of the Espionage Act, Abrams and five companions were convicted on four counts of violating the Montana-spawned 1918 Sedition Act, which had become federal law in May. Like many other sedition cases, the trial featured considerable prejudice by the judge and a speedy verdict (one hour and six minutes).[21] Abrams, Samuel Lipman, and Hyman Lachowsky were each sentenced to twenty years and fined $1,000. Mollie Steimer, barely twenty-one, received a fifteen-year sentence and a $500 fine.[22]

In an opinion written by Justice John Clarke, issued exactly eight months after the *Frohwerk* and *Debs* decisions, the court majority had little trouble disposing of the case, argued less than three weeks earlier.[23] To them, the defendants' pro-Bolshevik statements were proscribed by the Sedition Act even though Abrams and company were manifestly anti-German. Using "bad tendency" rhetoric, Clarke then concluded that "the plain purpose of their propaganda was to excite, at the supreme crisis of the war, disaffection, sedition, riots, and, as they hoped, revolution, in this country . . ."

This time, however, Holmes, joined by Justice Louis D. Brandeis, could not go along. Even taking the strongest possible charge, that the radicals' appeal to the consciences of munitions workers would affect the supply of arms to Germany, he argued, "Intent . . . to cripple or hinder the United States in the prosecution of the war" had not been proven. The leaflets had not posed a "clear and imminent" danger to the government. Holmes made it clear that this mild change in wording really signified a sea change in his thinking. This time he was focusing on the *immediate* danger posed by speech. Employing several different variations in wording, he finally settled on this:

> I think that we should be eternally vigilant against attempts to check the expression of opinions that we loathe and believe to be fraught with death unless they so imminently threaten immediate interference with the lawful and pressing purposes of the law that an immediate check is required to save the country.[24]

To Holmes, his new test had not been met, not by a mile. By comparison with Schenck, Frohwerk and Debs (and perhaps to justify why they merited long prison sentences), Holmes made Abrams and company look like the gang who couldn't shoot straight. He described their propaganda as "the surreptitious publishing of a silly leaflet by an unknown man" and "these poor and puny anonymities."[25]

Holmes' more libertarian formulation for the limits of dangerous speech would eventually have profound repercussions, affecting the way Americans regarded their liberty of conscience, and thereby transforming the political and social currents of the nation. But it was not only the test, but also the philosophy behind it that Holmes so eloquently expressed in the final paragraph of his famous dissent that would herald the dawn of free speech in America:

> Persecution for the expression of opinions seems to me perfectly logical. If you have no doubt of your premises or your power and want a certain result with all your heart you naturally express your wishes in law and sweep away all opposition.[26]

Coming three days after the first Palmer raids, Holmes' observation seemed to spotlight the frenzied sentiments of the majority, which had expressed its will in harsh laws like the Espionage Act, the Sedition Act, postal censorship laws, and the deportations of radicals.

> But when men have realized that time has upset many fighting faiths, they may come to believe even more than they believe the very foundations of their own conduct that the ultimate good desired is better reached by free trade in ideas—that the best test of truth is the power of the thought to get itself accepted in the competition of the market, and that truth is the only ground upon which their wishes safely can be carried out.[27]

Holmes—historian, scholar, polymath, philosopher, old Civil War soldier—could no doubt have recalled a hundred different illustrations of cherished beliefs coming undone. Several more immediate examples suggest themselves: disillusionment by those on the winning side of the war, for world peace seemed as elusive as ever; the agonies of defeat for the losers, whose own faith in their cause had been crushed; the feeling of betrayal that progressives like Holmes felt, for the war they had initially supported had transmogrified into a horror of repression.

Free trade in ideas was at the core of Holmes' belief. It was in part a reflection of his philosophy of Social Darwinism, in this case the survival of the most workable or fittest idea. But he also would have realized that the test of truth needed more breathing room than any "bad tendency" judgment was likely to give it, hence the importance of words like "immediate" or "imminence" in his proposed test. Even hateful and dangerous ideas, "opinions that we loathe and believe to be fraught with death," could be traded unless the imminent danger test were met.

Holmes' own radical idea, then, was his endorsement of a test and an underlying theory that worked together to expand constitutional protection for free speech.[28] It represented a paradigm shift in thinking about dangerous speech, and perhaps a significant shift in Holmes' own philosophy. Degrees of perceived danger before the state is justified in shutting down speech are often represented as points on a scale—"bad tendency" at one point, "clear and present danger" at another, and so forth. But Holmes propelled the First Amendment into almost a different dimension.

The bad tendency test presupposed criminal or dangerous intent. It said the state must control both acts and speech that might prove dangerous. It implied little faith in individuals to sort things out, and it also implied a powerful, controlling, or even autocratic state. Its intellectual patrons were Aristotle and Hobbes. And yet the man who had carried Hobbes' *Leviathan* on his graduation day at Harvard, whose long career as a jurist favored the will of the majority and a communitarian philosophy, had chosen an approach to free speech that was the yin to Hobbes' yang. Holmes' test and theory said "Let's wait and see" and "individuals (whose government it is) can choose the best idea." It bespoke a libertarian approach informed by the thought of Mill and Locke.

Holmes' thoughts, while path-breaking, were not original. Anyone who reads John Stuart Mill's *On Liberty* side by side with Holmes' paragraph in the Abrams case will be struck by the parallels. But taken as a whole, as the philosophical foundation and the practical test for a more expansive notion of free speech, Holmes' paradigm resonated in the American spirit. The marketplace of ideas rang true not only with those who summoned forth the competitive tenets of capitalism, but also as an endorsement of the ethos that overlaid that economic theory in the United States with a virtually bottomless belief in opportunity. Law professor Rodney Smolla notes, "The American love of the marketplace of ideas metaphor stems in no small part from our irrepressible national optimism." And, he adds, the freedom of speech that Holmes endorsed rang an even deeper chord as "part of the human personality itself, a value intimately intertwined with human autonomy and dignity."[29]

Holmes' dissent in *Abrams* was itself a kind of tiny spark of revolutionary thought. It would break down established patterns of thought and elevate the importance of free speech in a democratic society. As Holmes would have realized, however, his more-expansive notion of free speech in the marketplace of ideas would take a long time to be accepted.

The Road to Acceptance

When the U.S. Supreme Court affirmed the conviction and fifteen-year sentence of Mollie Steimer, the fresh-faced compatriot of Jacob Abrams, she was twenty-one.[30] When that same court in 1969 endorsed, for the first time, a free speech test that would have reversed her sedition conviction on First Amendment grounds, she was seventy-one, living in Mexico.[31] The Court would never have reached that point, however, had it not been for a crucial decision in 1925 that revolutionized the scope of free speech protection.

Defended by Clarence Darrow, a twenty-nine–year-old socialist named Benjamin Gitlow had been convicted under New York's criminal anarchy law, making it a crime to advocate the overthrow of organized government by force or violence. He was sentenced to five to ten years in prison. Gitlow was a leading member of the Left Wing Section of the New York Socialist Party. The party's windy thirty-four–page manifesto that he published was so dry in its dialectic that if read aloud by an agitator would incite violence only against himself, one observer cracked.[32] And even if it did urge revolution, Darrow argued, what of it? "For a man to be afraid of revolution in America would be to be ashamed of your own mother."[33]

The trial court jury, however, concluded that Gitlow broke the law, and the Supreme Court agreed. The manifesto "urges in fervent language mass action which shall progressively foment industrial disturbances and through political mass strikes and revolutionary mass action overthrow and destroy organized parliamentary government." As such, the jury concluded, it "advocates . . . the necessity . . . of overthrowing . . . organized government by force or violence, or by . . . any unlawful means."[34]

The law was valid, wrote Justice Edward T. Sanford. There was no need to apply even the toothless clear and present danger test that Holmes

Figure 30. Charlotte Anita Whitney and John F. Neylan, her attorney, appealed her criminal syndicalism conviction. The U.S. Supreme Court affirmed her conviction in 1927, despite Justice Louis D. Brandeis's stirring defense of free speech. California Governor Clement C. Young pardoned her soon thereafter. Courtesy of The Bancroft Library, University of California, Berkeley.

had used in the *Schenck* case because the New York legislature had, in effect, already classified certain speech, no matter how remote or theoretical, as criminally dangerous. "A single revolutionary spark may kindle a fire that, smouldering for a time, may burst into a sweeping and destructive conflagration," Sanford explained.[35] If anything, the court was going backwards on free speech protection.

However, Sanford then wrote, almost in passing, "For present purposes we may and do assume that freedom of speech and of the press—which are protected by the First Amendment from abridgment by Congress—are among the fundamental personal rights and 'liberties' protected by the due process clause of the Fourteenth Amendment from impairment by the States."[36]

Here was a statement more revolutionary than Gitlow's. The Supreme Court was expanding "Congress shall make no law . . ." to every state legislature, potentially to all state action affecting expressive rights. The court was appointing itself the final arbiter of future questions in which a defendant could claim that a state's action infringed his or her First Amendment rights. A court that not so many years before had staunchly protected private property rights against state regulation was now opening the door to protecting expression rights against state intrusion (and to protecting other individual rights of citizens).

From this point forward, the federal courts would be deeply immersed in a wide variety of free speech issues. Of course, if the appellate courts were to merely emulate the *Gitlow* majority and rubber-stamp state decisions, the court's greatly expanded power wouldn't have meant a thing. It would take a combination of the extension of First Amendment doctrine to the states and the courts' willingness to give more breathing room to free speech to meaningfully expand this right.

The *Gitlow* case also gave Holmes the chance to further expound on his new, industrial-strength clear and present danger test: "It is said that this manifesto was more than a theory, that it was an incitement. Every idea is an incitement. It offers itself for belief and if believed it is acted on unless some other belief outweighs it or some failure of energy stifles the movement at its birth. The only difference between the expression of an opinion and an incitement in the narrower sense is the speaker's enthusiasm for the result. Eloquence may set fire to reason. But whatever may be thought of the redundant discourse before us it had no chance of starting a present conflagration."[37]

In other words, real incitement to violence, the kind that the state can justifiably act on, needs to present real and immediate danger. Holmes' co-conspirator, Louis D. Brandeis, would drive that point home two years later.

Brandeis deserves just as much credit as Holmes, if not more, for attempting to push the court toward free expression in the crucial postwar years. The Jewish progressive "attorney for the people" had been appointed to the court by President Wilson in 1916, gaining his seat only after a bruising confirmation battle. Business interests had opposed the man who had attacked "the curse of bigness" in railroad monopolies and banking and insurance practices. Like Holmes, he had changed his mind after voting with the rest of the court on the first free speech cases. After the *Abrams* case, he took the lead in writing the dissents in a half-dozen more free-speech cases, while the majority continued to stubbornly affirm convictions under the Espionage Act, as well as under state sedition, syndicalism, and anarchy laws.[38]

Brandeis' greatest contribution to the strengthening of the First Amendment—and to the popularization of this notion—was his stirring rhetoric in the 1927 case of Charlotte Anita Whitney against the state of California.[39] A Wellesley-educated spinster, Mayflower descendant, and niece of arch-conservative former justice Stephen J. Field, Whitney was a former teacher, a socialist and a suffragist who supported socialist causes. She had reportedly spent most of her savings bailing out people whom she thought to be political prisoners.[40]

In November 1919, Whitney, then fifty-two, attended a convention in Oakland to form a California branch of the Communist Labor Party. The party, she urged, should use the electoral process to gain popular support for its objectives. But a majority of the delegates rejected political action. Instead, they backed the national party's more militant platform, adopted the previous summer, including the goal "to create a unified revolutionary working class movement in America, organizing the workers . . . in a revolutionary class struggle to conquer the capitalist state . . ." The national party had also lauded the IWW for its sacrifices in the class war. By adopting this platform, the California CLP was implicitly endorsing revolutionary Bolshevist principles and aligning itself at least in spirit with the IWW.[41]

As with other such laws, California's 1919 criminal syndicalism law was written with the IWW in mind. It made it a felony to belong to any group that taught "the commission of crime, sabotage . . . , or unlawful acts of force and violence or unlawful methods of terrorism as a means of accomplishing a change in industrial ownership or control or effecting any political change."[42]

Although Whitney was not a member of the IWW and her party had only stood with the organization on the national level, Whitney was arrested in 1920 after giving a public lecture in Oakland and charged with violating the California law. In a four-week trial in which most of the witnesses testified about IWW violence (also marked by her attorney's and a juror's death from influenza, and her own serious illness), Whitney was convicted and sentenced to one to fourteen years in prison at San Quentin. Public donations helped her make bail.[43]

Represented on appeal by John F. Neylan, a prominent San Francisco lawyer, and by two of the leading civil liberties lawyers of the day, Walter Pollak and Walter Nelles (who had also represented Benjamin Gitlow), Whitney's case reached the U.S. Supreme Court after a tortuous seven-year legal battle. Writing for the majority, Justice Sanford affirmed her conviction, citing no previous free speech opinions except the *Gitlow* case in holding that "a state in the exercise of its police power may punish those who abuse [freedom of speech] by utterances inimical to the public welfare, tending to incite to crime, disturb the public peace, or endanger the foundations of organized government and threaten its overthrow by unlawful means."[44] He rejected Whitney's contention that she had no control over the convention's rebuff of the more-moderate course she had advocated and its adoption of a national platform that subjected her to the criminal law.[45]

Joined by Holmes, Brandeis came to the defense of free speech in a brilliant exposition of free speech and with an extension of Holmes' test.

Whitney's conviction, Brandeis noted, was merely "for a step in preparation, which, if it threatens the public order at all, does so only remotely."[46] He argued somewhat hopefully that the court hadn't yet decided "what degree of evil shall be deemed sufficiently substantial to justify resort to abridgment of free speech and assembly." The majority, of course, had long ago decided on the bad tendency test. Brandeis suggested a tougher, more explicit test: "In order to support a finding of clear and present danger it must be shown either that immediate serious violence was to be expected or was advocated, or that the past conduct furnished reason to believe that such advocacy was then contemplated."[47]

Brandeis backed up his test with a show of rhetorical fireworks, enlisting America's revolutionary patriots in a rousing parade of free speech virtues, celebrating the deliberative and rational virtues of citizenship in a democracy:

> Those who won our independence believed that the final end of the state was to make men free to develop their faculties, and that in its government the deliberative forces should prevail over the arbitrary. . . . They believed liberty to be the secret of happiness and courage to be the secret of liberty. They believed that freedom to think as you will and to speak as you think are means indispensable to the discovery and spread of political truth; that without free speech and assembly discussion would be futile; that with them, discussion affords ordinarily adequate protection against the dissemination of noxious doctrine; that the greatest menace to freedom is an inert people; that public discussion is a political duty;

and that this should be a fundamental principle of the American government.[48]

He invoked the evils that the revolutionaries a century and a half earlier knew so well and were determined to overcome:

[T]hey knew that order cannot be secured merely through fear of punishment for its infraction; that it is hazardous to discourage thought, hope and imagination; that fear breeds repression; that repression breeds hate; that hate menaces stable government; that the path of safety lies in the opportunity to discuss freely supposed grievances and proposed remedies . . .[49]

And he lauded their courage:

Fear of serious injury cannot alone justify suppression of free speech and assembly. Men feared witches and burnt women. It is the function of speech to free men from the bondage of irrational fears.[50] Those who won our independence by revolution were not cowards. They did not fear political change. They did not exalt order at the cost of liberty.[51]

With those magnificent words marching in ranks across the printed page (see Appendix II for full text), Brandeis threw down a giant challenge to that and future generations of judges, lawmakers, and citizens. Are you afraid of radicals like Benjamin Gitlow and Eugene Debs and Anita Whitney, of ordinary people like Ben Kahn and Janet Smith, Martin Wehinger and Tony Diedtman? Do they pose such a danger to ordered liberty that we should sacrifice our constitutional principles, our identity as a nation, in order to save it?

The high court's answer to Brandeis' challenge would oscillate greatly over the next eight decades, but the general trend would be to answer, No, we are not afraid. We do not fear change or experimentation or even the crassest, foulest, or most provocative speech. We do not fear hate-spewing bigots, jack-booted thugs, religious zealots, vicious satirists, or dissenters who spit on or burn the flag. Yes, there is a limit, but we will set the thermostat to the highest point on the scale, for to do less than that will enervate our nation, weaken our foundation, and repress ideas that in a self-governing nation *must* be heard.

Praising Brandeis as he pardoned Ms. Whitney a month after the Supreme Court had affirmed her conviction, California's governor C. C. Young said freedom of speech is the "indispensable birthright of every free American."[52] But what Brandeis said went deeper: Freedom of speech is indispensable to a healthy democracy.

In trumpeting the virtues of civic courage, argues First Amendment scholar Vincent Blasi, Brandeis was really saying that the future of a nation depends on its character, on "how it responds to the challenge of threatening ideas." Freedom of expression allows a people to meet such ideas with "confidence, initiative, and openness to change," the central qualities of a vibrant democratic nation.[53]

True patriotism today, noted historian Arthur M. Schlesinger Jr. in a 2004 speech on "The Right to Disagree" at Swarthmore College, "consists of living up to a nation's highest ideals."[54] Honoring "those who won our independence" means acting on the courage that they exemplified by preserving the widest possible latitude for freedom of expression. "War does not nullify the Bill of Rights," Schlesinger said. "Even when the Republic faces mortal dangers, the First Amendment is still in the Constitution."[55]

The false patriotism of blind loyalty that underlay so much of the repression of World War I could be summed up in an old slogan: "My country right or wrong." Senator Carl Schurz of Missouri, who emigrated from Germany in the mid-nineteenth century and became a leading Republican, had the perfect rejoinder in 1872 when called unpatriotic by a colleague for questioning arms sales during the Franco-Prussian War. "Our country, right or wrong—when right to be kept right; when wrong to be put right," Schurz shot back, to thunderous applause from the Senate gallery.[56]

The freedom of expression implicit in that remark is so important, Schurz would later write, that on it depends "our dignity, our free institutions and the peace and welfare of this and coming generations of Americans."[57]

The generation of World War I failed to protect freedom of expression. What will we do? ✦

Appendix I

Espionage Act of 1917, Title I, Section 3. Enacted June 15, 1917.

Whoever, when the United States is at war,

shall willfully make or convey false reports or false statements with intent to interfere with the operation or success of the military or naval forces of the United States or to promote the success of its enemies and whoever, when the United States is at war, shall willfully cause or attempt to cause insubordination, disloyalty, mutiny, or refusal of duty, in the military or naval forces of the United States, or shall willfully obstruct the recruiting or enlistment service of the United States, to the injury of the service or of the United States, shall be punished by a fine of not more than $10,000 or imprisonment for not more than twenty years, or both.

Montana's Sedition Law of 1918. Approved February 22, 1918.

An Act Defining the Crime of Sedition, and to Prescribe Punishment Thereof, and Declaring This Act to be an Emergency Law Necessary for the Preservation of Public Peace and Safety.

Be it enacted by the Legislative Assembly of the State of Montana:

SEC. 1. Whenever the United States shall be engaged in war, any person or persons who shall utter, print, write, or publish any disloyal, profane, *violent*, scurrilous, contemptuous, *slurring*, or abusive language about the form of government of the United States, or the Constitution of the United States, or the soldiers or sailors of the United States, or the flag of the United States, or the uniform of the army or navy of the United States' or any language **calculated** to bring the form of government of the United States, or the Constitution of the United States, or the soldiers or sailors of the United States, or the flag of the United States, or the uniform of the army or navy of the United States into contempt, scorn, contumely, or disrepute, or shall utter, print, write or publish any language calculated to incite or inflame resistance to any duly constituted Federal or State authority in connection with the prosecution of the War, or who shall display the flag, of any foreign enemy, or who shall by utterance, writing, printing, publication or language spoken, urge, incite or advocate any curtailment of production in this country of any thing or things, product or products necessary or essential to the prosecution of the war in which the United States may be engaged, with intent by such curtailment to cripple or hinder the United States in the prosecution of the War, or in time of war in which the United States shall be engaged shall wilfully make or convey false reports or statements with intent to interfere with the operation or success of the military or naval forces of the United States, or promote the success of its enemy or enemies, or whoever in time of war in which the United States shall be engaged shall wilfully cause, or attempt to cause, disaffection in the military or naval forces of the United States, or who shall by uttering, printing, writing, publication, language spoken or by any act or acts, interfere with, obstruct, or attempt to obstruct, the operation of the national selective draft law or the recruiting or enlistment service of the United States to the injury of the military or naval service thereof shall be guilty of the crime of sedition.

SEC. 2. Every person found guilty of the crime of sedition shall be punished for each offense by a fine of not less than $200.00 nor more than $20,000.00, or by imprisonment in the State Prison for not less than one year nor more than twenty years, or by both such fine and imprisonment. In the event of a fine imposed for violation of any of the provisions of this Act and not paid, the guilty person shall be imprisoned for a period represented by credit of $2.00 per day until the amount of fine is fully paid.

SEC. 3. This Act is hereby declared to be an emergency law and a law necessary for the immediate preservation of the public peace and safety.

SEC. 4. This Act shall be in full force and effect from and after its passage and approval.

The Federal Sedition Act of 1918. Enacted May 16, 1918.

Wording defining the criminal act is exactly the same as Section 1 of Montana's law, except that two words, in **bold italics**, were deleted, and "**calculated**" was changed to "intended."

Appendix II

Excerpt from Justice Louis D. Brandeis' opinion in
Whitney v. California, 274 U.S. 357 (1927).

This Court has not yet fixed the standard by which to determine when a danger shall be deemed clear; how remote the danger may be and yet be deemed present, and what degree of evil shall be deemed sufficiently substantial to justify resort to abridgement of free speech and assembly as the means of protection. To reach sound conclusions on these matters, we must bear in mind why a State is, ordinarily, denied the power to prohibit dissemination of social, economic, and political doctrine which a vast majority of its citizens believes to be false and fraught with evil consequence.

Those who won our independence believed that the final end of the State was to make men free to develop their faculties, and that, in its government, the deliberative forces should prevail over the arbitrary. They valued liberty both as an end, and as a means. They believed liberty to be the secret of happiness, and courage to be the secret of liberty. They believed that freedom to think as you will and to speak as you think are means indispensable to the discovery and spread of political truth; that, without free speech and assembly, discussion would be futile; that, with them, discussion affords ordinarily adequate protection against the dissemination of noxious doctrine; that the greatest menace to freedom is an inert people; that public discussion is a political duty, and that this should be a fundamental principle of the American government. They recognized the risks to which all human institutions are subject. But they knew that order cannot be secured merely through fear of punishment for its infraction; that it is hazardous to discourage thought, hope, and imagination; that fear breeds repression; that repression breeds hate; that hate menaces stable government; that the path of safety lies in the opportunity to discuss freely supposed grievances and proposed remedies, and that the fitting remedy for evil counsels is good ones. Believing in the power of reason as applied through public discussion, they eschewed silence coerced by law—the argument of force in its worst form. Recognizing the occasional tyrannies of governing majorities, they amended the Constitution so that free speech and assembly should be guaranteed.

Fear of serious injury cannot alone justify suppression of free speech and assembly. Men feared witches and burnt women. It is the function of speech to free men from the bondage of irrational fears. To justify suppression of free speech, there must be reasonable ground to fear that serious evil will result if free speech is practiced. There must be reasonable ground to believe that the danger apprehended is imminent. There must be reasonable ground to believe that the evil to be prevented is a serious one. Every denunciation of existing law tends in some measure to increase the probability that there will be violation of it. Condonation of a breach enhances the probability. Expressions of approval add to the probability. Propagation of the criminal state of mind by teaching syndicalism increases it. Advocacy of law-breaking heightens it still further. But even advocacy of violation, however reprehensible morally, is not a justification for denying free speech where the advocacy falls short of incitement and there is nothing to indicate that the advocacy would be immediately acted on. The wide difference between advocacy and incitement, between preparation and attempt, between assembling and conspiracy, must be borne in mind. In order to support a finding of clear and present danger, it must be shown either that immediate serious violence was to be expected or was advocated, or that the past conduct furnished reason to believe that such advocacy was then contemplated.

Those who won our independence by revolution were not cowards. They did not fear political change. They did not exalt order at the cost of liberty. To courageous, self-reliant men, with confidence in the power of free and fearless reasoning applied through the processes of popular government, no danger flowing from speech can be deemed clear and present unless the incidence of the evil apprehended is so imminent that it may befall before there is opportunity for full discussion. If there be time to expose through discussion the falsehood and fallacies, to avert the evil by the processes of education, the remedy to be applied is more speech, not enforced silence. Only an emergency can justify repression. Such must be the rule if authority is to be reconciled with freedom. Such, in my opinion, is the command of the Constitution. It is therefore always open to Americans to challenge a law abridging free speech and assembly by showing that there was no emergency justifying it.

Notes

Introduction

1. Zellick, "Patriots on the Rampage: Mob Action in Lewistown, 1917–1918."
2. *Democrat-News* (Lewistown, Montana), April 23, 1917, cited in Zellick, 31.
3. *Whitney v. California*, 274 U.S. 357 (1927).
4. *New York Times v. Sullivan*, 376 U.S. 254 (1964).

Chapter 1

1. Flynn, *The Rebel Girl: An Autobiography, My First Life (1906–1926)*, 103.
2. Koelbel, *Missoula the Way It Was*, 102.
3. Ibid.
4. *Missoula: The Garden City* (1909), 3–5 passim. Quoted in Venn, "The Wobblies and Montana's Garden City," 18.
5. Evans, "Montana's Role in the Enactment of Legislation Designed to Suppress the Industrial Workers of the World," 32.
6. *Industrial Worker*, Sept. 16, 1909.
7. Lavender, *Land of Giants: The Drive to the Pacific Northwest, 1750–1950*, 421.
8. Flynn, "Memories of the Industrial Workers of the World."
9. Harbor Allen, "The Flynn," *American Mercury* 9 (December 1926): 426–33, quoted in Fargo, *Spokane Story*, 218.
10. Ibid.
11. Flynn, *The Rebel Girl*, 95–102.
12. Baxandall, *Words on Fire*, 10.
13. *Industrial Worker*, Sept. 16, 1909.
14. Ibid.
15. Fred W. Heslewood, "Barbarous Spokane," *International Socialist Review* 10, no. 8 (Feb. 1910): 711, quoted in Townsend, *Running the Gauntlet: Cultural Sources of Violence Against the IWW*, 72.
16. Foner, ed., *Fellow Workers and Friends*, 29.
17. Heslewood, "Barbarous Spokane."
18. Flynn, *The Rebel Girl*, 102.
19. Renshaw, *The Wobblies*, 116.
20. Dubofsky, *We Shall Be All*, 201.
21. Renshaw, *The Wobblies*, 50.
22. Cobb-Reiley, "The Meaning of Freedom of Speech," 123, citing *Historical Statistics*, 168 (D765–78), and 139 (D182–232).

23. Dubofsky, *We Shall Be All*, 7.

24. Ibid., 201.

25. Renshaw, *The Wobblies*, 51.

26. Tyler, *Rebels of the Woods*, 26.

27. Tyler, *Rebels of the Woods*, 88.

28. Abraham Glasser, *The Lumber Industry of the Pacific Northwest and the Inland Empire*, Glasser File, 1917, Record Group 60, Department of Justice, National Archives. The "Glasser File" contains drafts of reports and supporting papers on the labor unrest in the lumber areas of the Northwest and in Butte, Montana, 1917–1920.

29. Rexford G. Tugwell, "The Casual of the Woods," *Survey* 44 (July 3, 1920): 472. Quoted in Dubofsky, *We Shall Be All*, 148.

30. *Industrial Worker*, September 23, 1909.

31. U.S. Bureau of the Census, *Historical Statistics of the United States* (Washington, 1960), 44.

32. Dubofsky, *We Shall Be All*, 6.

33. Tyler, *Rebels of the Woods*, 6.

34. Dept. of Commerce and Labor, Bureau of Corporations, *The Lumber Industry*, 1, (Washington, 1913–1914: 10, quoted in Rowan, *The IWW in the Lumber Industry*, 2.

35. Rowan, *The IWW in the Lumber Industry*, 2.

36. Evans et al., *The American Century*, 76.

37. Ibid., 77.

38. Dubofsky, *We Shall Be All*, 23.

39. Tyler, *Rebels of the Woods*, 7.

40. Lukas, *Big Trouble*, 225.

41. Ibid., 226.

42. Ibid., 1–2.

43. Ibid.

44. Ibid., 96.

45. Industrial Workers of the World, *Proceedings of the Founding Convention of the IWW* (1905; reprint, New York: Merit Publishers, 1969), 152, quoted in Gaylord, "Politics and Syndicalism, a Case Study of the IWW."

46. Kornbluh, ed., *Rebel Voices: An IWW Anthology*.

47. *Industrial Union Bulletin* (Chicago), Sept. 19, 1908 and Oct. 24, 1908.

48. Ibid.

49. Lukas, *Big Trouble*, 748.

50. *Industrial Worker*, Sept. 16, 1909.

Chapter 2

1. *Anaconda Standard*, Oct. 2, 1909.

2. Foner, ed., *Fellow Workers and Friends*, 217.

3. Dubofsky, *We Shall Be All*, 186.

4. James P. Cannon, *Notebook of an Agitator* (New York: Pathfinder Press, 1958), 32–36, quoted in Dubofsky, *We Shall Be All*, 186.

5. *Industrial Worker*, Oct. 7, 1918.

6. Ibid.

7. Ibid.

8. *Industrial Worker*, Oct. 20, 1918; Flynn, *The Rebel Girl*, 104.

9. *Butte (MT) Miner*, Oct. 1, 1918.

10. *Industrial Worker*, Sept. 30, 1909.

11. *Daily Missoulian*, Oct. 2, 1918.

12. Flynn, *The Rebel Girl*, 104.

13. Ibid.

14. *Daily Missoulian*, Oct. 6, 1918.

15. Flynn, *The Rebel Girl*, 104.

16. *Butte Miner*, Oct. 4, 1909.

17. *Daily Missoulian*, Oct. 6, 1909.

18. Foner, ed., *Fellow Workers and Friends*, 28.

19. Flynn, *The Rebel Girl*, 105.

20. Ibid.

21. *Butte Miner*, Oct. 8, 1909.

22. Venn, "The Wobblies and Montana's Garden City," 28.

23. *Butte Evening News*, Oct. 9, 1909.

24. Ibid.

25. See Woods' testimony in *U.S. Commission on Industrial Relations, Final Report*, Vol. 11, 10550–58, and also Woods, "Reasonable Restrictions Upon Freedom of Assemblage," 29.

26. Woods, "Reasonable Restrictions," 32.

27. Wertheimer, "Free-Speech Fights," 152.

28. Foner, ed., *Fellow Workers and Friends*, 13–14.

29. Ibid., 12.

30. Flynn, *The Rebel Girl*, 107.

31. Foner, ed., *Fellow Workers and Friends*, 33.

32. IWW Headquarters for Spokane Free Speech Defense (Coeur d'Alene, ID) to all locals of the United Brotherhood of Carpenters and Joiners of America, January 9, 1910, DOJ File 150139, RG 60.

33. Dubofsky, *We Shall Be All*, 178.

34. Ibid., 1.

35. Foner, ed., *Fellow Workers and Friends*, 36; Flynn, *The Rebel Girl*, 107.

36. Ibid., 53.

37. Ibid., 43.

38. Ibid., 33.

39. Ibid., 124.

40. Dubofsky, *We Shall Be All*, 196.

41. Foner, ed., *Fellow Workers and Friends*, 134. Dubofsky, *We Shall Be All*, 196.

42. Ibid., 9.

43. Ibid., 15.

44. Ibid.

45. Ibid., 18; Foner, ed., *Fellow Workers and Friends*, 19. Top honors for intolerant remarks are shared by Judge Davis in Minot, N.Dak., who when asked, "Judge, can't you do something to prevent the beating down of innocent men?" replied, "Prevent Hell. We'll drive the God Damned Sons of Bitches into the river and drown them. We'll starve them. We'll kill every damn man of them or drive them together with the Socialists from the city!"

46. Ibid., 19.

47. DOJ File 150139–8.

48. *San Diego Union*, May 28, 1912, 4.

49. Weinstock, *Report on Recent Disturbances in the City of San Diego*, 7–9.

50. Ibid., 20.

51. Taft to Hilles, Sept. 7, 1912, DOJ File 150139–28.

52. Wickersham to Taft, Sept. 16, 1912, DOJ File 150139–29.

53. Industrial Workers of the World, *Proceedings of the Founding Convention of the IWW*, 152.

54. Daniel O' Regan, "Free Speech Fight in Spokane 4" (November 2, 1914); *Reports of the U.S. Commission on Industrial Relations*, 1912–1915, quoted in Rabban, *Free Speech in its Forgotten Years*, 116.

55. *San Diego Evening Tribune*, May 10, 1912, quoted in Rabban, *Free Speech in Its Forgotten Years*, 115.

56. *Commonwealth v. Davis*, 162 Mass 510, 511 (1895).

57. Excellent contemporary scholarship in the history of free speech in the United States includes Rabban, *Free Speech in Its Forgotten Years*; Wertheimer, "Free-Speech Fights"; Cobb-Reiley, "The Meaning of Freedom of Speech and the Press in the Progressive Era"; and Blanchard, *Filling the Void*.

58. *Gitlow v. New York*, 268 U.S. 652 (1925).

59. *Solidarity*, August 23, 1913.

60. Rabban, *Free Speech in Its Forgotten Years*, 88.

61. "Why Free Speech is Denied the IWW," *Industrial Worker*, Nov. 17, 1909, quoted in Rabban, *Free Speech in Its Forgotten Years*, 85.

62. Reprinted in *Industrial Worker*, Dec. 9, 1916.

Chapter 3

1. Emmons, *The Butte Irish*, 264.

2. Ben Reitman, "Impressions of the Chicago Convention," *Mother Earth* 7 (October 1913): 241–42, quoted in Brissenden, *The IWW: A Study of American Syndicalism*, 2nd ed., 317.

3. Kornbluh, *Rebel Voices*, 159.

4. Kornbluh, *Rebel Voices*, 161.

5. Brissenden, *The IWW: A Study of American Syndicalism*, 288.

6. Ibid., 282.

7. Kornbluh, *Rebel Voices*, 161.

8. Brissenden, *The IWW: A Study of American Syndicalism*, 289.

9. *Hearings on the Lawrence Strike* (Washington: Government Printing Office, 1912), 75, cited in Brissenden, *The IWW: A Study of American Syndicalism*, 284.

10. Ibid., 290.

11. W. M. Leiserson, *The Labor Market and Unemployment*, Commission on Industrial Relations, Unpublished Reports, HF 1452 L5, 6, cited in Townsend, *Running the Gauntlet*, 145, 146.

12. Flynn, "Memories of the Industrial Workers of the World."

13. Dubofsky, *We Shall Be All*, 292–300.

14. Dispatch signed "R.E.P.," *Weekly People*, Dec. 9, 1916, quoted in Brissenden, *The IWW: A Study of American Syndicalism*, 338; Carleton H. Parker and Cornelia Stratton Parker, *The Casual Laborer* (New York: Harcourt, Brace, and Howe, 1920), 121, quoted in Townsend, *Running the Gauntlet*, 170.

15. Flynn, *Sabotage*.

16. Joe Hill, *Ta-ra-ra-Boom-de-ay*, *I.W.W. Songbook*, 9th Edition, in Kornbluh, 143.

17. Flynn, "Memories of the Industrial Workers of the World."

18. *Chicago Daily News*, Sept. 22, 1914, quoted in Brissenden, *The IWW: A Study of American Syndicalism*, 328.

19. Dubofsky, *We Shall Be All*, 277.

20. *The World's Work* 26 (1913): 417, quoted in Conlin, *Bread and Roses Too*, 100.

21. Conlin, *Bread and Roses Too*, 95–117.

22. Dubofsky, *We Shall Be All*, 334.

23. David Honig, "One Big Union," *The Weekly*, May 8, 1985 as printed in *Landmarks* 4, no. 1: 69–73. http://www.tpl.lib.wa.us/cgi-win/fulltcgi.exe/Industrial_Workers_of_the_World/labor/indwrkrs.iww

24. Mackenzie, "Logging in Western Montana Since 1910."

25. Anaconda Forest Products Collection, File 230–145-9.

26. *Industrial Worker*, July 2, 1910, quoted in Kornbluh, *Rebel Voices*, 257–58.

27. Rajala, "A Dandy Bunch of Wobblies," 216; Kornbluh, *Rebel Voices*, 259.

28. Anaconda Forest Products Collection, 230–145-31.

29. *Industrial Worker*, May 29, 1913, quoted in Rajala at 214.

30. Ibid., 86.

31. Aarstad, "Montana's Other Strike: The 1917 IWW Timber Strike," 56.

32. Tyler, *Rebels of the Woods*, 63.

33. Morgan, "The Industrial Workers of the World," 139–52.

34. See Tyler, *Rebels of the Woods*, Chapter 3, as well as Smith, *The Everett Massacre*; Dubofsky, *We Shall Be All*; and Bird et al., *Solidarity Forever*.

35. Jack Miller, also known as Jack Leonard, interview by Bird and Shaffer for their documentary, *The Wobblies*, reprinted in Bird et al., *Solidarity Forever*.

36. Tyler, *Rebels of the Woods*, 62.

37. Kenneth Ross to A. W. Cooper, Oct. 11, 1917, Anaconda Forest Products Collection, 230–27–13.

38. U.S. Department of Labor, *Report of President's Mediation Commission*, Jan. 9, 1918, printed in Secretary of Labor's Annual Report, 1918, 19–21, quoted in Glasser file.

Chapter 4

1. Walker C. Smith, *!War! United States, Mexico, Japan* (New Castle, Pa.: IWW Publishing Bureau, 1911) in DOJ File 150139–3.

2. Albert Brooks was arrested and convicted in Dillon, Beaverhead County, Montana (see Chap. 14).

3. Carleton H. Parker, *The Casual Laborer, and Other Essays* (New York: Harcourt, Brace, and Howe, 1920), 102, quoted in Peterson and Fite, *Opponents of War, 1917–1918*, 50.

4. Kennedy, *Over Here: The First World War and American Society*, 30.

5. Cooper, *Pivotal Decades: The United States, 1900–1920*, 167.

6. Hart, *History of the First World War*, 78–96.

7. Keegan, *The First World War*, 135.

8. Ibid., 82.

9. Ibid., 83.

10. 65th Cong., 1st Sess., *Congressional Record* 55 (April 4, 1917): S 213.

11. French censorship was perhaps even more severe, but was a minor factor in the filtering of information to and from the United States compared to that of Great Britain.

12. Peterson, *Propaganda for War*, 12ff.

13. Walter Millis, *Road to War: America 1914–1917* (Boston: Houghton Mifflin, 1935), 147, quoted in Peterson, *Propaganda for War*, 14.

14. Peterson, *Propaganda for War*, 14–15.

15. Ibid., 26–27.

16. United States Committee on Public Information. Four-Minute Men.

Bulletin No. 11, issued July 23, 1917, "Why We Are Fighting." (Washington, D.C.: U.S. Government Printing Office, 1917) quoted in Cornebise, *War As Advertised: The Four-Minute Men and America's Crusade 1917–1918,* 129.

17. Viereck, *Spreading Germs of Hate* (New York: H. Liveright, 1930), 16. The fact that this chronology was reprinted in 1933 in pro-Nazi propaganda published by the Hamburg Fichte-Bund does raise questions about who was manipulating whom. (World War I Pamphlet Collection, Special Collections, Mansfield Library, University of Montana, Missoula).

18. Reprinted in the *Helena Independent* on May 7, 1917.

19. Ibid.

20. Ponsonby, "The Corpse Factory," 121.

21. 65th Cong., 1st Sess., *Congressional Record* 55 (April 2, 1917): H 118–120.

22. Ibid., 120.

23. Ernest Stires, *The High Call* (New York: E. P. Dutton & Co., 1917), 66–70, quoted in Gamble, *The War for Righteousness,* 154.

24. McKim, Randolph, *For God and Country* (New York: E. P. Dutton & Co., 1918), 113–29, quoted in Gamble, *The War for Righteousness,* 158.

25. Reprinted in *Fergus County Argus,* April 20, 1917.

26. *Congressional Record*—Senate, April 4, 1917, p. 219.

27. *Congressional Record*—Senate, April 4, 1917, p. 223.

28. *Congressional Record*—Senate, April 4, 1917, p. 208.

29. Ibid., p. 215.

30. Reprinted in *Fergus County Argus,* April 20, 1917.

31. *Solidarity,* February 17, 1917, quoted in Dubofsky, *We Shall Be All,* 353.

32. Bill Haywood to Frank Little, May 6, 1917, quoted in Renshaw, *The Wobblies,* 217.

33. Peterson and Fite, *Opponents of War, 1917–1918,* 40–41.

34. Preston, *Aliens and Dissenters,* 91.

35. Just after the Everett massacre in November 1916, the song's lyrics were reprinted in the Seattle *Post-Intelligencer* under the headline, "Hymn of Hate, Battle Song of the IWW." DOJ File 150139.

36. *Helena Independent,* Aug. 19, 1917.

37. *Helena Independent,* Feb. 16, 1918, and Feb. 18, 1918.

38. Dowell, *A History of Criminal Syndicalism Legislation in the United States,* 76–77.

39. "Onward, Christian Soldiers, Marching as to War," War Eagle Series, March 7, 1918, World War I Pamphlet Collection, Box 75, Special Collections, Mansfield Library, University of Montana, Missoula.

40. Gamble, *The War for Righteousness,* 174.

Chapter 5

1. Gutfeld, "The Speculator Disaster in 1917," 14; Glasser, "The Butte Miners Strikes 1917–1920," 3, Glasser File.

2. *Helena Independent*, June 9, 1917.

3. Writers' Project of Montana, *Copper Camp*, 175.

4. *Copper Camp*, 177–79.

5. Emmons, *The Butte Irish*, 148–49.

6. State of Montana, *Third Biennial Report of the Department of Labor and Industry, 1917–1918*, 10–11, quoted in Calvert, *The Gibraltar: Socialism and Labor in Butte, Montana, 1895–1920*, 103.

7. *Copper Camp*, 173.

8. Toole, *Twentieth Century Montana*, 147.

9. Emmons, *The Butte Irish*, 370.

10. *Copper Camp*, 19.

11. All from *Copper Camp*.

12. Howard, *Montana: High, Wide and Handsome*, 85.

13. Emmons, *The Butte Irish*, 367.

14. Glasser, "The Butte Miners Strikes 1917–1920," 1.

15. Emmons, *The Butte Irish*, 367.

16. Gutfeld, *Montana's Agony*, 18. Wage rates in July went up to $5.25, according to Lewis O. Evans' *Address to the Chamber of Commerce*, 12.

17. Albert Rees, *Real Wages in Manufacturing, 1890–1914* (Princeton: Princeton University Press, 1961), Table 10, quoted in Townsend, *Running the Gauntlet*, 143.

18. Glasser File, "Butte Miners' Strikes, 1917–1920," 8–13.

19. Glasser File.

20. Montana State Legislature, *Report of Committee Appointed by the Sixteenth Legislative Assembly to Investigate the High Cost of Living*, 1919, MHS.

21. *Helena Independent*, July 14, 1917.

22. Ibid.

23. Ibid.

24. *Strike Bulletin*, June 10, 1917, quoted in Kustudia, "The Press and Propaganda Coverage of the Butte Labor Strike of 1917," 6.

25. Ibid.

26. *Copper Camp*, 170.

27. Byrkit, "The IWW in Wartime Arizona," 152.

28. Emmons, *The Butte Irish*, 367–69.

29. *Strike Bulletin*, June 10, 1917, quoted in Kustudia at 6.

30. Emmons, *The Butte Irish*, 368.

31. See Calvert, *The Gibraltar*; Emmons, *The Butte Irish*; Malone, *The Battle for Butte: Mining and Politics on the Northern Frontier 1864–1906*; Gutfeld,

Montana's Agony; Wetzel, "The Making of an American Radical: Bill Dunne in Butte"; Toole, *Twentieth Century Montana*.

32. Calvert, *The Gibraltar*, 71–76.

33. According to Emmons, members of a radical Irish faction, the Pearse-Connolly Club, had started to form the union when they were denied a parade permit for draft registration day on June 5. They marched against the draft anyway, fearing that they might be called upon to fight Ireland, engaged in its own insurrection against England and looking to Germany for assistance.

34. There were no more survivors. The final death toll varies from 165 (*Butte Miner*, June 18, 1917, quoted in Emmons, *The Butte Irish*) to 168 (Granite Mountain memorial plaque).

35. Toole, *Twentieth Century Montana*, 145.

36. Emmons, *The Butte Irish*, 381.

37. Ibid., 383.

38. Emmons, *The Butte Irish*, 383.

39. *Butte Daily Post*, June 13, 1917, quoted in Gutfeld, *Montana's Agony*, 17.

40. *Butte Miner*, June 16, 1917.

41. Emmons, *The Butte Irish*, 367.

42. See Calvert, *The Gibraltar*; Emmons, *The Butte Irish*; Gutfeld, *Montana's Agony*.

43. Emmons, *The Butte Irish*, 383.

44. *Anaconda Standard*, July 20, 1917.

45. Emmons, *The Butte Irish*, 374.

46. Harries and Harries, *The Last Days of Innocence*, 180; Kennedy, *Over Here*, 71–72.

47. *Anaconda Standard*, July 21, 1917.

48. Wetzel, "The Making of an American Radical: Bill Dunne in Butte," 15.

49. *Anaconda Standard*, July 23, 1917.

50. *Outlook* 116 (July 18, 1917): 434, quoted in Dubofsky, *We Shall Be All*, 384.

51. *Anaconda Standard*, July 19, 1917.

52. George H. Sands to Woodrow Wilson, August 21, 1917, DOJ File 186701–13–12.

53. U.S. Department of Labor, *Statement of Conditions of Aeroplane Spruce Supply in Northwest*, Labor Department File 33–574, in Glasser File, Box 7.

54. Emmons, *The Butte Irish*, 372.

Chapter 6

1. Lewis. O. Evans, *Address to Chamber of Commerce*, August 29, 1917.

2. Glasser File, "Butte Miners' Strikes, 1917–1920," 6.

3. Dowell, *A History of Criminal Syndicalism Legislation*, 147.

4. Marguerite Green, *The National Civic Federation and the American Labor*

Movement, 1900–1925 (Washington, D.C.: Catholic University of America Press, 1956), 101, footnote 40, quoted in Townsend, *Running the Gauntlet*, 105.

5. Robert F. Hoxie, *Trade Unionism in the United States* (New York: D. Appleton and Company, 1917), quoted in Townsend, *Running the Gauntlet*, 108.

6. A. Parker Nevin, "Some Problems of American Industry," *American Industries* 14 (March 1914): 13, quoted in Townsend, *Running the Gauntlet*, 113.

7. Townsend, *Running the Gauntlet*, 33–34.

8. *Strike Bulletin*, July 25, 1917, quoted in Garrity, "The Frank Little Episode and the Butte Labor Troubles of 1917," 20.

9. Townsend, *Running the Gauntlet*, 42.

10. Tyler, *Rebels of the Woods*, 60.

11. *Helena Independent*, Aug. 1, 1917. Among other IWW nicknames collected by *Anaconda Standard* editor William Eggleston were Implacable Wreckers of the World, Imps of the Wicked World, Irate Wasps of the World, I Work for Wilhelm and Infernal Wretches of the World.

12. Townsend, *Running the Gauntlet*, 41.

13. Ibid., 82.

14. Dowell, *A History of Criminal Syndicalism Legislation*, 37–38.

15. Flynn, "The Free-Speech Fight at Spokane," *International Socialist Review* 10 (December 1909): 483–89, quoted in Foner, ed., *Fellow Workers and Friends*, 41.

16. Walter V. Woehlke, "The IWW and the Golden Rule," *Sunset* 38 (February 1917): 65; "The Red Rebels Declare War," *Sunset* 38 (September 1917): 20, 75, quoted in Byrkit, "The IWW in Wartime Arizona," 11.

17. *New York Tribune*, Nov. 14, 1917, quoted in Peterson and Fite, *Opponents of War 1917–1918*, 149.

18. *Helena Independent*, sec. 2, July 29, 1917.

19. For a fresh, in-depth examination of Montana newspapers and the Anaconda Copper Mining Co., see Swibold, *The Copper Chorus: Mining, Politics and Journalism, 1889–1959*.

20. Kustudia, "The Press and Propaganda Coverage of the Butte Labor Strike of 1917," 41.

21. *Butte Miner*, June 13, 1917, quoted in Kustudia, "The Press and Propaganda," at 9.

22. *Anaconda Standard*, June 29, 1917.

23. *Boise Evening Capital News*, July 7, 1917, quoted in Dowell, *A History of Criminal Syndicalism Legislation*, 41.

24. *Anaconda Standard*, July 17, 1917.

25. *Butte Miner*, July 21, 1917, quoted in Gutfeld, *Montana's Agony*, 24.

26. *Strike Bulletin*, August 14, 1917, quoted in Kustudia, "The Press and Propaganda," at 37.

27. Vernon H. Jensen, *Heritage of Conflict: Labor Relations in the Nonferrous Metals Industry up to 1930* (Ithaca, N.Y.: Cornell University Press, 1950), 442, quoted in Kustudia, "The Press and Propaganda," at 36.

28. Johnson, "An Editor and a War: Will A. Campbell and the *Helena Independent*, 1914–1921," 13–17.

29. McGuckin, *Memoirs of a Wobbly*, 83.

30. Byrkit, "The IWW in Wartime Arizona," 5.

31. *Butte Miner*, August 1, 1917.

32. Mock and Larson, *Words That Won The War*, 123.

33. Stephen Vaughn, *Holding Fast the Inner Lines: Democracy, Nationalism and the Committee on Public Information* (Chapel Hill: University of North Carolina Press, 1980), 21, quoted in Harries and Harries, *The Last Days of Innocence*, 164.

34. Mock and Larson, *Words That Won The War*, 11.

35. Kennedy, *Over Here*, 143.

36. See Appendix I.

37. Mock and Larson, *Words That Won The War*, 80–81.

38. Townsend, *Running the Gauntlet*, 63.

39. Mock and Larson, *Words That Won The War*, 111.

40. Ibid., 161.

41. Ibid., 169.

42. State Department of Public Instruction *State Course of Study*, City Elementary Schools of Montana, (Helena, 1918).

43. "A Suggestive Outline for Teachers," *Teachers' Patriotic Leaflets*, Vol. 1, National Security League, New York, n.d., World War I Pamphlet Collection, Box 74, Mansfield Library, The University of Montana.

44. Mock and Larson, *Words That Won The War*, 113.

45. Ibid., 125.

46. Cornebise, *War as Advertised*, 11.

47. Ibid., 33.

48. Ibid., 65.

49. Ibid., 67.

50. Ibid., 80.

51. Ibid., 40.

52. *Four-Minute Men Bulletin* 21, Committee on Public Information, January 2, 1918, quoted in Mock and Larson, *Words That Won The War*, 123.

53. "German War Practices," CPI, Washington, D.C., World War I Pamphlet Collection, Box 73, Mansfield Library, The University of Montana.

54. Cornebise, *War as Advertised*, 119.

55. *Helena Independent*, July 21, 1917.

56. See Mock and Larson, *Words That Won The War*, 6–8 for an explanation of

how a hypothetical Midwestern family got its news and opinions about the war through the various offices of the CPI.

57. Morison and Commager, *The Growth of the American Republic*, vol. 2 (New York: Oxford University Press, Inc., 1933), 497, quoted in DeWeerd, *President Wilson Fights His War: World War I and the American Intervention*, 244.

58. Mock and Larson, *Words That Won The War*, 6.

59. Lillian Wald, Jane Addams, et al. to the President of the United States, April 17, 1917, DOJ File 9–4-108.

Chapter 7

1. *Daily Missoulian*, July 3, 1917.

2. *Helena Independent*, July 24, 1917.

3. Kornbluh, *Rebel Voices*, 295.

4. T. W. Gregory, memorandum to Asst. Attorney General Charles Warren, July 11, 1917, DOJ File 186701:1.

5. Circular, Department of Justice to United States Attorneys, July 17, 1917, DOJ File 186701:2.

6. *Anaconda Standard*, July 19, 1917.

7. *Anaconda Standard*, July 20, 1917.

8. The mining companies were able to keep tabs on what went on at workers' meetings through a system of spies and informants. For the meetings Little attended, reports were submitted by at least two informants.

9. Carl Dilling, report on MMWU meeting, July 25, 1917, Files of the Montana Council of Defense, MHS.

10. Ibid., July 26, 1917; Gutfeld, *Montana's Agony*, 24–25.

11. Ibid.

12. *Anaconda Standard*, July 28, 1917.

13. *Butte Daily Post*, July 28, 1917; DOJ File 186701–27.

14. *Butte Daily Post*, July 28, 1917; Gutfeld, *Montana's Agony*, 25.

15. *Anaconda Standard*, July 30, 1917.

16. *Helena Independent*, Aug. 1, 1917.

17. Burton K. Wheeler to attorney general, August 17, 1917, DOJ File 186233–207–2, quoted in Mothershead, memo to Bettman, February 13, 1918, DOJ File 189730 (renamed File 9–19–1707).

18. *Anaconda Standard*, July 31, 1917.

19. Ibid., August 2, 1917, quoted in Gutfeld, *Montana's Agony*, 28.

20. Ibid.

21. *Helena Independent*, Aug. 8, 1917.

22. *Helena Independent*, Aug. 4, 1917.

23. Ibid.

24. *Strike Bulletin*, Aug. 2, 1917, quoted in Kustudia, "The Press and Propaganda," 28–29.

25. Reprinted in *Daily Missoulian*, Aug. 3, 1917.

26. *Helena Independent*, Aug. 2, 1917.

27. Ibid., Aug. 7, 1917.

28. *Anaconda Standard*, Aug. 5, 1917.

29. Little's grave is near the southeast corner of Mountain View Cemetery in Grave 5, Lot 10, Block 20–1.

30. *Anaconda Standard*, Aug. 1, 1917.

31. The epigram is also attributed to Aeschylus and to Arthur Ponsonby.

32. Tyler, *Rebels of the Woods*, 153.

33. Evans, "Montana's Role in the Enactment of Legislation Designed to Suppress the Industrial Workers of the World," 77–78. By 1918, after the Russian Revolution had begun, a sixth reason was commonly employed as well: that "the Wobblies were disguised Bolsheviks, preparing to establish Lenin's Communistic regime in the United States."

34. *Helena Independent*, Aug. 2, 1917.

35. Gov. Samuel V. Stewart correspondence, MHS.

36. C. H. McLeod, Kenneth Ross, Martin J. Hutchens, E. H. Polleys and J. O. Newcomb to Honorable Henry L. Myers, Aug. 2, 1917, DOJ File 186701–27–1.

37. Ibid.

38. Wheeler, *Yankee From the West*, 85.

39. Senator H. L. Myers to the attorney general, August 3, 1917, DOJ File 186701–27–1.

40. *Helena Independent*, Aug. 4, 1917.

41. Dubofsky, *We Shall Be All*, 409.

42. Stoddard, unpublished manuscript of Burton K. Wheeler biography, K-6, MHS.

43. Agent E. W. Byrn, report on IWW activities, August 7, 1917, DOJ File 186701–27.

44. Ibid., Aug. 10, 1917.

45. Ibid.

46. Agent E. W. Byrn, report on IWW activities, Aug. 10, 1917, DOJ File 186701–27.

47. Henry L. Myers to William C. Fitts, Aug. 10, 1917, DOJ File 186701–27–8.

48. Ibid.

49. Fitts to Myers, Aug. 11, 1917, DOJ File 186701–27–8.

50. Rabban, *Free Speech in Its Forgotten Years*, 250.

51. 65th Cong., 2nd Sess., *Congressional Record* 55 (Aug. 11, 1917): S 5949.

52. 65th Cong., 2nd Sess., *Congressional Record* 55 (Aug. 11, 1917): S 5949–5950.

53. *An Act for the Punishment of Certain Crimes Against the United States* (July 14, 1798), *U.S. Statutes at Large* I (1798): 596–97, quoted in Smith, *Freedom's Fetters*, 442.

54. *Anaconda Standard*, Aug. 19, 1917, quoted in Stoddard, Wheeler manuscript, K-6, M-5.

55. Stoddard, Wheeler manuscript, M-5.

56. Hilton, "Public Opinion and Civil Liberties in Wartime 1917–1919," 219.

57. *Helena Independent*, Aug. 25, 1917.

58. 65th Cong., 2nd Sess., *Congressional Record* 55 (Aug. 23, 1917): S 6262–6265.

59. *Helena Independent*, June 16, 1918.

60. B. K. Wheeler to the attorney general, Aug. 21, 1917, DOJ File 186701–27–15.

61. Department of Justice, circular to United States Attorneys, July 17, 1917, DOJ File 186701–2.

62. T. H. MacDonald to Thomas W. Gregory, Aug. 21, 1917, DOJ File 186701–27–14.

63. Wade Parks to Thomas W. Gregory, Aug. 29, 1917, DOJ File 186701–27–17.

64. Ibid.

65. Evans, *Address to Chamber of Commerce*, Aug. 29, 1917.

66. Dubofsky, *We Shall Be All*, 394.

67. Preston, *Aliens and Dissenters*, 296.

68. Dubofsky, *We Shall Be All*, 395.

69. *Helena Independent*, Aug. 12, 1917.

70. Preston, *Aliens and Dissenters*, 106.

71. Tyler, *Rebels of the Woods*, 130.

72. *Helena Independent*, Aug. 14, 1917.

73. Tyler, *Rebels of the Woods*, 133; Evans, "Montana's Role," 70; Gov. Moses Alexander of Idaho, telegram to Gov. Stewart, Aug. 14, 1917, Stewart Correspondence, MHS.

74. Tyler, *Rebels of the Woods*, 134.

75. *Helena Independent*, Sept. 3, 1917; Evans, "Montana's Role," 72.

76. Dubofsky, *We Shall Be All*, 406.

77. Preston, *Aliens and Dissenters*, 128.

78. Dubofsky, *We Shall Be All*, 406.

79. Hough, *The Web*, 133.

80. William C. Fitts to Albert B. Fall, Aug. 30, 1917, DOJ File 186701–27–16.

81. Dubofsky, *We Shall Be All*, 406.

82. Chaplin, *Wobbly: The Rough and Tumble Story of an American Radical*, 209.

83. Preston, *Aliens and Dissenters*, 118–20.

84. Hough, *The Web*, 133.

85. Peterson and Fite, *Opponents of War*, 8, 63.

86. 65th Cong., 2nd Sess., *Congressional Record* 56 (April 6, 1918): S 4695.

87. Handwriting on letter from Myers to Fitts, Aug. 16, 1917, DOJ File 186701–55–5.

88. 65th Cong., 2nd Sess., *Congressional Record* 56 (April 6, 1918): S 4695.

89. Ibid.

Chapter 8

1. Peterson and Fite, *Opponents of War*, 63.

2. Preston, *Aliens and Dissenters*, 127.

3. *Espionage Act of 1917, U.S. Statutes at Large* 40, 65th Cong., 1st Sess. (June 15, 1917), Title XII.

4. Preston, *Aliens and Dissenters*, 145.

5. Ibid., 144–49.

6. Peterson and Fite, *Opponents of War*, 48.

7. *Espionage Act of 1917*, Title I, §3.

8. Rabban, *Free Speech in Its Forgotten Years*, 249.

9. Preston, *Aliens and Dissenters*, 119–21.

10. Ibid.

11. John Lord O'Brian to Charles G. Davis, December 26, 1917, DOJ File 9–19 General.

12. Alfred W. Dame to Hon. Woodrow Wilson, February 22, 1917, DOJ File 9–4 General.

13. Peterson and Fite, *Opponents of War*, 117–18; *United States v. Waldron* (Vt. 1918), 3–4, in U.S. Attorney General's Office, *Interpretation of War Statistics Bulletin* 79, (1918).

14. Alfred Bettman, memo to John Lord O'Brian, March 19, 1919, DOJ File 19551–11.

15. Ibid.; *United States v. Kirchner*, (N.d. W. Va. 1918), 2, *Interpretation of War Statistics Bulletin* 69 (1918).

16. Charles H. Ingersoll to Hon. Woodrow Wilson, Feb. 24, 1917, DOJ File 9–4 General.

17. Homer Cummings and Carl McFarland, *Federal Justice: Chapters in the History of Justice and the Federal Executive* (New York: MacMillan, 1937), 425, quoted in Peterson and Fite, *Opponents of War*, 120.

18. Harry N. Scheiber, *The Wilson Administration and Civil Liberties 1917–1921* (Ithaca, N.Y.: Cornell University Press, 1960), 48–49, quoted in Kennedy, *Over Here*, 83.

19. Edward C. Day to attorney general, February 12, 1919 and March 11, 1919, DOJ Files 187415–422, 187415–415.

20. U.S. District Court records, NARA, Seattle.

21. The copper king had fought the Amalgamated, the Anaconda's parent corporation, to a standstill with hundreds of mining claim lawsuits brought before bribed judges. However, the Amalgamated had forced Heinze's hand by shutting down all its operations, throwing fifteen thousand men out of work. This forced the legislature into special session to pass a bill making it easier to disqualify a judge for bias. In the next election, Bourquin replaced one of the crooked judges, while the Anaconda began its hegemony over the state's economy, politics, and newspapers.

22. Gutfeld, "Western Justice and the Rule of Law," 88. See also by Gutfeld: *Montana's Agony: Years of War and Hysteria 1917–1921;* "The Ves Hall Case, Judge Bourquin, and the Sedition Act of 1918," *Pacific History Review* 38 (1968): 163–78, and "Purveyors of Injustice: Bourquin on Ethics and the Legal System," *Tel Aviv University Studies in Law* 15 (2000): 237–55.

23. Wheeler to Walsh, June 18, 1917, DOJ File 186233.

24. Ibid.; Stoddard, Wheeler biography manuscript, M-4.

25. Ibid.

26. *Anaconda Standard,* Aug. 17, 1917, quoted in Stoddard, Wheeler manuscript, M-4.

27. *Helena Independent,* Aug. 30, 1917, quoted in Stoddard, Wheeler manuscript, M-6.

28. Stoddard, Wheeler manuscript, M-6.

29. Ibid., M-7, M-8.

30. *Great Falls Tribune,* Feb. 20, 1918.

31. Pitkanen's wife, Gertrude, achieved some notoriety as a baby broker, arranging for childless couples to "buy" babies from unwed or impoverished mothers. Years later, some of these children began to find each other through the Internet, and called themselves "Gertie's Babies."

32. *Bozeman Chronicle,* March 25, 1918.

33. *Anaconda Standard,* Nov. 4, 1917, quoted in Stoddard, Wheeler manuscript, M-10.

34. *Helena Independent,* Nov. 9, 1917, quoted in Stoddard, Wheeler manuscript, M-11.

35. *United States v. Hall,* 248 F. 150 (D.C. D. Mont. 1918); grand jury indictment in DOJ File 9–19–1707; trial transcript in DOJ File 9–19–1707.

36. Ibid.

37. Wheeler, *Yankee From the West,* 154.

38. *Senate Journal,* 15th Ex. Sess., 64.

39. Walter, *Montana Campfire Tales,* 162.

40. Stoddard, Wheeler manuscript, N-1.

41. *Anaconda Standard,* November 9, 1917, quoted in Stoddard, Wheeler manuscript, L-10.

42. Transcript of *U.S. v Hall*, DOJ File 9–19–1707.

43. *U.S. v. Hall*, *Helena Independent*, January 27, 1918, DOJ File 9–19–1707.

44. *U.S. v. Hall*, 153.

45. Ibid.

46. *Helena Independent*, Jan. 27, 1918.

47. *Helena Independent*, Jan. 27, 1918.

48. Ibid.

49. Will A. Campbell to Henry L. Myers, Jan. 27, 1918, DOJ File 9–19–1707.

50. Sen. Henry L. Myers to attorney general, Feb. 9, 1918, DOJ File 9–19–1707.

51. G. E. LaFollette to the attorney general, Feb. 2, 1918, DOJ File 9–19–1707.

52. DOJ File 9–19–1707.

53. O'Brian to Gregory, Feb. 27, 1918, DOJ File 9–19–1707.

54. *Ex parte Jackson*, 263 F. 110 (D.C. D. Mont. 1920).

55. The Honorable George M. Bourquin Memorial, Bourquin File, Vertical File, MHS.

56. *Montana Standard*, Nov. 17, 1958.

57. *Montana Standard*, Nov. 17, 1958.

58. *Ex parte Starr*, 263 F. 145 (D.C. D. Mont. 1920).

Chapter 9

1. *House Journal*, 15th Ex. Sess., 5.

2. Files of Governor Samuel Stewart, MS 35, Box 10, MHS.

3. Ibid.

4. Ibid.

5. *House Journal*, 15th Ex. Sess., 4; draft of speech in Gov. Stewart's files, MHS.

6. Files of Gov. Stewart, MS 35, Box 10, MHS.

7. McDorney, *Joys and Hardships of Homestead Life*, 18.

8. *Annual Report of Secretary of Labor 1918*. Historical Statistics, Series K 265–73, 297. Washington, 1919. M. L. Wilson, "Dry Land Farming in the North Central Montana Triangle," *Montana Extension Service Bulletin* 66 (June 1923): 13, quoted in Gutfeld, *Montana's Agony*, 94.

9. On February 14, 1918, northern spring wheat prices in Montana were quoted at between $1.71 and $1.91 per bushel. *Great Falls (MT) Tribune*, Feb. 14, 1918. Nine days later, President Wilson set the government guarantee for 1918 wheat at $2.00. See *Great Falls Tribune*, Feb. 24, 1918.

10. *House Journal*, 15th Ex. Sess., 5.

11. Draft of speech in Gov. Stewart's files, 5, 7.

12. Gutfeld, "George Bourquin: A Montana Judge's Stand Against Government Despotism," 51.

13. Gutfeld, *Montana's Agony*, 95.

14. Ibid.

15. *Daily Missoulian*, Feb. 19, 1918.

16. *Daily Missoulian*, Feb. 6, 1918.

17. Gov. Stewart's files, MHS.

18. Ibid.

19. *Daily Missoulian*, Feb. 14, 1918.

20. *House Journal*, 15th Ex. Sess., 26.

21. *Anaconda Standard*, Feb. 15, 1918, 10.

22. Waldron, *Montana Legislators 1864–1979*, 10.

23. Waldron, *Montana Legislators 1864–1979*, 10.

24. Twelve legislators did not attend the special session and one had died. See *House Journal*, 15th Ex. Sess.

25. *Daily Missoulian*, Feb. 14, 1918.

26. Ibid.

27. *House Journal*, 15th Ex. Sess., 4.

28. Butte Newswriters' Association, *A Newspaper Reference Work: Men of Affairs.*

29. Burlingame and Toole, *A History of Montana*, 44.

30. *Anaconda Standard*, Feb. 14, 1918.

31. Harries and Harries, *The Last Days of Innocence*, 210.

32. *Daily Missoulian*, Feb. 14, 1918.

33. *House Journal*, 15th Ex. Sess., 6.

34. Ibid.

35. Ibid.

36. Evans, "Montana's Role," 88.

37. Ibid.

38. *Great Falls Tribune*, Feb. 15, 1918.

39. Evans, "Montana's Role," 91

40. State of Montana, *Laws Passed by the Extraordinary Session of the Fifteenth Legislative Assembly*, 28–29.

41. See Rabban, *Free Speech in Its Forgotten Years.*

42. *Great Falls Tribune*, Feb. 6, 1918.

43. *House Journal*, 15th Ex. Sess., 62.

44. *Senate Journal*, 15th Ex. Sess., 17.

45. *House Journal*, 15th Ex. Sess., 30.

46. *Great Falls Tribune*, Feb. 17, 1918. Davis wasn't finished harassing the press. The next day, he introduced a resolution appealing to "the oft-demonstrated patriotism of the press" to eliminate the "useless duplication of news items and editorial expressions" by publishing just one or two daily newspapers in the state, thus releasing more than one thousand men for employment in industries needed for prosecution of the war. The measure did not pass.

47. *House Journal*, 15th Ex. Sess., 30.

48. *Senate Journal*, 15th Ex. Sess., 16.

49. *Anaconda Standard*, Feb. 17, 1918.

50. *House Journal*, 15th Ex. Sess., 49.

51. *House Journal*, 15th Ex. Sess., 72.

52. DOJ File 9–19, Box 758. The Texas legislature passed the first state sedition bill during World War I, weeks after America's entry into the war. Tennessee, however, had had a sedition law (Michie's Code, §11026) since 1858.

53. *Great Falls Tribune*, Feb. 19, 1918.

54. Evans, "Montana's Role," 89.

55. Evans, "Montana's Role," 94; Dowell, *A History of Criminal Syndicalism Legislation*, 17, 147.

56. Six senators did vote against House amendments to the bill. *Senate Journal*, 15th Ex. Sess., 36.

57. *Senate Journal*, 15th Ex. Sess., 18.

58. *House Journal*, 15th Ex. Sess., 48; *Great Falls Tribune*, Feb. 20, 1918.

59. *Senate Journal*, 15th Ex. Sess., 52.

60. *Senate Journal*, 15th Ex. Sess., 63; *Great Falls Tribune*, March 23, 1918.

61. *Great Falls Tribune*, March 23, 1918.

62. *Senate Journal*, 15th Ex. Sess., 63.

63. Ibid.

64. Walter, *Montana Campfire Tales*, 159.

65. Walter, *Montana Campfire Tales*, 160.

66. *Senate Journal*, 15th Ex. Sess., 64; *Great Falls Tribune*, March 23, 1918.

67. *Great Falls Tribune*, March 21, 1918.

68. Ibid.

69. *Great Falls Tribune*, March 22, 1918.

70. *Great Falls Tribune*, March 22, 1918.

71. *Helena Independent*, Jan. 30, 1918.

72. *Great Falls Tribune*, Feb. 4, 1918.

73. Walter, *Montana Campfire Tales*, 164; *Daily Missoulian*, Feb. 4, 1918.

74. *Great Falls Tribune*, Feb. 22, 1918.

75. *Senate Journal*, 15th Ex. Sess., 58.

76. *Great Falls Tribune*, Feb. 23, 1918.

77. Wheeler, *Yankee From the West*, 156.

78. Walter, *Montana Campfire Tales*, 166.

79. *Daily Missoulian*, March 22, 1918.

80. *Senate Journal*, 15th Ex. Sess., 71.

81. Ibid., 72.

82. Ibid., 74–76.

83. Walter, *Montana Campfire Tales*, 171.

84. Harry Fritz, discussion with the author, October 2003.

Chapter 10

1. *Saturday Evening Post*, Oct. 27, 1917, reprinted in "STOP Malicious Rumors—Help Win the War!" (Washington D.C.: National Committee of Patriotic Societies, n.d.), Sedition File, Montana Council of Defense files, RS 19, MHS.

2. *Daily Missoulian*, Jan. 24, 1918; *Helena Independent*, June 8, 1918.

3. Ibid., Aug. 9, 1917; Aug. 10, 1917.

4. Ibid., Oct. 18, 1917.

5. Ibid., Nov. 2, 1917.

6. *Daily Missoulian*, Jan. 29, 1918.

7. *Daily Missoulian*, April 19, 1918.

8. *Helena Independent*, July 20, 1917.

9. Ibid.

10. *Anaconda Standard*, Feb. 2, 1918; *Helena Independent*, Feb. 9, 1918, quoted in Evans, "Montana's Role," 86–87.

11. *Daily Missoulian*, April 7, 1918.

12. *An Act Providing for the Creation and Appointment of the Montana Council of Defense and County Councils*, 15th Leg., Ex. Sess. (1918), § 5.

13. See Fritz, "The Montana Council of Defense" for a full description of the MCD members.

14. Fritz, "The Montana Council of Defense," Appendix 4.

15. W. N. Smith to Chas. D. Greenfield, April 17, 1918, RS 19, Box 3, Folder 13, MHS.

16. Ike E. O. Pace to Chas. D. Greenfield, April 6, 1918, RS 19, Box 1, Folder 33, MHS.

17. Lewis C. Clark to Charles V. Peck, undated, RS 19, Box 4, Folder 32, MHS.

18. Ibid.

19. *Lewistown Democrat-News*, Feb. 11, 1918, quoted in Zellick, "Patriots on the Rampage," 38.

20. *Roundup Record*, March 29, 1918, quoted in Walter, "Patriots Gone Berserk," 78–85.

21. Zellick, "Patriots on the Rampage," 30–43.

22. Ibid.

23. Ibid.

24. *State v. Foster*, Fergus County Case No. 1122.

25. *State v. Schaffer*, Fergus County Case No. 1110.

26. Christensen, *Red Lodge and the Mythic West: Coal Miners to Cowboys*, 77. See also Lampi, *At the Foot of the Beartooth Mountains: A History of the Finnish*

Community at Red Lodge, Montana.

27. Ibid.

28. Johnson, "An Editor and a War," 212.

29. *Helena Independent*, Aug. 11, 1918.

30. Johnson, "An Editor and a War," 218.

31. Evans, "Montana's Role,"101.

32. Peterson and Fite, *Opponents of War*, 18.

33. Ibid., 19.

34. Kennedy, *Over Here*, 82.

35. Hough, *The Web*, 14.

36. Harries and Harries, *The Last Days of Innocence*, 305.

37. DOJ File 194086, Box 2934.

38. Gregory to Dr. R. E. Vinson, May 13, 1918, Gregory Papers, Box 1, Library of Congress, Washington D.C., quoted in Harries, *The Last Days of Innocence*, 307.

39. T. W. Gregory to Gilbert A. Currie, April 12, 1918, quoted in Peterson and Fite, *Opponents of War*, 20.

40. George Creel, "Our Aliens—Were They Loyal or Disloyal," *Everybody's* (March 1919): 37, quoted in Hilton, "Public Opinion and Civil Liberties in Wartime," 212.

41. R. VandenBerg to Governor Steward [sic], April 8, 1918, in RS 19, Box 1, Folder 22, MHS.

42. J. E. Lane, chairman of Fergus County Council of Defense, to Chas. D. Greenfield, RS 19, Box 1, Folder 22, MHS.

43. Meeting of the County Council of Defense held at the Office of the County Attorney, Nov. 1, 1918 (Butte, Mont.), Montana Council of Defense Records, RS 19, Box 4, MHS.

44. *Order Number Two*, Montana Council of Defense (March 15, 1918), MCD Collection, MHS.

45. R. Lewis Brown to State Council of Defense, Aug. 23, 1918, RS 19, Box 1, Folder 26, MHS.

46. A. H. Bowman, telegram to C. D. Greenfield, Aug. 10, 1918, RS 19, Box 1, Folder 3, MHS.

47. J. B. Collins to Chas. D. Greenfield, July 6, 1918, RS 19, Box 1, Folder 14, MHS.

48. *Helena Independent*, Aug. 6, 1918.

49. H. A. Simmons to State Council of Defense, Aug. 3, 1918, RS 19, Box 1, Folder 15, MHS.

50. *Order Number One*, Montana Council of Defense (March 15, 1918), MCD Collection, MHS.

51. Ibid.

52. *Daily Missoulian*, April 19, 1918.

53. *Anaconda Standard,* July 19, 1917.

54. John A. Fitch, "Baiting the IWW," *Survey* 33 (March 6, 1915): 634–35, quoted in Byrkit, "The IWW in Wartime Arizona," 149–70.

55. Ibid., March 13, 1918.

56. *Anaconda Standard,* March 10, 1918, quoted in Stoddard, Wheeler manuscript, L-12.

57. *Daily Missoulian,* March 12, 1918.

58. Ibid., April 21, 1918.

59. *Miles City Daily Star,* April 7, 1918.

60. Wheeler, *Yankee From the West,* 148. *Miles City Daily Star,* April 9, 1918; May 14, 1918.

61. *Billings Gazette,* May 7, 1918.

62. D. C. Dorman to J. A. McGlynn, May 3, 1918, MCD Collection, RS 19, Box 1, Folder 14, MHS.

63. *Miles City Daily Star,* May 13, 1918.

64. *Daily Missoulian,* May 14, 1918.

65. *Miles City Daily Star,* May 14, 1918.

66. Ibid.

67. Ibid.

68. Ibid.

69. Ibid.

70. *Daily Missoulian,* May 15, 1918.

71. Reprinted in *Miles City Daily Star,* May 13, 1918.

72. Atty. Gen. Samuel Ford to the Joint Session, May 27, 1918, MCD Collection, MHS.

73. Ibid.

74. *Daily Missoulian,* May 29, 1918.

75. Council of National Defense, "Loyalty and Sedition, Supplementary to Bulletin No. 99," (July 18, 1918), Sedition folder, MCD Collection, RS 19, MHS.

76. Open letter from Woodrow Wilson, July 26, 1918, Sedition folder, MCD Collection, RS 19, MHS.

77. Harries and Harries, *The Last Days of Innocence,* 307–8.

Chapter 11

1. Oscar Ameringer, *If You Don't Weaken* (New York: Henry Holt, 1940), quoted in Luebke, *Bonds of Loyalty,* 225.

2. *Daily Missoulian,* April 24, 1918.

3. Luebke, *Bonds of Loyalty,* 251.

4. *Daily Missoulian,* May 5, 1918.

5. John G. Brown to S. V. Stewart, April 18, 1918, RS 19–1-8, MHS.

6. John G. Brown to F. J. Ward, May 20, 1918, RS 19–4-29, MHS.

7. F. J. Ward to C. D. Greenfield, May 21, 1918, ibid.

8. John G. Brown to Mrs. A. M. Hoyt, May 11, 1918, ibid.

9. J. A. Devlin to Chas. D. Greenfield, May 3, 1918, ibid.

10. Emil Peterson to Chas. D. Greenfield, May 14, 1918, RS 19–1-30, MCD Collection, General Correspondence (1917–1918), Ha-Hi Misc., MHS.

11. Gertrude Buckhous to President E. O. Sisson, May 13, 1918, RS 19–4-29, MHS.

12. W. K. Dwyer to Chas. D. Greenfield, May 13, 1918, ibid.

13. Fritz, "The Montana Council of Defense," 102.

14. Fritz, "The Montana Council of Defense," 98.

15. See Luebke, *Bonds of Loyalty.*

16. *Our Times, Our Lives,* 420; Reuben Goertz, *Princes, Potentates and Plain People,* 19.

17. Rev. Fred O. Brose to Governor S. V. Stewart, April 29, 1918, RS 19–1-8, MHS.

18. Rev. D. Bergstedt to the state governor, May 21, 1918, RS 19–1-6, MHS.

19. Unsigned letter to S. V. Stewart, RS 19–1-3, MHS.

20. W. L. Lawson to Gov. S. V. Stewart, April 29, 1918, RS 19–1-8, MHS.

21. Walter H. North to S. V. Stewart, May 1, 1918, ibid.

22. Rev. Fred O. Brose to Chas. D. Greenfield, Jan. 4, 1919, RS 19–1-8, MHS.

23. Leon Shaw to C. D. Greenfield, Dec. 13, 1918, RS 19–3-16, MHS.

24. Fritz, "The Montana Council of Defense," 103.

25. Ibid., 104.

26. Ibid., 105.

27. *Helena Independent,* February 21, 1919.

28. Ibid.

29. A 1923 Supreme Court ruling in a Nebraska case, *Meyer v. Nebraska,* held language laws to be unconstitutional restrictions on individual rights.

30. Chas. D. Greenfield to Will A. Campbell, April 21, 1920, RS 19–1-15, MHS.

31. Ibid.

32. Fritz, "The Montana Council of Defense," 99.

33. *Butte Daily Bulletin,* January 12, 1920, quoted in Johnson, "An Editor and a War," 220–21.

34. Fritz, "The Montana Council of Defense," 89.

35. *Great Falls Tribune,* April 25, 1917.

36. *Lewistown Democrat-News,* April 23, 1917.

37. *Anaconda Standard,* July 22, 1917.

38. *Daily Missoulian,* April 10, 1917.

39. *Daily Missoulian,* March 16, 1918.

40. Ibid.

41. *Great Falls Tribune,* Feb. 6, 1918.

42. *Great Falls Tribune*, March 28, 1917.

43. Ibid.

44. *Great Falls Tribune*, April 5, 1917.

45. *Daily Missoulian*, Jan. 14, 1918.

46. *Daily Missoulian*, Feb. 19, 1918.

47. Ibid.

48. Wilson to Arthur Brisbane, April 25, 1917, Wilson MSS, Library of Congress, Washington, D.C., quoted in Preston, *Aliens and Dissenters*, 129 n. 34.

49. Hughes would become Chief Justice of the U.S. Supreme Court in 1930.

50. *Boston Transcript*, as reprinted in *Daily Missoulian*, May 6, 1918.

51. Luebke, *Bonds of Loyalty*, 241, 262 n. 22.

52. Henry Van Dyke, letter to the editor, *New Republic* 13 (December 22, 1917): 214, quoted in Peterson and Fite, *Opponents of War*, 149.

53. *Daily Missoulian*, March 19, 1918.

54. *Great Falls Tribune*, March 31, 1918.

55. *Helena Independent*, July 23, 1918; July 24, 1918; *Northwest Tribune*, July 26, 1918.

56. Harris, "Dr. E. B. Craighead's *New Northwest*: 1915–1920."

57. Ibid., 75; *New Northwest*, April 19, 1918.

58. Ibid., 65; *New Northwest*, July 26, 1918.

59. Ibid., 79–80; *New Northwest*, April 26, 1918.

60. Ibid., 78; *New Northwest*, April 26, 1918. See also Swibold, *Copper Chorus*.

61. Ibid., 68; *New Northwest*, December 5, 1919.

62. Preston, *Aliens and Dissenters*, 122.

63. Dubofsky, *We Shall Be All*, 434; Peterson and Fite, *Opponents of War, 1917–1918*, 235–47.

64. Reed was writing for *The Liberator* and other left-wing publications. He is quoted in Chaplin, *Wobbly*, 244–46.

65. Preston, *Aliens and Dissenters*, 119–20.

66. *Literary Digest*, reprinted in *Helena Independent*, Sept. 8, 1918.

67. *Helena Independent*, Aug. 18, 1918.

68. *Literary Digest*, reprinted in *Helena Independent*, Sept. 8, 1918.

69. Dubofsky, *We Shall Be All*, 443.

70. Ibid.

71. Preston, *Aliens and Dissenters*, 122.

72. Flynn had been granted a separate trial, which never took place for lack of evidence. She cut her ties to the IWW and joined the Communist Party. Convicted in the early '50s of violating the Smith Act, a peacetime sedition law that criminalized the advocacy of overthrowing the U.S. government by force or violence, Flynn spent two years at the women's penitentiary at Alderson, West Virginia. She died in the Soviet Union in 1964 and was buried in Chicago near

the remains of Big Bill Haywood. He, too, had died in the Soviet Union in 1928. He fled there after jumping bail in 1921, when the U.S. Supreme Court refused to consider an appeal of his conviction in the Chicago trial.

Chapter 12

1. Kennedy, *Over Here*, 78–80.
2. O'Brian to Walsh, March 6, 1918, DOJ File 9–19–1707.
3. O'Brian to Gregory, Feb. 27, 1918, DOJ File 9–19–1707.
4. Kennedy, *Over Here*, 80.
5. O'Brian to Sen. James W. Wadsworth, Feb. 13, 1918, DOJ File 187415–46.
6. 65th Cong., 1st sess., *Congressional Record* 55 (April 27, 1917): S 4559.
7. Ibid., S 4560.
8. Ibid., S 4639.
9. Ibid., S 4830.
10. Ibid., S 4771.
11. Ibid., S 4692.
12. Ibid., S 4714.
13. *Great Falls Tribune*, April 5, 1918.
14. Ibid.
15. *Congressional Record* 55 (April 27, 1917): S 4715.
16. Those responsible for the lynching were acquitted. During their trial, the eleven defendants wore red, white, and blue ribbons. While the jury deliberated for twenty-five minutes, a band "coincidentally" in the courthouse played "The Star-Spangled Banner" and "Over There."
17. *Congressional Record* 55 (April 27, 1917): S 4715, Appendix 338.
18. Ibid., S 4631.
19. Ibid., S 4633.
20. Ibid., S 4571.
21. *Congressional Record* 55 (April 27, 1917): S 4850.
22. Ibid., S 4629–4630.
23. Ibid., S 4835.
24. Ibid., S 4785.
25. Rabban, *Free Speech in Its Forgotten Years*, 121.
26. *Congressional Record* 55 (April 27, 1917): S 4694.
27. Ibid., S 4711.
28. Ibid.
29. Ibid., S 4835.
30. O'Brian to Walsh, April 16, 1918, Walsh MSS, Box 269, quoted in Polenberg, *Fighting Faiths*, 33.
31. *Congressional Record* 55 (April 27, 1917): S 4839.

32. Ibid., S 4639.

33. Ibid., S 4566.

34. Ibid., S 4631.

35. Ibid., S 6233.

36. Ibid.

37. Kennedy, *Over Here*, 81.

38. Chafee, *Free Speech in the United States*, 3rd Ed., 41.

39. *Congressional Record* 55 (April 27, 1917): S 6180.

40. Ibid., S 6179.

41. Ibid., S 6186.

42. Harold Evans to Woodrow Wilson, May 9, 1918, DOJ File 187415–88.

43. Alfred Bettman to John Lord O'Brian, May 10, 1918, O'Brian MSS, Box 18, LOC, quoted in Polenberg, *Fighting Faiths*, 35.

44. *Anaconda Standard*, May 28, 1918, quoted in Evans, "Montana's Role," 121.

45. Chafee, *Free Speech in the United States*, 163 ff. Australia's Unlawful Associations law, passed in 1916 with the IWW in mind, was the model for the bill.

46. See *Congressional Record* 55, S 6082 for text of bill as introduced to the Senate for debate.

47. Ibid., S 6084–6085.

48. *Congressional Record* 55 (April 27, 1917): S 6086.

49. Ibid., S 6087.

50. Ibid., S 6083.

51. Ibid., S 6091.

52. Dowell, *A History of Criminal Syndicalism Legislation*, 147.

53. *Congressional Record* 55, S 4640.

54. Chafee, *Free Speech in the United States*, 60 ff.

55. Gregory to Wilson, May 14, 1918, Wilson MSS, Reel 356, quoted in Polenberg, *Fighting Faiths*, 35.

56. Bettman to O'Brian, DOJ File 187415.

57. Chafee, *Free Speech in the United States*, 69.

58. John Lord O'Brian, "Civil Liberty in Wartime," *Report of the New York Bar Association* 42 (1919): 275, quoted in Stoddard, Wheeler manuscript, N-18—N-19.

59. Chafee, *Free Speech in the United States*, 68.

60. Ibid., 66.

61. Ibid., 68.

62. Office of the Attorney General, *Annual Report* (1918): 47; *Annual Report* (1919): 22; *Annual Report* (1920): 25. Also see *Congressional Record* 55, Appendix 528, and R. P. Stewart to Ben Neale, February 2, 1920, DOJ File 9–19–35–4.

63. Harry N. Scheiber, *The Wilson Administration and Civil Liberties* (Ithaca, N.Y.: Cornell University Press, 1960): 48–49, quoted in Kennedy, *Over Here*, 83.

64. Chafee, *Free Speech in the United States*, 70.

65. Max Eastman, "The Trial of Eugene Debs," *Liberator* 1, 9 (November 1918): 9, quoted in Chafee, *Free Speech in the United States*, 73.

66. Walter Nelles, "In the Wake of the Espionage Act," *Nation* (December 15, 1920), quoted in Hilton, "Public Opinion and Civil Liberties in Wartime," 221.

67. House Committee on the Judiciary, *Hearings on H.R. 291* 65th Cong., 1st Sess., 1917, 63, quoted in Rabban, *Free Speech in Its Forgotten Years*, 255.

68. Hilton, "Public Opinion and Civil Liberties in Wartime," 216.

69. Ibid., 218.

70. Chafee, *Free Speech in the United States*, 78.

71. Ibid., 79.

72. O'Brian to C. B. Van Dusen, responding to a letter from Van Dusen to the attorney general, May 9, 1919, DOJ File 187415–509.

73. Chafee, *Free Speech in the United States*, 69.

74. Bettman to Bell, November 20, 1918, referencing letter from Bell to attorney general, November 15, 1918, DOJ File 9–19.

75. Ibid.

Chapter 13

1. *Ex parte Starr*, 263 F. 145, (D.C. D. Mont. 1920).

2. *Helena Independent*, July 28, 1918.

3. Ibid., July 20, 1918.

4. *Jefferson County Courier*, Sept. 19, 2001, 11.

5. *Daily Missoulian*, March 30, 1918.

6. Wheeler, *Yankee From the West*, 145.

7. *Helena Independent*, June 4, 1918.

8. Ibid., June 2, 1918; Wheeler, *Yankee From the West*, 147.

9. Ibid., Oct. 17, 1917; Nov. 17, 1917, quoted in Johnson, "An Editor and a War," 107, 108.

10. Wheeler, *Yankee From the West*, 147. Wheeler said the tales were spread mostly by W. A. Clark Jr., the son of the copper baron, who was jealous of Rohn for corresponding with Clark's former wife.

11. *Helena Independent*, June 3, 1918.

12. *State v. Steck*, Lewis and Clark County Case No. 1454.

13. *State v. Diedtman*, Lewis and Clark County Case No. 1460.

14. *State v. Heil*, Lewis and Clark County Case No. 1456.

15. *State v. [John] Milch*, Lewis and Clark County Case No. 1455.

16. *State v. [Joe] Milch*, Lewis and Clark County Case No. 1457.

17. *State v. Lembrecht*, Lewis and Clark County Case No. 1458.

18. *State v. Reno*, Lewis and Clark County Case No. 1459.

19. *Helena Independent,* July 20, 1918.

20. Ibid.

21. *Helena Independent,* July 21, 1918.

22. Johnson, "An Editor and a War," 151–152.

23. *Helena Independent,* July 21, 1918.

24. Ibid., July 23, 1918.

25. Ibid., July 28, 1918.

26. Ibid., August 1, 1918.

27. *State v. Diedtman,* 69 Mont. 13, 190 Pac. Rptr. 117 (1920).

28. Ibid.

29. Ibid.

30. *State v. [Joe] Milch,* Lewis and Clark County Case No. 1457.

31. *Helena Independent,* Dec. 30, 1918.

32. Montana Bureau of Vital Statistics.

33. Rolla L. Thomas, *The Eclectic Practice of Medicine* (Cincinnati: Eclectic Medical Institute, 1907), quoted in http://www.ibiblio.org/herbmed/eclectic/thomas/main.html.

Chapter 14

1. Defendant's Proposed Bill of Exceptions, *State v. Kahn,* Carbon County Case No. 457, 14.

2. Fritz, "The Montana Council of Defense," 141.

3. Defendant's Proposed Bill of Exceptions, *State v. Kahn,* 3–4, 15–17.

4. Ibid., 17.

5. Ibid., 10–13.

6. Ibid., 8–9.

7. Ibid., 31.

8. U.S. Census Office, *1920 U.S. Census,* Cottonwood Township, Powell County, Montana.

9. *State v. Kahn,* 183 Pac. Rptr. 107 (Mont. Sup. Ct. 1919).

10. Ibid., 109, citing *Schenck v. U.S.,* 249 U.S. 47 (1919).

11. Ibid., 107–10.

12. See appendix I.

13. *Miles City Daily Star,* Oct. 3, 1918.

14. *State v. Starr,* Rosebud County Case No. 292.

15. Ibid.

16. *State v. Bausch,* Yellowstone County Case No. 1441; *Billings Gazette,* March 29, 1934. Bausch returned to Billings on parole after twenty-eight months at Deer Lodge. A son, Norman, was born eleven months later, In the middle of the Depression, Norman, at home with his grandparents, was struck and killed by a car.

17. *Billings Gazette*, April 16, 1918.

18. *Daily Missoulian*, March 24, 1918.

19. *State v. Effinger*, Missoula County Case No. 1121.

20. *State v. Heuer*, Gallatin Case No. 6146A.

21. *Bozeman Daily Chronicle*, March 24, 1918.

22. *Townsend Star*, April 18, 1918.

23. *Bozeman Daily Chronicle*, March 26, 1918.

24. *Bozeman Daily Chronicle*, April 8, 1918.

25. *Daily Missoulian*, May 8, 1918.

26. *State v. Burans*, Case No. 1130.

27. *State v. Griffith*, Yellowstone County Case No. 1458, affidavit in support of motion for a new trial.

28. *State v. Griffith*, 219, 56 Mont. 241, 184 Pac. Rptr. (1919).

29. See Chapter 4.

30. *Anaconda Standard*, March 1, 1918.

31. Montana State Penitentiary records, 240, MHS.

32. *State v. Brooks*, Supreme Court of Montana Case No. 4419 (April 8, 1920): 9.

33. Ibid., 4.

34. Ibid., 7.

35. Affidavit by Harlow Pease, *State v. Brooks*, May 13, 1920.

36. See Chapter 10.

37. *State v. McGlynn*, Carter County.

38. *State v. McGlynn*, 199 Pac. Rptr. 708, 709 (Mont. Sup. Ct. 1921).

39. Ibid.

40. *1920 U.S. Census*, Cottonwood Township, Powell Co., MT (Deer Lodge Prison).

41. See *Miles City Daily Star*, June 7, 1918; June 8, 1918; June 9, 1918, for accounts of Rohde's trial.

42. *State v. Rohde*, Custer County Case No. 847.

43. *Miles City Daily Star*, June 9, 1918; June 11, 1918.

44. *Miles City Daily Star*, June 9, 1918.

45. *Miles City Daily Star*, June 9, 1918.

46. *State v. Wehinger*, Custer County Case No. 854.

47. Brown, *The Frontier Years*, 181.

48. *State v. Rodewald*, Rosebud County Case No. 290.

49. *State v. Klippstein*, Richland County Case No. 119-C.

50. *State v. Smith*, Custer County Case Nos. 874, 875. After Powder River County was created, the bulk of the Smiths' court files were transferred to the county courthouse in Broadus in 1920.

51. *Miles City Daily Star*, June 5, 1918; June 11; Oct. 11, 12, 13, 15, 16 and 20.

52. *State v. Christiansen*, Custer County Case No. 877; *Miles City Daily Star*, October 18, 1918.

53. *Miles City Daily Star*, Oct. 20, 1918.

54. *Miles City Daily Star*, Oct. 20, 1918.

55. *1920 U.S. Census*, Cottonwood Township, Powell Co., Mont. (Deer Lodge Prison).

Chapter 15

1. Often referred to—even by himself—as William F. Dunn, his given name was Willis Francis Dunne. He himself contributed to further confusion by dropping the final 'e' from his surname during this period, and by calling himself either Will Dunn or Bill Dunn.

2. *Helena Independent*, June 6, 1918.

3. See Wetzel, "The Making of an American Radical."

4. Ibid., 1–26.

5. Ibid., 27.

6. Johnson, "An Editor and a War," 164.

7. Montana Council of Defense, *Hearings Held at the State Capitol*, May 31, June 1 and 2, Helena, 1918. Despite the dates in the title, the testimony includes a transcript of the MCD hearings on June 5 and 6. Referred to henceforth as "MCD Hearings."

8. Unpublished letter to the editor of the *Daily Missoulian*, September 19, 1918, W. F. Dunne Collection, NYU Library, Series 3, Folder 15.

9. Wetzel, "The Making of an American Radical," Johnson, "An Editor and a War," and Fritz, "The Montana Council of Defense," contain accounts of Dunn's loyalty hearing before the MCD and subsequent events.

10. MCD Hearings, 1341; *Helena Independent*, June 6, 1918.

11. MCD Hearings, 1366; Johnson, "An Editor and a War," 172.

12. *Helena Independent*, June 6, 1918, quoted in Johnson, "An Editor and a War," 173.

13. Ibid.

14. Johnson, "An Editor and a War," 175, citing minutes of MCD Hearings, 83–86.

15. *Helena Independent*, Aug. 13, 1918.

16. *Butte Weekly Bulletin*, Aug. 16, 1918, quoted in Johnson, "An Editor and a War," 177.

17. Wetzel, "The Making of an American Radical," 28.

18. *Helena Independent*, Aug. 23, 1918.

19. *Butte Daily Bulletin*, March 11, 1919, republishing verbatim the transcript of the Montana Council of Defense hearings; Johnson, "An Editor and a War," 184.

20. Ibid.

21. Preston, *Aliens and Dissenters*, 114.

22. Wetzel, "The Making of an American Radical," 104.

23. Dunn to the *Missoulian*, Sept. 19, 1918, W. F. Dunne collection. See n. 29.

24. DOJ File 195397.

25. Wheeler, *Yankee From the West*, 161; *Ex parte Jackson*, 263 F. 110 (D.C. D Mont. 1920): 111–14.

26. *Helena Independent*, Sept. 16, 1918.

27. Ibid., Sept. 15, 1918.

28. *Butte Daily Bulletin*, Sept. 18, 1918, quoted in Wetzel, "The Making of an American Radical," 106.

29. Dunn to the *Missoulian*, Sept. 19, 1918, W. F. Dunne collection. See n. 29.

30. *Butte Daily Bulletin*, Jan. 15, 1919. Typed transcript in DOJ File 195397.

31. Transcript of trial, *State of Montana v. William F. Dunne*, Helena case no. 4411 (1919): 309, quoted in Wetzel, "The Making of an American Radical," 106.

32. *Helena Independent*, Feb. 20, 1919.

33. Transcript of trial, *State v. Dunne*, 127; Wetzel, "The Making of an American Radical," 107.

34. Id., 180, *Helena Independent*, February 21, 1919.

35. Transcript of trial, *State v. Dunne*, 134–35; Johnson, "An Editor and a War," 194.

36. Wetzel, "The Making of an American Radical," 107 n. 25.

37. Transcript of trial, *State v. Dunne*, 300, 320; Wetzel, "The Making of an American Radical," 108–9.

38. *Helena Independent*, Feb. 25, 1919.

39. Wetzel, "The Making of an American Radical," 111.

40. Ibid., 110.

41. Wetzel, "The Making of an American Radical," 62.

42. *Helena Independent*, June 27–29, 1919.

43. Harris, "Dr. E. B. Craighead's *New Northwest*," 84; *New Northwest*, July 11, 1919.

44. DOJ File 195397–30.

45. Samuel V. Stewart to A. Mitchell Palmer, April 25, 1920, DOJ File 195397–33.

46. *State v. Smith*, 57 Mont. 563, 190 Pac. Rptr. 107 (1920); *State v. Dunn*, 57 Mont. 591, 190 Pac. Rptr. 121 (1920).

47. *State v. Smith*, 190 Pac. Rptr. at 116.

48. Wetzel, "The Making of an American Radical," 115.

49. Ibid.

50. *Helena Independent*, May 4, 1920; Johnson, "An Editor and a War," 207.

51. *Butte Daily Bulletin*, May 10, 1920.

52. William Crowley, conversation with the author, May 6, 2004. Crowley

added that all of his grandfather's files were lost in a fire in Butte.

53. *State v. Ferkovich*, Musselshell Co.

54. State Board of Pardons, *Order of Sentence Commutation*, Oct. 3, 1921, in the matter of the commutation granted by the Governor to Martin Ferkovich, Case No. 1715; legal notice published in *Roundup Record*, Oct. 14, 1921.

55. Wetzel, "The Making of an American Radical," 117.

56. Ibid.

57. Ibid., 122–27.

58. Ibid., 126.

59. Toole, *Twentieth Century Montana*, 273. See also Swibold, *The Copper Chorus.*

60. Johnson, "An Editor and a War," 256–57.

61. Ibid.

62. Wheeler, *Yankee From the West*, 150.

Chapter 16

1. Gardiner, A. C., *Portraits and Portents* (New York: Harper & Row, 1926), 13, cited in Murray, *Red Scare*, 17.

2. Chafee, *Free Speech in the United States*, 142.

3. Palmer, "The Case Against the Reds," 173–85.

4. Murray, *Red Scare*, 58.

5. Cooper, *Pivotal Decades*, 321.

6. Goldstein, *Political Repression in Modern America*, 142.

7. See Morgan, *Skid Road: An Informal Portrait of Seattle*, 199–219; and Friedheim, *The Seattle General Strike.*

8. *Seattle Post-Intelligencer*, Feb. 11, 1919, 4.

9. Evans, *American Century*, 176.

10. Preston, *Aliens and Dissenters*, 199.

11. Senate Resolution 213, Oct. 19, 1919, *Charges of the Illegal Practices of the Department of Justice*, Hearings before a Subcommittee of the Senate Committee on the Judiciary (Washington, D.C. 1921), reprinted in Congressional Record, 67 Cong. 4 Sess., Feb. 5, 1923, 3017.

12. Murray, *Red Scare*, 185.

13. "Shipping Lenine's Friends to Him," *Literary Digest*, 64 (Jan. 3, 1920): 14–15.

14. Preston, *Aliens and Dissenters*, 221; *Charges of Illegal Practices* reprint 3005–27.

15. Post, *The Deportations Delirium of Nineteen-Twenty*, 231.

16. *Attorney General A. Mitchell Palmer on Charges Made Against Department of Justice by Louis F. Post and Others*, Hearings before the Committee on Rules, House of Representatives (Washington, D.C. 1920), 27, cited in Murray, *Red Scare*, 219.

17. Post, *Delirium*, 134–37.

18. *Colyer v. Skeffington*, 265 Fed. 17, D. Mass (1920); Chafee, *Free Speech in the United States*, 204; Murray, *Red Scare*, 213.

19. Post, *Delirium*, 90.

20. Post, *Delirium*, 167.

21. Cobb-Reiley, "The Meaning of Freedom of Speech," 191.

22. Post, *Delirium*, 253.

23. Post, *Delirium*, 185; *Ex parte Jackson*, 263 (D.C. D. Mont. 1920).

24. Post, *Delirium*, 159–60.

25. *Charges of Illegal Practices* reprint 3013.

26. *Investigation of Administration of Louis F. Post in the Matter of Deportation of Aliens*, Hearings before House Committee on Rules, 66th Cong., 2nd Sess., Parts 1 and 2 (1920).

27. In Butte, juries' refusal to convict Wobblies under Montana's criminal syndicalism law during a period of postwar labor trauma led the Anaconda Company to urge deportations. But a confidential report by a special investigator deemed the Company at least as culpable for the unrest as the radicals and counseled against deportation. See Preston, *Aliens and Dissenters*, 232–33 and sources cited therein.

28. Post, *Delirium*, 147.

29. Link, ed., *The Papers of Woodrow Wilson*, 306–7.

30. Evans, *The American Century*, 186.

31. *Charges of Illegal Practices* reprint 3015.

32. Post, *Delirium*, 93.

33. Murray, *Red Scare*, 79–81.

34. Preston, *Aliens and Dissenters*, 194.

35. "Drastic Sedition Laws," *Literary Digest* 64 (Jan. 24, 1920): 18; (Feb. 7, 1920): 8; Murray, *Red Scare*, 230; Chafee, *Free Speech*, 169.

36. Ibid.

37. "The Dead-Line of Sedition," *Literary Digest* 64 (March 6, 1920): 17–19.

38. Chafee, *Free Speech*, 178–95.

39. Ibid.

40. Montana's criminal syndicalism law was declared unconstitutional in a 1920 trial, but the decision was never appealed and the law remained on the books until 1999.

41. Dowell, *Criminal Syndicalism*, 147.

42. Dowell, *Criminal Syndicalism*, 47.

43. Chafee, *Free Speech*, 327.

44. Chafee, *Free Speech*, 167.

45. Dowell, *Criminal Syndicalism*, 14.

46. Goldstein, *Burning the Flag*, 9.

47. Murray, *Red Scare*, 234. (Murray admits the figures are "not too reliable but the only ones available.")

48. Chafee, *Free Speech*, 247.

49. Ibid.

50. Murray, *Red Scare*, 236; Chafee, *Free Speech*, 269.

51. Chafee, *Free Speech*, 273–74; "The Dead-Line of Sedition," *Literary Digest* 64 (Jan. 24, 1920): 19–20.

52. Chafee, *Free Speech*, 281.

53. Chafee, *Free Speech*, 275.

54. Murray, *Red Scare*, 245.

55. *Cleveland Plain Dealer*, Sept. 18, 1920, 6, cited in Murray, *Red Scare*, 259.

56. *Charges of Illegal Practices* reprint 3026–27.

57. See William Preston Jr.'s epilogue to *Aliens and Dissenters*, 2nd ed., 277–95.

58. Arthur M. Schlesinger Jr., *The Crisis of the Old Order* (Boston: Houghton-Mifflin 1957), cited in Goldstein, *Political Repression*, 167.

59. Cobb, "The Press and Public Opinion," *The New Republic* (Dec. 31, 1919): 144.

60. Ibid.

Chapter 17

1. Record 5 (insert), in *Schenck v. United States*, 249 U.S. 47 (1919) (Nos. 437 & 438) (filed May 3, 1918) (U.S. Supreme Court Records & Briefs, vol. 249), in 1st Amendment Online, University of Minnesota Law School, http://1stam.umn.edu/.

2. In the Supreme Court of the United States, October Term, 1917, *Schenck v. U.S.*, Brief of Plaintiffs-in-Error, http://www.yale.edu/lawweb/avalon/curiae/html/249–47/001.htm.

3. *Towne v. Eisner*, 245 U.S. 418, 425 (1918).

4. *Schenck v. U.S.*, 249 U.S. 47, 52 (1919).

5. Polenberg, *Fighting Faiths*, 214.

6. *Frohwerk v. U.S.*, 249 U.S. 204 (1919).

7. *Frohwerk v. U.S.* at 209.

8. Schlesinger (ed.), *Writings and Speeches of Eugene V. Debs*, 417–33.

9. *Debs v. U.S.*, 249 U.S. 211, 214–15 (1919).

10. *Debs v. U.S.* at 212.

11. Salvatore, *Eugene V. Debs*, 296.

12. Rabban, *Forgotten Years*, 274–75.

13. *Debs v. U.S.* at 215.

14. Lochner v. New York 198 U.S. 45 (1905).

15. Frankfurter, *Mr. Justice Holmes and the Supreme Court*, 62.

16. *Jacobson v. Massachusetts*, 197 U.S. 11, 27 (1905).

17. Both Polenberg and Rabban have good explications of this process in their respective books.

18. *Masses Publishing Co. v. Patten*, 245 F. 102 (2d Cir. 1917).

19. See Freund, "The Debs Case and Freedom of Speech"; Chafee, "Freedom of Speech," and Chafee, "Freedom of Speech in Wartime." The latter two articles, published in 1918 and 1919, led to Chafee's book, *Free Speech in the United States*, first published in 1920.

20. See Richard Polenberg, *Fighting Faiths,* an excellent exegesis of the Abrams case and its liberating effect on First Amendment jurisprudence.

21. Polenberg, *Fighting Faiths*, 138.

22. Polenberg, *Fighting Faiths*, 146.

23. *Abrams v. U.S.*, 250 U.S. 616 (1919).

24. Id., 630.

25. Id., 628.

26. Id., 630.

27. Id.

28. See Robert Post, "Reconciling Theory and Doctrine in First Amendment Jurisprudence," (January 1, 2001) Boalt Working Papers in Public Law, University of California, Berkeley, Paper 106, http://repositories.cdlib.org/boaltwp/106.

29. Rodney Smolla, "Freedom of Speech Overview," First Amendment Center, http://www.firstamendmentcenter.org/speech/overview.aspx?topic=speech_overview, accessed Aug. 1, 2004. See also Smolla, *Free Speech in an Open Society*.

30. Steimer and her co-defendants were incarcerated for about two years before being deported in 1921. See Polenberg, *Fighting Faiths*, 341 ff.

31. *Brandenburg v. Ohio*, 395 U.S. 444 (1969). Arguably, the court might have reached such a result much sooner, as it did overturn a state conviction for criminal syndicalism in 1927 in *Fiske v. Kansas*, 274 U.S. 380, but the court did not articulate a speech test in that case. Instead it held that there was insufficient evidence to convict Fiske, an IWW organizer, Biographical information about Steimer is from Polenberg, *Fighting Faiths*, 368.

32. Chafee, *Free Speech in the United States*, 319.

33. "The Red Ruby," Address to the jury by Benjamin Gitlow, Communist Labor Party, n.d., 9, Debs Collection, Indiana State University, http://debs.indstate.edu/g536r4_1900.pdf.

34. *Gitlow v. New York*, 268 U.S. 652, 666 (1925).

35. *Gitlow v. New York*, 268 U.S. at 669.

36. Id.

37. Id., 672.

38. "Speech" in this context includes free press cases. Brandeis wrote the dissent in *Schaefer v. U.S.*, 251 U.S. 466 (1920); *Pierce v. U.S.*, 252 U.S. 239 (1920); *Gilbert*

v. Minnesota, 254 U.S. 325 (1920), in which Holmes voted with the majority; *U.S. ex rel Milwaukee Social Democratic Publishing Co. v. Burleson,* 255 U.S. 407 (1921); *Whitney v. California,* 274 U.S. 357 (1927), counting their concurrence as a dissent; and *U.S. v. Burns,* 274 U.S. 328 (1927). Holmes wrote the opinion for the two dissenters in *Abrams; Gitlow v. New York,* 268 U.S. 652 (1925) and *U.S. v. Schwimmer,* 279 U.S. 644 (1929).

39. *Whitney v. California,* 274 U.S. 357 (1927).

40. Blasi, "The First Amendment and the Ideal of Civic Courage: The Brandeis Opinion in *Whitney v. California,*" 656.

41. Ibid., 657–58.

42. *Whitney v. California,* 360.

43. Young, "The Pardon of Anita Whitney," 310–11.

44. *Whitney v. California,* 371.

45. Id., 369.

46. Id., 373.

47. Id., 376.

48. Id., 375.

49. Id.

50. Id.

51. Id., 377.

52. Young, "The Pardon of Anita Whitney," 312.

53. Blasi, "Civic Courage," 695. Blasi examines the philosophical roots of Brandeis' First Amendment ideas in the Greeks of fifth-century BC Athens such as Pericles and Euripides.

54. Schlesinger Jr., "The Right to Disagree: An Endangered Species."

55. Ibid.

56. Senator Carl Schurz, remarks in the Senate, February 29, 1872, *The Congressional Globe,* 2nd Sess., 42nd Congress, Part II, p. 1287. According to a biographer, "The applause in the gallery was deafening." Trefousse, *Carl Schurz: A Biography,* 180.

57. Schurz, "The Policy of Imperialism," 119–20.

Selected Bibliography

Aarstad, Richard R. "Montana's Other Strike: The 1917 IWW Timber Strike." Thesis, University of Montana, 2000.

Amick, Robert M. Jr. "The 1919 Election: Broadsides and Ballots in Butte," *Montana Journalism Review* 15 (1972): 38–47.

Baxandall, Rosalyn. *Words on Fire: The Life and Writings of Elizabeth Gurley Flynn.* New Brunswick, N.J.: Rutgers University Press, 1987.

Bird, Stewart, Dan Georgakas, and Deborah Shaffer. *Solidarity Forever: An Oral History of the IWW.* Chicago: Lake View Press, 1985.

Blanchard, Margaret A. "Filling the Void: Speech and Press in State Courts Prior to Gitlow." *The First Amendment Reconsidered,* Bill F. Chamberlin and Charlene J. Brown, eds., New York: Longman Publishing, 1982.

———. *Revolutionary Sparks: Freedom of Expression in Modern America.* New York: Oxford University Press, 1992.

Blasi, Vincent. "The First Amendment and the Ideal of Civic Courage: The Brandeis Opinion in *Whitney v. California.*" *William and Mary Law Review* 29, 2 (Summer 1988): 653–97.

Bobitz, Bradley C. "The Brandeis Gambit: The Making of America's 'First Freedom' 1909–1931." *William and Mary Law Review* 40, 2 (Feb 1999): 557–641.

Brissenden, Paul. *The I.W.W.: A Study of American Syndicalism.* New York: Russell & Russell, 1957.

Brown, Mark H., and W. R. Felton. *The Frontier Years: L. A. Huffman, Photographer of the Plains.* New York: Bramhall House, n.d.

Burlingame, Merrill K., and K. Ross Toole. *A History of Montana.* New York: Lewis Historical Publishing, 1957.

Butte Newswriters' Association. *A Newspaper Reference Work: Men of Affairs and Representative Institutions of the State of Montana.* Butte, Mont.: Butte Newswriters' Association, 1914.

Byrkit, James W. "The IWW in Wartime Arizona," *Journal of Arizona History* 18 (Summer 1977): 149–70.

Calvert, Jerry W. *The Gibraltar: Socialism and Labor in Butte, Montana, 1895–1920.* Helena: Montana Historical Society Press, 1988.

Chafee, Zechariah Jr. *Free Speech in the United States.* 3rd ed. Cambridge: Harvard University Press, 1946.

———. "Freedom of Speech." *The New Republic* 17 (1918): 66.

———. "Freedom of Speech in Wartime," *Harv. L. Rev* 32 (1919): 932.

Chaplin, Ralph. *Wobbly: The Rough-and-Tumble Story of an American Radical.* Chicago: University of Chicago Press, n.d.

Christensen, Bonnie. *Red Lodge and the Mythic West: Coal Miners to Cowboys.* Lawrence: University Press of Kansas, 2002.

Cobb, Frank I. "The Press and Public Opinion." *The New Republic* 21 (1919): 144–47.

Cobb-Reiley, Linda. "The Meaning of Freedom of Speech and the Press in the Progressive Era: Historical Roots of Modern First Amendment Theory." Dissertation, University of Utah, 1986.

Coburn, Christine. "The Attitude of Montana Newspapers Toward Sedition and Free Speech During World War I." Thesis, University of Montana, 1972.

———. "The Impeachment of Judge Crum." *Montana Journalism Review* 19 (1976): 41–50.

Commission on Industrial Relations. *Final Report, 1915.* Department of Labor, Record Group 174, National Archives. Washington, D.C.

Conlin, Joseph R. *Bread and Roses Too: Studies of the Wobblies.* Westport, Conn.: Greenwood Pub. Corp., 1969.

Cooper, John Milton, Jr. *Pivotal Decades: The United States, 1900–1920.* New York: W.W. Norton & Co., 1990.

Cornebise, Alfred E. *War as Advertised: The Four-Minute Men and America's Crusade 1917–1918.* Memoirs of the American Philosophical Society 156. Philadelphia: American Philosophical Society, 1984.

Dawson County Family Stories. *Our Times, Our Lives.* Glendive, Mont., 1989.

DeWeerd, Harvey A. *President Wilson Fights His War: World War I and the American Intervention.* New York: MacMillan, 1968.

Dowell, Eldridge Foster. *A History of Criminal Syndicalism Legislation in the United States.* The Johns Hopkins University Studies in Historical and Political Science 1. Baltimore: Johns Hopkins Press, 1939.

Dubofsky, Melvyn. *We Shall Be All: A History of the Industrial Workers of the World.* Chicago: Quadrangle Books, 1969.

Emmons, David M. *The Butte Irish: Class and Ethnicity in an American Mining Town.* Chicago: University of Illinois Press, 1989.

Evans, Harold, with Gail Buckland, and Kevin Baker. *The American Century.* New York: Alfred A. Knopf, 1998.

Evans, Lewis O. *Address to Chamber of Commerce.* Missoula, Mont. 29 Aug. 1917.

Evans, Robert Emlyn. "Montana's Role in the Enactment of Legislation Designed to Suppress the Industrial Workers of the World." Thesis, Montana State University, 1964.

Fargo, Lucile F. *Spokane Story.* New York: Columbia University Press, 1950.

Flynn, Elizabeth Gurley. *I Speak My Own Piece.* 1955. Reprinted as *The Rebel Girl: An Autobiography, My First Life (1906–1926).* New York: International Publishers, 1973.

———. "Memories of the Industrial Workers of the World," address to students and faculty members, Northern Illinois University, DeKalb, Nov. 8, 1962.

———. *Sabotage.* Cleveland: IWW Publishing Bureau, 1915.

Foner, Philip S., ed. *Fellow Workers and Friends: I.W.W. Free Speech Fights As Told By Participants.* Contributions in American History 92. Westport, Conn.: Greenwood Press, 1981.

Frankfurter, Felix. *Mr. Justice Holmes and the Supreme Court.* Cambridge: Harvard University Press, 1961.

Freund, Ernest. "The Debs Case and Freedom of Speech." *The New Republic* 19 (1919): 13.

Friedheim, Robert L. *The Seattle General Strike.* Seattle: University of Washington Press, 1979.

Fritz, Nancy Rice. "The Montana Council of Defense." Thesis, University of Montana, 1966.

Gamble, Richard M., *The War for Righteousness: Progressive Christianity, the Great War and the Rise of the Messianic Nation.* Wilmington: Intercollegiate Studies Institute, 2003.

Garrity, Donald A. "The Frank Little Episode and the Butte Labor Troubles of 1917." Thesis, Carroll College, 1957.

Gaylord, Luther M. "Politics and Syndicalism: A Case Study of the IWW." Industrial Workers of the World: http//www.iww.org/culture/articles/Gaylord1.shtml (August 16, 2003).

Goertz, Reuben. *Princes, Potentates and Plain People: The Saga of the Germans from Russia.* Sioux Falls, S. Dak.: Center for Western Studies, 1994.

Goldstein, Robert J. *Burning the Flag: The Great 1989–1990 American Flag Desecration Controversy.* Kent, Ohio: Kent State University Press, 1996.

———. *Political Repression in Modern America.* Cambridge: Schenkman Publishing, 1978.

Gutfeld, Arnon. "George Bourquin: A Montana Judge's Stand Against Government Despotism." *Western Legal History* 6 (1993): 51–68.

———. *Montana's Agony: Years of War and Hysteria, 1917–1921.* Gainesville: University Presses of Florida, 1979.

———. "The Speculator Disaster in 1917: Labor Resurgence at Butte, Montana." *Arizona and the West* 11 (1969): 27–38.

———. "Western Justice and the Rule of Law: Bourquin on Loyalty, the 'Red Scare' and Indians." *Pacific History Review* 64 (1996): 85–106.

Harries, Meirion, and Susie Harries. *The Last Days of Innocence: America at War 1917–1918.* New York: Random House, 1997.

Harris, Lyle E. "Dr. E. B. Craighead's *New Northwest:* 1915–1920." Thesis, University of Montana, 1967.

Hart, Liddell. *The Real War 1914–1918.* 1930. Reprinted as *History of the First World War.* London: Pan Books, 1970.

Henderson, Harley, and Lawrence F. Small. *Montana Passage.* Helena, Mont.: Falcon Press, 1983.

Higham, John. *Strangers in the Land: Patterns of American Nativism, 1860–1925.* New Brunswick, N.J.: Rutgers University Press, 1955.

Hilton, O. A. "Public Opinion and Civil Liberties in Wartime 1917–1919." *Southwestern Social Science Quarterly* 28,3 (December 1947): 201–24.

Hinerman, Lenore. *Homesteading Our Heritage.* Glasgow, Mont.: North Valley County Bicentennial Comm., 1980.

Hough, Emerson. *The Web: The Authorized History of the American Protective League.* New York: Arno Press, 1969.

Howard, Joseph Kinsey. *Montana: High, Wide and Handsome.* Lincoln: University of Nebraska Press, 1983.

Industrial Workers of the World. *Proceedings of the Founding Convention of the IWW.* Chicago: IWW Pub. Bureau, 1905.

Johnson, Charles S. "An Editor and a War: Will A. Campbell and the *Helena Independent,* 1914–1921." Thesis, University of Montana, 1970.

———. "The Montana Council of Defense." *Montana Journalism Review* 16 (1973): 2–16.

Keegan, John. *The First World War.* New York: Alfred A. Knopf, 1999.

Kennedy, David M. *Over Here: The First World War and American Society.* New York: Oxford University Press, 1982.

Kent, Philip. *Montana State Prison History.* Deer Lodge, Mont.: Powell County Museum and Arts Foundation, 1979.

Koelbel, Lenora. *Missoula The Way It Was.* N.p.: Pictorial Histories Publishing Co., 1972.

Kornbluh, Joyce, ed. *Rebel Voices: An IWW Anthology.* Ann Arbor: University of Michigan Press, 1964.

Kustudia, Michael. "The Press and Propaganda Coverage of the Butte Labor Strike of 1917." Thesis, University of Montana, 1988.

Lampi, Leona. *At the Foot of the Beartooth Mountains: A History of the Finnish Community of Red Lodge, Montana.* Coeur D'Alene, Idaho: Bookage Press, 1998.

Lavender, David. *Land of Giants: The Drive to the Pacific Northwest 1750–1950.* Garden City, N.Y.: Doubleday, 1958.

Lewis, Anthony. *Make No Law: The Sullivan Case and the First Amendment.* New York: Random House, 1991.

Link, Arthur, ed. *The Papers of Woodrow Wilson.* Princeton, N.J.: Princeton University Press, 1980.

Luebke, Frederick C. *Bonds of Loyalty: German Americans and World War I.* De Kalb: Northern Illinois University Press, 1974.

Lukas, J. Anthony. *Big Trouble.* New York: Simon & Schuster, 1997.

MacConnel, June. "Fritz and Wilma Haynes." *They Came and Stayed: A Rosebud Community History.* Billings, Mont.: Western Printing and Lithography, 1977.

Mackenzie, Don. "Logging in Western Montana Since 1910," interview by Mike Ryan, Feb. 22, 1982, Oral History 55–22, K. Ross Toole Archives, University of Montana.

Malone, Michael P. *The Battle for Butte: Mining & Politics on the Northern Frontier 1864–1906.* Helena: Montana Historical Society Press, 1995.

———, Richard B. Roeder, and William L. Lang. *Montana: A History of Two Centuries.* Seattle: University of Washington Press, 2001.

McClelland, John M. *Wobbly War: The Centralia Story.* Tacoma: Washington Historical Society Press, 1987.

McDorney, Mary. *Joys and Hardships of Homestead Life, or Thirty-Two Years on a Montana Homestead.* Missoula, Mont., 1982

McGuckin, Henry E. *Memoirs of a Wobbly.* Chicago: C. H. Kerr, 1987.

Miller, John C. *Crisis in Freedom: The Alien and Sedition Acts.* Boston: Atlantic-Little, Brown, 1951.

Mock, James R. *Censorship 1917.* Princeton, N.J.: Princeton University Press, n.d.

———, and Cedric Larson. *Words That Won The War.* Princeton, N.J.: Princeton University Press, 1939.

Montana Council of Defense. *Hearings Held at the State Capitol,* May 31, June 1 and 2, 1918, Helena, 1918.

———. *Orders Made and Promulgated by the Montana Council of Defense.* Helena, April 22, 1918.

Morgan, Murray C. "The Industrial Workers of the World." In *The Last Wilderness.* New York: Viking Press, 1955.

———. *Skid Road, an informal portrait of Seattle.* Seattle: University of Washington Press, 1980 (Rev. ed.)

Murphy, Paul L. *The Meaning of Freedom of Speech.* Westport, Conn.: Greenwood Publishing Co., 1972.

Murray, Robert K. *Red Scare: A Study in National Hysteria, 1919–1920.* Minneapolis: University of Minnesota Press, 1955.

National Popular Government League. *To The American People, Report Upon the Illegal Practices of the United States Department of Justice.* Washington, D.C. National Popular Government League, 1920.

Palmer, A. Mitchell. "The Case Against the Reds." *Forum* 63 (1920): 173–85.

Peterson, H. C., and Gilbert C. Fite. *Opponents of War, 1917–1918.* Madison: University of Wisconsin Press, 1957.

Polenberg, Richard. *Fighting Faiths: The Abrams Case, the Supreme Court, and Free Speech.* Ithaca, N.Y.: Cornell University Press, 1999.

Ponsonby, Arthur. "The Corpse Factory," *The Journal for Historical Review* 1, 2 (1980): 121–30.

Post, Louis F. *The Deportations Delirium of Nineteen-Twenty.* Chicago: Charles H. Kerr & Co., 1923.

Preston, William, Jr. *Aliens and Dissenters: Federal Suppression of Radicals, 1903–1933.* 1964. 2nd ed. Chicago: University of Illinois Press, 1994.

Rabban, David M. *Free Speech in Its Forgotten Years.* Cambridge: Cambridge University Press, 1997.

———. "The IWW Free Speech Fights and Popular Conceptions of Free Expression Before World War I." *Virginia Law Review* 80 (1994): 1054–1159.

Rajala, Richard A. "A Dandy Bunch of Wobblies: Pacific Northwest Loggers and the IWW, 1900–30." *Labor History* 37 (1996): 205–34.

Renshaw, Patrick. *The Wobblies: The Story of Syndicalism in the United States.* Garden City, N.Y.: Doubleday & Company, 1967.

Rowan, James. *The IWW in the Lumber Industry.* Seattle: Shorey Book Store, 1969.

Salvatore, Nick. *Eugene V. Debs: Citizen and Socialist.* Chicago: University of Illinois Press, 1982.

Schlesinger, Arthur M. (ed.). *Writings and Speeches of Eugene V. Debs.* New York: Hermitage Press, 1948.

Schlesinger, Jr., Arthur M. "The Right to Disagree: An Endangered Species." Address at Swarthmore College, Feb. 10, 2004.

Schurz, Carl. "The Policy of Imperialism." In *Speeches, Correspondence and Political Papers of Carl Schurz, Vol. 6.* New York: G.P. Putnam's Sons, 1913

Smith, James Morton. *Freedom's Fetters.* Ithaca, N.Y.: Cornell University Press, 1956.

Smith, Jeffery A. "The Political Costs of Press Controls: Woodrow Wilson and Wartime Suppression." Paper, Association for Education in Journalism and Mass Communication, Anaheim, Ca., Aug. 1996.

Smith, Walker C. *The Everett Massacre: A History of the Class Struggle in the Lumber Industry.* Chicago: I.W.W. Publishing Bureau, 1920.

Smolla, Rodney A. *Free Speech in an Open Society.* New York: Alfred A. Knopf, 1992.

Spritzer, Don. *Roadside History of Montana.* Missoula: Mountain Press Publishing, 1999.

State Department of Public Instruction. *State Course of Study.* City Elementary Schools of Montana, Helena, 1918.

Stoddard, Dayton, unpublished manuscript of Burton K. Wheeler biography, Montana Historical Society, Helena.

Stone, Geoffrey R. "Reflections on the First Amendment: The Evolution of the American Jurisprudence of Free Expression." *Proceedings of the American Philosophical Society* 131, 1 (March 1987): 251–60.

Strum, Philippa. *Brandeis: Beyond Progressivism.* Lawrence: University Press of Kansas, 1993.

Swibold, Dennis L. *The Copper Chorus: Mining, Politics and Journalism, 1889–1959.* Helena: Montana Historical Society Press, 2006.

Toole, K. Ross. *Montana: An Uncommon Land.* Norman: University of Oklahoma Press, 1959.

———. *Twentieth Century Montana: A State of Extremes.* Norman: University of Oklahoma Press, 1972.

Townsend, John Clendenin. *Running the Gauntlet: Cultural Sources of Violence Against the I.W.W.* New York: Garland Publishing, 1986.

Trefousse, Hans L. *Carl Schurz: A Biography.* Knoxville: University of Tennessee Press, 1982.

Tyler, Robert L. *Rebels of the Woods: The I.W.W. in the Pacific Northwest.* Eugene: University of Oregon Press, 1967.

Venn, George A. "The Wobblies and Montana's Garden City. *Montana: The Magazine of Western History* (Autumn 1971): 18–30.

Viereck, George S. *Spreading Germs of Hate.* New York: H. Liveright, 1930.

Waldron, Ellis L. *Montana Legislators 1864–1979: Profiles and Biographical Directory.* Missoula: Bureau of Govt. Research, University of Montana, 1980.

Walker, Samuel. *In Defense of American Civil Liberties: A History of the ACLU.* Oxford: Oxford University Press, 1990.

Walter, Dave. *Montana Campfire Tales: Fourteen Historical Narratives.* Helena: Two Dot Books, 1997.

———. "Patriots Gone Berserk: The Montana Council of Defense, 1917–1918." *Montana Magazine* (September/October 2001): 78–85.

Weinstock, Harris. *Report on Recent Disturbances in the City of San Diego and the County of San Diego, California.* Sacramento: State Printing Office, 1912.

Wertheimer, John W. "Free Speech Fights: The roots of modern free-expression litigation in the United States." Dissertation, Princeton University, 1992.

Wetzel, Kurt. "The Making of an American Radical: Bill Dunne in Butte." Thesis, University of Montana, 1970.

Wheeler, Burton K., with Paul F. Healy. *Yankee From the West.* Garden City, N.Y.: Doubleday & Co., 1962.

Wilson, M. L. "Dry Land Farming in the North Central Montana Triangle." *Montana Extension Service Bulletin* 66. n.d.

Woods, Arthur. "Reasonable Restrictions Upon Freedom of Assemblage." *American Socialist Society: Papers & Proceedings* 9 (1915): 29.

Writers' Project of Montana. *Copper Camp: The Lusty Story of Butte, Montana, the Richest Hill on Earth.* Helena: Riverbend Publishing, 2002.

Young, Gov. C. C. "The Pardon of Anita Whitney." *The New Republic* (Aug. 10, 1927): 310.

Zellick, Anna. "Patriots on the Rampage: Mob Action in Lewistown, 1917–1918." *Montana: The Magazine of Western History* (Winter 1981): 30–43.

Legislative records and reports

Montana State Legislature. *House Journal.* 15th Cong., Ex. Session, 1918.

Montana State Legislature. *Senate Journal.* 15th Cong., Ex. Session, 1918.

State of Montana. *Laws Passed by the Extraordinary Session of the Fifteenth Legislative Assembly.* Helena: State Publishing, Co., n.d.

Montana State Legislature. *Report of Committee Appointed by the Sixteenth Legislative Assembly to Investigate the High Cost of Living.* Helena, 1919.

Archives

Butte-Silver Bow Public Archives: Kaiyala and McGlynn Collections, newspaper collections and vertical file.

Missoula Public Library: *Missoulian* microfilm records.

Montana Historical Society: Marguerite Greenfield, Montana Council of Defense, Montana State Prison and Gov. Sam Stewart collections; newspaper microfilm collection; Barclay Craighead, Lester H. Loble, and Burton K. Wheeler papers; vertical files.

National Archives and Records Administration: Committee on Public Information files, RG 63; Department of Justice files, RG 60; Land Entry Files; Montana Federal District Court files (NARA, Seattle).

The New York Public Library: Papers of Francis Patrick Walsh.

The New York University Library: W. F. Dunne Collection (microfilm copy, University of Montana).

The University of California, Berkeley, Bancroft Library.

The University of Montana, K. Ross Toole Archives: Anaconda Forest Products, Kenneth Ross, Oral History, World War I Pamphlet, and newspaper microfilm collections.

Wayne State University, Walter P. Reuther Library, Archives of Labor and Urban Affairs.

Other Agency Reports

Montana State Attorney General. *Report and Official Opinions of the Attorney General of the State of Montana: Nov. 30, 1916 to Nov. 30, 1918*. Helena, Mont.: Independent Publishing Company, 1919.

————. *Report and Official Opinions of the Attorney General of the State of Montana: Nov. 30, 1918 to Nov. 30, 1920*. Helena, Mont.: Independent Publishing Company, 1921.

U.S. Bureau of the Census. *Historical Statistics of the United States*. Washington, D.C. 1960.

U.S. Commission on Industrial Relations. *Final Report and Testimony*. S. Doc. No. 415, 64th Cong., 1st Sess. 10573 (1916).

U.S. Department of Justice. *Interpretation of War Statistics Bulletin, 1918–1919*.

U.S. Department of Justice. Office of the Attorney General. *Annual Report, 1918, 1919, 1920*.

Cases cited

Abrams v. U.S., 250 U.S. 616 (1919).

Brandenburg v. Ohio, 395 U.S. 444 (1969).

Colyer v. Skeffington, 265 Fed. 17, D. Mass (1920).

Commonwealth v. Davis, 162 Mass 510 (1895).

Debs v. U.S., 249 U.S. 211 (1919).

Ex parte Jackson, 263 F. 110 (D.C. D. Mont. 1920).

Ex parte Starr, 263 F. 145 (D.C. D. Mont. 1920).

Fiske v. Kansas, 274 U.S. 380.

Frohwerk v. U.S., 249 U.S. 204 (1919).

Gilbert v. Minnesota, 254 U.S. 325 (1920).

Gitlow v. New York, 268 US 652 (1925)

Jacobson v. Massachusetts, 197 U.S. 11, 27 (1905).

Lochner v. New York, 198 U.S. 45 (1905).

Masses Publishing Co. v. Patten, 245 F. 102 (2d Cir. 1917).

Meyer v. Nebraska, 262 U.S. 390 (1923).

New York Times v. Sullivan, 376 U.S. 254 (1964).

Pierce v. U.S., 252 U.S. 239 (1920).

Schenck v. U.S., 249 U.S. 47 (1919).

Schaefer v. U.S., 251 U.S. 466 (1920).

State v. Diedtman, 69 Mont. 13, 190 Pac. Rptr. 117 (1920).

State v. Dunn, 57 Mont. 591, 190 Pac. Rptr. 121 (1920).

State v. Griffith, 219, 56 Mont. 241, 184 Pac. Rptr. (1919).

State v. Kahn, 183 Pac. Rptr. 107 (Mont. Sup. Ct. 1919).

State v. McGlynn, 199 Pac. Rptr. 708,709 (Mont. Sup. Ct. 1921).

State v. Smith, 57 Mont. 563, 190 Pac. Rptr. 107 (1920).

Towne v. Eisner, 245 U.S. 418 (1918).

U.S. ex rel Milwaukee Social Democratic Pub. Co. v. Burleson, 255 U.S. 407 (1921).

U.S. v. Burns, 274 U.S. 328 (1927).

U.S. v. Hall, 248 F. 150 (D.C. D. Mont. 1918).

U.S. v. Kirchner (N.D. W. Va. 1918).

U.S. v. Schwimmer, 279 U.S. 644 (1929).

U.S. v. Waldron (Vt. 1918).

Whitney v. California, 274 U.S. 357 (1927).

Index

Abrams, Jacob, 249–50, 252–53, 255
ACM. *See* Anaconda Copper Mining
    Company (ACM)
Adams, John, 3
AFL. *See* American Federation of Labor
    (AF of L, AFL)
Albany Socialists, 239–42
Alien and Sedition Acts (1798), 29,
    100–101, 127, 171, 236
Amalgamated Copper Company, 15, 65.
    See also Anaconda Copper Mining
    Company (ACM)
American Communist Party. *See*
    Communist Party, American
American Defense Society, 140
American Federation of Labor (AF of L,
    AFL), 17, 34, 44, 66, 236; miners
    and, 70–71, 72; World War I, 57–58
American Industry, 77–78
American Protective League (APL), 105,
    106, 140
Ameringer, Oscar, 148
Anaconda Copper Mining Company
    (ACM), 2–3, 15, 95–99, 111*i*, 125*i*, 185;
    Butte miners' strike, 63–68;
    Industrial Workers of the World
    (IWW) and, 74; influence, political
    and economic, 79–81, 137, 213,
    279n21; Lumber Department,
    41–43, 46; Myers and, 126; sedition
    prosecutions, role in, 217, 219,
    221–22, 225, 226, 228
Anaconda Standard, 79–80, 91–93, 123–24,
    155, 174, 183; free speech, 174; loyalty,
    155; lynching of Frank Little, 96
Ancient World (West), 148
anti-Germanism, 137–42, 148–54,
    183–93, 204–8

APL. *See* American Protective League
    (APL)
Associated Press, 155
Atherton, Gertrude, 79, 202

"bad tendency" test, 108, 158, 178, 202,
    247; Brandeis and, 257; Clarke and,
    250; Holmes and, 245, 252
Baer, Elizabeth, 244
Baker, Newton, 104
Baldwin, James, 95
Bausch, Herman, 198–99
Bell, Sherman, 16
Berger, Victor L., 239
Berkman, Alexander, 232
Bettman, Alfred, 173, 176
Big Blackfoot Milling Co., 99
Billings Gazette, 79–80, 153
Bill of Rights, 4
bindlestiffs, 12–14
Bisbee (Arizona), 71–74, 91, 163
Bolshevism, 222, 228, 230, 233, 240–41
Borah, William E., 169, 175
Bourquin, George M., 93, 234, 279n21;
    Espionage Act and, 110–18, 111*i*,
    113–14; military forces, domestic use
    of, 217; Montana sedition law, 120,
    180–81; Ves Hall acquittal, 120, 166,
    225
Bozeman, 142, 160, 199, 200
Bozeman Chronicle, 96
Bradley, Omar, 217
Brandeis, Louis D., 4, 250, 255–59;
    Whitney v. California, excerpt from
    opinion in, 262–63
Brennan, William, 4
British War Propaganda Bureau, 51–52
Brooks, Albert, 202–3
Brose, Oscar, 151, 152–53
Brown, John G., 148–50, 154
Bryan, William Jennings, 49, 56
Buford, 232
Burans, Thomas, 200

Burleson, Albert S., 30, 147, 172, 239

Butte, 15, 66–70; Anaconda Copper Mining Company (ACM), 125*i*, 126; Dunn, 68, 70–71, 158–59, 159*i*, 220; Haywood, 44; labor strife, 60–71, 74, 76, 80–82, 90–96; miners' strike, 217–19; mining deaths, 60–62; sedition, 114–15, 117–18, 141–43, 184–86, 197–98, 212–26; vigilantism, 99. *See also* Little, Frank

Butte and Anaconda Joint Strike Bulletin, 64

Butte Bulletin, 158, 215, 217, 219–20, 223, 224

Butte Daily Bulletin, 212, 213, 216, 223

Butte Daily Post, 92

Butte Miner, 21, 23, 79–80

Butte Miners Hall, dynamiting of, 67*i*

Butte Miners Union (BMU), 65–66

Butte Post, 66, 79–80

Byrn, E. W., Jr., 99

California Commission for Immigration and Housing, 39

Campbell, Thomas E., 72

Campbell, Tom (MMU), 70, 95, 96

Campbell, Will, 81–82, 81*i*, 88, 133–34, 220, 226; Council of Defense, 135, 185; Dunn and Smith trials, 212, 220, 224; lynching of Frank Little, 96; Montana Loyalty League, 139–40

Canning, Matt, 225

Cannon, James P., 20

Central Valley (California) riot, 38

Chafee, Zechariah, Jr., 235, 236, 237

Chaplin, Ralph, 19

Charteris, J. V., 54

"Children's Crusade," 35–36

"Christians at War," 58–59

Christian Science Monitor, 55, 56

Citizens Alliance, 16

Civil War, 3

Clark, Lewis C., 137–38

Clark, William A., 15, 65, 69*i*, 83

Clarke, John, 250

Clark Fork River, 7

Cleveland Plain Dealer, 241

CLP. *See* Communist Labor Party (CLP)

Cobb, Frank I., 242–43

Coeur d'Alene, 15, 19, 26

Cold War, 4

Colorado, 16

Committee on Public Information (CPI), 51, 83–89, 140, 147; *Under Four Flags,* 86*i*; Four Minute Men, 87; "Why We Are Fighting," 52

Communist Labor Party (CLP), 229, 256

Communist Party, American, 225–26

Congress, 91, 173–74, 178, 232, 235–40; declaration of war, 156–57; sedition legislation, 100–102, 164, 167–68, 241, 243, 245; Wilson's war message to, 54–57

Congressional Record, 241

Conley, Frank, 142, 196, 211

Council of National Defense, 70, 135

Councils of Defense, Montana, 2, 81, 120, 137*i*, 148, 150–51; anti-Germanism, 137–42; investigative powers, 135, 137; local, 137, 142, 144, 153–55, 159, 194–95; loyalty issues, 138–41, 155; Mennonites and, 154; Order Number Three, 148, 151, 153, 161

CPI. *See* Committee on Public Information (CPI)

Craighead, Edwin, 160–61

Creel, George, 83–84, 87, 140, 147

Cripple Creek, 16

Crismas, William J., 126

Crum, Charles L., 115–16, 129–32, 198

Daily Missoulian, 22, 79–80, 124; sedition legislation and, 155–56; war rumors and, 134

Daily Worker, 225

Daly, Marcus, 15, 65, 79

Darrow, Clarence, 19, 27, 253

Davey, Martin L., 236

Davis, Clarence C., 128, 281n46

"Deadly Parallel, The " (*Solidarity*), 57–58

Debs, Eugene, 17, 49, 56, 140, 196, 246–47

Democrat-News (Fergus County), 2

deportations, 117, 217–18, 234, 296n27; Palmer and, 231–32

Diedtman, Tony, 187–93, 189*i*

Dixon, Joseph M., 213, 225

Donoghue, Mortimer M., 128

Dubofsky, Melvyn, 40, 161, 163

due process of law, 5, 31, 126, 163–64, 218, 231–34; Fourteenth Amendment, 31, 248, 254

Dunn, William F. (Dunne), 68, 70–71, 158–59, 159*i*, 293n1; sedition trial of, 212–26; *Strike Bulletin*, 75

Dwyer, John V., 198

Effinger, Louis, 199

Elm Orlu mine (Ella-ma-loo), 66

Employers' Association of Washington, 45

Equity Society, 129

Espionage Act, 84, 88, 93, 100, 164, 246–48; excerpt, 260; prosecutions under, 108–10, 177–80, 250. *See also* "bad tendency" test

Estabrook, Frank W., 29

Eureka Lumber Company, 43

Evans, Lewis O., 67, 74, 93, 103

Evening Capital News (Boise), 80

Everett (Washington), 44–45

expression, freedom of. *See* First Amendment; free speech during World War I; free speech fights, pre-war

Fall, Albert, 169

farming, 118–21. *See also* Non-partisan League (NPL)

farm workers, migratory, 37–38

Faulds, J. R., 159

Federalists, 3

Ferkovich, Martin, 225

Finns, 57, 70, 80, 139

First Amendment, 4, 31, 127, 244, 253; Brandeis, 4, 250, 255–59; newspapers and, 155–58; Oliver Wendell Holmes, Jr., 30, 244–47, 248–53, 257; wartime limitations on, 154–58. *See also* free speech; free speech fights, pre-war

Fitts, William C., 99, 100, 105

Flynn, Elizabeth Gurley (Gurley Flynn), 8–11, 19, 36*i*, 78–79, 161, 287–88n72; free speech fights, 20–22, 25–26; Lawrence textile workers' strike and, 35; *Sabotage*, 38–40; Subversive Activities Control Board and, 40

Ford, Sam, 95–96, 144–46, 201

Four Minute Men, 87

Frankfurter, Felix, 235, 248

free speech, 47, 154–58; censorship, 51, 269n11; propaganda techniques and, 51–54; on streets, in parks and other public locations, 30–31; wartime limitations on, 154–58. *See also* First Amendment

free speech fights, pre-war, 267n57; Everett, 44–45; Missoula, 20–25; San Diego, 27–30; Spokane, 25–26

Frenette, Edith, 22, 26

Fresno Republican, 240

Freund, Ernest, 235

Fritz, Harry, 132

Frohwerk, Jacob, 245–47, 250

Gerard, James W., 79

Gibson, Charles Dana, 85

Gitlow, Benjamin, 253, 256, 258
Gitlow v. New York, 255, 267
Goldman, Emma, 34, 232
Gompers, Samuel, 57, 70, 236
Gore, Thomas P., 171–72
Great Falls Tribune, 127, 156, 158
Great Northern Railroad, 11, 122, 218
Green Corn Rebellion, 57
Greenfield, Charles D., 135, 142, 152
Gregory, Thomas W., 30, 39, 99, 102, 140, 147, 165i; Espionage Act, 117, 164–65, 172–73, 175; Industrial Workers of the World (IWW) and, 90–91, 99, 101–3, 105; loyalty issues, 140; military forces, domestic use of, 217
Grierson, Henry, 130
Griffith, John A. "Jack," 200–202

Hagerty, Thomas J., 17
Hall, Ves, 120, 130–31, 164, 166, 225, 244
Hardwick, Thomas W., 171, 175
Harnois Theater, 7, 10, 23
Hart, Albert Bushnell, 87
Hathaway, Maggie Smith, 126
Hay, M. E., 26
Haynes, Felkner "Fritz," 129, 130, 131
Haywood, Big Bill, 10, 16, 34, 36i, 162, 231; Lawrence textile workers' strike, 35
Heil, Frank, 187, 193
Heinze, Fritz Augustus, 15, 65, 112, 279n21
Helena Independent, 79–80, 81–82, 92–93, 96, 102, 162
Herve, Gustave: "Patriotism and the Worker," 47–48
Heuer, Julius, 199–200
Higgins, Ronald, 128, 131
Hill, Jim, 41
Hill, Joe, 19, 27, 37

History of the American People (Wilson), 236
Holmes, Oliver Wendell, Jr., 196; First Amendment, 30, 244–47, 248–53, 257
Hoover, J. Edgar, 232
House of Representatives, Montana, 122–23, 128–31
House of Representatives, U.S., 166, 173, 175, 233, 239
Howard, Joseph Kinsey: Montana, High, Wide and Handsome, 62
Hoxie, Robert, 75
Hughes, Charles Evans, 157, 240
Hunter, Frank, 144, 204–5
Hutchens, Martin, 124
Hutterites, 151

Idaho, 14, 15, 19, 42, 65, 129; IWW, 23, 26, 101, 104, 134; syndicalism, 237
Industrial Union Bulletin, 18
industrial unionism, 34
Industrial Worker (Spokane), 14, 21–22, 25, 41
Industrial Workers of the World (IWW), 1, 7, 8, 10, 13, 15; California Central Valley riot, 38; Chicago trial, 161–63; Committee on Public Information and, 83–89; Espionage Act and, 164; founding of, 16, 18–19; free speech fights, 20–33, 44–45; "harvest stiffs" and, 37–38; Idaho, 23, 26, 101, 104, 134; intolerance of, 27–30, 267n45, 273n11, 276n33; Lawrence textile workers' strike, 35–37; lumber industry, 40–46, 72–73; Lumber Workers Industrial Union No. 500, 43; mining industry, 66–70, 71, 73–74; Missoula, 24, 67, 98–99, 156; Montana sedition prosecutions, 200–204; newspapers and, 78–83; passive resistance, 31–32; patriotism, 47–48; political action, 17–18; Red

Scare, 230–32, 242; sabotage, 18, 38–40, 45, 75, 98, 237–38; socialism and, 17; Spokane, 14, 26, 78, 104; strategies, 16, 17*i*, 18, 30, 34–35; World War I and, 90–100, 105–6, 143
Ingalls, Emma A., 126
International Brotherhood of Electrical Workers, 71
IWW. *See* Industrial Workers of the World (IWW)

Japan, 48
Jefferson, Thomas, 228
Jerome (Arizona) Loyalty League, 71
Johnson, Charles, 226
Johnson, Hiram, 27, 29, 97, 171, 242
Jones, Jack, 8, 19, 21

Kahn, Ben, 194–96, 195*i*, 258
Kansas City Journal, 163
Kenyon, William S., 55
King, William, 166–67
Kirchner, H. E., 109
Klingle, C. A., 129
Klippstein, Theodore, 208
Kootenai River valley, 43
Korea, 48
Kultur, 149

labor unrest, postwar, 229–31
Lachowsky, Hyman, 250
La Follette, Robert, 49, 157
Lamb, L. W., 201
Landis, Kenesaw Mountain, 161–62, 239
Lawrence textile workers' strike, 35–37
Lee Newspapers, 226
Le Matin, 53
Lembrecht, August, 187, 193
Lemon, Courtenay, 32–33
Lenin, V. I., 229
Lewistown, 1–2, 137–39, 148, 155

Lewistown News-Democrat, 155
Lind, John, 103–4
Lipman, Samuel, 250
Literary Digest, 49, 157, 236
Little, Frank, 20–21, 71–73, 74, 88; industrial sabotage and, 40; lynching of, 90–94, 94*i*, 95*i*, 96–98, 163, 168, 213; World War I, 57
Loble, Lester, 182, 184, 186–90, 220–22, 226
Lodge, Henry Cabot, Sr., 55–56
Logan, Andrew, 22
Lohe, Richard, 187
London, Meyer, 173
Los Angeles Times, 26–27, 162–63
Lucas, H. F. "Harry," 197–98
lumber industry, 12–14, 40–46; Anaconda Copper Mining Company (ACM) and, 42; Kootenai River valley, 43; Northern Pacific Railroad, 41; shingle weavers, 44–45; strikes, 46, 72–73; working conditions, 41–42
Lumber Workers Industrial Union No. 500, 43
Lusitania, 54, 56, 115, 194

MacDonald, T. H., 102
Maclean, John N., 200
Majors, Ed, 187, 212
Marshall, Louis, 157
Martin, Robert, 143–44
McDonald, Muckie, 66
McGlynn, J. A. "Mickey," 144–45, 203–4
McGuckin, Henry, 82–83
McKim, Randolph, 55
McLeod, C. H., 99
McNamara, J. J. and J.B., 27
McNulty, F. J., 71
McRae, Donald, 44–45
Mennonites, 151, 154
Metal Mine Workers Union, 66
Mexico, 48, 54
migrant farm workers, 37–38

Milch, Joe, 187
Milch, John, 187, 193
Miles City Daily Star, 204–5, 209–10
military forces, domestic use of, 9*i*,
　104, 217–18
Milwaukee Leader, 239
Milwaukee Railroad, 7
Miner, 83
mining industry, 60, 61*i*; Bisbee strike,
　71, 73–74; Butte strike, 66–70;
　Jerome Loyalty League, 71; spies
　and informers in, 15, 66, 275n8;
　wartime demands on, 64–65; work-
　ing conditions, 63–65
Missoula, 7–10, 9*i*, 20–25; Chamber of
　Commerce, 103, 121; Craighead
　and, 160; free speech, 20–24; IWW,
　24, 67, 98–99, 156; Little, 20–21,
　71–73; lumber industry, 12–14; sup-
　pression of dissent, 142–44, 150
Missoula Mercantile Co., 99
Montana, High, Wide and Handsome
　(Howard), 62
Montana Bankers' Association, 99–100
Montana Council of Defense, 81, 120
Montana Federation of Labor, 128
Montana Legislative Assembly, 122–29
Montana Loyalty League, 139–40, 154
Moore, Fred H., 45
Morgan, J. P., 14, 46, 231
Moyer, Charles, 19, 66
Muffly, C. S., 129
Myers, Henry L., 55, 59, 98–99, 99,
　167*i*, 170; sedition legislation,
　100–102, 126, 168

National Association of Manufacturers
　(NAM), 75
National Civil Liberties Bureau, 178
National Security League, 140
Nazis, 270n17
Nebeker, Frank, 105
Nelles, Walter, 178, 256

neutrality, U.S., 49, 52, 62
Nevin, A. Parker, 75
New Northwest, 160
New Republic, The, 157
newspapers and World War I, 78–82
New York Assembly, 239–42
New York Sun, 53–54
New York Times, 157, 240–41
New York Times v. Sullivan, 4
New York Tribune, 79
New York World, 236, 242–43
Neylan, John F., 256
Non-partisan League (NPL), 120–21,
　143, 160, 203
Norris, George, 50, 56
North, Walter Henry, 152
Northern Pacific Railroad, 14, 41
Northwest Tribune, 159
NPL. *See* Non-partisan League (NPL)

O'Connor, James F., 126
Orchard, Harry, 19
Otis, Harrison Gray, 26–27
Overalls Brigade, 18

Palmer, A. Mitchell, 229, 231–36, 241,
　251
Pancner, John, 31, 42
Parker, Carleton, 48
Parks, Wade, 102–3
Parry, David M., 75
passive resistance, 31–32
PATRIOT Act, 4
patriotism, 48–49, 84, 87, 259; World
　War I and, 133–47
"Patriotism and the Worker" (Herve),
　47–48
Peabody, James H., 16
Pearse-Connolly Irish Independence
　Club, 70, 272n33
Pearson's Magazine, 32
Pettibone, George A., 19
Philippines, 48

Pittsburgh Leader, 240
Pohl, Carl von, 184–87
Poindexter, Miles, 169, 232
Pollak, Walter, 256
Pollard, T. F., 194–96
Post, Louis F., 233–35, 233*i*
Pound, Roscoe, 235
Prager, Robert Paul, lynching of, 168, 288n16
President's Mediation Commission, 46
Pressed Steel Car Company, 11–12

Rankin, Jeannette, 56, 95, 142–43
Rebels of the Woods (Tyler), 76–77
Red Lodge, 139, 142, 182, 194
Red Scare, 3, 219, 222, 226, 238–39, 241–42; end of, 235; labor unrest and, 228–30; Palmer raids, 231–33; press and, 242–43
Reed, James A., 56, 171, 175
Reed, John, 161–62
Reitman, Ben, 34
Reno, Leo, 187, 193
"Right to Disagree, The" (Schlesinger), 259
Rockefeller, John D., 14
Rockefeller, William, 65
Rockefeller family interests, 15, 47
Rodewald, Fred, 207–8, 206*i*, 207*i*
Rogers, William, 65
Rohde, Herman, 204–5
Rohn, Oscar, 184–86, 214
Roosevelt, Theodore, 29, 157, 170
Ross, Kenneth, 43, 46, 99
Rowan, James, 14, 44, 104
rustling card, 66–68, 69, 72, 95, 185
Ryan, John D., 95

sabotage, 18, 38–40, 45, 75, 98, 237–38
Sabotage (Flynn), 38–40
San Diego, 27–30
San Diego Evening Tribune, 28, 30
San Diego Union, 27, 28, 29

Saturday Evening Post, 133
Scanlon, Joseph, 205
Schenck, Charles T., 244
Schlesinger, Arthur M., Jr.: "Right to Disagree, The," 259
Schurz, Carl, 259
sedition legislation, 3, 31, 111, 113, 236–38, 261; Bourquin and, 110–18, 120, 166, 180–81, 225; enforcement issues, 106, 110, 175–80; Montana, 119–32, 260–61; national, 100–101, 106, 164–74; Senate Bill 2789, 100–101, 106; states, 237–38, 282n52; Wheeler and, 102, 120, 180, 215–17, 220–21
sedition prosecutions, 181–83, 204, 208–11; Anaconda Copper and, 217, 219, 221–22, 225, 226, 228; anti-Germanism, 183–93, 204–8; disloy-alty, 194–200; IWW, 181, 200–204; Non-partisan League (NPL), 203; socialist editors, 212–25
Senate, Montana, 122–23, 126, 128–32
Senate, U.S., 100–101, 166–75, 241, 259; Committee on Military Affairs, 165; Judiciary Committee, 166
"sharks," 10–11
Shaw, George Bernard, 181
Sherman, Lawrence Y., 169
shingle weavers, 44–45
side-door Pullmans, 8
Simmons. H. A., 142
Smith, Bruce, 212–24
Smith, Walker C., 47
Smith, William K. and Janet, 208–11
social divisions, 14–16
Socialist Party, 17, 49, 139, 229, 239, 244, 246
Solidarity, 56; "The Deadly Parallel," 57–58
Somers Lumber Co. (Great Northern), 11
South Butte Mining Company, 184
Southern Pacific Railroad, 14

Speculator Mine disaster, 60–62, 61*i*, 64
Spencer, A. C., 196
Spokane, 25–26; citizens militia, 26; free speech fights, 25–26; Gurley Flynn, 10, 14; IWW, 14, 78, 104
Spokane Spokesman-Review, 78–79
Spreckels, John D., 27, 28
Stalin, Joseph, 225–26
Standard Oil, 14, 65
Starr, Earnest V., 198–99
Steck, Adam, 187
Steimer, Mollie, 250, 253, 298n30
Sterling, Thomas, 235
Steunenberg, Frank, 19
Stewart, Sam, 2, 66, 81–82, 95, 98, 124*i*; Council of Defense, Montana, 143; Council of National Defense, 135; free speech and, 168; military forces, domestic use of, 104–5; sedition legislation, 103–4, 119–21, 123–26, 128, 225
St. John, Vincent, 18, 27
Stone, Arthur, 156–57, 157
Stout, Tom, 2, 155
Strike Bulletin, 75, 96
strikes, 229–31
Subversive Activities Control Board, 40
Sunset, 79
Supreme Court, U.S., 4, 31, 104, 239; free speech, 127, 202, 244–59, 298n31. *See also* "bad tendency" test; *specific justices*
Sweet, Thaddeus C., 240
syndicalism, 75, 101, 128–29, 256, 296n40

Taft, William Howard, 29, 47
terrorist bombings, 231, 241
Thomas, Charles S., 174
timber beasts, 12–14
Times (London), 54
Townley, A. C., 143
Tracy, Thomas, 45
Trading With the Enemy Act, 84

Tucker, Herman, 21
Tuscania, 124
Tyler, Robert: *Rebels of the Woods*, 76–77
Under Four Flags: Committee on Public Information, 86*i*
United States Steel, 14, 63
Unlawful Associations bill, 174–75

Vanderveer, George W., 45, 162, 201
Van Dyke, Henry, 157
Vardaman, James K., 170–71
vigilantism, 26, 27–30, 45, 71–72, 78, 140

Waldron, Clarence, 109
Waldru, Eberhard von, 184–92
Walker, Sharpless, 204–5, 209–10
Walsh, Frank P., 235
Walsh, John H., 18
Walsh, Thomas J., 3, 167*i*, 227, 235–36, 241–42, 243; Espionage Act, 164, 166; syndicalism, 101; Unlawful Associations bill, 174
Walter, Dave, 132
war hysteria, 133–35
Warren, Charles, 100
Wehinger, Martin, 206–7, 206*i*, 207*i*, 258, iii
Weinstock, Harris, 27–29
West, Willis Mason: *Ancient World*, 148, 150
Western Federation of Miners (WFM), 10, 15, 16, 17, 20, 66
Western News, 92–93
Western Pine Association, 46
Weyerhaeuser, George, 14
wheat prices, 120, 280n9
Wheeler, Burton K., 3, 93–95, 102, 110–15, 110*i*, 227; governorship, 213; patriotic fanaticism and, 118, 184, 186; Robert Martin and, 144; sedition prosecutions, 102, 120, 180,

215–17, 220–21; Ves Hall acquittal,
131; *Yankee from the West*, 227
Whitney, Charlotte Anita, 254*i*, 256–57,
259
Whitney v. California, excerpt from
Brandeis' opinion, 262–63
"Why We Are Fighting" (Committee
on Public Information), 52
Wickersham, George W., 28–30
Wilkes, John, 239
Williams, Ben, 32, 56-57
Williams, John, 169
Wilson, Woodrow, 29, 49, 54–55, 70,
84–85, 105; administration, 30, 49;
free speech, 157, 242; *History of the
American People*, 236; patriotism and,
147; sedition legislation, 173
Windsor, H. H., 157–58
Wobblies. *See* Industrial Workers of the
World (IWW)
Woehlke, Walter V., 79
Woods, Arthur, 24
Word, Lee, 190–92, 220–25
World War I, 49–59, 147; atrocity
rumors, 52–54; brutality of, 50–51;
Committee on Public Information,
51–52, 83–89, 140; free speech limita-
tions, 154–58; hysteria, 133–35; news-
papers and, 78–82; propaganda,
50–54; U.S. neutrality, 49, 52, 62

Yankee from the West (Wheeler), 227
Young, C. C., 259

Zastrow, Charles, 182
Zellick, Anna, 138
Zimmerman telegram, 54